Food and Beverage Cost Control

by

Donald A. Bell

University of Nevada at Las Vegas

McCutchan Publishing Corporation
2526 GROVE STREET • BERKELEY, CALIFORNIA 94704

ISBN 0-8211-0135-8
Library of Congress Catalog Card Number 83-62769

Printed in the United States of America

Cover design by Terry Down, Griffin Graphics, Berkeley, Calif.
Book design and production editing by Kim Sharrar, MPC

Contents

Exhibits

Section I

Introduction

1 Overview of Control

What Is Control?

The purpose of this book is to provide an understanding of food and beverage operations control. *Control* is one of the most frequently used words in the foodservice managers' vocabulary. We are always talking about it. We talk about food cost control, food quality control, bar control, labor control, operating expense control, the need for more controls, control systems, and so forth. The obvious place to begin is by defining *control*. For our purposes *control* will be defined with two terms: the first is information, the second is action. Control is partly achieved by gathering suitable information. There can be no control without information. The more information available, the greater the potential for control. Information by itself is worthless, however; someone must be willing to act upon it. For example, if you know that your bar cost is 6 percentage points too high for the month of April, you do not have control. If you know that the entire cost variance can be traced to one bar, you do not have control. If you

know that only one bartender is involved, you still do not have control. If you fire the bartender, hire a suitable replacement, train him or her properly, and take steps to assure that whatever had been going on can no longer occur, then you have control.

Information is necessary for control, but too many managers in the foodservice business think that because they have all sorts of statistics about their operations they are in control of those operations. Nothing could be further from the truth. Of the two elements, information and action, action is the more important. A manager sitting in an office surrounded by stacks of computer print-outs is not as effective as one who is out among the employees and customers doing something. In the first case, the manager may know exactly what to do, but he is not doing it. In the second, the manager may make mistakes through lack of complete information, but as least she is doing something. Much of what she is doing will be effective simply because she is close to what really counts in this business—the people.

The first lesson to be learned about control is

that management must acquire the right information. This is essential. Information cannot be implemented, however, without really knowing the operation, and nothing will happen without your willingness to take action. You cannot run a foodservice operation from an office on your seat. You must be on your feet, out in the operation, with your people and your guests.

The necessity for action implies a second aspect to information. It does not only flow up from the operation to management. Control is also achieved by information flowing downward from management to the operation, to the people who ultimately must implement all action, the employees.

Types of Information

Management can accumulate two types of information: *historical* and *analytical*. Historical information merely informs management that something has happened. Analytical information, on the other hand, tells management why something happened, when it happened, where it happened, who was involved, and so on. Historical information is not a useful basis upon which to make decisions. The previous example about the bar cost percentage that was 6 percent higher than it should have been is a good illustration of historical information. You are informed that the cost was 6 percent high. This is really not very meaningful. You obviously have a problem, your job may even be in danger, but what are you going to do about it? Is it a cost problem or a sales problem? Is a bartender stealing liquor, or is he stealing money? Are the other employees stealing alcoholic beverages? Are the suppliers cheating you somehow? Do you have a portion-control problem? What bar is involved, or are there problems on all the bars? Is your problem in the banquet department or in the dining room?

Historical information is exactly that; it informs and it is history. We are told that we can learn from history. This is true, but this kind of history will not teach us much of anything at all. Recall that the second part of the control equation is action. How can any action be taken on this information? Analytical information will, however, provide us with a basis for intelligent action. Referring again to the earlier example, the bar cost problem was isolated as to its location; only one bar was involved. The problem was then isolated as to personnel; only one bartender was involved. In this case, management was in a position to take action and to do so quickly and effectively.

Effective control is built on information systems. We even have a fancy term for them now. We talk about our MIS, our management information systems, but not all information is useful. Management should ensure that most of what they are gathering is of an analytical nature, not historical. Our experience is that the distinction is often blurred, and much of what foodservice managers have available to them only informs; it does not explain how or why.

Anticipate—Don't React

Based on the information received, management will make decisions and send information back down through the operation. This can take two forms: *corrective* or *preventive*. Corrective implies that management is attempting to correct something that has already gone wrong. They are trying to solve yesterday's problems today. Preventive decision making occurs when management has some rational expectation of what will or what is likely to happen. Such expectations would, of course, arise from an effective information system. This implies that management is spending their time making analyses and decisions to control what is going to occur, not what has occurred, trying to solve tomorrow's problems before they happen. There are two kinds of managers. One we will call the reactive type, and the other the anticipating type. We even have a term for the first type of management—the firefighting style. This manager works very hard, spending long hours in the operation day after day, but all he ever does is put out fires. Putting out a fire when you are aware of one is commendable of course. But more commendable would be to take some action that assures future fires cannot start. Many managers pride themselves on their ability to put out fires. We would rather work in an establishment where fires do not occur. The anticipating type of manager will be more concerned with looking ahead and trying to head off potential problems.

We once knew a manager who was assigned to a restaurant in a shopping center and was totally astounded when his January sales dropped to about half of what they had been in December. The operation had been open for about seven years, and this had happened every year. When the next year came, he was again surprised at how slow it was. This experience is not at all unusual.

As another example of what we are talking about, let us imagine an operation whose midsummer sales are about 20 percent lower than they were in the late spring. The reactive manager will probably become increasingly uneasy with the continued decline. One day he will decide it cannot be tolerated any longer. Profits are either being seriously eroded or have disappeared entirely. Being a good manager, he tries to stimulate sales and cut costs. He will run some ads in the paper, put together a promotion or two, call a waitress meeting and urge them to give better service. Next he will lay off waitresses and buspersons, perhaps a dishwasher, and a cook or two. All these actions will be taken in haste, with few, if any, well thought out or properly prepared. If any of these actions work, it is as much due to luck as anything else.

The anticipating manager in the same situation of a midsummer slump will have made careful and detailed income and expense forecasts long before the summer arrived. She may have realized that the summer business would be slow because past records indicate this as a regular occurrence. She may have to do nothing more than evaluate past sales records to realize she is going to have a problem in a few months. Or it could be that she is aware of changing economic conditions that will affect her operation or her location. Two courses of action are open to her, just as there were to the other manager. She can attempt to reverse the sales decline or cope with it by cost cutting. The first is always preferable, so she would investigate that. It could be that, especially since she has sufficient planning time, she can develop an innovative promotional program.

If, on the other hand, it is not realistic to increase sales, the cost cutting approach must be taken. Again, because there is time, it can be properly planned and organized so that the negative impact upon the organization will be minimal. She may prepare new employee schedules to use during the summer months. She may not replace people she knows will be leaving. She may have to decide to let some employees go, but that decision can at least be made rationally, without the pressure of having to make it quickly as the other manager did. In like manner, she will evaluate the entire organization for reasonable ways to reduce expenses. This manager is anticipating events and attempting to control them in her business's favor. Most managers in the foodservice industry are competent enough so that when they know what is going to happen they can cope with it. It is the unexpected that throws them. When a person does not know what is likely to occur, he may not be able to cope and may just react automatically to whatever occurs. Such a person, being managed by circumstances instead of managing circumstances, is a firefighter.

Another term, equally appropriate, is *management by crisis*, which means that managers move from one crisis to another, never fully in control of their operations. Unfortunately many individuals in the hospitality industry pride themselves on their ability to cope with continual crises and chaos. They love it. They thrive on it. They like the "excitement." We would rather the excitement came from satisfying guests, developing stable enthusiastic employees, and, best of all, profits.

We are not stating that management can, or should, spend all their time looking forward. We once heard a very successful foodservice operator state that, at best, management can anticipate 30 to 40 percent of what is going to happen. This means that 60 percent or more of what occurs on a day-to-day basis cannot be predicted with any accuracy. It also reemphasizes the necessity for management to spend time in the operation, to know the operation, so that they can better cope with the uncertainty. What we are suggesting is that managers have attitudes. Some take a strictly defensive attitude, and most of what they do is of a reactive nature. Others, generally the most successful operators, attempt to anticipate. Their attitude is to look ahead.

Accuracy and Timeliness

Information must be accurate, and it must be timely. The consequences of inaccurate information do not really have to be pointed out. Timely information means that management gets it quickly. If you were informed that the bartender who never showed for work a week ago also left with $2,500.00, you could at best regard the information as interesting. It would not, however, be very useful. If someone came dashing up to you yelling that the bartender was just then leaving with $2,500.00, you would find it both interesting and useful (especially if you could run faster than the bartender). Without accurate and timely information, decisions are made improperly; they are made too late, or they are not made at all. Calvin Coolidge is sometimes praised for his performance as president because he did nothing. Few political scientists regard this as a satisfactory approach to running the government of the United States, and even fewer foodservice owners or executives would accept it as a management technique.

How to Gather Information

Information can be obtained *physically* or *electronically*. Traditionally, we have had to rely on physical or manual information retrieval systems in the foodservice business. These are time consuming and often inaccurate. They can also be expensive, more so than they seem to be. Many operators will resist automated or electronic systems because of expense when, in truth, they may not be any more expensive than their manual counterparts. This is especially true when such managers are getting quality information from the electronic system. The term we brought up previously—MIS—is taken

today to mean some sort of computerized or electronic system. Many are available to choose from, and the choice is becoming wider. Chapter 13 provides a detailed discussion of what computers can do in foodservice systems and how to evaluate and select the proper system for your operation.

Basic Control Concepts

Food Control

Food control is unique and is differentiated from beverage control by two factors: (1) Quality control is as important as cost control, and (2) food control is primarily a product control problem. The underlying reason for both is the variability of foods. You are never quite sure what condition the food will be in when it arrives, and food products are subject to change and deterioration every hour you hold them in your establishment. Quality control is thus of prime importance, and a lot of time, effort, and expense is necessary to assure that quality products are consistently served. Control, as our discussion thus far should have made clear, is enhanced by *predictability*. The more unpredictable something is, the more difficult it will be to control. You can get to the point where you have no control simply because you have no idea what is going to happen. The nature of food is to be unpredictable because it is, after all, a natural product. It is not manufactured in a factory, and you cannot purchase a thousand identical units. Food control is difficult because of the product itself, and so it is a product control challenge. Food control does not ignore the potential for personnel problems; people can, and do, steal and waste food. The first objective of a food cost and quality control program, however, is to control the product; second, it is to control personnel. This will be emphasized throughout Section 2: Food Operations Management.

Beverage Control

As stated, beverage control is much different from food control. With beverages, because of their consistency, stability, and predictability, quality control is not a significant problem. You can generally depend on the quality you purchase to be the same as the quality you serve to your guests. You can, of course, purchase poor quality alcoholic beverages, but this is not what we refer to. For this reason, the product itself is easy to control, especially compared to food. Personnel are another matter entirely, however. Beverage control is primarily a personnel problem and secondarily a product problem. Therefore, if one has control over an alcoholic beverage system, she is most likely effectively monitoring the activities of people. This concept will be emphasized in Section 3: Alcoholic Beverage Operations Management.

Role of Accounting in Control

The importance of accounting is that it can yield information that enables management to be aware of the operation's true state of affairs. An accounting system should not only provide analyses of past costs and sales, but it should also produce information for sales and expense projections. This is consistent with the concept of looking forward, not backward. The potential value of modern data processing to an accounting system is a key to effective control, which is why we will place great emphasis on MIS.

It must be recognized that accounting type controls are very important, but at least as important is the control gained by constantly inspecting the premises, procedures, and policies, and by supervising and observing the personnel. As stated earlier, a foodservice operation cannot be managed just from an office; there must be a balance. Thus, some of the control procedures and methods we discuss will seem to be of a commonsense nature. They often are, but experience indicates that they are not followed.

Forecasting

What Is Forecasting?

Forecasting, in the sense that we are going to discuss it here, is the formal projection of income and expenses over a specific time period. This period seldom exceeds one year for operating management. Projections covering longer periods are and should be made, but our discussion will be limited to short-range income and expense planning.

Importance of Forecasting

Management must have a reasonable expectation of income and expenses on which to base operating decisions. Learning to make rational projections is therefore one of the most important skills that management can acquire. The importance of an accurate forecast as an operating tool can be illustrated quite simply. How would you like to have your actual operating statement for the year to come? Do you think it would be useful to know exactly what your food and beverage sales will be, month by month—not only your sales but all your expenses? You would know your food costs, your beverage costs, your labor costs, and all of your operating expenses. It is unlikely that you would be totally satisfied with this operating statement. You could probably find specific instances where sales and/or expenses could be improved. You might even find signs of impending disaster. Would this document be useful to you in making decisions over the coming year? Obviously it would.

As we pointed out, the more certain you are that something will happen, the better you can cope with it. You cannot, of course, obtain an actual operating statement for a future period, but you can do the next best thing—that is to predict, as rationally as possible, what the future is likely to be. When you have done that, you have prepared an operating forecast. You cannot predict the future with total accuracy, but you must make an attempt. Management that does not do so is management that has no expectations, management that is not prepared to cope with anything. In reality, they are making no attempt to *manage*. Such people merely operate from day to day. They do not control their business; it controls them!

Forecasts are also useful in evaluating the efficiency of management. Chains and corporations do not like surprises. They prefer to be able to plan the organization's direction with some confidence. A manager who cannot foresee what is going to happen in his or her unit would be, and should be, evaluated negatively. An effective forecast, as we shall see, can be produced only by a manager who really knows his or her unit, and such a forecast is a valid evaluation criterion.

What Periods Do Forecasts Cover?

Forecasts are generally made according to the frequency of the income statement. Since most organizations prepare statements on a monthly basis, those are the units used. The months are generally combined into quarters, and the quarters into a year. A system for revision should be set up because no matter how carefully the figures are compiled, changes in the economic environment are bound to occur as the year progresses. The need for updated projections can be critical in the last two quarters.

Consider a forecast that was completed in November of 1983 for the year 1984. The first quarter (January, February, and March) would probably be quite accurate, but by the time the final quarter arrives (October, November, December) substantial changes may have occurred in many of the assumptions those figures were based on. Perhaps in the spring a major sales conference had been booked for October. Perhaps a recession, which had only been feared, turned out to be real, and sales over the third quarter were down significantly. Or perhaps the economic recession holding sway when the forecast was made seemed to be ending earlier than expected. Or inflation could cause menu prices to rise, which would result in higher dollar sales. In all these cases, the original forecast would no longer be valid and should be revised.

Forecasts must also be revised to keep current with constantly increasing costs. Meat prices could unexpectedly increase in the spring, and this would affect the food cost forecast. Revision is necessary to keep the forecast as accurate as possible. Unless a forecast is accurate, it is not useful. In fact, it could even be harmful. A forecast is an indication of what is expected. If it is accurate, intelligent and rational operating decisions can be made. If it is not accurate but believed to be, decisions will be made that will be ineffective or even dangerous to the profitability of the establishment.

An example would be when a manager expects sales to increase by some 15 percent during the last two quarters. In this case, a rational decision may be to increase the payroll, hiring and training some new people. If the sales increase does not materialize, the unit would be overstaffed and would sustain unwarranted expenses. On the other hand, if sales did increase unexpectedly, the operation may not be able to adequately service the increase, and the total effect could be detrimental. In the first case, management took action that they should not have taken, and in the second they did not take action they should have. Both cases were caused by an inaccurate forecast.

Income Projection

The first step in forecasting, and the most difficult one, is projecting income. Here, management is trying to predict the future, and that is always a risky thing to do. Accurate sales forecasting requires a great deal of information about the operation and the environment.

Historical Operating Information. What has happened in the past is one of the best indications of what can be expected to occur in the future. The farther back the manager can track sales history, the more useful the information is. It follows then that forecasting sales for a new unit with no history will be extremely difficult. The response of a seasoned restaurateur to the question of how to project sales for a new operation is apropos. He said to use a computer, hire a consultant, evaluate all the economic indicators, take traffic counts, talk to the chamber of commerce, and so forth. When you have come up with the most rational, most intelligent sales projection you can possibly develop, cut it in half. If you cannot make a profit on the sales that remain—don't open. This is good advice and, if followed, there would be fewer failures in the foodservice business than there are. One of the most common reasons for failure is that sales did not meet expectations, and so expenses could not be covered.

Sales projections must be realistic. Another example is that of an individual who took over a location where the two previous tenants (both restaurants) had gone bankrupt. There were at least 300 commercial foodservice operations in this city, and the highest volume any of them were doing was $2 million per year. The next highest was about $1.7 million. Probably only one or two others were even grossing a million per year. His projection for the first year was $2.3 million! He had it all on paper and didn't see how he could miss. The volume the first year was about $450,000. There was no second year.

Evaluate Current Conditions. While historical results are of great value, they have to be evaluated according to what current and recent operating conditions are. If the unit has shown a consistent sales growth of 10 percent per year over the last five years, but for the last two quarters has had a difficult time even maintaining the sales level, this could indicate an end to the growth. It could also just be a temporary problem that was anticipated. At any rate, management must always modify historical trends in light of current conditions.

Expected Operating Conditions. This refers to the future economic, social, and political environment. If a recession were expected, it would not make any sense to project increased sales merely because you have grown in the past. Tax legislation could also have an effect on your customers' spending patterns. The problem here is that the information available seldom lends itself to clear interpretations. Put two economists in the same room with the same information, and one will forecast a depression while the other will predict prosperity. Add another, and you will probably get an entirely different prediction. In spite of this difficulty, it would be unwise to ignore general information about the economy as a whole.

Management Expertise. There is no substi-

tute for qualified management when making operating projections. Managers who are experienced and knowledgeable and have a detailed understanding of the unit being evaluated will be able to make surprisingly accurate projections. Inexperienced managers will not be able to do this, nor will unqualified managers be able to. Statistics and computer print-outs are not a satisfactory substitute for operating knowledge. We cannot emphasize strongly enough how necessary it is to really know the unit for which the forecast is being made. Chains sometimes move managers frequently, so they often have only a superficial knowledge of the operations they are managing.

Separate the Operation into Units. Do not think of your operation as a single entity. It consists of several income sources, each potentially much different from the others. Each of these must be considered independently. To illustrate income forecasting, we will discuss an operation that serves three meals per day, serves both foods and alcoholic beverages, has a lounge, and does catering. The sources of income would be as shown in Exhibit 1.1.

It is necessary to look at the units separately because each income source may well represent a different market. The customers who patronize

Exhibit 1.1. Sources of Income

Food	Beverages
Dining room	Dining Room
breakfast lunch dinner	lunch dinner
Catering	Catering
	Lounge
	lunch cocktail hour dinner evening

the establishment for breakfast are not necessarily the same as those who come in for lunch. The same thing is true of the lunch and dinner customers. This restaurant may even have four different food markets since the catering customers could also constitute a separate and specific market segment. The same is true with alcoholic beverage sales. Some of these sales are from the dining room and catering departments; the customer base is whoever is in those areas, but the evening lounge business could be completely different.

In this case, there are actually several distinct businesses operating under one roof. Some may be thriving while others could be doing poorly. Evaluation of total sales would not show the individual unit's patterns.

Differentiating between the days of the week is also necessary in most commercial operations. Restaurants seldom show the same sales pattern each day of the week. Lunch may be fairly consistent during the week, but it can change dramatically on the weekend. Friday and Saturday night will generally be peak times for the dinner meal period, while Monday can be very slow. This is true for both the dining room and the lounge. The catering department has its patterns as well, and they are usually unique to that department.

When you put your sources together with the days of the week, you have a sales forecast work sheet. Examples of a food work sheet and a beverage work sheet are shown by Exhibits 1.2 and 1.3.

Food Sales Forecast. Initial projections in the dining room will be made by guest count, by meal period, and by the day of the week. The key concept in the dining room is that sales are the result of people. The most important statistic is guest count. Sales result from customers spending at a specific rate. The check average is

Exhibit 1.2. Food Sales Forecast Work Sheet

Income Source	M	T	W	T	F	S	S	Total
Dining Room								
Breakfast CC (customer count) check average sales								
Lunch CC check average sales								
Dinner CC check average sales								
Dining room food								
Catering								
Total Food Sales								

Exhibit 1.3. Beverage Sales Forecast Work Sheet

Income Source	M	T	W	T	F	S	S	Total
Dining Room								
Lunch								
CC								
check average								
sales								
Dinner								
CC								
check average								
sales								
Dining room beverage								
Lounge								
Lunch								
Cocktail hour								
Dinner								
Evening								
Lounge total								
Catering								
Total Beverage Sales								

therefore very important but only *after* you get a customer in the door. If you have no guests, the check average is meaningless. We recommend therefore that you project the dining room sales by guest count. Follow the procedure outlined earlier. Past history is probably the most important of the projection criteria you will use, but you will not want to ignore economic trends, social conditions, and so forth. In fact anything that could have an impact on the number of customers coming into your operation should be considered when doing a guest count forecast.

What we are going to do here is establish a reasonable level of business for one week. This will be referred to as a "typical" week. It represents your most realistic appraisal of what is going to happen in an ordinary week. We have a different technique for handling atypical periods, such as Mother's Day, New Year's Eve, and other holidays, and it will be discussed later. Once the guest count projections are made, you make a check average forecast. Again, the operating history will be your best guide. If your records indicate that the customers have been spending an average of $3.75 at lunch and you do not anticipate price increases or any other changes that would affect that, it would be rational to forecast $3.75.

In this manner you fill in the food forecast for the dining room. When completed, you will have projected the guest counts for each day of the week and for each of the three meal periods. The sales are the result of multiplying the various guest counts (referred to on the work sheet as

CC, which means customer count) by their check averages. Total the sales for each day and then for the week. Exhibit 1.4 shows a completed food work sheet. The dining room sales are projected to be $11,273.95.

Catering sales are handled differently. Guest counts do not have the same significance in catering as they do in the dining room. This is due to the great variance in types of groups you will cater to. Early in the week you might do a luncheon for the Lions Club, the next night a bowling banquet, late Saturday morning a brunch for the Ladies Garden Club, and that evening a wedding. The Lions had 25 people and you charged $5.50 per person. The bowlers were shopping around town for a deal, and you ended up serving 75 at $7.00 per person (tip and tax included). The lady gardeners provided 30 guests, and you charged them $4.50 each

(reasoning that it was better than nothing). Saturday night you hit the jackpot, however. You served 250 people a prime rib dinner and charged $12.50 per person and the bar bill was over $1,600.00!

Guest counts and check averages are not meaningful when these types of variances occur with regularity, and in the catering business they do. In making a catering projection, therefore, you work with dollar figures. It actually is fairly easy to make accurate forecasts. This type of business is generally contracted long before the event takes place. Therefore you just go through your banquet bookings and add them up, week by week, and month by month. When making the forecast for the last couple of quarters, however, you have to be aware of the effect that future bookings and cancellations will have. You will pick up contracts you do not now have and will

Exhibit 1.4 Food Sales Forecast Work Sheet—Completed

Income Source	M	T	W	T	F	S	S	Total
Dining Room								
Breakfast								
CC	56	62	65	60	70	21	---	334
check average	1.75	1.75	1.75	1.75	1.75	2.15		1.775
sales	98.00	108.50	113.75	105.00	122.50	45.15	-0-	592.90
Lunch								
CC	112	124	130	130	155	38	250	939
check average	3.25	3.25	3.25	3.25	3.25	2.50	4.00	3.42
sales	364.00	403.00	422.50	422.50	503.75	95.00	1,000.00	3,210.75
Dinner								
CC	86	100	112	120	160	175	---	753
check average	9.65	9.65	9.65	9.65	10.00	10.50		9.92
sales	829.90	965.00	1,080.80	1,158.00	1,600.00	1,837.50	-0-	7,471.20
Dining room food	1,291.00	1,476.50	1,617.05	1,685.50	2,226.25	1,977.65	1,000.00	11,273.95
Catering								
Total Food Sales								

Exhibit 1.5 Beverage Sales Forecast Work Sheet—Completed

Income Source	M	T	W	T	F	S	S	Total
Dining Room								
Lunch								
CC	112	124	130	130	155	38	---	689
check average	.95	.95	.95	.95	1.50	1.25		N/A
sales	106.40	117.80	123.50	123.50	232.50	47.50	-0-	751.20
Dinner								
CC	86	100	112	120	160	175	---	753
check average	2.10	2.10	2.10	2.10	2.40	2.50		N/A
sales	180.60	210.00	235.20	252.00	384.00	437.50	-0-	1,699.30
Dining room beverage	287.00	327.80	358.70	375.50	616.50	485.00	-0-	2,450.50
Lounge								
Lunch	$53.00	$60.00	$65.00	$65.00	$120.00	$50.00		413.00
Cocktail hour	120.00	120.00	125.00	125.00	200.00	100.00		790.00
Dinner	75.00	80.00	100.00	100.00	120.00	130.00		605.00
Evening	150.00	170.00	175.00	200.00	300.00	300.00		1,295.00
Lounge total	398.00	430.00	465.00	490.00	740.00	580.00		3,103.00
Catering								
Total Beverage Sales								

probably lose some as well. The business increase potential is especially high when you see that you have several prime weekends still open for the last quarter of the year. You reasonably expect to fill them with holiday parties, although nothing is on the books yet. In this case, you simply make an educated guess, based upon what normally happens. If you know your market, your operation, and have good records, you will be quite accurate.

Beverage Sales Forecast. The procedure used in making the beverage forecast is similar to that

used with food. In the dining room, the guest count is the basis for projecting sales; in catering, it is done by dollars. Exhibit 1.5 shows the completed beverage forecast work sheet.

The source of income in the dining room is the same guest base as was used for food projections. we have made two assumptions here. Alcoholic beverages are not served at breakfast or on Sunday. Therefore, only the lunch and dinner guest counts are used. The check average is not as meaningful here as it was with food. The reason is that every dining room guest orders food, but not everyone orders a drink. The dining room is expected to produce $2,450.50 during an average week.

The catering forecast for beverages is handled exactly the way it was done with food. Dollars should be used, and most of the information will come from the catering functions book.

Lounge forecasting is also best done by dollars. Guest counts are not as reliable an indicator as with food because of the variance in spending patterns. One bar customer may drink two beers, while another could have five martinis. The check averages are too inconsistent (not always, but in most cases) for the guest count to be the most useful forecasting criterion. The bar history is our best guide. And as with the other areas, we make whatever modifications seem indicated by the current and expected economic and social conditions. Our forecast in Exhibit 1.5 is $3,103.00.

Total food and beverage sales, exclusive of catering sales, for this operation are $16,827.45. Food sales are $11,273.95, or 67 percent of total sales. This is what the operator expects under normal conditions. The middle of winter may not constitute normal conditions, nor may early September when school begins. Christmas week is not a typical week. There are several more examples in which sales would be expected to deviate substantially from the average.

The procedure is to begin making the forecast for the coming year, using this average or typical week as the base. As you move through the year, week by week, you modify the forecast according to what ordinarily occurs in your operation. You begin the year, for example, with New Year's Day. If you were closed on New Year's Day, and it fell on a Friday, it would have a major effect on that week's forecast, since Friday is your busiest day (you actually do over 21 percent of your business on that one day). Saturday is your next busiest day, and although you would be open on that day, it would certainly not be normal. It generally takes a while for business to pick up after the Christmas and New Year's holidays. Thus you have no sales for Friday and greatly reduced sales for Saturday. Even if the rest of the week were normal, which it probably would not be, this is going to be a very slow sales week. This

"week," by the way, consists of only three days—Friday, Saturday, and Sunday.

This is another problem that should be recognized in forecasting. Whenever you use a twelve-month calendar for operating statements, and nearly all businesses do, you have an imbalance built in. Each month does not have the same number of days, nor do they have the same days. Using our sales pattern as an example, imagine the difference between two months, one of which had five Fridays and Saturdays and the other five Sundays and Mondays. The sales per week could be exactly the same, but because of the imbalance in the days of the week, there would be a significant difference in total monthly sales.

This causes interpretation problems with the operating statement as well. Since the sales are the same on a weekly basis, all the expenses are likely to be the same, especially the payroll. The net profit, however, as shown by the operating statement, will not be the same. In fact, one month could show a loss and the other a profit. Neither figure is correct. The two should be combined and an average of the two would show the true profitability. Although this causes problems in forecasting sales from month to month, our technique of doing it a day and a week at a time makes the necessary adjustment. You move through the entire year in this manner, modifying the typical week upwards or downwards as conditions indicate. When you finish, the total is your projected sales for the year.

This should be a realistic figure. Sales forecasts are often done by using yearly dollar totals. In other words, the operator will look at the current year's sales and last year's sales, evaluate the economy, and so forth, and then come up with a prediction for the following year. What we have done is much different. Ours is a defensible figure because it is based on guest counts and check averages, it recognizes the difference among daily sales patterns and seasonal sales patterns, and it accounts for the sales mix among departments and between product lines, such as food and beverage. This is a rational approach. When it is done by an experienced manager who knows his or her operation and who has access to the proper information, it will yield very accurate forecasts.

After they have been compiled, sales projections should be entered in the operating forecast work sheet (Exhibits 1.6 and 1.7). The

Exhibit 1.6. Operating Forecast Work Sheet

	$	%	Comment
SALES Food Beverage Total sales			
Cost of Sales Food Beverage Total cost of sales **Gross Profit**			
Controllable expenses Labor direct payroll management fringe costs total labor Supplies—cleaning Supplies—operating Supplies—paper China, glassware, silver, and linen Contract expenses Utilities Music and entertainment Administrative and general Advertising and promotion Repairs and maintenance Total controllable expenses			
Income before occupation expenses			
Occupation costs Rent, property taxes, and insurance			
Profit before interest and depreciation			

Exhibit 1.7 Operating Forecast Work Sheet—Completed

	$	%	Comment
SALES			
Food	716,245	67.8	*SALES MIX %% OF FOO*
Beverage	340,756	32.2	*67.76% BEN TO*
Total sales	1,057,001	100.0	*32.24% TOTAL SALES*
Cost of Sales		*COST OF SELLING*	
Food	272,173	38.0 *NOT A SALES MIX*	*38.0*
Beverage	89,234	26.2	*716,245 272,173*
Total cost of sales	361,407	34.2 *TOTAL COST*	
Gross Profit *= GROSS MARGIN SOMETHING*	695,594	*DIFFERENCE* 65.8	
Controllable expenses			
Labor			
direct payroll	250,000	23.7	
management	46,000	4.4	
fringe costs	45,000	4.3	
total labor	341,000	32.3	
Supplies—cleaning	5,283	0.5	
Supplies—operating	7,925	0.75	
Supplies—paper	5,280	0.5	
China, glassware,			
silver, and linen	31,698	3.0	
Contract expenses	5,290	0.5	
Utilities	29,585	2.8	
Music and entertainment	8,453	0.8	
Administrative and general	63,396	6.0	
Advertising and promotion	36,981	3.5	
Repairs and maintenance	20,075	1.9	
Total controllable expenses	554,966	52.5	
Income before occupation expenses	140,628	13.3	
Occupation costs			
Rent, property taxes, and insurance	70,000	6.6	
Profit before interest and depreciation	70,628	6.7	

totals in Exhibit 1.7 were arrived at using the formulas at the bottom of this page.

Forecasting Expenses

Once the sales projections have been made, the various expenses necessary to support *this specific* level of business must be forecast. Expense forecasting is much easier than income forecasting because in the latter you are attempting, as pointed out, to predict the future. With expense forecasting, however, you are usually only making decisions as to how much you want to spend, and this is a critical difference. A sales forecast that is inaccurate may be the result of external factors beyond the control of management. Expense forecasts that prove to be wrong almost always result from lack of internal control.

Food Cost Forecasting. The most important point about the food cost is that it is predetermined by management. In other words, when the forecast is made, management is actually deciding what they want it to be; they are not trying to predict what it *might* be. Achieving it is, of course, another story, but that is an operating problem, a question of control. Another key point with food costs is that it is a true variable cost and thus should be forecast by a percentage, not dollars. What we mean by a *true variable cost* is that the cost of food should always maintain the same ratio to food sales, regardless of how high or low those sales are. If you sell a chicken that costs $2.50 for $6.00, your food cost will be 41.7 percent. If you sell 100 chickens, you food cost will be 41.7 percent. If

you sell 2,451 chickens, your food cost will be 41.7 percent! Volume of sales, therefore, does not affect the expected food cost percentage. What does affect it, however, are the following factors:

Sales mix

Product costs

Product selling prices

The sales mix is important because if you sell five chickens and five lobsters, you will have one food cost percentage, but if you sell three chickens and seven lobsters, you will have another. Product costs are important because if your supplier raises the prices of chickens, your cost could increase to $2.75 from $2.50, giving you a new food cost percentage of 45.8 percent. The selling price is obviously important because a change in the menu price from $6.00 to $6.50 would drop the food cost percentage to 38.5 percent (assuming the cost were still $2.50). These are the only factors that will have an impact on the food cost percentage. Volume has nothing to do with it. The only effect volume can have is on waste and efficiency, and this is an operating problem—not a planning problem— and is thoroughly discussed in Chapter 4. For forecasting purposes, it is only necessary that management know what products they will sell, how much the products will cost, and what they will be selling them for.

Management must have net profit objectives, and they should establish cost parameters for the various operating expenses so that the profit can

---

Formulas for calculating totals in Exhibit 1.7

Food—dining room = $11,273.95 x 52 weeks   = $586,245.40
       catering   = $130,000.00
Total food sales = $716,245.40

Beverage—dining room = $2,450.00 x 52 weeks = $127,400.00
           lounge   = $3,103.00 x 52 weeks = $161,356.00
           catering   = $ 52,000.00
Total beverage sales = $340,756.00

Total sales = $1,057,001.40

be achieved. In other words, in order to make a certain percentage or dollar profit, management must decide how much to spend on food, on beverages, on labor, on operating supplies, on energy, on rent, and so forth. In most of these areas, they will not have much control, but even in those cases, they must know what their costs will be and adjust the other expenses accordingly. This is one way to establish the food cost percentage. Someone decides that the operation cannot meet its financial objectives unless the food cost is no higher than 38 percent. Once this decision is made, operating management must structure the unit so that this objective is met. They have to have reasonable expectations of what the sales mix and the product costs will be. They have to know how much they will be charging for the various menu items. This will give them the projected food costs. If it is not satisfactory, and it may not be, management has to go back to the drawing board. Adjustments will have to be made in the sales mix, the product costs, and the menu pricing structure.

For purposes of our discussion, let us assume that the goal established by the company or the owner was a food cost of 38 percent and that management was able to plan menus so that this percentage would be attained. The sales would be multiplied by 38 percent, and the food cost of $272,173 ($716,245.00 x .38) would be entered in the operating forecast work sheet (Exhibit 1.7).

Beverage Cost Forecast. This is done the same as the food forecast. Beverage cost is a true variable cost, and thus its percentage should remain stable regardless of what the sales levels are. The factors that could cause the beverage percentage to change are the same as with food: sales mix, product costs, and product selling prices. Management needs to know what these are, and they need to know what the cost objectives are. Once these are known, the forecast can be made with reasonable certainty that it is accurate. A point about both food and beverage cost percentages which will be covered in some detail in the food and beverage sections is that without knowledge of what sales mixes are and knowledge of what food and beverage product costs are management does not, and

cannot, know what the cost percentage should be. Under such circumstances, intelligent planning cannot be done, nor can the operation be adequately managed.

In planning the beverage cost, management will have to project specific costs for the various income sources and for the different types of products sold. The catering department will not have the same cost structure as the lounge does. The lounge will differ from the dining room where, among other factors, most of the wine will be sold. This is significant because wine generally has the highest percentage cost of any of the alcoholic beverages. Our beverage cost forecast is based on these assumptions:

Expected cost percentage
   Catering = 30%
   Lounge   = 18%
   Dining room = 35%

Projected dollar costs
   Catering: $15,600 ($ 52,000 x .30)
   Lounge: $29,044 ($161,356 x .18)
   Dining room: $44,590 ($127,400 x .35)

Total cost: $89,234.00

Cost percentage: 26.2%

If this cost is not consistent with the organizational goals, then it's back to the drawing board. The sales have been rationally projected, so the only recourse, at this point, is to adjust the selling prices or the product costs so that the financial objectives can be met. But we will assume that these costs are acceptable, and they will be entered into the operating forecast work sheet (Exhibit 1.7).

Cost of Goods Sold Forecast. The cost of goods sold is the combination of food and beverage costs. The dollar figures are added together, and the percentage is calculated from this total. The total cost is $361,407 ($272,173 + $89,234), and the cost of goods sold percentage is 34.2 percent ($361,407 ÷ $1,057,001). These are entered on the forecast work sheet.

Payroll Forecast. Labor cost is not a variable cost as are food and beverage costs. This means that this cost cannot be expected to maintain a fixed relationship to sales. We stated that if you expected a 38 percent food cost, unless one of the three cost factors changed, the cost should be 38 percent no matter what the sales level happened to be. You cannot do this with payroll cost. If, for example, a 30 percent payroll is the ideal cost for an operation in a month where the volume is $100,000.00, in those months where the volume exceeded $100,000.00, the percentage should be expected to be lower. The reverse is also true. If the volume should drop much below $100,000.00, the percentage would normally increase. Volume does affect payroll costs.

Labor cost is a semivariable cost. When sales increase, you may not need any more employees since many employee categories are not responsive to the guest counts. You need only one potwasher to clean the soup kettle regardless of whether the kettle was used to make 4 gallons of soup or 10 gallons. One cashier can take money from either 100 guests nightly or 175. One manager will be needed, one chef, and so on. If there is a large increase in sales, you will have to increase some categories of employees, such as waiters, waitresses, buspersons, perhaps dishwashers and some cooks, but nearly always by a lesser amount than the sales increase. The result could be, for example, that the sales went up 12 percent, but the payroll dollars increased only 4 percent. The net effect would be that the overall payroll percentage would drop. If the sales were to drop by 12 percent, you may not be able to cut any hours from the payroll. Or if you can, it will almost certainly be less than 12 percent. The payroll percentage would increase in this case.

Because of these factors, payroll should be forecasted as a dollar figure and then converted to a percentage. The recommended procedure for forecasting the dollar cost is to use the employee schedules and cost them out. The schedules, in turn, are dependent on the guest patronage levels. What we are suggesting is that management should evaluate each level of sales and develop staffing guides to assure that the needs of the guests can be satisfied with the least commitment of labor at each level. This is easy to say, but it is one of the most difficult tasks that foodservice management has.

We do not mean to imply that the payroll percentage is not important. If it exceeds the figure management has specified for minimum profitability, the firm could no longer be viable. One thing should be clearly recognized however. The payroll dollars that are projected by this method represent management's best estimate of the minimum numbers of employees necessary to service the business according to the organization's standards. If this dollar cost results in an unacceptably high percentage, the establishment has a real problem. The payroll forecast can be reduced. That is no problem at all. If it is, however, the level of service will drop, and this in turn could affect the volume. Here you really have to go back to the drawing board, sometimes to the extent of reevaluating the entire concept since some very basic changes will have to be made in the operating system.

The payroll forecast should be separated, at minimum, into direct labor (employees), management, and fringe costs or employee benefits. Each should be forecast independently. The direct wages will come from the employee schedules or staffing guides. This figure would be expected to change throughout the year as the volume levels change. Management payroll is a fixed cost; it is not responsive to volume and will be the same for each month. If salary increases are anticipated for either management or employees, they should be reflected in the months they will occur. Employee benefits are a function of the total payroll costs, and most of the time they are forecast by percentage. We have used 15 percent of the total payroll dollars, direct and management, to obtain the fringe costs. This is a realistic cost for most foodservice operations today. If a unit's records showed that their fringe costs were higher or lower than this, they would of course use the actual figure. The forecast work sheet shows that the employee wages are expected to total $250,000.00 for the year and that this will yield a percentage of 23.7 percent. Management wages are $46,000.00, or

4.3 percent, and fringes come to $45,000.00 (4.3 percent). The total payroll is $341,000.00, and the overall labor percentage is 32.3 percent. We will assume that this percentage is consistent with the financial objectives. These figures are entered into the forecast work sheet (Exhibit 1.7).

Other Controllable Expenses. Although these expenses individually are much smaller than the previous ones, when you total them, they are considerable. The industry reports controllable expenses, exclusive of payroll, as ranging from about 18 percent to nearly 24 percent. These types of expenses are generally forecast using percentages as guidelines. Most are more or less semivariable types of costs; that is, they will vary in relationship to sales, but they usually require large sales changes to affect the percentages. In such cases, percentages will be reasonably consistent. Inconsistent operating percentages are usually an indication of a poorly run unit. A few of the categories should be handled similar to the way in which we did the direct wages. The proper dollar cost should first be established, and the percentage calculated from that. In this category are contract expenses, utilities, music and entertainment, and advertising and promotion. We will look at each of these separately.

Contract Expenses. This expense normally includes all contracted services. Examples would be:

Night cleaning service

Exterminator

Restroom sanitation service

Hood cleaning and fireproofing

Carpet shampooing

Armored truck cash pickup service

Window washing

There are many other such services, but these will give you an idea of what the category covers. These are easy to forecast since you have a contract. The forecast is whatever the contract total is. The percentage is derived from the dollar total. In Exhibit 1.7 we show an expense of $5,290.00 (0.5 percent).

Utilities. Energy expense is an important topic among hospitality operators, and that is what this expense consists of. It includes gas, electricity, water, heat, air conditioning, and so forth. The forecast would generally be based on the expected dollar expense. The operator would examine her or his recent utility bills, modify them for expected rate increases, and make the forecast. There are many things that operators can do to reduce energy expenditures, but these have little to do with the forecast. They should be addressed in both the planning and operating phases, but once you have a history, these expenses are relatively easy to forecast.

Music and Entertainment. The forecast is simple to make. Your contract with the musicians and entertainers is the basis for the forecast. If you do not have long-term contracts, you should have an entertainment budget that allows you to spend a certain amount of money. This then becomes the forecast.

Advertising and Promotion (A and P). Although many operators project A and P expenses by using a percentage, we feel that this is wrong. The most rational method is to project your advertising and promotion *needs* and then determine what it will cost to implement them. If you anticipate a Mother's Day promotion, what are you going to do? Be specific. How much will it cost? That expense becomes part of the A and P forecast for May. If you are going to do certain things to promote New Year's Eve or weddings in June or an early-bird special in the dining room or a new cocktail hour concept or a special group of musicians you intend to bring into the lounge—cost them out. The cost becomes your forecast for those specific periods. You will not necessarily have a consistent dollar cost over the year. In fact, it would be unusual if you did. As with all your expenses, there should be organizational guidelines as to acceptable percentages. If you plan to promote too heavily, it may not be justified since you could be exceeding the guidelines.

Semivariable Controllable Expenses. The remaining expenses have a fairly consistent relationship with sales and can be forecast using a percentage. The source of the percentage would be the historical records. When these records indicate specific costs that you consider excessive, you must be careful about forecasting improved costs. There is a reason why they are high, and without a plan of action properly implemented, they are not going to change. This is a mistake that is often made. Managers will look at, for example, a total supplies cost of perhaps 6 percent and realize that it is well above the industry average and probably higher than it should be. The temptation is to lower the forecast cost to 4.5 percent and hope you can solve the problem. First you had better know what the problem is, and second have a strategy developed to cope with it before you forecast an improvement.

These other controllable expenses are recorded on Exhibit 1.7. They total $213,966.00 or 20.2 percent, which is about in the middle of the industry range.

Occupation Costs. This cost is not a forecast; it is your only true fixed cost and can be expected to remain at the same dollar level whatever happens to the sales. There are some exceptions to this, such as when a sliding rent scale is in effect, but the statement is generally valid. These expenses include rent, property taxes, and insurance. In our example, the cost is $70,000.00 per year, and this gives us a percentage of 6.6 percent, which is on the high end of foodservice industry averages.

The remaining task is to subtract all the costs from sales and see whether or not you made any money. In Figure 1.7 we had a profit (before interest and depreciation) of $70,628.00. The profit percentage was 6.7 percent. This is on the low side of average industry performance which shows that profits before interest and depreciation range from 6 to 10 percent.

What Do You Do Next? You may think that you are now finished. It would be nice to report to you that this is all there is to it; we would,

however, be misleading you. *If* you were totally satisfied with the forecast, in all respects, you would be finished. It is more likely, however, that there are some areas that you are not happy with. Back to the drawing board!

The most obvious area of dissatisfaction would be sales because everything except food and beverage cost is somewhat, if not entirely, dependent on the sales totals. What if the sales had been $75,000.00 higher? That is only $1,500.00 per week and does not seem to be unreasonable. This sales increase probably would have no effect on the following costs:

Payroll (not a major sales increase so we assume no additional personnel will be required)

Contract cleaning

Utilities

Music and entertainment

Repairs and maintenance

The sales increase would have almost no effect on these costs:

Supplies (cleaning and operating)

China, glassware, silver

Administrative and general

Paper supplies and linen would probably go up more than the others since they are more closely tied to sales. Food and beverage costs would, of course, increase. The net effect could be something like this:

Sales increase = $75,000.00
Food sales = $50,850.00 (67.8% of total sales)
Beverage sales = $24,150.00
                (32.2% of total sales)
Food cost increase = $19,323.00
                (38% x $50,850.00)
Beverage cost increase = $6,327.00
                (26.2% x $24,150.00)
Gross profit increase = $49,350.00

Nearly all of this $49,350.00 will go to the bottom line for we have established that most of the other costs are not affected by this volume increase, and those that are, are affected only minimally. Let us be generous and estimate that another $4,350.00 will be spent to support this increased volume. That still leaves us with $45,000.00 profit. Some of you may have noticed that there was no discussion of the effect of the volume increase on advertising and promotion expenses. The reason is that advertising and promotion expenses are not affected *by* sales; they have an effect *on* sales. What we mean is that we are going to have to do something to get this extra business, and whatever we do will cost us money. As long as we spend less than $45,000.00, we come out ahead. $45,000.00 will buy a lot of advertising!

If you are dissatisfied with the sales totals, the way you forecasted the sales will aid you in planning how to augment them. You have, after all, detailed statistics on how many guests you expect for lunch on a typical Tuesday. You know how many people will be coming in for breakfast on Thursday, how many for dinner on Saturday, and so on. You have similar detail on the expected beverage income, lounge income, and catering income. A careful evaluation of all these sources should indicate where you are weak and can use improvement. This, incidentally, helps to focus your promotional effort. If you know

that you need lunch customers on Monday, Tuesday, Wednesday, and Thursday, you can develop specific promotions to build business at those times. If you perceive that the early week dinner business is slow and that you are packed on the weekend, it would be a mistake to run some ads in the paper proclaiming the qualities of your establishment. What would probably happen is that you would be overcrowded on the weekend and still slow on the weekdays. In this case whatever you do should be focused on building dinner trade early in the week. The point here is that if the sales are inadequate to support the projected expenses, you have the information necessary to attack the problem intelligently.

You have also developed, in the preparation of this forecast, a detailed knowledge of all your expenses. You should be able to rationally examine the total cost structure to see if there are any areas that could be improved.

This process that we have labeled *forecasting* is very consistent with the philosophy discussed at the beginning of this chapter. Look ahead, not behind. Use what has happened to better plan for what lies ahead, and most important of all, know your operation. A manager who prepares a forecast along the lines we have outlined will not only have a reasonably accurate document to use as a management tool but will also have a much greater understanding of the unit's operation.

Section II

Food Operations Management

In the foodservice industry, product cost along with labor cost accounts for what is known as the "prime cost." Two basic types of products are sold in foodservice operations: foods and alcoholic beverages. Of these two, food is by far the larger. Many operations do not even serve alcoholic beverages, so their entire product cost is food. An approximate average sales mix for units that do sell wines, spirits, and beers is 75 percent food, 25 percent beverage. Cost percentages vary widely, but the average for food is about 40 percent and for beverages about 26 percent. Any operation showing these kinds of figures would have a total product cost of 36.5 percent.

Food = .40 x .75 or		.30%
Beverage = .26 x .25 or		.065%
Total Percentage Cost		.365

This means that of each dollar received in food sales, $.40 will be spent on the food itself. From every dollar of total sales, food will account for $.30. Thus the expense item we are studying

accounts for a significant part of the total operating expenses. As an expense item, food is also controllable to a high degree by operating management. Food costs—as well as beverage costs—are technically true variable costs, the types most responsive to management control. Fixed costs do not change and are therefore not manageable. Semivariable costs, such as payroll, share the characteristics of both fixed and variable costs. They can swing towards one or the other, depending on conditions. With food, we are interested not only in cost control but quality control as well. Achieving cost and quality control of a food system is quite difficult due to the unpredictability of the basic products.

A food control program has two objectives. One is to put management in a position to predict the exact nature of a product when it is served to a guest. They should know what it looks like, smells like, tastes like, feels like, and so on. This is quality control. The other objective is to put management in a position to know what the total product cost will be, and this is cost control. Both are equally important, and attaining one without the other would eventually lead to failure. Operations can fail due to lack of guests, and quality control is a large factor in this situation. Operations can also fail because of an inability to make the forecasted profit on food sold. This is what cost control is all about.

First, we will examine the factors that influence food costs. Second, we will look at the analytical tools and techniques that enable management to correctly interpret what has occurred and then to make rational decisions toward correcting problems. Finally, we will discuss how to control a food system.

2 Factors Affecting Food Cost and Quality

Menu

Of all the factors that can affect food costs, the menu is probably the most critical one. The menu affects both what a food cost *should* be and the difficulty of attaining that figure. In both cases, the responsibility is primarily on planning management rather than operating management.

A menu built around lower-cost items will have a lower potential percentage cost than will a menu composed of lobster tails and steaks. It would be a mistake to assume that lower-cost menus are limited to operations such as fast food, cafeterias, coffee shops, and family restaurants. The management of many fine dining establishments have made efforts to put foods on their menus that yield high profits. Mexican dinner house chains are a good example of this and so are the many so-called casual restaurants. Their managers show great imagination and creativity in the development and presentation of products that have great appeal and also yield excellent profits. Thus the first cost aspect of menu planning is the "standard" or "potential"

cost. This is the cost if everything goes properly. The potential cost is partially a function of the type of establishment, but as pointed out, creative planning can make the market less of a constraint.

The second cost aspect of the menu is in the degree of control difficulty. This simply refers to the difficulty management encounters in trying to attain the projected potential cost. In general, the fewer the items on the menu, the more effective the control measures are because the operation is less complex. Two contrasting extremes illustrate this point. One very traditional restaurant has a large and extensive menu composed of about forty entrees. Preparing these forty entrees—from scratch— requires hundreds of ingredients. The other restaurant has a very limited menu. There are three kinds of steaks, lobster tails, crab legs, and a rib roast. Very few ingredients are needed to support this menu. The steaks, lobster tails, and crab legs are all purchased already portioned, and the rib roast is purchased oven ready. Obviously other ingredients are required: potatoes, vegetables, desserts, salad ingredients, and so forth. Even so, this restaurant will be purchasing very few items relative to the first one.

All foodservice operations must perform the same functions. They must purchase, receive, store, issue, produce, and serve food. Yet there is a significant difference in the complexity of these functions in the two restaurants given as examples. If the objectives of control are to assure predictability and consistency in both the quality and cost of products served, these objectives can be more readily met in the limited-menu restaurant.

Sales Mix

The potential cost of a menu is not stable. It will vary according to the mix of products sold. Seldom if ever will a menu be developed in which all products have the same cost percentage. Usually each item will be different from the others, sometimes very much so. A crepe costing $1.75 to produce may sell for $5.25 (33.3 percent food cost), while lobster tail on the same menu that costs $6.50 sells for $12.95 (50.2 percent food cost). The food cost and the profit are dependent on the sales ratio of crepes to lobsters. This sales mix can be somewhat controlled by the design and layout of the menu. By highlighting and properly locating items yielding maximum profits (although not necessarily the lowest percentage), menu planners can move sales in a predetermined direction. Operating management can have a great deal of control over the sales mix. Training service people in effective techniques of personal selling, promoting, and merchandising are all proven ways to maximize menu profits.

Many foodservice operators do not realize their unique position in the world of retailers. When guests enter a restaurant, they have already made a decision to purchase. In most other types of sales establishments, the customers are only prospective customers. Usually they are in the middle of the purchase decision sequence, and they may or may not finally decide to buy something. Since restaurant patrons have already made that decision, the management challenge is to assure that the customer's choice is the most profitable one. Some guests, of course, will have already decided what to purchase before they enter, but many will not. It is the job of all customer-contact personnel, the menu, and in-house merchandising to influence product selection. Often, foodservice operations miss acting on this responsibility. When this happens, it is difficult to reach maximum profits. These sadly unrealized profits due to sales mix have nothing to do with efficiency of the operation. The establishment could be quite well run and clean, the food could be excellent, and the service both attentive and warm. It would not make any difference. Unless the menu product mix is optimized, profits will be limited.

Market Consumption Trends

Market trends are related to the above concept since they will have an effect on the sales mix. When a food fad appears or, for a variety of reasons, people change their consumption habits, this can alter the cost structure. Trends can change the sales mix of existing products, or they can cause items to be added to the menu. When this occurs, there is a period of uncertainty, waiting for a new sales pattern to emerge. Then time is necessary to evaluate the pattern. These things can happen when a new style of preparation suddenly becomes very popular, such as with the *nouvelle cuisine*. It also can occur when people cut down on beef and demand more variety in poultry and seafood dishes. It happens as well when the consumer becomes interested in certain types of ethnic foods. The taste for Mexican food during the late 1970s is a prime example. Changes also take place when there is great interest in "natural" foods or "health" foods or "organic" foods.

These factors can be as much an opportunity as they are a problem. Successful foodservice operators say, "Tell me what the people want, and I'll figure out a way to make money on it!" A classic example of this in the area of beverage sales was the effect on profits of the white wine boom in the late 1970s and early 1980s. Restaurant patrons in massive numbers began ordering white wine before dinner instead of the traditional mixed drinks. Mixed drinks typically sold at higher prices, and they were certainly more profitable. Costs were adversely affected by the new drinking habits. When the trend persisted, some operators found ways to make money on it using strategies such as promoting wine cocktails, developing strong house wine programs, increasing dinner wine sales, and switching the spirit drinks to the end of the meal. Management must be aware of consumption patterns and the effects of these on costs and profits. They must also be prepared to take action when a seemingly negative trend occurs in order to turn it around.

Seasonal Variations in Sales Mix

The sales mix can be expected to vary over the course of a year, often enough so as to alter standard costs. As in the previous example, some operators refuse to accept declining profits merely because it is summer or winter or whatever. They find foods to sell that will appeal to the market and make money as well. These seasonal variances in the sales mix should not cause any problems since they are predictable. Summer comes yearly, and winter arrives at about the same time each year. The fall season with schools reopening and football is a regular occurrence. Yet many operators sit, seemingly helpless, when the seasonal sales patterns change, and their costs and profits fluctuate.

Selling Prices

Selling prices have an obvious effect not on dollar costs but on cost percentages. They are, however, only one of the three elements that make up a standard cost percentage. The others are the dollar cost of each product and the sales mix. Too many times the selling price is viewed as either the sole savior or villain when trying to manage costs. The point is that pricing can be considered as a cost-reduction measure, but it should not be used to the exclusion of the other two. We have already discussed the potential benefits of manipulating the sales mix. The

operator should consider product dollar cost reduction as a strategy as well for it will reduce the percentage by reducing the dollar cost. This can be much less noticeable to the consumer than raising the price. The use of pricing strategies to reduce costs often yields only short-term benefits, whereas concentration on other measures can offer a substantial payoff over a longer period.

Standards

The issue of standards implies that a proper, right, or acceptable product or action has been established. The existence of and enforcement of standards greatly helps attain the consistency and predictability needed in managing a food system. Lack of standards, on the other hand, is one way to insure that the cost and quality of products delivered to the guests will vary constantly. In such cases, there is no control. Standardization of *all* foods, *all* ingredients, *all* methods of preparation, *all* plating and presentation, *all* serving techniques is essential to control. The relationship between controls and standards is that standards are set for the establishment, and controls are whatever management does to insure that the standards are met. Without standards, how would management know whether the controls were effective? What would management control if there were no standards?

Sales Volume

The relationship between food cost percentage and sales volume is often misunderstood. Many foodservice people expect that as volume increases, the cost percentage should come down. As pointed out, however, a standard food cost is the result of three factors: the costs of products, selling prices, and sales mix. Volume is not used to calculate a potential or standard food cost. Therefore, from a theoretical standpoint, volume should have no effect on food cost percentages, only on food cost dollars. This is so because food cost is a true variable cost. The dollar cost will vary as more or fewer products are sold, but the percentage relationship between cost and sales should remain the same. If a chicken dish with a food cost of $2.50 is sold for $6.75, the cost percentage will be 37 percent. If ten chicken orders are sold, the food cost will be $25.00, and the percentage 37 percent. If forty orders are sold, the food cost will increase to $100.00, but the cost percentage should still be 37 percent. Regardless of the number of chickens sold, the cost percentage should remain the same. Volume, therefore has no effect on cost percentage. This is a factual statement so long as the three basic food cost percentage factors do not change.

If volume influences either the product's actual dollar cost or the sales mix, then the food cost percentage could change. Volume, therefore, is not a primary influence upon cost percentage, but it may well be a secondary one. Volume is a factor when it changes the basic variables. Continuing with the chicken dish as an example, if the sales increased substantially, the establishment might be able to get a better purchase price on chicken. Sellers of virtually all products, unless they are in a monopoly position, will reduce prices on larger volume purchases. If the chicken costs less, the serving cost of the meal will drop, and the result is that the food cost percentage will decrease. The decrease is not due directly to the volume, however. It is due to the fact that increased volume enabled a reduction in the product's dollar cost, and this created a different set of percentage variables. Another way in which volume could indirectly influence the expected percentage is by altering the sales mix. When there are significant increases in guest count, the consumption patterns can be expected to change somewhat. If the sales mix changes, the standard percentage is likely to change as well.

A third effect of volume is to lower the actual percentage but not the standard percentage. The standard percentage by definition will be attained when everything is done perfectly, when there are no mistakes. This, of course, is uncommon. Mistakes are made, food is wasted, yields are inconsistent, food is stolen or eaten, it

may spoil and be discarded. In such cases, the potential food cost is not reached; and the actual food cost exceeds the potential. Volume can cover up these mistakes. If only ten chickens are being sold daily and one order is wasted, eaten, stolen, or spoiled, the operation has lost 10 percent of its product. This would have a large negative impact on the costs. If, however, the sales were eighty chickens daily, the loss of one chicken would not be felt nearly as much. Volume thus reduces the inefficiency factor. What has happened is not that the increased volume dropped the food cost percentage but that the increase in volume enabled the operation to get closer to its standard cost. But volume can also cause the opposite effect: if the volume is excessive, *increased* waste could occur, which would raise costs.

For these reasons, it is technically incorrect to expect volume changes to raise or lower food cost percentages, but volume can create conditions that can do so. Decreases in volume generally have little impact on the product costs, but they can have a serious effect upon waste and efficiency. Sales losses put a lot of pressure on a cost control program.

Personnel

In discussing this topic, we would like to focus on the quality of the personnel. Skilled food-handling employees can contribute to the operation by assuring that standards are met. Unskilled and/or poorly trained kitchen employees perform so inefficiently that actual costs are higher than calculated or expected costs. This is so obvious that it does not require explanation, but not so obvious is how temporary this situation can be. Hiring and training is the key to quality personnel. Foodservice operations often do a poor job of hiring personnel. They do not necessarily hire people who are physically unqualified; rather they put people to work who are socially and/or psychologically unqualified to perform the required tasks. It is not a mistake to hire an individual who has never cooked before. It is a mistake to hire someone who has no sense of quality or any appreciation for the tastes, colors, and textures of food. These are the types of personal attributes to look for in someone to hire for a foodservice operation. You can teach specific skills. Too often hiring is done based on skills or experience, with little if any regard for personal characteristics.

Once qualified people are hired—qualified in terms of the previous discussion—they must be properly trained. Foodservice operations also tend to do a poor job of training employees. There are many exceptions to this statement. Any successful foodservice establishment spends much time, effort, and expense on training. For every such successful operation, however, there are dozens that do not.

Unqualifed employees who are inadequately trained will not, cannot perform at the level necessary to attain standard costs. *Inexperienced* workers, when properly selected and adequately trained, can perform at this level. The point is that although personnel considerations are a major factor in food costs, they need not be a negative factor.

Equipment and Facilities

This is a critically important component of food control and, moreover, it is primarily the responsibility of the planners and operations designers. Operating management can reverse mistakes made in the planning and design but only at substantial expense. New equipment and facilities redesign and/or reconstruction are usually very expensive.

There must be adequate space and proper equipment to receive foods easily. An efficient purchasing department would be worthless unless the receiving department assures that the products they specify and order actually are delivered and properly stored and accounted for.

Poorly designed storage facilities and ineffective storage equipment can undo a well-planned control program. Sufficient space for storage of delivered goods must be built in. Otherwise foods are overcrowded or else stored in unsuitable areas. Overcrowding creates operational problems, possibly even microbiological hazards. Storage in undesirable areas often results in food spoilage or contamination as well.

The temperature in storage areas must meet the food requirements. If it does not, the minimum consequence will be reduced shelf life, and the outcome could well be an outbreak of food-caused illness. The section on food control will cover recommended storage temperatures for various foods.

Access and security are other elements to consider in storage equipment. The type of storage facilities and their location will greatly influence these factors. Security depends upon equipment, location, and operating policies. Some equipment and certain locations are easier to secure against unauthorized entry than others. In general, security is enhanced by reducing accessibility to an area. The fewer people authorized to enter a storage area, the greater the control. The more difficult it is for an employee to circumvent this restriction, the more effective the control. The type of facilities, the equipment, and its location can enhance or detract from the effectiveness of controls. In this regard, need for access is also a factor. The more often employees require access to storage areas, the greater the control difficulty. The need for accessibility may not be a controllable factor, but designing facilities to cope with it adequately is.

The effect of production areas and equipment on food cost is obvious. Waste is an important food-cost factor, and waste can often be blamed on inadequate or improperly specified equipment. The best and most dedicated employees cannot turn out products of standard cost with nonstandard equipment. Consistency is the key to cost and quality control, and it cannot be attained without a well-designed and well-equipped facility. This is the responsibility of planning management. To saddle operating management with inadequate facilities and equipment and then expect a high degree of cost control is irrational. Competent managers can overcome these handicaps, but such competence should ideally be restricted to solving operating problems, not planning deficiencies.

Purveyors

Suppliers can save foodservice operations money, or they can cost them money. Selecting the proper purveyors in the first place and maintaining a professional and profitable relationship is an important part of any good food-control system. The most obvious way a purveyor can help is in pricing, but there are other ways. Low prices are the result of an efficient operation. A supplier who is wasting money due to a poorly managed warehouse, delivery system, personnel, and so forth will not stay in business any more than a similarly operated restaurant. Competitive pricing—a better term than low prices—that is not the result of a professional operation can hold for only a short time. It is far better for a foodservice operator to work with a stable supplier who can maintain competitive pricing over time. Foodservice buyers are notoriously flighty, switching regularly from one supplier to another in the quest for better prices. They overlook the true expense in time alone of establishing a suitable seller-buyer relationship, in which each knows and understands the needs of the other, their strengths and weaknesses. The supplier must know a great deal about the specific products and services required by the food operation. The restaurateur must know what range of products the supplier has and what their storage and delivery capabilities are. Learning all of this takes time. The expense represented by this time invested should ideally be amortized over as long a period as possible. When one supplier follows another in and out of a food operation as though they were in a revolving door, this initial expense is repeated endlessly.

In addition to pricing, the purveyor can influence costs in other ways. Their payment policies could enable the foodservice operator to manage their cash flow better. This is possible either by extending credit over a longer period (increasingly rare) or by discounting if a bill is paid more quickly than usual. Suppliers can also reduce an operation's costs when they agree to make more frequent deliveries. In essence, they perform a warehousing and storage role for the foodservice establishment. In general, though, pricing remains the most effective avenue for a purveyor to influence costs. In fact, suppliers who extend credit and carry inventory for their customers may not be competitive and thus may be unable to offer lower prices.

Specifications

The importance of specifications is that without them products cannot be consistent. Many products could be shipped under such general labels as prime rib, canned tomatoes, filet mignon, green beans, sole, and so on. But the label alone does not mean anything. Without consistency, there cannot be any control. Control here again involves the actions taken to assure that all standards are met. Without specifications, there are no standards to meet, therefore nothing to control.

The quality of specifications is also important. Well-written specifications can save money by assuring that the right products are purchased. This is defined as the product best suited for a particular use. Crushed tomatoes are more suitable for sauces than are whole tomatoes, which have to be crushed first for use in sauces. Using whole tomatoes for sauces would increase handling costs, and they cost more as well. The prices of the food products bought reflect their attributes. If not careful, foodservice buyers will pay for attributes they cannot use, such as canned tomatoes in large solid pieces for sauces, or appearance in extra fancy fruit cocktail which is then to be used in a gelatin salad.

Specifications can therefore affect costs in two ways. They establish the basic food standards, and they should assure use of the optimum products at all times. The optimum product is that product which delivers maximum performance for minimum cost. It is not necessarily the best product, nor is it the least expensive. It is simply the most suitable from both a performance and a cost standpoint.

Receiving Procedures

Higher costs result when foods are not properly or competently checked on delivery. Delivery mistakes, accidental and otherwise, do occur. The operator who pays for products not delivered, who pays higher than agreed-upon prices, or who pays standard prices for substandard goods can expect increased costs. The receiving dock is where the operation takes physical possession of and legal title to food products. This is where purchasing and delivery mistakes begin to cost money. Both kinds of mistakes, purchasing and delivery, can be troublesome and time consuming. When they are caught during receiving, though, they have little impact on profits. Moreover, when spotted and reviewed with those responsible, the mistakes are likely not to be repeated.

Spoilage

Spoilage is deterioration of a food product so that it cannot be used for its specified purpose. Spoilage is a significant contributor to increased costs in the restaurant business. Increased costs due to spoiled food are not limited to microbiological contamination, although that is certainly one form of spoilage. Celery that has become too flaccid to be used in salads is spoiled for that use although it is not contaminated. No one would get sick eating it, but no one would be much interested in eating it either. Because the celery is not contaminated, it does not necessarily have to be discarded. It could still be used in a soup or stew, but it is not ideally suited for those products and the celery is spoiled in regards to its intended usage.

Food spoilage is generally caused by excessive holding periods and/or storing food under improper conditions, primarily at the wrong temperature. Food is often simply kept too long, and therefore it deteriorates. All foods have a finite and distinctive shelf life. Some, like fresh seafood, may be only a day or two. Other foods, such as some frozen goods, may be kept well for a year or more. Either type of product held past its specified time will suffer quality deterioration, as a minimum consequence. If held improperly, the shelf life decreases, often dramatically. The foodservice operator, to paraphrase a well-known wine commercial, should "sell no food past its time." But this is costly unless the operator can prevent spoilage. Delay or prevention of spoilage is therefore a main objective of the storage function.

Stock Levels and Inventory Turnover

Carrying excess inventory can increase costs in two areas: financial and operational. If too much stock is on hand (low inventory turnover), the business has money tied up. This is an opportunity cost in that, were the money available, it could be used to generate income. Instead it is sitting in storerooms, freezers, refrigerators, and kitchens. Since it is excess inventory, it is not even doing any good there. The cost of money is becoming so high that most successful managers demand that investments in inventory be kept to a minimum and that increases in this investment be justified.

The other way inventories can increase food costs is by disrupting day-to-day operations. Large amounts of stock on hand can result in some or all of the following:

1. *Waste*: A cook sees a lot of stew meat in the refrigerator. Instead of 10 pounds as the recipe calls for, the cook puts 13 pounds into the stew, reasoning that the meat will not be missed, and the stew will taste better. There is a tendency for employees to get careless with products when there seems to be a large supply. This is probably even more true with nonfood items such as paper towels, aluminum foil, plastic wrap, and cleaning supplies—all expensive.

2. *Spoilage*: As we discussed in the preceding section, this is due primarily to long holding periods. Relatively large inventories that do not turn at an adequate rate inevitably lead to spoilage. This is a

problem unique to food. Most alcoholic beverages are stable, and virtually all operating and cleaning supplies are too.

3. *Pilferage and Theft*: The reasoning in this case is similar to that used with waste: there is so much, it won't be missed. It is particularly risky to hold excess amounts of desirable products such as steak, shrimp, and lobster tails.

Storage Temperatures

The shelf life of food is determined by time and temperature. Refrigerated at proper temperatures, most foods can maintain their normal storage times, whether it is a day or a week. Some foods can have their holding times greatly extended by frozen storage. The lower the temperature, the longer these foods can be kept. At freezer temperatures, there is no microbiological activity; therefore, there can be no contamination due to bacteria, yeasts, mold, or other biological agents. Chemical activity does not stop in a freezer, however. Fats, proteins, and carbohydrates are still subject to alteration. Thus the food is subject to spoilage through quality deterioration. The rate of chemical reaction decreases rapidly as temperatures drop, 2 or 2.5 times for each 10 degrees C. (18 degrees F.) change. This means that in freezers the temperature is fully as important as in other storage areas. Holding foods much above -18 degrees C. (0 degrees F.) will hasten deterioration, as will fluctuating temperatures. Freezer temperatures should be both as low and as consistent as possible.

Foods are perishable. Most must be refrigerated, although certain types of fresh foods (potatoes) and processed foods (canned) can be held at ambient temperatures. There is no one recommended cold storage temperature. Different classes of foods—meat, dairy products, fresh produce—all have different requirements. In general, though, these foods must be held below 7 degrees C. (45 degrees F.). That is the temperature at which pathogenic bacteria begin to reproduce and multiply. Assuring that all cold storage areas maintain temperatures no higher than 4.5 degrees C. (40 degrees F.) provides a reasonable safety margin. Meats are the most perishable and easily contaminated products and should be held at the lowest temperature. Fresh produce, on the other hand, cannot be held at the same temperatures as meats because products such as lettuce would probably begin to freeze, and quality deterioration would be rapid.

While many foods do not require cold storage, temperature is still important. Canned goods are safe from contamination stored at any temperature. The processing (if done properly) assures against the presence and/or growth of organisms that could cause illness. Spoilage in the form of quality deterioration does occur, however, and its rate is determined by the temperature. Freshly packed canned peaches will show sharply cut edges, firm flesh, bright color, and clear syrup. Peaches held for a long time or held at excessively high temperatures will be much different. The edges will begin to lose the sharp distinction of the cut, the flesh will soften, the color will fade, and the syrup will be cloudy. The nutritional value will also decrease. The peaches are certainly safe to eat, but they will no longer look, feel, or taste as good as before. They will not be as good for you either. Ambient temperature storerooms should never be warm, and the cooler the better. It is recommended they be around 21 degrees C. (70 degrees F.), although a few degrees higher would not cause any problems. Temperatures above 27 degrees C. (80 degrees F.) should definitely be avoided. There are some storerooms in foodservice operations with temperatures exceeding 38 degrees C. (100 degrees F.)!

Inadequate Security

Loss of products due to pilferage and theft is an unfortunate fact of life in the foodservice industry. Food, particularly certain kinds, is an especially attractive product to most employees. Once stolen, it is easily disposed of as well. The food thief does not require the services of a "fence." Theft and pilferage are best discouraged by adequate management information systems.

Few people will take something when they realize its absence will be quickly noted. When management knows at all times what they have and where it is, and when they follow up constantly on this information, theft is not a serious problem. When goods can be removed, and either they are not missed or they are missed only days or weeks later, they *will* disappear. The most important aspect of security, therefore, is knowledge of product counts and locations, and this must be supplemented with physical security. Reducing access to food-storage areas and reducing the times when areas must be left open are both effective security measures.

It is fairly common, however, to find foodservice managers who do not know exactly what is on hand in their operations. This makes it impossible to tell if and when anything is missing. Some managers also allow virtually all employees free access to food-storage areas and compound these errors by failing to restrict times of access. Small wonder that loss of products is a problem. The wonder is that the problem is not worse than it is.

Food-handling Policies

By this we mean the total food-handling procedures of an operation. Management must pay great attention to receiving, storing, producing, and serving food. The dual objectives, again, are to place food of a standard quality and standard cost before the guests.

Waste and Production Scheduling

Waste, like spoilage, is a major contributor to high food costs. Waste is caused by several factors, the most important being poor production planning. One of the most important and complex tasks in foodservice operations is the planning of how, when, and how much food to prepare. This task is often allowed to just evolve on its own. Management often confuses writing a menu with production planning. The menu is only the beginning. Effective planning should cover the following sequence:

1. The menu dictates what is to be prepared.

2. Production forecasting is done for every product served. It is not enough to know that pea soup must be made. Someone must determine exactly how much will be sold. Ideally, by the end of a meal period, no food would be left and nothing would have run out before the end. This is impossible, but the objective should be to come as close as possible to the ideal. Leftovers increase costs because they seldom bring full sales prices when recycled. More often, they cannot be recycled and are simply lost or discarded.

3. Now that the total production demand is known, the recipes should be carefully evaluated. The objective is to bring the prepared or semiprepared foods to the point of service as efficiently as possible. This requires that all the factors of production be integrated properly. These are: ingredients (products), personnel, space, equipment, and time. The overall design of the facility and equipment availability are critical to good production planning. Kitchens in which a cook is dicing onions for a soup at 8:00 A.M., another (or the same) cook dicing onions at 9:30 A.M. for a sauce, and a pantry person dicing onions at 10:15 A.M. for tuna salad have not paid much attention to production scheduling. The recipes should be examined to find ingredients and processes in common. In this case, the common factors are onions and dicing. It would be a much more efficient use of equipment, space, time, and personnel if all the onion dicing were done in one location, at one time, by one person. In this case, it might be worthwhile to use a food-chopping machine. Each individual probably chopped the onions by hand since the individual needs were small. By consolidating the tasks, using a machine may be justified. In this case, one person could probably chop all the onions in much less time than each spent individually, and time, space, personnel, and product would all have been used more productively.

Because of its perishability, food cannot be produced as efficiently as durable goods can. Automobiles made on mass production lines can be held safely until sold, even if that takes several months. The planning of auto production is done according to the principles of economies of scale. Nonetheless, food production systems can adopt some of these same mass production techniques and so become more efficient. Lack of control over production results in wasted food and poor utilization of the factors of production.

A unique problem faced by the foodservice industry is that each operation typically has responsibility both for manufacturing and retailing goods. Most businesses that make products do not have to sell them to the ultimate consumer. Foodservice operations do. Considering the importance of manufacturing standard products to sell, operators need to perform the planning of production more competently than is generally the case. Merely to give the kitchen staff the next day's menu along with instructions as to the general level of volume expected is not good production planning, but it passes for production planning in far too many operations.

Excessive Preprep Activities

Preprep activities are those that prepare ingredients to incorporate into menu items. Peeling, chopping, dicing, and cutting into strips or squares are all examples of preprep activities. Control is made more difficult since the unpredictability of the completed products increases as preprep activities increase. The purpose of control is to insure consistency within the parameters of the standards. Preprep activities are unpredictable because the specific yields are usually unknown. How many 3-ounce tossed salads will you get from a case of lettuce? How many strip steaks will be obtained from a boneless loin? What will 50 pounds of potatoes weigh after peeling? How many pounds of onions will be left after you peel and chop ten pounds? How many pounds of shrimp are required to yield 4 pounds after boiling and shelling? Of course, yield tests can, and should, be performed on all these and similar activities. The problem with yield testing, however, is that it is done on natural products, and they are never exactly the same. Even with the best specifica-

tions, there will be significant variances over time on virtually all raw, unprocessed products.

The purchase of preprepared and/or portioned foods is not a decision to be made solely on this factor, but it does increase the cost and product quality predictability. This, in turn, enhances control, which may also reduce costs. Purchasing 10 pounds of prepared salad greens assures forty 4-ounce portions every day of the year. The product is always the same. The yield should also be the same—potential yield, that is. The servings can still be issued over or under the standard portion. The cost of preprepared or portioned food is also much more stable. A portioned strip steak costing $3.75 to purchase will cost exactly $3.75 to serve. Such an approach also provides much greater assurance that the steak will be the desired weight, that it won't have too much fat or too long a tail. Likewise a 30-pound bag of peeled potatoes yields 30 pounds of potatoes for boiling. By necessity, restaurant kitchens have traditionally had to perform all these "prep" activities. Old habits die hard, and this is a very costly habit.

Yields

Inconsistent yields were suggested as the main reason preprep work could lead to higher costs, but yields are a prime culprit for cost problems in general. The closer the food is to its original state, the more inconsistent the yields will be. Some foodservice operators avoid any sort of processed foods on the grounds that their success depends upon their ability to produce distinctive products. They believe that the purchase of undifferentiated processed foods would interfere with their success. This is not necessarily true, however. When the objective is a unique menu and food products, imagination and creativity are much more important than the form in which foods are purchased.

Yields can vary for any number of reasons. Many of these are product related, such as seasonal variations. Most foods have seasonal peaks and valleys, and there will be periods during the year when decent yield will be so difficult to obtain with certain products, that buyers may temporarily decide not to purchase them. There are also variations due to excessive or low rainfall, not enough or too much sun, and all sorts of other climate and weather changes.

Operational problems can lead to inconsistent yields. The specifications may be loose, permitting all sorts of products to be used. Proper equipment is also essential to accurate and consistent yields. A malfunctioning peeler, a dull knife, an oven that runs too hot, or an inaccurate portion scale can all result in reduced yields.

Personnel are a major cause of yield problems. They may be incapable of doing a job properly due to poor selection, training, or supervision. Employees who are otherwise competent could have a bad day due to temporary personal problems, and everyone will make mistakes from time to time. Inconsistent yields can thus be due to a combination of product problems, operating and equipment problems, and personnel problems.

Food Variances

Food is a difficult product to control because it is so inconsistent. Of the many products handled in a foodservice operation, food is the most challenging because it has more variances than any of the others.

1. *Quality*: The quality can range all over the scale. The operator can count on the fact that there will be differences in the product from time to time, even with excellent specifications. Contrast this with other products. A particular Scotch will be the same from month to month, year to year. The dishwashing soap will be the same, as will the frilled toothpicks and paper cups. All of these, even the Scotch, are basically manufactured products made to specific standards. A case of lettuce grown under poor weather conditions could weigh about 30 pounds and yield only 22 pounds of usable product. A few months later, the same product could be delivered at a weight of 60 pounds with a net

yield of 56 pounds. To compound the operator's problem, the 30-pound case probably costs more. Food is a living product that is grown. Inevitably there are going to be quality variations. They are seldom as pronounced as the lettuce example, but that is an actual example and indicates the possible extremes.

2. *Packaging*: Most products are packaged with consistency. Wines and distilled spirits, for example, nearly always come in cases of twelve bottles, each containing 750 milliliters. Food is packaged in cardboard, metal, glass, and plastic. Some foods come in amounts of less than 1 ounce (saffron for example), while others such as flour or sugar may weigh 100 pounds. Food comes in solid form, liquid form, and even air (aerosol cans of cream topping). Canned goods are packaged in very small containers, very large containers, and many sizes in between.

3. *Shelf life*: Some foods should be used in a day or two after purchase while others can be held for a year or more with no deterioration when properly stored.

4. *Storage areas*: Food has to be stored at specific temperatures and in a variety of storage situations. Thus foods are stored in freezers, both walk-in and reach-in. Food is also stored in refrigerators, also walk-in and reach-in. Some refrigerators are for meats, others for vegetables, others for dairy products, and still others for leftovers and foods-in-process. Some foods do not require cold storage, but they will be found in storerooms, all over the kitchen, and even in the dining room.

The potential cost and quality control problems are enormous. How does one control a variety of products that must be held at several different temperatures and are stored literally all over the operation, some in areas that are totally open and unsecured?

5. *Price fluctuations*: Most products are expected to show some price movement, but many foods are extreme in the degree to which their prices change. Meat prices tend to be quoted on a weekly basis, while fresh produce

often has daily quotations! These two are the most variable, but few foods have as much price stability as the nonfood products used by operations. Distilled spirits, china, glassware, flatware, cleaning supplies, kitchen tools, and so on all have greater price predictability. If you asked the buyer what the price on any of these items was expected to be in four to six months, you would probably get a confident answer. Ask the same question about many foods, and if you even get an answer, it will be anything but confident.

6. *Processing complexity*: Another factor about food which complicates control is that cooking and food production are quite complex activities requiring great technical skill and food knowledge. During production, food generally undergoes physical changes and often chemical changes as well. Even with skilled workers, the results of these changes are not always the same. Some degree of uncertainty is always present. Up to now we have been discussing the variances in the raw product prior to the actual production, and the difficulties those variances pose. Here, we are saying that even when consistently identical foods are introduced into the production system, there will still be inconsistencies in quality and cost.

Recipes

Recipes are a dominant cost factor. It is fashionable to discount the importance of recipes on several grounds: good cooks don't require them; classic food cannot be produced from standardized recipes; the logical place of recipes is in the institutional sector. It should be understood that there is absolutely no fixed relationship between recipes and the *level* or degree of food quality. The most elaborate and creative food can come from recipes. The proper and desired relationship is between recipes and consistency of quality—and, of course, cost. A recipe is intended to assure that a product is prepared the same way all the time, using the same ingredients and the same techniques. If this is done and if there is some consistency in the

ingredients used, the finished product will meet a predetermined standard and will attain the predicted cost. These are the dual objectives of food control, and recipes are essential to achieving them.

Consistency in food ingredients is not a normal occurrence, but management should take whatever steps are necessary to assure the maximum consistency possible. Management should also attempt to have the ingredients used in the same way at all times. Finally, there must be cost and quality standards. The purpose of ingredient and preparation technique consistency is to insure meeting the cost and quality standards.

Standardized recipes as an effective control tool are of fairly recent origin. The drawback to their use is that unless standardized ingredients are used, they will not yield standardized products. In the United States, due to advancements in growing, harvesting, and processing foods as well as improvements in transportation, food standardization has reached a very high level and can be expected to progress even more. There are some operators who deplore this, apparently regarding the purchase, delivery, and use of consistently standard foods as unseemly, somehow constricting their creativity. Today imagination and creativity should be directed towards menu development and food presentation, not towards attempting to cope with the bewildering inconsistency of products coming in the back door. It is irrational to ignore the continuing stabilization and standardization of foods available. At the least, it is a poor business decision, and one thing that should never be forgotten is that a foodservice operation is a business. Admittedly, it is a very specialized one, but a business nonetheless. Many operators forget this and become overly concerned with the techniques and art of running restaurants. Unless you can put something on the bottom line, however, you run the distinct risk of becoming a starving artist.

The way recipes are written has an effect on both food and labor costs. In the section dealing with production control, proper formats for standardized recipes will be discussed. It is important to know that material, personnel, and time can all be wasted by poorly written recipes. The recipe format also affects accuracy of ingredient measurement and precision in product precosting.

Food Prepared But Not Sold

The food-handling system could work perfectly up to the service function and break down there. The two main dangers here are overproduction and service personnel cheating.

Overproduction may or may not be the responsibility of the production personnel. If it is, management has made a serious error: allowing kitchen employees to control production forecasting. If management controls this as it should, production becomes a management responsibility. A true executive chef, by the way, manages the kitchen. It would be proper for such a chef to handle this responsibility. In such a case, management *is* making the critical production forecasting decisions.

Whenever overproduction takes place, costs are nearly always negatively affected. Few prepared foods are unaffected by holding, which means that leftovers must usually be reprocessed or used for employees' meals. In the first case, there are probably reduced sales. In the second, there are no sales.

The other case of prepared foods not being sold happens when dining-room servers pick up food from the kitchen, serve it, collect the money, and keep it. If there are any records of the sales, such as guest checks, they simply destroy them. Here we have a perfect example of how the food system itself could literally work to perfection, yet still incur high costs. When cost problems show up, it is the unfortunate habit to blame the kitchen, whereas it could be a dining-room problem.

3 Analysis of Food Systems

The purpose of analysis is to generate information about what is happening in the operation so the right decisions can be made and any problems can be solved. Analysis is actually a comparison process. The actual results, be they costs, sales, or whatever, are compared to the standards—or what should have occurred. In analysis, therefore, you are constantly comparing the "what is" to "what should be."

Percentage Analysis

Percentages are often misused in foodservice operations, particularly with food and beverages. They can be used in analysis, but they have only limited usefulness for decision making, which is their most common use. Another common misconception about percentages is that they are directly related to profits. Nothing could be further from the truth. We will discuss this point in detail.

Food cost is a variable cost and, as pointed out, should be expected to rise or fall along with sales—generally maintaining the same ratio of cost dollars to sales dollars. In other words, the percentage should not vary. We have discussed the conditions where fluctuating sales values may cause the percentage to vary: waste and production efficiency. These conditions change the standard percentage. The standard percentage is, therefore, a legitimate analytical benchmark when it is accurate. It is accurate only when three basic conditions are known:

1. Total product cost of every menu item
2. Selling price of every menu item
3. Numbers of each item sold

Unless these figures are exact, or nearly so, the standard (potential or ideal) percentage cannot be calculated.

Discussion of the Standard Percentage Factors

Product Cost. Few operators know with any degree of accuracy what it actually costs to serve each product. There are several reasons for this. First, it is difficult to know actual costs due to the variances in quality, yield, and prices. Because of this difficulty, recipe costing is frequently not even attempted. It is likely in fact that

39

establishments which do precost their recipes are in the minority by a substantial margin. Of all those who do precost, the ones who do it accurately are also in the minority. Accurate recipe costs soon become inaccurate if not updated on a regular basis. All this analysis is time consuming, and to be honest, the results are only an approximation of what the costs should be. Too many variables exist for the type of product-costing accuracy that manufacturing industries can claim. There are even significant differences in costing accuracy among various types of food services. A limited-menu restaurant with only six portion-controlled items should be able to precost with nearly total accuracy. A family-style Italian restaurant with fifty menu items, all prepared from scratch, will have a much lower accuracy potential. But this is beside the point. Unless an operation has a precost, whether actual or only a reasonable estimate of the product costs, it is impossible to use a percentage figure for cost analysis. If a precost is not done, one of the three elements in the percentage calculation is missing, so how can the calculation be made?

Selling Price. Here the necessary information is always available. A problem would arise if otherwise identical products were sold at different prices, such as happens in the bar with drinks being sold at a lower price during the "cocktail" hour and at a higher price when the entertainment begins. This would be uncommon with food, and it can safely be assumed that this portion of the percentage calculation is available.

Sales Information. The third piece of information necessary is the quantity sold of every item on the menu. This should not be limited to entrees but should also include appetizers, side items, desserts, and beverages. Entree information alone is very useful, but the absence of the other menu components will skew the results. Many foodservice units do not have even the entree sales, and very few have access to total sales counts. Thus, a second of the three necessary calculation elements is not often available, and the determination of an accurate percentage is impossible.

With these three pieces of information, the standard percentage can be calculated. See Exhibit 3.1. To calculate the standard cost, list the various menu items with the number sold, item cost, and item selling price, as shown. The next step is to ascertain the total cost of selling each item. This is obtained by multiplying the number sold by the per-unit cost. With chicken, for example, if we sold fifty orders at a cost of $1.75 each, the total cost of selling chicken *should be* $87.50. This is done with all the menu items, and they are then added together. This figure, $560.99, is what the total food cost should be in dollars. The third step is to calculate the sales. The same procedure is followed for this. Thus, the sales resulting from selling fifty orders of chicken at $4.25 each is $212.50. The total sales of this menu would be $1,433.90. The last step is to divide the total cost, $560.99, into the total sales, $1,433.90, to obtain the standard percentage. The result, 39.12 percent, is the

Exhibit 3.1. Calculation of Standard Food Cost Percentage

Item	Number Sold	Cost	Selling Price	Total Cost	Total Sales
Chicken	50	$1.75	$4.25	$ 87.50	$212.50
Steak	82	3.78	8.95	309.96	733.90
Sole	24	2.15	6.50	51.60	156.00
Roast ribs	39	2.87	8.50	111.93	331.50
	195			$560.99	$1,433.90

Standard %:
$$\frac{\$560.00}{\$1,433.90} = 39.12\%$$

food-cost percentage which should result as a consequence of selling these four items in this specific ratio at these costs and prices. If the sales mix changes, or if the costs change, or if the menu is repriced, there would be a new percentage. As long as management knows what sales and costs are, the percentage becomes a useful figure; otherwise it is not.

How the Standard Percentage Can Be Used

The value of the standard percentage is that it provides a frame of reference for management. It offers a figure managers can then compare to the actual cost percentage. This is of value since actual performance must always be checked against the standard. Using percentages in this way enables management to tell quickly if the food-handling system is working properly. If the percentage is high, there *might* be a problem. There are only three areas in which to look for

the answer. First, the selling prices could have been lowered. This would increase the standard percentage because it would lower the sales without affecting the cost. See Exhibit 3.2. Price variances have increased the standard cost to 40.99 percent. Whenever prices are changed, the new standard cost percentage must be calculated, or else management will not have an accurate reference to compare the actual cost with.

We have kept the other variables constant for the purposes of this example, but repricing or changing the menu will usually cause some changes in the sales mix. The sales mix is the second factor management should investigate when cost percentages vary from the standard. In Exhibit 3.3, we have changed the quantities of each menu item sold and then recalculated the percentage. The new figure is 37.6 percent. Again the other two variables, selling price and cost, were held constant. Sales mix changes can

Exhibit 3.2. Effect of Pricing Change on Standard Percentage

Item	Number Sold	Cost	*Selling Price	Total Cost	Total Sales
Chicken	50	$1.75	$4.00	$ 87.50	$200.00
Steak	82	3.78	8.50	309.96	697.00
Sole	24	2.15	6.25	51.60	150.00
Roast ribs	39	2.87	8.25	111.93	321.75
	195			$560.99	$1,368.75

Standard %: $\dfrac{\$560.00}{\$1,368.75} = 40.99\%$

Exhibit 3.3. Effect of Sales Mix Change on Standard Percentage

Item	*Number Sold	Cost Selling	Price	Total Cost	Total Sales
Chicken	61	$1.75	$4.25	$106.75	$259.25
Steak	46	3.78	8.95	173.88	411.70
Sole	30	2.15	6.50	64.50	195.00
Roast ribs	58	2.87	8.50	166.46	493.00
	195			$511.59	$1,358.95

Standard %: $\dfrac{\$511.59}{\$1,358.95} = 37.6\%$

result from a variety of things. One of the most important is pricing, but merchandising, menu design, and personal selling techniques can also have a considerable impact. An important lesson to learn here is that the percentage went down, but this was not due to any greater operating efficiency. In other words, this operation is not suddenly being managed better (or worse), and the food has not necessarily improved. The guests are purchasing different foods, and this has had a dramatic effect on the expected cost percentage. Management can and should attempt to sell the most favorable mix of items, but this is not a question of cost control. Food cost percentage changes are not necessarily attributable to control problems.

If there were no changes in either the prices or sales mix, any variation in the percentage would have to be due to the third element, product cost. Exhibit 3.4 shows the effect due to increases in the product cost. In this case the percentage went up to 41.1 percent. This is also not necessarily the result of a breakdown in the control system. When products cost more to purchase, the serving cost will obviously increase unless compensations are made.

It is critical that management be able to pinpoint what the problems are. Let us take the example of an operation that has just experienced an increase in food-cost percentage. Following the procedures just outlined, management would first check the pricing. Knowing there had been no menu changes, they could then eliminate that as a potential answer. Next they check the sales mix. Let us further assume that no difference occurred there either. The cause of the cost increase must then be product dollar costs that were higher than anticipated. At this point, the existence of a problem is apparent, but whether it is a control problem or not remains unknown. Product cost calculations must be checked. If it is found that there are no significant increases in the prices paid for food, then there is a control problem. What has happened is that the menu items are costing more to serve than they should. The potential causes of this are many, and more sophisticated analytical techniques are required to determine the exact problem. It could be stealing, waste, or spoilage; possibly poor purchasing, receiving, or production; the service people could be selling food and keeping the money; or it could be a portion-control problem. We could go on and on, but the point is that the percentage cost increase *is* control related; and much more information is required to determine the specific cause(s).

Percentages are best used as a monitoring tool. They can indicate when the relationship between costs and sales is out of line. They cannot, however, indicate why. They will not even indicate that they are out of line unless standard percentages are used. If the requisite information for a standard percentage is not available, it is not realistic to use percentages for anything. Foodservice operators tend to overrely on percentages. Many establishments actually tend to have several percentages. One is the desired percentage the operation is required to

Exhibit 3.4. Effect of Cost Change on Standard Percentage

Item	Number Sold	*Cost Selling	Price	Total Cost	Total Sales
Chicken	50	$1.86	$4.25	$ 93.00	$212.50
Steak	82	3.95	8.95	323.90	733.90
Sole	24	2.40	6.50	57.60	156.00
Roast ribs	39	2.95	8.50	115.05	331.50
	195			$589.55	$1,433.90

Standard %: $\dfrac{\$589.55}{\$1,433.90} = 41.1\%$

maintain. The source for this figure could be the parent company, the chain headquarters, an independent operator's idea of a profitable figure, what some competitor is averaging, or whatever. Then there is the actual food cost percentage, which may well be different from the desired one. Whether it is above or below does not really matter. The fact is that it is different and so now there are two figures to contemplate. If this establishment were to calculate a standard percentage based upon their own specific prices, costs, and sales mix, they could possibly come up with still another percentage, completely different from the first two. No two operations are exactly alike. Even when the menus and selling prices are the same, even in the rare event that the product serving costs are the same, it is highly unlikely that the sales mix would also be the same. The result is a different standard percentage, and all the central office pressures in the world will not change that fact.

The reliance on percentages also obscures the really important and significant factor—profitability. Attention should be on the dollars that a menu contributes to profits, not on the percentage. In our examples we did not look at dollar profits, but this is what they are:

Exhibit 3.1: $872.91 ($1,433.90 - 560.99)

Exhibit 3.2: $807.76 ($1,368.75 - 560.99)

Exhibit 3.3: $847.36 ($1,358.95 - 511.59)

Exhibit 3.4: $844.35 ($1,433.90 - 589.55)

This clearly shows that all the changes from the original menu resulted in decreases in profits. In two cases the percentage went up; in one it went down. Which would you rather have, a low percentage or increased profit? Percentages cannot be used for decision making because they do not accurately show profitability. To repeat, percentages are best used as a monitoring tool.

Standard Cost Analysis

This system does not concern itself with percentages at all. In fact, there are no percentages since it ignores sales. Cost analysis does not determine as a standard what the proper percentage should be but rather what the proper dollar cost should be. The total food cost dollars are then compared to what they should be. Discrepancies, if noted, will be investigated. One of the drawbacks of the previous analysis system was that it could only pinpoint possible problems in terms of selling prices, sales mix, and/or product cost. From a control standpoint, product cost is the major concern. The cost analysis system concentrates on the cost and provides management with more useful data.

In order to establish the cost standard, two of the three percentage standard requirements are needed. They are the quantities of all menu items sold and the total cost of each product. The cost of each product is multiplied by its sales to get the total potential cost from that specific item. Then the costs of all menu items are totaled. The result is what the dollar food cost should be if everything was done properly. For an example, refer again to Exhibit 3.1. Previously we used it to calculate the percentage, but it can provide the standard dollar cost as well. On Exhibit 3.1, the standard cost is $560.99. Any actual food cost higher or lower than $560.99 *could* indicate a deviation. The first thing to do is to determine whether the variance is caused by the cost or by the sales mix. If the sales mix has changed (Exhibit 3.3), there is a new standard cost, and that one is the frame of reference. In this case, Exhibit 3.3 shows a cost of $511.59. This is why deviations both over and under the standard must be investigated. If an actual food cost of $540.00 had been compared to the original standard of $560.99, an operator would probably feel that the system was working fine, but further investigation would show that the $540.00 should really be compared to $511.59. Instead of spending *less* money on food, this operation has actually spent *more*. Therefore, the first step is always to assure that sales mix changes have not altered the standard cost.

If there is a cost variance and it cannot be attributed to the sales mix, then it is cost related. But it may not necessarily be due to a control breakdown. Exhibit 3.4 shows the effect of product cost increases on the standard cost, which rises to $589.55. If management were not aware of how much the serving costs increased, they would misinterpret the data. If, for example, the cost actually were about $590.00, management would surmise they had a control problem when none exists at all.

If changes in the standard cost are not justified by product costs and/or sales mix variances, any deviations from the standard cost are then control related. This is the point at which the percentage analysis stopped, whereas dollar costs can generate much more detailed information about what has actually happened. The dollar costs for the various menu items can be compared to the actual costs. What management now needs to know is which food areas (if any) can the problem be traced to? Some foods can be compared using the total costs. With others, additional calculations must be made. With menu items such as coffee, milk, juices, some desserts and appetizers, the cost of the named item is the total or nearly total cost of the entire serving. In this instance, use the total calculated product standard cost. If the projected cost for coffee were $50.00, compare that with the actual coffee cost. The objective of this is to determine whether the cost variances can be traced to a few specific items or whether all products show deviations from their standards. The latter, by the way, may be a worse problem. If the entire cost problem is due to portion-controlled strip steaks, management can safely assume they have a security problem. On the other hand, if nothing sticks out, the problem is most likely general sloppiness in most or all phases of the food handling system. In this case more variables are involved, and correction would probably take longer and prove more difficult.

Most menu items, however—especially the entrees—require a different analysis approach. The chicken cost is $1.75 per order (Exhibit 3.1), but this includes foods other than the chicken, such as rolls, butter, table condiments, perhaps a potato and/or other vegetable. The procedure is to look at the recipe cost analysis and see how much of the $1.75 is for the chicken itself. If it were $1.02, then multiply $1.02 times the sales count of fifty for a standard cost of $51.00 for the chicken alone. Compare $51.00 to the actual cost of chicken, determined by physical inventory. Doing this with the major menu components will quickly reveal what the problems are and where they occur.

This, then, is standard cost analysis. It puts the emphasis where it belongs, on the product cost. Food control is difficult and challenging, and this is mostly due to the nature of the products. The quality changes all the time, yield variances are common, price changes occur constantly, availability is not always certain, and waste is a real problem as is spoilage. All these are problems that occur either only with food, or to a greater degree with food than with other products. As a result, a food control system is primarily concerned with protecting and monitoring physical goods. The standard cost system meets this need quite well.

Product Analysis

This technique is used specifically to determine whether the cost variances are due to food utilization inefficiencies or errors in calculating the costs. If the former, this method will pinpoint specific products. It requires information on the total products sold and the products used by the operation. The products sold become the standard, and the ones actually used are compared to it. See Exhibits 3.5, 3.6, and 3.7.

Exhibit 3.5

Exhibit 3.5 gives the total sold for selected menu items. The easiest way to get this information is from computerized point-of-sale (POS) machinery. These systems can be expensive but often not much more so than electronic register systems, which are very common today. Some of the sophisticated POS equipment available has the capability of reporting the sales of a hundred or more menu items. Some will even calculate usage of other ingredients when a product is sold. Recording

Exhibit 3.5. Sales Analysis

Menu Items	Orders Sold
New York strip	157
Lobster tail	49
Roast ribs	294
Beef stew	78
Chicken a la king	42
Steamed shrimp	104
Coffee	2,150
Tossed salad	1,400
Orange juice	439

the sales, for example, would result in recording not only the use of one hamburger patty, but also one bun, one ounce of lettuce, one tomato slice, two pickle chips, one frilled toothpick, and 1.5 ounces of dressing. The advantage of obtaining such information should be obvious. The question the operator should ask is not, "Can I afford it?" but "Can I afford *not* to have it?"

Most foodservice operations do not currently have this type of sales reporting capability, but the information can easily be obtained. A table-service operation typically has guest checks with the orders noted on them. A cashier must process each one of these checks. If the cashier had a list of the menu items, the sales could be tallied prior to filing the checks. See Exhibit 3.8. These can be typed and duplicated and thus easily changed when the menu changes. Specials can be written in daily. This takes the cashier virtually no additional time, since each check has to be handled individually anyway. If not done at the collection point, the checks can be abstracted later. The process then is identical but takes longer, and someone has to be specifically assigned to it. From a labor productivity standpoint, this would not be as desirable. If it is the only way to get the information, however, it should be done. One method of sales count retrieval that is not recommended is to take usage counts in the kitchen. For example, say the broiler is issued twenty new steaks, and four steaks are available from the previous evening. At the end of the evening two steaks remain. The

number of steaks used is twenty-two, but this does not mean twenty-two were sold! Actual sales information is still required. This method of calculating the product usage is worthwhile, but the objective of obtaining kitchen counts is to compare them with the dining room sales count.

A system that works well in a cafeteria and could easily be used in a table-service operation is to equip the cashier with a push-button counter. These can be purchased with multiple keys. All the cashier or food checker has to do is press the appropriate button for each item. Whatever way this information is obtained, it is necessary. As pointed out in percentage analysis, a standard percentage *cannot* be established without accurate sales counts. This is possibly the single most useful and needed type of information that management can generate.

Exhibit 3.6

Exhibit 3.6 involves a different approach. Many products cannot be tracked by tabulating the menu sales, unless you have equipment that also calculates the meal components. It is still possible to project the usage of these foods based on standards. In the examples given in Exhibit 3.6, the ideal consumption of butter pats, salad dressing, parsley for garnish, and dinner rolls is planned.

Exhibit 3.6. Usage Projections for Other Foods

Butter pats (3,000 guests x 1.5 pats)	4,500 each
Salad dressing (1,400 salads x 1.0 oz.)	11 gallons
Parsley (1,020 dinners/one bunch = 20 guests)	51 bunches
Dinner rolls (1,020 x 1.0 each)	85 dozen

Exhibit 3.7

Exhibit 3.7 is an example of a work sheet estimating the actual numbers of each item that could have been sold based on actual consumption arrived at by physical inventories. Each product should be evaluated independent of the others.

Exhibit 3.7. Actual Product Usage

INVENTORY USAGE = OI + PURCHASES - CoI.

	Opening Inventory	Purchases	Closing Inventory	Total	Total Orders Used
New York strip (12 oz.)	40 ea.	230 ea.	95 ea.	175 ea.	175
Lobster tail (10 oz.)	21 ea.	60 ea.	30 ea.	51 ea.	51
Roast ribs (lb.)[1]	365 lb.	420 lb.	269 lb.	516 lb.	343
Beef stew meat (lb.)[2]	15 lb.	20 lb.	5 lb.	30 lb.	80
Chicken meat (lb.)[3]	16 lb.	0	8 lb.	8 lb.	32
Shrimp (lb.)[4]	40 lb.	15 lb.	23 lb.	32 lb.	112
Coffee (lb.)[5]	15 lb.	75 lb.	10 lb.	80 lb.	3,200
Tossed salad mix[6] (20 lbs. per case)	2 cs.	20 cs.	4 cs.	18 cs.	1,440
Orange juice (qt.)[7]	18 qt.	48 qt.	8 qt.	58 qt.	464
Butter pats (90/lb.)	23.5 lb.	45 lb.	18 lb.	50.5 lb.	3,030
Salad dressing (gal.)	5.0 gal.	12 gal.	3.25 gal.	13.75 gal.	1,760
Parsley (bunch)	6 bu.	53 bu.	5 bu.	54 bu.	1,080
Dinner rolls (doz.)	4 doz.	90 doz.	7 doz.	87 doz.	1,044

Notes

1. Ribs NAMP #109 20-22 lb. (Ave. = 21 lb.) 14 orders/rib
2. Stew meat 6 oz. per order
3. Chicken meat (a la king) 4 oz. per order
4. Shrimp 16-19/lb. (Ave. = 17.5) 5 shrimp/order
5. Coffee 1 cup/order, 6 oz./cup, 40 cups/lb.
6. Tossed salad mix 4 oz./order
7. Orange juice 4 oz./order

Exhibit 3.8. Sales Count Record

Date:1/17/83   **Day:Monday**

Menu Items	Number Sold	Total Sold
New York strip	卌 卌 II	12
Lobster tail	卌 I	6
Roast ribs	卌 卌 卌 卌 II	22
Beef stroganoff	卌 III	8
Beef stew	IIII	4
Chicken a la king	III	3
Steamed shrimp	卌 卌 卌 II	17
Daily special:		
Stuffed pork chop	卌 卌 IIII	14

Strip Steak. This is a product purchased by the piece or portion controlled. Figures show 175 steaks were used or consumed by the operation, yet according to the sales counts (Exhibit 3.5), only 157 were sold. There are 18 steaks missing. They could have been stolen, eaten, burned, or sold with no record of the sale (or any income from the sale). They could have been invoiced and paid for without even having been received. There could have been an inventory mistake, although if it was in the opening inventory, it can never be proven.

Lobster Tail. The inventories show that fifty-one individual lobster tails were consumed during the period. The sales analysis (Exhibit 3.5) shows only forty-nine being sold. The situation is similar to that of the steaks; physical goods are missing. The variance, however, is only two tails, which may be due to mistakes rather than theft. The management decision may be to caution the cooks to be more careful in handling the tails.

Roast Ribs. This type of product is quite unlike the strip steaks and lobster tails. They were both preportioned and handled by count. The roast ribs meat must be portioned each time there is an order. This presents obvious control complications. Our usage calculations show an estimated consumption of 343 orders. This is calculated as follows:

Pounds of ribs actually consumed = 516 pounds

Number of roasts @ 21 pounds/roast
= 24.5 roasts

Number of orders @ 14/roast = 343 orders

Therefore, the ribs used during the period should have produced 343 orders. This is the standard. To the standard, we compare the number of orders actually sold, 294. There is quite a significant variance. One possible explanation is overportioning. Of 24.5 roasts divided into 294 orders you would get twelve slices per roast rather than the specified fourteen. This is entirely possible. Further investigation could show that the production cooks were roasting at too high a temperature,

resulting in increased cooking losses and lighter roasts. The service cooks might then have adjusted the portion size to keep from cheating the guests. The actual problem in this case is not in the portioning but in the cooking. The solutions are to review roasting procedures with the kitchen, to check the oven thermostats (the roast cook could be a victim of malfunctioning equipment), and to emphasize to the line cooks that although they made a rational portion adjustment, they should have immediately pointed out the problem to management. It is unlikely that any ribs were stolen, although that is a possiblity to be considered if the investigation shows no cooking or portioning problems. Another potential cause might be that the dining room servers picked up the orders, but the sales were not recorded. The results from any of these would be the same—products used were not being sold and profits are lost. This analysis only indicates the basic problem of lost sales. Management must investigate to determine the cause of the problem. Once this has been established, it should not be difficult to rectify the problem. Problem solving in foodservice operations is difficult because operators often cannot identify the specific problem. When all they know is that a cost variance exists, they have no realistic hope of quickly reversing the situation. Analysis should identify not only the problems but also the probable cause(s).

Beef Stew. The usage analysis (Exhibit 3.7) indicates 30 pounds consumed, which should serve eighty people. The sales analysis (Exhibit 3.5) shows that seventy-eight people paid for beef stew. This variance is slight, indicating a *very minor* portioning problem, which may or may not be worthwhile discussing with the line cooks. If there had been a major variance, the most logical assumption would still be a portioning problem. In such a case, however, it could be the fault of the line cooks, due to overportioning, or the production cook, for using more meat than the recipe required. The analysis indicates the existence or lack of existence of a problem, but management must know their operation and be totally familiar with the food-handling procedures in order to use the information effectively. A million-dollar computer could give inexperienced or incompetent or unenergetic management fabulous information that would not solve anything.

Chicken à la King. This product should be analyzed like beef stew. If there are variances between usage and sales, it is most likely being overportioned on the line or else prepared improperly. Theft and/or pilferage cannot be ruled out but are not as likely as with steak and lobster. The data show a usage of eight pounds for thirty-two orders (Exhibit 3.7) and sales of forty-two orders. This is a significant variance, but it shows more orders served than should have been! The usual portioning and production explanations are applicable here, only in reverse. The line cooks could be underportioning, or the production cooks could be using less chicken meat than the recipe calls for, or both of these could occur. Another potential explanation would simply be a calculation mistake. The opening or closing inventories could be wrong, or the purchases could be. The opening inventory cannot be checked now (although the figure can be; it could have been incorrectly transcribed). The ending inventory can be checked, though, and should be. The purchases for the period should also be verified. When usage is less than sales, check the figures first. If they hold up, as far as you can determine, investigate preparation and portioning.

Steamed Shrimp. This is a product served by count, five pieces to an order. There can be no possibility of control unless the specifications clearly state the count per pound. In this case, the count is 16 to 19. It is common to allow a range. Then the operator should use a midrange count to calculate the cost and number. The average of 16 to 19 is 17.5, so each pound of shrimp is presumed to consist of 17.5 pieces. On this basis, the 32 pounds of shrimp consumed (Exhibit 3.7) should have yielded 112 portions. Since only 104 orders were sold, there is a variance. Overportioning is a potential problem. If the kitchen had put 5.38 shrimp on each order instead of 5, the difference would be explained. Realistically, however, it is difficult to imagine cooks not being able to count to 5, whereas with items such as stew or à la king, it is easy to make a portion error.

The most likely explanations are either that some shrimp were stolen (forty shrimp or about 2.25 pounds), eaten without authorization, or delivered off-specification—that is, *larger* than specified. All these explanations are realistic. Shrimp are an attractive and desirable commodity, and employees would be happy to eat them or take them home if they thought they could get away with it. If this type of analysis were used regularly, however, employees would realize that the loss would be noticed and would not take the risk. In such a case, the more likely cause of the variance would be oversized shrimp. Observance of the portion count with heavier pieces would result in excess pounds used. The solution is to work both with the receiving clerks and purveyors to correct the problem. Again, analysis plus knowledge of the product and the food-handling system are necessary to identify the specific cause. Solutions are readily accomplished from that point.

Coffee. There were 80 pounds of coffee used (Exhibit 3.7). At 40 cups (of 6 ounces each) to a pound, there is a potential for 3,200 cups being served. The actual count was 2,150 (Exhibit 3.5), and the discrepancy has to be checked. Probable causes are employees drinking coffee, and coffee being made too far ahead and/or in large batches, both of which can result in leftovers. It is also possible that some coffee was stolen. If this operation uses small one-pot coffee packages, theft should be seriously considered. That type of packaging is very attractive to employees, many of whom have similar sized brewers at home. Management should determine how much of the variance is due to employee drinking, and then they must decide whether it is excessive or not. It would not necessarily be a mistake for management to allow the employees to drink as much as they want. It would be a mistake for management not to know how much employees were drinking. As long as policies are based on actual data, they are usually pretty rational.

Tossed Salad Mix. Eighteen cases of 20

pounds each were used. This should have fed 1,440 people at 4 ounces each (Exhibit 3.7). From Exhibit 3.5 we see that 1,400 orders were obtained and sold. This might seem to be a reasonable variance and probably doesn't warrant any follow-up. On the other hand, the count should be very close since the product being purchased, tossed salad mix, should have 100 percent yield. It is doubtful anyone would want to steal salad mix. With significant variances, the explanation is probably overportioning. Another cause of poor yield would be overproduction: too much salad mix is put out for service each day with consequent spoilage and loss.

Orange Juice. Inventory depletions of orange juice were 58 quarts or 14.5 gallons (Exhibit 3.7). The portion size is 4 ounces. This means that 464 orders could have been sold. Actual sales were 439. Probable cause? The employees are drinking the orange juice. It is not a portioning problem (the glasses should hold only 4 ounces). It is probably not being stolen, nor is there much danger of spoilage since it is always kept refrigerated, and turnover is quick. What is happening is that the employees occasionally have a glass of orange juice. It is not a serious problem, but if it is against policy, management should follow up on it.

One recurring problem in most of these product analyses is the necessity to guess at how much food, coffee, orange juice, and so on is being consumed by the employees. If all employee meals and snacks were written and recorded, management could interpret the data more quickly and accurately. If this were done on coffee and orange juice, for example, the sales figures from Exhibit 3.5 would include employees' legitimate consumption. Any variances from this would be unacceptable.

Other Foods. This category would include butter pats, salad dressing, parsley, and dinner rolls. The same process is followed with these and all other foods. The actual usage is determined (Exhibit 3.7) and compared with the usage projection (Exhibit 3.6). This process is more accurate if the sales counts include

authorized employee meals and snacks as well as promotional food that may not be paid for. The objective is to determine whether any food cannot be accounted for. Knowledge is the key here. So long as management knows where all the food is going, they have control or at least the potential of control. If they do nothing, the losses will continue. But this is not a lack of control; it is a problem of incompetent and/or lazy management. If they did not know what was happening to the steaks, there would be a control problem. If they did not even realize any steaks were missing, there would be a severe control problem! Data is not itself any control. Someone must be willing to act on the information before it becomes an effective control system.

Product analysis should be an ongoing process. It does not have to be done on every product. It cannot be done accurately on all products, but it certainly should be performed on all entrees or main entree components and as many other foods as possible. It should not be limited to the end of the month either since a daily comparison of kitchen-product usage with dining-room sales is an excellent control device.

Inventory Analysis Systems

Once a standard cost percentage has been established, it can be used as a monitoring tool. It becomes a frame of reference indicating whether or not the food-handling system is working well or if it is going off in some unanticipated direction. The most common time to make the comparison between the standard and actual percentages is at the end of the month (or operating period) when physical inventories are taken. Management may decide to make comparisons more frequently, since waiting until the end of the month or period to find problems could mean significant profit losses, especially in high-volume operations. Taking a full physical inventory is both time consuming and expensive. Other ways have been developed to gather the necessary information. One such system is called a "cost estimation system." See Exhibit 3.9. The costs are determined in three ways. Product categories such as meats, fish,

Exhibit 3.9. Cost Estimation Work Sheet

Product	Opening Inventory	Purchases	Closing Inventory	Total Used	Unit Price	Total Cost
Meat/Fish/Poultry						
Pork loin - lb.	36 lbs.	115 lbs.	54 lbs.	97 lbs.	2.17/lb.	$210.49
Shrimp - lb.	8.5 lbs.	27 lbs.	6 lbs.	29.5 lbs.	6.95/lb.	205.03
Filet mignon						
10 oz. ea.	45 ea.	174 ea.	34 ea.	185 ea.	3.28 ea.	606.80
Top sirloin - lb.	24 lb.	212 lb.	31 lb.	205 lb.	2.97/lb.	608.85
Chicken	16 lb.	159 lb.	19 lb.	156 lb.	.89/lb.	138.84
Total						$1,770.01 (19.6%)
Produce						
Head Lettuce - cs.	1.5 cs.	6.0 cs.	.75 cs.	6.75 cs.	8.53/cs.	$57.58
Tomatoes - cs.	1.0 cs.	5.0 cs.	0.5 cs.	5.5 cs.	10.94/cs.	60.17
Green pepper - bu.	0.25 bu.	2.0 bu.	.75 bu.	1.5 bu.	17.65/bu.	26.48
Onions - lb.	13 lb.	100 lb.	22 lb.	91 lb.	.36/lb.	32.76
Lemons - 120/l	0.3 cs.	1.0 cs.	0.5 cs.	.8 cs.	20.40/cs.	16.32
Total						$193.31 (2.1%)
Dairy						
Milk - 1/2 pt.		$26.64				$26.64
Cream - qt.		16.15				16.15
Sour cream - lb.		8.65				8.65
Eggs - doz.		19.04				19.04
Butter - lb.		54.75				54.75
Total						$125.23 (1.4%)
Groceries (Staples)						$542.00 (6.0%)
Bakery						
Bread – lb.		$43.50				$43.50
Hamburger buns – doz.		17.95				17.95
Hot dog buns – doz.		16.45				16.45
Rolls – doz.		21.32				21.32
Pie shells – ea.		18.54				18.54
Cake – ea.		21.19				21.19
Total						$138.95 (1.5%)
Total Food Cost						$2,769.50
Total Food Sales						$9,027.58 (30.6%)

poultry, and produce are physically counted. Their cost, as Exhibit 3.9 shows, is calculated as precisely as possible. This is done just as it would be at the end of an accounting period. Exhibit 3.9 is not intended to be complete. It lists only a few products in each category for illustration purposes.

The second way to generate the costs is to use only the dollar purchases, as shown with dairy and bakery products. This ignores the opening and closing inventories, the assumption being that they are the same or nearly so. If there is no difference between the inventories, the purchases equal the cost.

Opening inventory	20
+ Purchases	80
= Goods available for sale	100
- Ending inventory	20
= Goods used/sold	80

Therefore, purchases equal goods used or sold.

This system works only when inventories tend to be stable. The two categories used in Exhibit 3.9, dairy and bakery, are the kinds of products that are often delivered daily or several times a week. The more frequent the delivery, the more consistent the inventory levels are. For example, if a foodservice operation uses twenty units of a product daily and has a single weekly delivery, the inventory situation could look like this.

Day	Inventory Level	Delivery
Monday	20	140
Tuesday	140	—
Wednesday	120	—
Thursday	100	—
Friday	80	—
Saturday	60	—
Sunday	40	—
Monday	20	140

If, however, there were deliveries Monday through Saturday, the inventory levels would be as follows:

Day	Inventory Level	Delivery
Monday	20	20
Tuesday	20	20
Wednesday	20	20
Thursday	20	20
Friday	20	20
Saturday	20	40
Sunday	40	—
Monday	20	20

In the first example, the inventory could not be ignored in calculating the cost, while in the second it could.

For the other food category, groceries or staples, we can use a percentage estimation. The figure used is 6 percent, and 6 percent of $9,027.58 (sales total) equals $542.00, which is added to the other costs. The source of the 6 percent is operating experience. If the actual cost, as determined by an inventory at the close of each operating period, is consistently 6 percent, then this percentage can be used with accuracy. So long as there is consistency in the actual cost percentage from period to period, this percentage can be used. If the actual cost shows variance, this system cannot be used. In many operations, particularly if they are well-run, this product category will show a stable cost percentage, at least for the short run.

The result of determining the cost by physical inventories, purchases, and percentage estimation is, in Exhibit 3.9, $2,769.50, or 30.6 percent. Percentages are useful as monitoring tools. This procedure provides an estimated cost percentage to compare with the standard. If the standard is about 30 to 31 percent, the operation is probably under control. If there is an unacceptable difference, an investigation would be necessary. If the estimated cost percentage is significantly lower than the standard, perhaps two or three percentage points, a calculation mistake was probably made (assuming, of course, the standard was accurate and calculated as described earlier in this chapter). In this case, the figures should be checked. It is more likely, though, that any variance will show up as an overage. Then management should look at the percentages of each category for comparison to a category standard. This standard, unfortunately, often cannot be calculated as precisely as the overall food cost can. Evaluation of past inventories, costs, and percentages will quickly show, however, whether sufficient consistency exists to establish a standard. In Exhibit 3.9, if the standard were 28.5 percent, the estimated cost of 30.6 percent would warrant further analysis. Let us assume the following standards for the various categories:

Meats/Fish/Poultry	17.5%
Produce	2.0%
Dairy	1.5%
Groceries	6.0%
Bakery	1.5%
	28.5%

It can readily be seen that all categories except meats/fish/poultry are in line. Groceries are using the standard as the estimated cost, so the problem could be there as well. The dairy and bakery categories, because of bypassing the inventory level in the calculation, could also be inaccurate. The most logical explanation here, though, would likely be a control problem with meats, fish, and poultry. The procedure then would be to use the product analysis technique described previously. If the problem is centered on a few items, it will quickly become apparent. The cost overage could also be spread evenly among all the categories, but that would indicate an overall control breakdown too large to have occurred suddenly. We are considering a situation where the normal expectation is for actual costs to be fairly consistent with expected costs. In that case, excessive costs are generally due to a few specific causes. In a poorly run operation with little or no control, this analysis would be worthless since it would reveal that there are problems with all foods, and that would be apparent by just observing the operation!

Inventory Turnover Analysis

When ignored, inventories have the disconcerting habit of growing over time. It is probably a fair statement to say that nearly all foodservice operations are carrying excess inventory. In many cases, the problem is not a major one, but it does exist. Often, it is a significant problem. A true example will illustrate this point. The top management of a foodservice chain with some thirty units thought they were too heavy in inventories (food, beverage, and supplies) and cash banks. A directive was sent to all unit managers to evaluate their operations and reduce, by whatever margin they felt was reasonable, their inventories and cash banks. Within two months, the company had gained over $75,000.00! This money did not show up on the operating statements, but it did increase the cash flow. In other words, the organization had $75,000.00 they had not had prior to that. Where had this money been? It was sitting in storage areas and cash drawers. The following example will show how this works.

Unit A: Before reducing food inventory

Opening inventory	= $ 5,500.00
Purchases	= 20,000.00
Food available for sale	= $25,500.00
Ending inventory	= 5,500.00
Cost of Sales	= $20,000.00

Sales = $60,000.00
Cost % = 33.3%

Unit A: After reducing inventory

Opening inventory	= $ 5,500.00
Purchases	= 19,500.00
Food available for sale	= $25,000.00
Ending inventory	= 5,000.00
Cost of Sales	= $20,000.00

Sales = $60,000.00
Cost % = 33.3%

By reducing the inventory, the operation had to purchase only $19,500.00 instead of $20,000.00

worth of food to support the same sales and make the same profit. Thus, the income statement is not affected, but the operation has saved $500.00. The same would apply to all other inventories—beverages, supplies, china, glassware, and flatware. The average increase in cash flow per unit in the foodservice chain example was about $2,500.00 This is not unusual. Most organizations, if they made it a priority, could realize significant savings in this way. One method for tracking and controlling inventory is to calculate an inventory turnover (T/O) and compare it to a predetermined standard. The calculation is made with the formula:

$$\frac{\text{Cost of sales}}{\text{Average inventory}} = \text{T/O}$$

The cost of sales calculation has been given. In the examples just used, the cost of sales was $20,000.00. The average inventory is determined by adding the opening and ending inventories together and dividing by two. In the examples for Unit A they would be:

Before reduction:

$$\begin{array}{c} \$\,5,500.00 \\ +\ 5,500.00 \\ \hline \$11,000.00 \end{array} \quad \frac{\$11,000.00}{2} = \$5,500.00$$

After reduction:

$$\begin{array}{c} \$\,5,500.00 \\ +\ 5,000.00 \\ \hline \$10,500.00 \end{array} \quad \frac{\$10,500.00}{2} = \$5,250.00$$

The T/O calculations would be:

Before: $\dfrac{\$20,000.00}{5,500.00} = \underline{3.64}$

After: $\dfrac{\$20,000.00}{5,250.00} = \underline{3.81}$

What these figures mean is that before reduction, the inventory was used or sold 3.64 times during the period. After reduction, it was used or sold 3.81 times. One word of caution: use cost of sales in the calculation—not sales, which is sometimes used. What should the T/O figures be? There are no specific standards, for conditions vary widely. Each operation would have its own ideal T/O figure based on its suppliers' capabilities and delivery policies, its storage facilities and capacities, the menu and types of food purchased, its location, and its sales volume. The latter is an important consideration because the higher the volume the more efficiently the stock can be used. There is a minimum amount of food stock that must be maintained just to be open for business, regardless of the number of guests. As the guest count increases, the stock levels generally do not have to be augmented by the same amount. The T/O will increase. An effort should be made to determine the lowest stock level necessary to support a given level of business. The T/O resulting from this inventory level would be the standard T/O. Then the actual T/O would be calculated each month and compared to this standard. When deviations occur, management must attempt to justify them. If, for instance, the month ended on a Friday when deliveries were made for Saturday, Sunday, and part of Monday, a lower than standard T/O would result, but it would be justified. If a two-week supply of steaks were purchased near the end of the month in anticipation of a price increase, instead of the usual three-to-four-day supply, the resulting decrease in T/O would also be justified. If, however, no circumstances caused the variance, the inventory level would be either larger or smaller than desired, and management should take action. Turnover figures lower than expected (indicating larger stock levels) are generally considered the most detrimental to profits, but a higher T/O can cause problems too.

Low T/O: Excessive Stock

1. *Increased waste*: Personnel may get careless when they see large amounts of stock. The rationale goes like this: "It does not matter if I eat, burn, drop, or waste this because we have a lot of it."
2. *Increased risk of pilferage*: Same reason-

ing: "No one will miss this. There is a lot more."

3. *Increased risk of theft or spoilage*: All food is perishable. The more you have on hand, the longer it will take to use it, and the greater the risk of deterioration and/or spoilage.

4. *Opportunity cost*: Excessive inventories mean money is tied up in unneeded products. This same money could be used in presumably more profitable ways. This is a critically important factor in periods of high interest rates when the value of money is higher than normal.

High T/O: Low Stock Level

The problem here is that the probability of running out of food is high and increases as the T/O goes up. The financial efficiency may increase but at the cost of disrupting production, employee morale, and guest satisfaction. One should not want to risk the first or second, and the third, guest satisfaction, cannot under any circumstances be compromised.

Menu Profitability Analysis

Using the menu as the focal point for a profitability analysis must be an unusual concept since so few foodservice operators do it. We have described how certain menu information must be available to establish the standard dollar and percentage costs. These are the product costs, product sales counts, and product selling prices. When these are available, the profits can also be calculated. That is what this section is all about, profits—how to calculate them, and how to increase them. The concept to be discussed was developed by Professor Donald I. Smith, director of Michigan State University's School of Hotel, Restaurant, and Institutional Management, while he was active in foodservice management. It was refined into its present form by Professor Smith and the school's faculty. We present the ideas here in a limited manner. (For a complete presentation see *Menu Engineering*, Kasavana, M. L., and Smith, D. I., Lansing, Michigan: Hospitality Publications, 1982.)

The gross-profit theory of menu analysis (or menu engineering) provides, among other things, the popularity and profitability of each menu item. This enables management to find that mix of selling prices, costs, and sales counts that will maximize profits. It also indicates which items on the menu require repricing, featuring, eliminating, repositioning, or recosting. Further, it provides a quantitative method of evaluating the success of a new menu compared to a previous one. Along the same line, it provides a means of evaluating similar or identical menus from different operations, such as in a foodservice chain.

The two key factors that go into the dollar profits are the total number of guests and the average gross profit from each guest. Gross profit is those dollars remaining after the product cost is deducted. An operation makes a net profit when the gross profit is sufficient to pay labor, operating, and fixed costs with something left over. A high gross profit does not guarantee overall profitability, but it is obviously the place to start. A term commonly used for gross profit is *contribution margin* (CM), which simply means the dollars contributed by the items, individually or collectively. Profits are thus the result of multiplying the number of guests by the average contribution margin. Profits can be increased by serving more guests and/or raising the average CM. It is important to realize the CM can be increased by reducing the cost or raising the selling price. Too often foodservice operators use pricing as the major or only means of increasing contribution margins. Relying primarily upon upward pricing frequently results in decreased guest counts. The bottom line of this should be obvious. The average CM can also be increased by selling more of the high-CM and less of the low-CM menu items. The average CM can be increased by selling additional, nonentree menu items. Increasing prices is not the only way to increase CM, and it can certainly be self-defeating to rely on such a strategy. We will discuss these ideas in greater detail as we review the technique.

The first step is to gather the necessary data: selling prices, sales counts, and product costs.

Selling prices are the most available and come from the menu. Sales counts are not always accessible, but we have described retrieval methods. The source for product costs is precosted recipes. Precosting recipes is covered in detail in the production controls section of chapter four. Once this data has been accumulated, the gross profit analysis chart (Exhibit 3.10) can be completed. The purpose of this chart is to provide the current level of profitability. Revisions and changes will be made with the objective of increasing the profit dollars.

A separate chart should be used for each meal period. Nonentree categories such as appetizers, desserts, and side items should have their own analyses as well. The reason for this is that there are such wide variances among contribution margins. A relatively good luncheon item, for example, may produce a CM of $3.00 while a poor dinner product could have a CM of $4.50. These figures cannot be compared to each other. If they are, no meaningful conclusions can be drawn. An appetizer with a CM of $1.75 cannot be thrown in with an à la carte vegetable that produces a CM of $.75. Luncheon menu items must be compared to other luncheon entrees, appetizers to appetizers, desserts to desserts, and so forth. The chart is then completed as follows:

Column A—Menu item name.

Column B—Number sold. This is called the menu mix or MM.

Column C—Menu mix percent (MM%). The actual number sold of each product must be converted to a percentage so the sales can be compared from one period to another. For example, if the sales for an item changed from 52/night to 41/night, the usual interpretation would be that there is a problem. If the percentage stayed the same (52 is 17 percent of 306 guests and 41 is 17 percent of 241 guests), there would be no problem due to sales mix (although the reduced guest count would pose a problem).

Column D—Item food cost. The total dollar cost to serve each menu item.

Column E—Item selling price.

Column F—Item CM. The contribution margin of each product. This is calculated by deducting the cost (D) from the selling price (E) of each item.

Column G—Menu cost. This is the total cost of serving each menu item. It is obtained by multiplying the number sold (B) by the cost per product (D).

Column H—Menu revenues. The total sales generated by each menu item, which is obtained by multiplying the number sold (B) by the selling price (E).

Box I—Total menu cost. This is also the standard cost, the food cost dollars which should have been used. It is the total of column G, the costs of each menu item.

Box J—Total menu revenues. The total of all the product sales in column H.

Box K—Standard sales percentage. This is calculated by dividing the total cost (I) by total sales (J). If a percentage is desired for cost monitoring, this is the only way an accurate figure can be obtained. As mentioned and will be brought out again in this analysis concept, the objective of menu revisions should be increased dollar profits.

Column L—Menu CM. This shows the total gross profit from each item on the menu. It can be calculated in two ways: (1) Multiply the number sold (B) by the CM or gross profit of each product (F). (2) Deduct the total cost for each product (G) from the total sales (H). It is a good idea to calculate it both ways as a check against errors.

Box M—Total Menu CM. The total of column L.

Box N—Total guest count. The total of column B. This was previously identified as one of the two profit factors.

Box O—Average CM. This is the other profit factor—the average gross profit per guest. It is obtained by dividing the total CM (M) by the

Exhibit 3.10. Menu Engineering Work Sheet Form

Restaurant: _____   Date: _____   Meal Period: _____

(A) Menu Item Name	(B) Number Sold (MM)	(C) Menu Mix %	(D) Item Food Cost	(E) Item Selling Price	(F) Item CM (E-D)	(G) Menu Costs (D*B)	(H) Menu Revenues (E*B)	(L) Menu CM (F*B)	(P) CM Category	(R) MM% Category	(S) Menu Item Classification	(T) Profit Factor
Column Totals:	N					I	J	M				

Additional Computations: $K = I/J$ $O = M/N$ $Q = (100/\text{Items})(70\%)$

total guest count (N). This figure becomes very important in the analysis because it is an excellent frame of reference for profitability. The profit of each product on the menu can be compared to the average profit. Each menu item can then be classified as having greater than average profitability or less than average.

Column P—CM category. This is the result of the relative profitability classification. Each item will be marked either high (average CM or above) or low (less than average CM).

Box Q—Minimum menu mix (MM). Just as each food on the menu can be classed as high or low in profitability, they can be ranked according to the other profit criteria—numbers sold. Here we want to determine a dividing point for popularity as was done with profit, or a minimum level of popularity. Below this we would want to make a change. The last sentence is a key one because it justifies the way we make the calculation. The easiest way is to take an average, just as was done with CM. This is accomplished by dividing 100 percent (total number of guests) by the number of products on the menu. For example:

$$10 \text{ menu items} = 100 \div 10 = 10\%$$
$$20 \text{ menu items} = 100 \div 20 = 5\%$$
$$5 \text{ menu items} = 100 \div 5 = 20\%$$

The trouble with these figures is that few foodservice operators would feel that these are reasonable *minimum sales requirements* for each product. It is therefore recommended that a percentage of this average be used as the minimum. The percentage recommended is 70 percent. Experience has shown this to be reasonable for most operations. The calculation is then made as follows:

1. The mathematical average is obtained as above.
2. The mathematical average is multiplied by 70 percent to obtain the minimum percentage.

$10 \text{ menu items} = 100 \div 10 = 10; 10 \times 70\% = 7\%$
$20 \text{ menu items} = 100 \div 20 = 5; 5 \times 70\% = 3.5\%$
$5 \text{ menu items} = 100 \div 5 = 20; 20 \times 70\% = 14\%$

This figure is then compared with the sales percentages of each menu item, so they can be classified as *high* MM or *low* MM.

Column R—MM percent category. Each menu item is classified high or low according to the above calculation.

Column S—Menu item classification. Using the two profit parameters, popularity (MM) and profitability (CM), all menu items can be classified in one of four categories:

1. Higher than average popularity. Higher than average profitability. These items are called *stars*.
2. Higher than average popularity. Lower than average profitability. These are called *plow horses*.
3. Lower than average popularity. Higher than average profitability. These are called *puzzles*.
4. Lower than average popularity. Lower than average profitability. These products are aptly termed *dogs*.

Once the categories are determined, the classification sheet (Exhibit 3.11) can be completed by placing the menu items in the appropriate spaces.

Column T—Profit factor. Up to now we have concentrated on the numbers of items sold and the profit margin per item. This data is useful, but we have yet to look at each product's share of the total menu profit. This is what the profit factor (PF) shows. The PF is calculated as follows:

1. Total CM (M) ÷ number of items on menu = average CM/menu item
2. Each product CM ÷ average CM = PF

For example, if a ten-product menu produced a $10,000.00 CM, the average CM would be $1,000.00 per product. If product A has a CM of $900.00, product B, $600.00, and product C, $1,450.00, the calculations would be as follows:

$$\text{A. } \frac{\$900}{\$1,000} = .9 \quad \text{B. } \frac{\$600}{\$1,000} = .6 \quad \text{C. } \frac{\$1,450}{\$1,000} = 1.45$$

Exhibit 3.11. Menu Engineering Classification Sheet

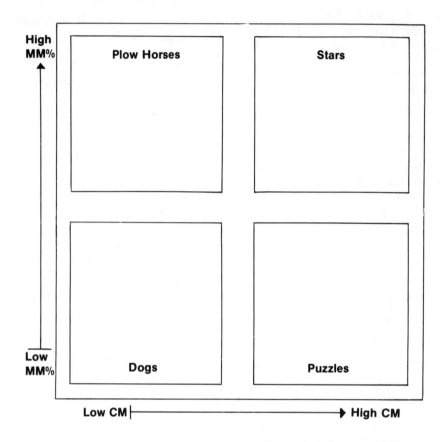

The interpretation is that product A produces 90 percent of the average profit. In other words, it nearly succeeds in carrying its own weight from a profit viewpoint. Product B, on the other hand is not producing profits for the operation—only 60 percent of the average. Product C is very profitable, accounting for some 145 percent of the average CM. The PF thus indicates the relative profitability of each menu item. It provides a more sensitive analytical data base than the four-way classification sheet does. There could, for example, be two plow horses, one because the profit margin is very low—it could be the lowest of all—and the MM is high enough to qualify for above average but just barely. In such a case, barely acceptable sales counts combined with terrible profitability would result in low total profits and a low PF. The other plow horse nearly has an average profit and has a huge sales count. In this case, the total CM would probably be large and so would the PF. Although both are plow horses, the first is nearly a dog and the second, nearly a star. The PF makes this clear.

The ideal menu would show a PF range of .9 to 1.1. This menu would be balanced. It is a mistake to assume very high PF figures are good. Because of the way they are calculated, the average of all the PF figures is 1.0. Therefore, any PF numbers above 1.0 must be balanced by others below 1.0. The higher some products go, the lower the other products will be. There are two kinds of problems with this.

1. Highly profitable menu items are thus offset by marginally profitable products. The operation is purchasing, receiving, storing, preparing, and serving products that do not produce profit margins sufficient to justify all this effort.

2. An extraordinarily profitable product can leave the operation very vulnerable to changes in the food market system. If the product cannot be obtained or if the quality is temporarily poor or the cost increases more rapidly than anyone anticipated, the operation would be in deep trouble and have relatively few options for reversal. Most corporations attempt to diversify for this very reason; they want to spread the risks of doing business by being in several businesses at once. A menu yielding a range of PF's of .3 to 3.6 is unbalanced, inefficient, and may ultimately be unprofitable. A menu with a PF range of .9 to 1.1 is well balanced, and the food-handling system will be more efficient.

In Exhibit 3.12, the work sheet has been completed. We will summarize the critical data and then analyze it to see whether or not the profitability can be improved. This menu is producing a gross profit of $12,177.48 (Box M). The average CM or profit per guest is $5.73 (Box O), and the MM percentage is 6.36 percent (Box Q). Any products that have a CM (column F) of $5.73 or over are considered more profitable than average and are classed as high CM. Menu items $5.72 and below are classed as low CM. All products with an MM percentage (column C) of 6.36 percent or above are highly popular. Any of 6.35 percent or below are low-popularity foods. Each of the eleven menu items are rated as either H (high) or L (low) for both CM and MM percentage and classified as a star, plow horse, puzzle, or dog (column S in Exhibit 3.12 and Exhibit 3.13). Finally, the profit factors for each item are given (column T).

Analysis of Data (Exhibit 3.13)

Stars. These items are both popular and profitable. The guests like them, and the operation makes an excellent profit on them. Little appears to be needed here other than maintaining the current situation. But this can be deceptive. The menu is unbalanced—the profit factors show that. Too much of the profit is being accounted for by too few of the menu items. The profit should be either spread more equally or concentrated even more by ruthless elimination of nonprofitable or less-profitable items. Stars should be tested for price elasticity. The price is said to be inelastic if the quantity sold does not vary when prices increase or decrease. In other words, the demand for the product(s) is not price responsive. If the price is elastic, raising or lowering the price can have a dramatic effect upon sales counts. A product that is highly elastic would respond well to price changes. Management could thus increase or decrease sales counts by using pricing strategies. Dropping a price to stimulate sales could result in increased total profit. Increasing a price to sell less of a product that causes handling problems could also be a profitable decision. When a product is inelastic, however, the strategies change. It would be foolish to ever reduce the price of an inelastic product since the sales will be unaffected. This means that the guest does not see any added value at the lower price. The effect is to reduce the CM—you might just as well throw money away. On the other hand, it would be smart to increase prices of such items. If they are truly inelastic, the guest will not see any reduced value at the higher price, and will buy it anyway. In fact, not to raise the price is also the equivalent of throwing profits away. Another strategy for stars is to assure the maximum degree of quality control. These are the most popular and most profitable foods on the menu, and they absolutely must be served in top condition at all times. Mistakes with such items can have disastrous consequences.

The stars on this sample menu (Exhibit 3.13) are crab legs, prime rib (12-ounce portion), and New York strip steak. We have to make some assumptions to set our strategy. One is that the demand for crab legs is inelastic, crab legs being a prestige or status item. We can price them higher without affecting the demand; thus we

Exhibit 3.12 Menu Engineering Work Sheet—Completed

Restaurant: _____   Date: _____

Meal Period: _____

(A) Menu Item Name	(B) Number Sold (MM)	(C) Menu Mix %	(D) Item Food Cost	(E) Item Selling Price	(F) Item CM (E-D)	(G) Menu Costs (D*B)	(H) Menu Revenues (E*B)	(L) Menu CM (F*B)	(P) CM Category	(R) MM% Category	(S) Menu Item Classification	(T) Profit Factor
Stuffed sole	295	13.9	3.95	7.95	4.00	1,165.25	2,345.25	1,180.00	L	H	Plow Horse	1.07
Crab legs	393	18.5	6.44	13.95	7.51	2,530.92	5,482.35	2,951.43	H	H	Star	2.67
Shrimp	100	4.7	4.71	7.50	2.79	471.00	750.00	279.00	L	L	Dog	.25
Fried chicken	253	11.9	2.69	6.50	3.81	680.57	1,644.50	963.93	L	H	Plow Horse	.87
Pork chops	132	6.2	3.48	8.85	5.37	459.36	1,168.20	708.84	L	L	Dog	.64
Beef liver	38	1.8	2.92	6.95	4.03	110.96	264.10	153.14	L	L	Dog	.14
Prime rib 12 oz.	349	16.4	5.71	11.95	6.24	1,992.79	4,170.55	2,177.76	H	H	Star	1.97
Prime rib 20 oz.	59	2.8	8.85	17.95	9.10	522.15	1,059.05	536.90	H	L	Puzzle	.49
New York strip	304	14.3	5.26	11.75	6.49	1,599.04	3,572.00	1,972.96	H	H	Star	1.78
Beef wellington	65	3.1	4.88	13.50	8.62	317.20	877.50	560.30	H	L	Puzzle	.51
Veal marsala	137	6.4	5.19	10.25	5.06	711.03	1,404.25	693.22	L	H	Plow Horse	.63
Column Totals:	N 2,125					I 10,560.27	J 22,737.75	M 12,177.48				

Additional Computations:

$$K = I/J \quad \frac{10,560}{22,738} = 46.4\%$$

$$O = M/N \quad \frac{12,177}{2,125} = \$5.73$$

$$Q = (100/\text{Items})(70\%) \quad \frac{100}{11} = 9.09 \times .7 = 6.36\%$$

Exhibit 3.13 Menu Engineering Classification Sheet—Completed

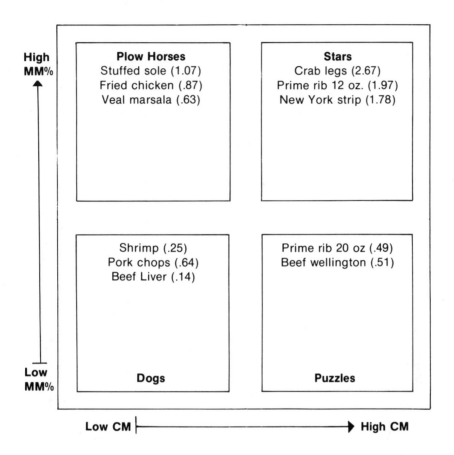

will raise the price to $14.50 (Exhibit 3.14). Another assumption will be that the demand for the smaller cut of prime ribs is elastic and can be tied into the large cut. What we want to do is sell more of the large cut since the profit on this is higher. One way to do that is increase the price of the 12-ounce portion (from $11.95 to $12.95), which should decrease sales. Our objective then is to push those lost sales into the larger, more profitable portion. The strategy for increasing the popularity of the 20-ounce cut will be discussed in the puzzles section. The demand for strip steak is seen as somewhat elastic, and it is quite profitable now, so we won't make any changes.

Another analysis factor to consider is handling cost. The exact costs of receiving, storing,

processing, and serving foods cannot be as precisely determined as can product costs, but an estimation can be made. With the prime rib, lower overall sales (both portion sizes) could be harmful because when a rib is roasted, it should be sold that night. Leftovers result in cost control problems. Steaks are purchased frozen and portioned so they do not present these problems. The number of steaks sold should not affect the profitability. Thus, our strategy is to switch prime rib sales to the larger, more profitable, size and to leave strip steak sales (and profits) the same.

Plow Horses. These foods are popular, but they do not attain the average profitability. A general overall strategy is to increase the CM. In most cases, it would be self-defeating to attempt

Exhibit 3.14 Menu Engineering Work Sheet—Revised

Restaurant: _____   Date: _____

Meal Period: _____

(A) Menu Item Name	(B) Number Sold (MM)	(C) Menu Mix %	(D) Item Food Cost	(E) Item Selling Price	(F) Item CM (E-D)	(G) Menu Costs (D*B)	(H) Menu Revenues (E*B)	(L) Menu CM (F*B)	(P) CM Category	(R) MM% Category	(S) Menu Item Classification	(T) Profit Factor
Crab legs	412	19.4	6.44	14.50	8.06	2,653.28	5,974.00	3,320.72	H	H	Star	2.20
Prime rib 12 oz.	309	14.5	5.71	12.95	7.24	1,764.39	4,001.55	2,237.16	H	H	Star	1.48
New York strip	319	15.0	5.26	11.75	6.49	1,677.94	3,748.25	2,070.31	H	H	Star	1.37
Stuffed sole	258	12.1	3.95	8.50	4.55	1,019.10	2,193.00	1,173.90	L	H	Plow Horse	.78
Fried chicken	266	12.5	2.40	6.50	4.10	638.40	1,729.00	1,090.60	L	H	Plow Horse	.72
Veal marsala	184	8.7	5.19	10.75	5.56	954.96	1,978.00	1,023.04	L	H	Plow Horse	.68
Prime rib 20 oz.	119	5.6	8.85	16.95	8.10	1,053.15	2,017.05	963.90	H	L	Puzzle	.64
Beef wellington	69	3.2	4.88	14.95	10.07	336.72	1,031.55	694.83	H	L	Puzzle	.46
Pork chops	189	8.9	3.48	8.85	5.37	657.72	1,672.65	1,014.93	L	H	Plow Horse	.67
Column Totals:	N					I	J	M				
	2,125					10,755.66	24,345.05	13,589.39				

Additional Computations:

$$K = I/J = \frac{10,755.66}{24,345.05} = 44.2\%$$

$$O = M/N = \frac{13,589.39}{2,125} = \$6.39$$

$$Q = (100/\text{Items})(70\%) = \frac{100}{9} = 11.1 \times .7 = 7.8\%$$

to increase sales. Price increases should be considered for these products. Plow horses are often very elastic. The theory here is that if sales drop, these items will be replaced by other menu selections that probably have higher profit levels. That combined with the increased CM from the higher prices should raise profit levels. Some plow horses could be house specialities, however, and the operator has to be very careful with these. We are talking here about the products that bring people in the door. It is okay to increase a price when the effect will be a switch to another menu item. It cannot be done when there is a risk of losing a customer. In this case, the strategy should be to increase the CM not on the entree but by promoting and merchandising side items such as cocktails, wines, desserts, and so on. Since the problem with plow horses is low-item CM, it would normally not be wise to lower prices. This would make the CM even worse. It is also not a good idea to promote these items, thereby increasing sales and probably cutting profits. Cost reduction should be considered along with price increases as a method for raising the CM. The recipes and food specifications should be carefully evaluated to see whether the serving cost can be reduced without lowering the perceived value of the product.

The profit factors are of critical importance with plow horses. Some items can, by sheer weight of numbers sold, account for significant total profits, and must be handled carefully. These may be the house image makers referred to earlier. The stuffed sole, for example, is a popular product but has the third lowest individual item profit ($4.00). Perhaps the reason for its popularity is that it is underpriced. It is probably not the house specialty type of product since several others outsell it. Increasing the price to $8.50 would improve the CM considerably, and switching the lost sales to almost any other menu item would be more profitable than selling sole at the present price. Another justification for increasing the CM is that the handling costs and potential waste are high. The fried chicken produces nearly the average total profit (pf = .87), but the profit per

order is very low (second lowest in fact), meaning the operation has to sell a lot of chicken. Chicken is quite perishable, so potential waste and spoilage would be a factor if sales were low, but handling costs probably are not. The operation needs more profit but doesn't want to sell any less. Their strategy could be to reduce the serving cost. A change in the presentation—less expensive garnish, smaller portions, change to longer-lasting frying fat, and so forth—could result in lowering the portion cost. The veal marsala must be handled very carefully. Its profit factor is poor, only .63. It also barely qualifies as a plow horse for if the sales were 135 rather than 137, it would be a dog. This product is expensive to purchase and handle. It is also difficult to prepare properly. The present profits do not justify the costs and risks. The correct strategy should be either to improve the total CM, or get rid of it. Here is a rare case in which promotion of a plow horse could be considered. Veal often is regarded as an elegant and desirable dish, so it would be worthwhile attempting to increase both the price and the sales count. This should involve a change in plate presentation, change in menu location, change in menu presentation, skilled salesmanship on the part of the service staff, and proper promotion and merchandising. It can, however, be accomplished.

Puzzles. These are exactly what the name implies. They are puzzling and frustrating because they are profitable, yet do not sell well. A number of strategies are appropriate here. The product quality must be evaluated. If a menu item does not sell well, the most common reasons would be:

1. Poor product—low standard or not produced up to the standard.
2. Unpopular product—what is wildly popular in one location could be thought awful in another.
3. Overpriced.

All these will result in poor value perception and reduced consumer demand. A poor product can be improved—although it may be difficult to convince the guests that it really has improved—

and this should be tried. An unpopular product should be dumped. Why waste time trying to sell something no one wants. Rather, determine what they do want and sell that. If pricing is the problem, adjust it. Since puzzles do not sell well, but are profitable, the price can often be reduced to stimulate sales, especially when the demand is elastic. Because the original profit is high, you may still have an acceptable item CM. In specialized cases, price increases could be attempted. Say, for example, there is a menu item that is highly desirable but only to a few people—the restaurant equivalent of a Mercedes automobile or Dom Perignon champagne. Products like this will never be big sellers, but people who desire them will pay for them. Therefore, raise the price. Sales are not likely to be affected, and the CM will increase.

Since puzzles move slowly, shelf life, waste, spoilage, leftovers, and labor cost must be evaluated. Total product profits are usually low with puzzles because it doesn't matter how much money you make per sale, if you have no sales! Even a fair level of profits could be misleading if there are a lot of the other costs just mentioned.

The two puzzles in our example are prime rib, large cut, and beef wellington. The rib strategy has been discussed. We want to sell more large cuts and fewer small cuts but not any fewer prime rib orders overall. The price on the 12 ounce was increased, and we will reduce the cost of the 20 ounce. By doing this we hope to increase demand for the larger portion by increasing its relative value to the prime rib consumers.

The wellington is one of those status-type products a few guests are willing to pay high prices for. Another way to put it is that like some of the stars, the demand may be inelastic. The strategy is to increase the price and hope the sales remain unchanged. Our example shows they do. But were they to drop, the item should be removed from the menu.

Dogs. These cannot ordinarily be allowed to remain on a menu. Two possible justifications for keeping them would be:

1. The most influential guest loves the product and you must carry it even if no one else purchases it.
2. It is a product you feel will become popular. The gamble is that it will. If it should, chances are you will have a real head start on the competition.

In the first instance, the strategy should be to increase the price so it at least achieves the average CM and thereby becomes a puzzle. This, of course, may not always be possible but must be considered. In the second case, if you feel the gamble is justified, you carry the product even though it may not be profitable. It is an investment in future profits.

The dogs here are in two profit categories. The shrimp and liver are terrible, while the pork chops are not too bad or at least give some hope for improvement. The pork chops are a dog because both the CM and sales count are below average, but are very close in both cases. It would be worthwhile to attempt to increase sales and move it up to the plow horse category. As always with a low-popularity product, check the product quality. Our strategy would be to promote it strongly, to change its image and value perception. Our assumption is that we can increase the sales level significantly.

The shrimp yields by far the lowest profit on the entire menu, indicating that it is probably underpriced; yet the sales are poor. The product is either very bad or just not popular. We will assume that trying to improve the profit margin would reduce the sales even more. The best strategy is to eliminate the product. This should not cost us any customers, since no one appears to like the item very much now. The liver decision is easy. This item is often unpopular. In this case, it is very unpopular and not very profitable either. We will drop it from the menu. Since the assumption was that total guest count would remain the same, any sales lost from these two products will be distributed among the remaining menu items roughly according to their MM percent.

Exhibit 3.14 gives the profitability results of the revised menu, and Exhibit 3.15 depicts the new classifications of the menu items. The total

Exhibit 3.15 Menu Engineering Classification Sheet—Revised

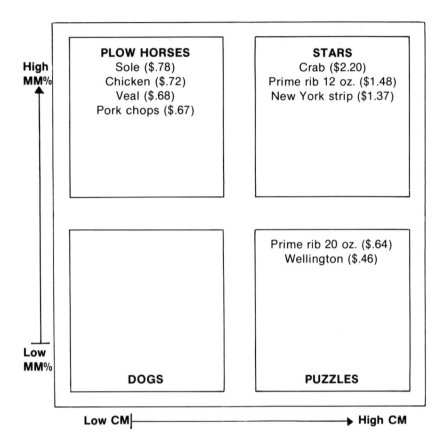

menu CM (box M) has increased to $13,589.39 from $12,177.48, an improvement of $1,411.91 or 11.6 percent. This is all that is really important. The standard cost percentage (box K) has gone from 46.4 percent to 44.2 percent, but this has nothing to do with the profitability. Profits are measured in dollars. As long as the dollar profit increased, the menu revision was positive regardless of whether the percentage went up or down. If a menu change results in a decrease in total CM, the revision would be negative regardless of the percentage. The point here is that this was a successful revision because CM increased, not because the percentage dropped. It would have been successful even had the percentage increased. The reason the profit went up was that the average CM per guest went from $5.73 to $6.39 (O), which means an

additional profit of $.66 was made on each guest. This additional profit will nearly all be net profit. Since the same number of guests are being served, there should be no additional need for personnel. It should not require any more energy to heat or cool the dining room, and no more linen is needed. The rent will not go up. Virtually all the nonproduct costs of serving 2,125 people are fixed, regardless of what they eat or how much they spend, so increased gross profits have a really major effect upon net profits.

The profit factors (column T) are much more balanced, the range being from $.46 to $2.20. Formerly it was $.14 to $2.67. This is still not ideal, but much improved. The two extremes, crab legs ($2.20) and wellington ($.46) have purposefully been placed in those positions. We perceived that both the crab legs and the wellington could be priced higher without affecting demand. The crab legs are popular so the profit is very high, the wellington is not that popular, but we have decided the revised profit level more than justifies its menu retention. It would now be foolish to drop it, since it has the highest CM on the menu and selling any other product in its place would reduce total profits.

The improved balance is also shown by the classification sheet (Exhibit 3.15). Profits will generally be improved when a menu revision results in:

1. Eliminating the dogs
2. Limiting the number of puzzles
3. Maximizing the stars

When these are accomplished, the remaining items will be plow horses, and under these revised conditions, they will be profitable.

4   Food Cost and Quality Control

Food control is primarily a product-control challenge. The control of personnel activities is also important since people make mistakes and they do steal. However, the product itself, with all its inconsistencies, greatly complicates cost and quality control. All foodservice operations perform the same functions. What differentiates them is the complexity of each. They all buy, receive, store, prepare, and serve food. We shall therefore take a functional approach and examine each of these in turn.

Purchasing

Purchasing is obtaining the right *quality* and the right *quantity* at the right *time* and the right *price* from the right *supplier*. Once management has established the standards for each of the above, control is whatever management does to assure that these standards are met. Operators often speak of the profit-making potential of the purchasing function but, in truth, no profits are to made from purchasing properly. There is, however, an enormous potential for loss from improper purchasing. Many would argue

heatedly over the statement that there are no profits to make in purchasing. But if purchasing is obtaining the right quality and quantity at the right time and so on, and all these elements are done properly, there will be a standard cost. To go below this cost implies that perhaps the right product was not delivered, or there was too little of it, or it came at the wrong time from the wrong supplier, or we paid too little for it. Therefore, "saving" money in purchasing is done by cutting standards, and that is not a healthy way to insure long-term profits. On the other hand, if a product quality mistake is made, or the food is delivered late, or too much is purchased, or an excessive price is paid, or you are dealing with an incompetent or unscrupulous supplier—any one of these can increase the operating costs significantly. We take the position that there is no money to be made from doing the job properly—any profits realized will be standard profits. If the job is performed poorly, money will be lost. As an example, if a buyer were to begin purchasing spare ribs from a different supplier at $.20 per pound less, the conventional attitude would be "I am saving $.20

per pound." Our attitude would be, "You have not been purchasing from the right supplier at the right price. Therefore you have been losing $.20 per pound, and what you are now paying is the correct price!" Another equally valid answer depending on circumstances would be, "You are not getting the same quality of product, and it is not worth any more than you are paying for it." In both cases, though, there are no savings from paying a lower price. Either you should have been paying it all along, or it is now the correct price, considering the change in the product standard.

What is the *right* quality? Quality is defined in the *Oxford American Dictionary* as "a degree or level of excellence, as in *goods of a high quality*." We may not, however, be interested in "high quality" or the "highest quality." An example of a high-quality automobile could be a Cadillac, though some might consider a Mercedes "higher quality." To an individual requiring a vehicle to haul lumber, neither would be the right quality. In purchasing, the term *quality* has no meaning unless it is related to use and ultimate cost, which may be a lot different from price! The right or best quality is that which can be purchased at the lowest cost to satisfy the intended function. Quality has no meaning in purchasing, cannot be understood, unless it is related to function and ultimate cost. The ultimate cost is the cost of serving the product, which is seldom the same as the price paid for a product. A product costing $4.00 per pound with a 90 percent yield is less expensive to serve than is a product costing $3.00 per pound with a 66 percent yield:

$$\$4.00 \div .90 = \$4.44$$
$$\$3.00 \div .66 = \$4.55$$

This is so obvious that it is difficult to understand why so many food buyers make purchasing decisions primarily upon price.

There are two determinations that must be made.

1. What is the quality necessary to perform a function? This is a technical consideration as to suitability.

2. What is a proper cost? This is an economic consideration of price and availability.

The first, the technical question, can best be answered by chefs, kitchen managers, food and beverage directors, and so on. The second, the economic question, is handled by the purchasing agent. In many operations, these may all be the same person, which points out an advantage of larger size and scope of operations. Larger operations can afford specialists, each making decisions related to their background and training. Smaller units must necessarily have generalists who are always better at some jobs than others. In other words, the chef may be a marvelous technician, but this does not qualify this same person as an effective and knowledgable buyer.

There are two components of a quality and cost control program. They are *specifications* and *standardization*.

Role of Specifications

In order to assure the lowest cost of products served and in order to assure that quotes by purveyors can be compared, it is necessary to have very specific and individualized products. Product quality must be related to ultimate functions. For example, tomatoes can be purchased in a variety of forms: fresh, canned whole, canned pieces, canned crushed, diced, and pureed. In addition, there are several varieties of tomatoes grown and shipped. There are also many quality ranges within each of the types of canned tomatoes. The specification should be consistent with the use. If they are required for slicing on sandwiches, fresh tomatoes—ripe and juicy—are needed. If they are to be stuffed for a luncheon salad plate, fresh tomatoes are also required but perhaps with a firmer texture. If creole sauce or stewed tomatoes are served, the canned pieces would be best, while an Italian-type pasta sauce would call for crushed or chopped tomatoes. Purchase of the so-called "best" canned tomatoes for the pasta sauce would result in using whole peeled tomatoes, firm, with no blemishes, gouges, or discolorations. This product would then be crushed or chopped for the sauce. The operator is paying a premium for the qualities just described, but these qualities are not apparent in the finished product. The product requirement is for tomato bulk, color, acidity, and flavor. These can be met just as satisfactorily with less expense using canned crushed tomatoes. Not only will the food cost be lower due to higher drained weight, but personnel cost will be reduced, and there will be less need for equipment.

Specifying the wrong product results in higher product, labor, and operating costs without improving the product's value in the eyes of the guest. A basic rule of purchasing is to pay whatever is necessary to meet your food standards but not to pay an extra penny for qualities that either will not be perceived by the guests or will give you a higher standard than you want to serve. An example of the latter would be prime steaks. If the decision is to serve choice steaks, it is a mistake to purchase prime. Prime is higher or better quality, but it goes beyond the standard regarded as suitable for that specific operation. If the standard is prime, then, of course, prime would be the best or most suitable quality.

Role of Standardization

Management must maintain a position of anticipating events rather than reacting to them. Standardization of products and procedures aids in assuring cost and quality consistency. Management should be in a position to predict the cost and quality of products when served to the guests—hence the importance of standardization. Without specifications, there cannot be any cost or quality standardization because the menu item ingredients will be variable and unpredictable. Even with excellent specifications, there are product variances. Without specifications, nearly anything is likely to be delivered—and used!

Purchase Decisions Versus Order Decisions

Certain types of decisions should be made only by management; that is, they should not be delegated. These are called *basic purchase decisions,* and there are three of them.

1. What to purchase
2. How much to stock
3. Whom to purchase from

The first—what to buy—is the specification. This decision cannot be left to the discretion of kitchen employees or food buyers, although it often is. Input into the decision will obviously come from many sources, one of which is the food personnel. The final decision, however, should be made by those who are responsible for the entire operation and who consider all the needs including financial, operating, and marketing. Other personnel, even chefs, tend to make such important decisions mostly, if not solely, upon production requirements. These are probably the most important, but they are far from being the sole criteria. The right product, to reiterate, is that product best suited to a particular need at the lowest ultimate cost. This includes marketing and financial requirements as well as production needs. This then is the first of the three basic purchasing decisions. It is best made in the planning or organizing as opposed to the operating stage. It is difficult in an already-operating establishment to make these decisions properly. They should be determined *prior* to opening, after adequate evaluation of product needs and product availability.

The second decision, that of deciding how much to stock, is an inventory-level decision. This also cannot reasonably be delegated. The question of how much stock to carry will be discussed under inventory control. It is a complex decision, demanding that many factors be evaluated—cost of money, space available, cost of space, risk, perishability, delivery, ability of suppliers, types of products, and so on. This, like product specification, should be decided as early as possible and is not likely to be as adequately thought out once the operation is off and running.

The last basic purchasing decision, the supplier, is equally important. The right supplier is the one who can deliver exactly the product you desire in the amount needed at the requested time and at the lowest cost. Again, these criteria go well beyond production requirements and cannot be delegated to production personnel for that reason alone. The most powerful argument against lack of centralized control of purchasing is the possibility of illegal and fraudulent agreements between the suppliers and the buyers.

Once these three decisions are made, restocking or reordering can be delegated. In fact, under certain circumstances they should be because in fact no decision needs to be made at all. They can be repetitive functions and, as such, should not be performed by management. For example, assume canned peach halves, 35/40 ct., are specified as extra fancy quality, packed in #10 cans, in heavy syrup, to be purchased from the ABC Distributors and that a par stock of three cases is to be maintained. All three of the basic purchase decisions have been made: what to purchase, how much to stock, and from whom. The only thing left to decide is how much to have delivered this week. In order to make the order, the present inventory must be known. If there is one case on hand, the order will be for two cases of extra fancy peach halves from ABC. Anyone who can read, write, talk, and count can make this order. There are no substantive decisions being made; these have already been made. Not only can management effectively delegate this type of ordering task, but they should. In fact, since practically anyone can do it adequately, management should not do it. A manager's time is too valuable to spend on a task that will be repeated over and over again. Managers are well-advised to spend their time on activities other employees cannot do. It is common, though, to see management wasting time doing things that could be done just as well by a variety of other employees. Additionally, they also waste time and potential profits as well by repeatedly making decisions that ideally should be made only once. When a specification has been rationally established, it is unlikely that it will need revision. If it does, the need will occur only rarely. When there are no specifications or they are not well formulated, the operator actually makes a basic purchase decision, that of deciding what to purchase, virtually every time an order is placed! The results of this are that more time is

required, the ordering cannot now be effectively delegated, and, worst of all, there is absolutely no consistency among products over time. In the latter case, it becomes impossible to predict cost and quality standards. The result is lack of ability to analyze what has occurred and to control what will occur.

Without par stocks and policies on inventory levels, the decision of how much to purchase will be made over and over again—each time an order is placed. The result is fluctuating inventories—sometimes understocked, often overstocked—certainly out of balance.

The last decision, whom to purchase from, is such an important one that it should be made only after an exhaustive evaluation. Once made, hopefully it will not have to be changed. This is an area where stability is desirable. Good purveyors can be a great asset to a foodservice operator, and as stated, purveyors and operators should attempt to build mutually satisfactory relationships. When this decision is remade with each order, there can be no stability in the entire purchasing function. When buyers continually switch back and forth between sellers, they are making supplier selections over and over. When this happens, the decision is based mainly on price, and as pointed out, serving cost, not price, is the important factor.

Role of Price

Price is one of the most important purchasing criteria, but it is far from the most important one, at least to professional industrial buyers. A study of patronage motives of some four hundred industrial buyers found the following to be the most important factors (ranked in order of importance):

1. Reliability of seller
2. Continuous supply under all conditions
3. Accessibility of seller
4. Low prices
5. Quick, reliable delivery

Many foodservice buyers would prepare a list that looks like this:

1. Price
2. Price
3. Price

An axiom of purchasing is that a product is always available *if* you are willing to pay the price. The reverse is just as true but is not recognized as widely: There is always a product available, regardless of how little you wish to pay. What this means is that when you purchase by price, the purveyor can always meet your demands. The quality, yield, and ultimate cost of serving such products is, however, another story. Some buyers think that by demanding the lowest prices they are challenging the purveyor. This is a mistake, for nothing could be easier. The purveyor is challenged when the buyer demands performance over a wide range of factors and activities: product excellence, delivery, financial terms, custom fabrication, and so forth.

To put this discussion of purchasing in the perspective of a foodservice operator, try to decide which of the following types of guest would be easier to accommodate. One guest comes in, asks for the manager, and announces he or she wants a strip steak and won't pay over $5.00 for it, stating that any operator who could not satisfy this demand and make money does not belong in this business. The other guest desires a quality strip steak (at least top choice), well-aged (about three weeks), expects professional service, immaculate linen, quality glassware and china, and wants the environment to be comfortable and conducive to relaxation and enjoyment. This guest expects to pay a *fair* price for all this and will very obviously be more difficult to satisfy. The question each food buyer should ask herself or himself is: which customer do I resemble?

Another example would be an automobile purchase. No foodservice buyer would go into an auto dealership and ask, "What is your lowest price for a car?" The answer might be $400.00, which would probably send the buyer, expecting to pay up to $9,000.00, wild with joy. Until, of course, the $400.00 car is presented for inspection. It will probably be very old, rusting, have bald tires, no motor, and so on. "No, No, I mean your lowest price for a new car."

"Oh," the salesman replies, "Well, we have one for about $5,000.00." This still appears to be a pretty good deal, but then the car is brought out—four cylinders, no air conditioning, no radio, no power equipment.

"No, No. I want _____." When the salesman is finally given exact, specific, details, a meaningful price can be quoted. Meaningful because the buyer can then go to another dealer and get a quote on the *same* auto. It is simple to determine who has the lowest price, but without the specification (and that is what it is), price quotations mean nothing at all. This then is the importance of price: When prices are quoted on identical products, and all other factors are equivalent, the lowest price is truly a better price. In the absence of specifications and delivery arrangements, payment terms, and so forth, prices cannot be compared.

Role of Purveyor

The purveyor is in business to satisfy the needs of the foodservice operator, just as that operator is in business to satisfy the needs of his or her guests. Restaurant patrons are thus in a favorable position as long as they do not abuse their relationship by making demands harmful to the well-being of the establishment, such as free food, triple portions, and so on. The foodservice buyer should remember this in dealing with purveyors. The buyer cannot make ridiculous demands and expect to maintain a relationship. But if the suppliers want the business, they must be willing to accommodate the realistic needs of the buyers, and different buyers have different needs.

Paradoxically, it is becoming more difficult for suppliers to maintain the needed flexibility in dealing with their customers. One reason is the constant expansion of product lines. When a buyer bought fresh produce from a produce specialist, and that is all the person handled, it was expected that the supplier could and would be very flexible and responsive to a wide variety of customer requirements. When one supplier handles meats, seafood, poultry, produce, canned goods, tools and equipment, paper goods, and cleaning supplies and compounds, this supplier simply cannot be as flexible. The products tend to be more standardized, procedures and policies more fixed. Concurrent with this development has been the rising cost of money. This has made it imperative for suppliers to maintain tight inventories and move their product lines quickly. They are not as likely to stock unusual, limited-demand products. Purchasers, of course, can obtain these items, but they will probably have to be ordered by the supplier, resulting in a delay. This is fine when the need can be recognized in advance, but in this business we cannot always predict our needs in advance.

The cost of delivery is also a factor. It has increased tremendously, making it necessary for the supplier to make ever larger deliveries to maintain minimum profit margins on each delivery. Look at this comparison of delivery costs past and present for a produce dealer.

Past:

Truck - (Nonrefrigerated, since deliveries were mostly local) $6,000.00. Estimated life, 5 years or 60 months.

Capital cost = $100.00/month

Gas - 3,000 miles/month, 10 mpg, $.50/gallon for gas = $150.00/month

Driver - $10,000/year or $833.00/month

Total monthly cost - Truck - $ 100.00
Gas - 150.00
Driver - 833.00
$1,083.00

Present:

Truck - (Refrigerated—wider delivery territory, more time on road) $40,000.00. Estimated life, 5 years or 60 months.

Capital cost = $667.00/month

Gas - 4,500 miles/month, 15 mpg, $1.30/gallon for gas = $390.00/month

Driver - $22,000/year or $1,833.00/month

Total monthly cost - Truck - $ 667.00
Gas - 390.00
Driver - 1,833.00
$2,890.00

Trucks can be rented also. A 20-foot refrigerated truck would cost nearly $1,400.00 per month. To this would be added:

$ .15 per mile driven

$ .65 per hour for refrigeration unit

$25.00 per week for insurance

Diesel fuel for refrigeration unit at perhaps $300.00 per month

The total cost is at least $2,500.00 per month, and this is not considered to be a large truck. This is a simplistic cost estimation since it ignores overhead costs, warehouse capital and operating cost, computer cost, and so on. It does show clearly, however, that each time the truck makes a delivery, it is necessary to drop off much more food than before to maintain the same profit. The days when the truck could come six days per week and deliver one case of lettuce, one dozen lemons, one bag of onions, and the like are over. The supplier cannot afford it. A $50.00 average order could once have been the break-even point on profit. Today that point might be $400.00. These figures are not intended to be specific but only to illustrate the position suppliers are now in. Their operating costs have increased considerably while their profit margins have not. They thus must move more products. The answer is fewer and larger deliveries to each unit. When you think about it, the foodservice operator is in a similar position. A gross profit per guest of $1.00 may once have been adequate, but today each guest must produce $3.00 or $4.00 or more to maintain necessary profit margins.

One reason why purveyors have expanded product lines is to increase the order sizes. This is the full-service distribution concept. The rationale on the part of the purveyors is that the more kinds of products they have, the larger the deliveries will be. It may not be possible to demand that the operator purchase a $300.00 minimum produce order, but if soap, paper towels, light bulbs, china, glassware, flatware, kitchen tools, aluminum foil, portion-cut steaks, frozen lobster tails, a stock pot, frozen vegetables and french fries, butter, canned carrots, canned hash, and so forth can all be delivered, there would be no problem in meeting or exceeding the minimum. Another advantage for the suppliers is that they can balance demand because customers will almost never be in a situation where they have no needs. They may not need any oranges but are about to run out of frilly toothpicks and could use tongs and serving spoons. Diversification is as valid a strategy for a purveyor as for a multinational conglomerate.

The purveyors also balance their profit margins. Each product line is subject to its own set of economic rules. Selling produce may result in narrow profit margins. These relatively small profit margins are balanced by the inventory turnover. Tuesday sales (out) nearly always equal Tuesday purchases (in). Inventories, as a percentage of total sales, are quite small. Profit margin times T/O equals total profitability. In this case the equation has small margins multiplied by large turnovers. Handling heavy kitchen equipment, however, is much different. Dollar inventories can be huge, but they are offset by much higher profit margins. The financial result may well be similar, since the larger profit margins are multiplied by reduced stock turnover.

Another advantage of the one-stop shopping concept is that the purveyor can offer certain products at a lower price than specialists can. The full-line distributor might be able to beat the price of the soap company for cleaning compounds. The theory here is that the chemicals company has to make its profit only on soaps and various cleaning compounds. If the buyer purchases just dish machine soap, the price will probably have to be pretty high. After all, how large could the order be? The chemical company has considerable overhead to support by just selling soap. The chemicals supplier thus also attempts to include pot-washing soap, floor cleaners, degreasing compounds, and so on with the order. The full-line supplier is obviously able to spread the fixed delivery costs among many more products and may be able to offer even lower prices.

The same reasoning applies when they compete for the coffee business with coffee and

tea companies, or premix soft drinks with the soda organizations and so forth. One great disadvantage for the buyer is that the full-line distributor may have no maintenance expertise. When the buyer purchases soap from a chemicals company, the company will baby-sit the dish machine, train personnel, provide inspections, maintenance, even repair it. The full-line foodservice distributor may not have this capability. The coffee specialist may provide not only maintenance but also the brewing equipment as well. The soda company can provide equipment, expertise, service, and marketing assistance. The foodservice operator must determine the value of these services and deduct them from the product cost savings to ascertain which is the best course to follow. The decision becomes easier when the full-line food distributors have the service capability. An example would be when they hire chemicals specialists to work with their clients or when they provide soft-drink, coffee, or juice dispensers.

Another facet of one-stop shopping is that, because of the broad range of product lines, it is easy for the operator to meet minimum order requirements. All suppliers must have some policies on minimum orders. When a supplier handles only one line, this places severe restraints on the buyer's ability to meet reasonable order sizes. A $300.00 minimum order on a specialized product could mean deliveries less often than management would like and subsequent overstocking at delivery time. A purchaser ordering from a purveyor who can supply a wide range of products, however, would have little trouble meeting a $300.00 minimum, even with frequent deliveries. Multi-item suppliers also enable small operators, by concentrating their orders with one distributor, to achieve respectable order sizes.

There are several drawbacks to the one-stop concept. It is difficult for a purveyor to be all things to all people, that is, to be sufficiently expert in all areas. A produce specialist would know more about fresh fruits and vegetables than an organization that handles produce almost as a sideline. This is not true when the large distributor merges the specialist into the organization, however. Size alone is no guarantee of efficiency, but it seems obvious that a large company with national or wide regional distribution can financially justify hiring experts in the various areas.

We have made reference to the product lines to be carried by a full-line purveyor. They are:

1. Meats/seafood/poultry
2. Frozen and prepared foods
3. Bakery goods
4. Fresh and processed produce
5. Beverages: coffee, tea, soft drinks, juices
6. Kitchen equipment and tools
7. China, glassware, flatware, and other tabletop items
8. Paper goods and disposable items
9. Sanitation supplies
10. Linens
11. Dairy (eggs, cheese, and so forth)

Another example of the advantage of size is in the area of fresh and processed produce, number 4 on the list. A specialist may be unable, due to size and financial strength, to meet the increasing demand for processed produce, whereas a larger, stronger company could justify investing in the equipment and facilities necessary to get into that end of the business.

A possible drawback of a larger organization is that they may lose some of the flexibility necessary in dealing with foodservice operations. Take emergency orders for example: In the case of a smaller, local purveyor, the owners themselves could end up delivering the needed products in their own cars. In the case of a large company, one possibly located in another city or town, with a fully computerized warehouse having an automated picking system, responding on short notice to a client's needs might be impossible. Another factor is that the larger the organization, the more bureaucratic it becomes and the less able it is to respond to specific needs or to carry unusual products. It may have relatively inflexible delivery schedules and may carry only basic products that have a high demand. Such a supplier may not be willing, for

example, to carry prime meat because the demand is mostly for choice. Only a few, specialized foodservice operations require prime. The needs of the majority will determine what is stocked. A smaller, high-quality meat specialist may be needed to satisfy this specific demand. There are also certain types of fresh fruits and vegetables that the full-line distributors may not bother with because they cannot justify it economically. The full-line distributors are often best suited for dealing with institutional buyers—commercial chains and the noncommercial sector. There will be some exceptions to this generalization. In certain markets you may find a large, full-service distributor that became that way by being exceptionally responsive to customer demands.

"Good" Buys: Guidelines for Evaluation

Food buyers are often offered opportunities to "load up" on products at apparently low prices. We shall not consider the financial and operating implications of overstocking at this time (for this, see the inventory control section). The buyer cannot overlook these two factors in making a wise decision about any offer:

1. There are no savings unless and until the products are *used*.
2. Often a "good buy" may involve distressed goods.

As an example of the first point, a large hotel located in the downtown area of a large city was found by a consultant to have some 250 cases of canned tomatoes in an out-of-the-way basement storage area. They had obviously been there for some years. When the consultant inquired about them, the reply was, "Oh, the former food manager got a real deal on those a few years ago." Investigation revealed that four years earlier the manager had purchased over 400 cases at a savings of about $5.00 per case. The manager then proudly announced that he had "saved" the company $2,000.00. What exactly was saved? The hotel invested thousands of dollars in purchasing the tomatoes. Since nearly 250 cases were still there four years later, the operation had used only some 150 cases. Savings, if they do occur, are realized when the products are *used*, not purchased. In this case, since they had actually used about 150 cases, the savings were $750.00, spread over four years, $188.00 per year, or $15.63 per month! This hardly appears to justify an investment of several thousand dollars. In addition to that, the tomatoes were no longer any good. Canned goods will not become contaminated, but they will certainly deteriorate in quality over time, especially when storage temperatures are 90 degrees F. or higher, as was the case here. A few cans were opened at random, and they had deteriorated to the point where they were considered unusable. Where then were the savings?

A general guideline is that you actually save money when you use an item. A price reduction of $1.00 per pound on filets, for example, does not become realized until the steak is cooked and served. Until then, it is merely sitting in a freezer or refrigerator and may actually be costing rather than saving money.

The possibility that the goods are distressed must also be considered. When this is the case, serving costs could actually increase and quality will certainly decrease. The buyer must determine the reason for the goods being offered at a lower-than-normal price. The products will seldom be in top condition, although that is a possibility. When that happens, the decision is easier since the product quality can be taken out of the evaluation process. An example would be a supplier who is overstocked for one reason or another. The goods are perfectly sound, but under normal product movement conditions, it will take the supplier so long to work them off that eventually the quality will suffer. Another example could be when suppliers make a mistake and get into a product area they should not have. If a restaurateur can use such products, he or she can benefit from the suppliers' mistake. Another example would be when a supplier is attempting to introduce a new product. The supplier also could be pushing a product that is not moving as well as it ought to. The rationale of the low price is that if people try it, they will come back for more (hopefully at a normal price, however).

The buyer should distinguish between push and pull marketing strategies. The pull strategy implies that the seller attempts to create a demand for the product with the user, such as Heinz catsup for the table. A purveyor does not have to try to induce food buyers to purchase Heinz. They do so because their customers want and expect it. Push marketing, on the other hand, occurs when the buyer has the discretionary ability to specify products. They don't with Heinz catsup for the table, but they do for catsup to cook with. The sellers are then placed in the position where they must induce the buyer to purchase their particular brand. There are not apt to be many deals for sound products when they are marketed by the pull method, but push-type products will often be available in prime condition at excellent prices. Sales items of many large reputable suppliers may also be a function of the suppliers' buyers getting "deals" from their *good, consistent*, and *reliable* packers and passing the savings on to their customers. This is especially true when the food distributor can move such products quickly.

If there is something wrong with a special-price item, it could still be a good deal, but the buyer must know exactly what will be delivered. If the problem is that the shelf life is running out and the buyer knows it can be utilized immediately, it would be wise to make the purchase. A hotel purchasing agent was once contacted by a local supermarket a few days prior to Easter. Their problem was that they had grossly overestimated the number of ham steaks they would sell for Easter. The purchasing agent had ordered portioned ham steaks, but they had not yet been delivered. This hotel's order was canceled, and the ham steaks were picked up at the supermarket. The hotel did, in fact, save a considerable sum, but if the steaks could not all have been used on Easter Sunday, it would not have been a good deal.

All frozen products have a limited shelf life; the freezer merely extends it well beyond that of nonfrozen foods. Shrimp, for example, have a shelf life of about six to eight months at 0 degrees F. If a purveyor offered a substantial discount on shrimp they had stored for six months, it would be a wise purchase if the shrimp could be used in a few weeks. Otherwise it would not be. It is wise under such circumstances to inspect a few boxes selected at random.

Sometimes a supplier has an opportunity to pick up quantities of a product that will have to be used quickly. The supplier will not take the product unless there is some assurance or they feel certain that they can pass it on to their customers. The supplier is thus in the same position as the buyers we have described. They are interested in the "deal" only if they can turn it over immediately. The buyer should react the same way. Frozen cornish hens near the end of their storage life would be a great purchase if they were scheduled for a banquet the following weekend, or if they were a popular special item.

There are many such occasions when the product is presently sound, but it will not remain so for long. If it can be moved quickly, it could be a wise investment. One note of caution, however. It must be turned over without disrupting the operation. A restaurant manager once picked up a huge supply of tomato juice. He was unable to resist it because he was "saving" so much money. When it was pointed out that he had purchased about a six-month supply and that the $650.00 he saved actually worked out to $100.00 per month or about $3.33 per day, he immediately stated his intention to use it all during the coming month and realize the entire savings on one income statement. He did so, but the cost was considerable disruption of the menu balance. Dining room and cocktail waitresses were firmly instructed to sell Bloody Marys in preference to all other drinks. Of course, he did not bother to work up a Bloody Mary promotion; he just told everyone to "push" Bloody Marys. A great variety of foods were served with a tomato sauce, and all banquets were served tomato juice appetizers, regardless of whether they were ordered or not. He did use all the tomato juice in one month, and he did "save" some $600.00 that month, but the customers must certainly have been mystified!

How Many Purveyors Do You Need?

There is no set answer or standard, but there are some guidelines. In general, there are two types of economic leverage an operator can use when dealing with purveyors. One comes from concentrating the orders with as few suppliers as possible, thereby becoming an important customer to each one. If the operator can become important enough, she or he can use leverage to move the purveyor into concessions that might not otherwise be made. This should not be surprising since it is exactly how a foodservice operator would react to a good customer. Most successful operators will bend over backwards to accommodate all guests; but for really important guests, they will do things they might have to refuse a nonregular guest. If an unknown guest asked for a steak to be prepared in the dining room, he or she would probably be turned down, politely and with warmth and sincerity, of course—but turned down just the same. When regular high rollers show up, you would not only prepare it tableside but would purchase a dragon to flame it if they so desired.

The other type of leverage consists of having more than one purveyor for each product category in order to leverage them against each other. The buyer can then compare prices and products continuously.

The decision as to which is the best method depends on the product itself. When there is considerable quality and price variance, the second one will probably be more effective. Where there is little consistency management realizes that at any given time there are a variety of quality/price relationships. In this case the most effective way to insure the best quality available at the lowest reasonable price is to make two or more purveyors prove themselves nearly on a daily basis. This type of leverage is lost with only one purveyor. Meat, seafood, poultry, and fresh produce fit into the more-than-one-purveyor category best. The produce market changes on a nearly daily basis, and the buyer may not want to commit to one purveyor, thereby having no readily accessible frame of reference as to prices and quality. The meat, seafood, and poultry markets—while not as volatile—are also subject to a wide range of variances, and the same policy of multiple distributors is often advised.

With many products today, however, there is little product differentiation; the buyer can get the same or similar performance from many brands. When several purveyors all handle the same products, the supplier decision is based largely on nonproduct factors, such as inventory assistance, delivery policies, location, payment policies, marketing help, market research, and so on. In such cases, there is little reason to have many suppliers, and the buyer can exert maximum pressure upon the seller by becoming an important and valued customer. This concept is borne out by the fact that some foodservice industry distributors have a policy governing the maximum percentage of their sales that they will allow to any one customer. Again, look at it from the foodservice operator's viewpoint. If you had a single customer accounting for 25 to 30 percent of total sales, that customer could control the operation and force it into harmful policies and activities. The alternative would be losing one-quarter of the business, and few organizations in any industry could cope with that. Such a customer could even cause the unit to fail.

Another advantage of having fewer suppliers has already been covered. Fewer suppliers means larger orders, and this means that the fixed delivery cost, as a percentage of the order, declines. The result can and should be lower prices. Most distributors have flexible pricing with the prices tied to the order size, either in dollars, weight, or cases.

Rebates, Discounts, and Kickbacks

The difference between a rebate and a discount is that with a rebate, the buyer pays full invoice amounts and has money returned at a later date. With a discount, the face value of the invoice is not paid. A rebate would be called for when the purveyor, for whatever reason, does not wish to alter the price structure. A rebate allows the seller to have standardized pricing yet retain pricing flexibility where needed. Normally this practice is responsive to volume and is one of the ways operators can use volume purchases to reduce costs. Rebates are legal and quite ethical (for food, not alcoholic beverages) so long as the money is returned to the organization and not to any individual and as long as it is documented. This means that a record of the transaction must exist somewhere. When the money is given directly to an individual, such as the purchasing agent, and no records of the transaction exist, the practice is termed a kickback and is both illegal and unethical. This is done following an agreement between the purchaser and seller that the supplier's products will be used. The amount could be tied to volume, or it could be a flat payment. Another type of kickback occurs when the purveyor agrees to charge more than the normal price, with the purchasing agent getting the difference. For example, if the normal product price were $2.75 per pound, the invoice would be charged at $3.00 per pound, and the purchasing agent would receive $.25 for each pound. This is quite possible when management does not know what a fair price is and does not follow up and monitor the purchasing department and/or the purchasing agent. It would be particularly easy in an operation where the chef is responsible for purchasing. The implication here is not that chefs are dishonest but that assigning the purchasing and production responsibility to one individual violates the basic control precept of separation of functions. Where there is a purchasing agent and a chef, they would probably have to collaborate since a competent, honest chef would question the prices being paid.

Another form of kickback, probably not illegal but certainly unethical, happens when noncash payments are rendered. Gifts, vacations, or products can be given to the purchasing agent. There is often a thin line between the purveyor practice of giving gifts to insure continued goodwill and giving gifts to guarantee a particular level of patronage. A purchasing agent can easily be compromised, even in the absence of any intent to defraud the employer. Consequently, most corporations and chains have policies limiting the value of gifts employees can accept, and they make sure these policies are known to purveyors.

A discount, like a rebate, is an accepted and legitimate business practice. Discounts permit the buyer, under specific conditions and terms, to pay less than the invoice amount. A common practice is to give a discount for quick payment. If the invoice contains the term "1/10, net 30," the buyer, by paying the bill within ten days, can deduct 1 percent from the invoice total. Otherwise the full amount is due within thirty days. If the cost of money exceeds 1 percent per month, however, it would cost the establishment money to take advantage of the discount. Discounts may also be offered for volume purchasing. This is the most common way for operations to save costs via quantity ordering. Some purveyors may have separate price structures for various size orders, and, in effect, they are discounting. The net price, after discount, normally appears on the delivery invoice, and the purchaser pays the face value.

Other Purchasing Controls

Separation of Functions

As mentioned, this is a basic control concept. In a sense, larger organizations can be more effectively controlled because they can financially justify the use of different people for different functions. In purchasing, there are potential control problems when one employee is allowed both to purchase and to receive goods. This potential problem is compounded when that same individual also has responsibility for the storage areas. Control becomes nearly impossible when the production function is also assigned to this person. The magnitude of the problem becomes apparent when one realizes that this is exactly the case in many small operations that hire a chef who is given all this responsibility. Effective control implies separation of functions. The purchasing agent should not be responsible for receiving, storing, inventorying, or production. The purchasing function should also be separated from the accounting function. Where this is not possible, management must be aware that a potential control and security problem exists, and they must compensate for it.

There are no procedures or controls that must be followed absolutely. Every foodservice establishment is different and must be understood and operated as such. There are, however, certain controls and policies that make so much sense that if they are not implemented, there must be a good reason. Moreover, management must assure that no losses are occurring as a result of not following these controls. Separation of responsibilities is a case in point. If it is necessary to have one employee purchase and receive goods, management or ownership has to recognize the enhanced possibility of fraud and pay more attention to these areas than they normally would. Specifically, they should periodically do the receiving themselves—talk to the purveyors and occasionally do the ordering, spot-check the invoices, check with other purveyors on current prices and market conditions. In short, they should follow up to assure that the responsible individual is not taking advantage of the situation. You can never give up a control, but you may retain it in other ways.

Purchase Authorization

Management must assure that only authorized personnel can deal with purveyors. To do so, they must make the authorization a matter of record. The suppliers should have a letter specifically noting who can become involved in purchase transactions and make commitments on behalf of the organization. This letter, for legal purposes, should be sent by certified mail so the foodservice operator has legal documentation that the purveyor has been so informed. The alternative is to invite situations in which other employees make deals with the purveyors, a practice known as "back-door selling." This occurs when someone, the chef perhaps, bypasses the purchasing agent and deals directly with the purveyor. The control procedures for this are to have legally designated purchasing agents and for management to follow up and be totally aware of what is happening.

Another control is to limit the dollar commitments a purchasing agent can make. In the case of food, this limit must be high enough to permit normal operations but not so high as to enable the buyer to encourage kickbacks for large purchases. This, too, must be set forth in a written policy. The effect is that management must specifically authorize purchases of an unusual nature.

Every product purchased by the establishment should have an authorized purchaser. When this is not done, "personal" purchases could be made. Employees might order something for themselves and charge it to the organization or purchase various products and submit the invoices for reimbursement. No one other than essential personnel should have purchase authorizations, and the activities of authorized persons should be closely monitored. In this regard, it can be effective to use a purchase-order system. Other than daily or weekly product requirements, all needs must be estimated prior to ordering and approved by management via a purchase order. The authorization for payment would be the purchase order and delivery invoice. In the absence of a valid purchase order, the invoice will not be paid. The purveyor obviously needs to be aware of this policy, and there must legal and binding documentation.

Personnel Recruiting and Selection

If you have a thief working for you, there is not much you can do to prevent theft, pilferage, and/or fraud. Controls are ineffective against thieves because they are willing to risk discovery. A thief will break the lock on a storage area. A thief will clean out the cashier stand and run. If such persons really want your money and/or products, they generally can get them. *But* —and this is an important but—they have to run because theft surfaces nearly immediately, and the finger generally points at specific individuals. Most employees will not take something

that would be missed quickly. If honesty does not influence their actions, then fear of discovery does. Control is achieved by an effective management information system (MIS) and by management follow-up to assure employees that the information is checked, verified, and used.

An effective personnel recruiting and selection process is thus one of the most effective ways to counter dishonesty among employees. If you hire honest people, they could turn against you. But if they have a solid history of honest performance elsewhere, the chances are you will encounter no trouble. Hiring upright, decent people, providing adequate training, paying fair wages, and recognizing each employee as an individual and important element in the team will go a long way towards nullifying the temptations inherent in all foodservice operations.

COD Deliveries

The situation of having to pay for deliveries COD is terrible, yet it must be admitted that many independent operators find themselves in it. A distributor will sell products to anyone who wants them, but if there is the slightest hint of financial instability, the customer will be put on a cash-only basis. This means cash must be retained from the daily receipts to pay for deliveries. Chain operations are well insulated from this problem. The manager of a chain unit merely authorizes and forwards all invoices to the central office for payment. The bills will be paid promptly, regardless of whether the particular unit is profitable or not. With an independent, however, lack of profitability may make it impossible to meet short-term obligations. Often even profitable establishments may have cash-flow problems and be temporarily unable to pay their bills on time. When it comes down to either meeting the weekly payroll or putting off the suppliers, the suppliers usually lose.

Cash payments should be avoided whenever possible. Standard accounting procedures dictate that daily receipts should be deposited intact. It is sloppy accounting, and dangerous, to use cash register money to pay bills. The operation should establish a petty cash system and require that all payments be made from the petty cash funds. All such transactions must then be authorized, approved, and documented. Management must review the transactions on a daily basis, and they must question and justify each and every one. Dollar limits should be placed on petty cash transactions. It is also advisable to set up a sort of purchase order system so that a request must be submitted and approved prior to the purchase. Even emergency purchases can be handled in this manner. If the kitchen staff find themselves short of strawberries an hour before dinner, it should not be any problem to go to management and get approval for the expenditure. Management should, at any rate, be given the option of deciding whether the higher cost at the supermarket (the probable source of the strawberries under these circumstances) is justified. They may decide to do without strawberries that night. The way it should not be handled—but often is—is for the chef or kitchen supervisor to send someone out to buy the strawberries and then present the receipt to the cashier for reimbursement. This violates the petty cash concept and puts cash purchasing authorization into the hands of virtually all employees. When this is allowed, employees eventually will buy something for themselves and get reimbursed by the cashier.

Checking Invoices

Invoices should be checked on an ongoing basis for pricing or extension errors. In a chain operation, the manager cannot depend on the central accounting office, to whom the invoices are sent for payment, to do this. They often do, but that does not relieve operations management from the responsibility of assuring that all prices are correct and that no extension errors have been made. In an independent foodservice operation, the owner-manager has an obvious responsibility to do this.

Checking Prices

Management should be assured that they are paying fair prices. This is most effectively accomplished by proper purveyor selection and effective use of leverage as discussed previously, but management should follow up on the purchasing personnel by checking prices from time to time and by being aware of current market conditions.

Auditing of Purchasing Operations

An occasional audit, done by an outside firm, may be useful. The purchasing department and procedures would be only one aspect of the audit since you would have the rest of your food system evaluated as well. In purchasing you want the following areas in particular to be evaluated:

1. Purveyor's price structure
2. Invoices
3. Purchasing records
4. Payment methods
5. Payment checks and records

These audits are most effective when they are done at random and with no prior announcement. When employees know that their activities, procedures, and records are subject to surprise evaluations or audits, they will often refrain from fraudulent activity. Audits become a powerful deterrent.

Who Should Pay the Bills?

This area is perhaps the most important of the separation-of-functions concept. The people who deal with suppliers and do the buying must not be involved in the payment function. In the case of buyer-seller collusion, it would be easy to cover tracks and avoid detection if the buyer is also in charge of payment. Another danger is that the buyer could arrange for phony bills to be paid to himself or herself.

There should be some system established to assure that there is no possibility of paying an invoice more than one time. This is easy to do. The invoice can be stamped with the notation that it has been paid, the date paid, and the specific check number used for payment.

Purchase Records

There must be some sort of record kept when orders are placed. It may be practical to use a formal purchase order system only in the largest operations, but the information as to what was ordered, from whom, and when should always be available if needed. These records are necessary when doing food-cost analysis, and they should also be compared to receiving records. When there is a proper separation of duties, the purchaser will not do the receiving. In this case, unless the receiver knows what is supposed to be delivered, a short delivery could be accepted and the operation would run short. Or else the supplier, mistakenly or otherwise, could send more than was ordered, thereby increasing supplier profits.

Who is Getting Paid?

Check to assure that only legitimate suppliers are being paid and for legitimate merchandise. A listing of authorized purveyors and their addresses should be available, and management should assure that no checks are issued to anyone not on the list. The exception would be an extraordinary case already known to management, such as an emergency delivery from an unapproved supplier. The best time to check is before supplies are sent, but if not then at least records should be kept so they can be audited after the fact.

Relationships with Salespeople

In an operation where the three basic purchasing decisions have been properly made, it is not necessary to spend much time with sales personnel. The operators already know what they will be getting, but they should want to be apprised of new products as they become available, and a purveyor's sales representative can do this. The operators know where each product will be purchased, but they should attempt to stay current with developments in the marketplace that could modify these decisions. Thus some time should be spent occasionally with salespersons from other than authorized purveyors. When the supplier decisions have been made effectively, the need to meet with others may not be eliminated, but it is certainly reduced.

An operator who finds it necessary to constantly talk to a variety of salespeople in order to determine what to buy has not made those initial decisions properly or effectively. An operator who constantly talks with the sales representatives of many suppliers to decide whom to purchase particular products from has not made these decisions adequately. When decisions have been arrived at carefully in the planning phase, the purchaser will not have to spend much day-to-day operating time on these matters. It should be necessary to gather only such information as is required to verify that the policies in effect are still valid. The primary reason why many foodservice buyers spend hours and hours each week with salespeople is because they have not made the basic decisions correctly. In effect, they are deciding what to buy and whom to purchase it from on a weekly basis. Under such circumstances, it is necessary to talk to a lot of people and spend a lot of time as well.

Meetings with salespeople should be scheduled. The nature of foodservice operations dictates that much of what occurs is unpredictable. For this reason, management cannot have total control over their daily activity. It seems to make sense, therefore, that they schedule those activities that can be predicted and controlled. Visits with sales personnel fall into this category. It is foolish for a foodservice manager or purchasing agent to simply drop everything when a salesperson shows up. Set aside reasonable periods at times convenient to you with people you want to talk to—not necessarily those who want to see you.

When effective policies have been established as to the purchasing basics, the weekly order can often become nothing more than a restocking decision: for example, how many cases of frozen peas do we need this week? You already know the specific brand and package and from whom it will be ordered. With a par stock, if you have current inventory information, you even know how much to order. What could a salesperson do for you in that situation? Just pick up the telephone and place the order. Foodservice people waste an enormous amount of valuable time in ordering when much of it can be done over the phone.

Receiving

Receiving is a key function in a cost and quality control system because that is the point at which goods physically change hands, and the foodservice takes legal title to the products. If mistakes are made by the purchaser or purveyor, accidentally or otherwise, these need not cost the operation anything if the goods are not accepted. Up to this point, if mistakes are made they are only a potential expense. When those mistakes are signed for, they belong to the operator. In spite of this, it is common to underrate the importance of the receiving function, as one story illustrates. A consultant was evaluating the final list of equipment needed by a restaurant. The total dollar expenditure was nearly $150,000.00. The owner had crossed off the receiving scale, which saved a total of $250.00. When questioned about the decision, the owner answered, "We don't need it. They have one in my other restaurant, and it is not used." The other restaurant, incidentally, lost money—lots of it. After some discussion, the owner reluctantly allowed the scale to go back on the list.

The objectives of receiving are simply stated: to assure that the specific products ordered were received in acceptable condition, in the right quantities, at the desired time, at the agreed-upon price, and from an authorized supplier. While this may be simple to say, it is anything but simple to do in practice.

The Receiving Clerk

Food is quite complex, and the proper inspection of it can be equally complex and demanding. Effective and intelligent purchasing is worthless if substandard products are accepted into the operation. A fine kitchen is ineffective if it does not have adequate raw materials to work with. It is not necessary, however, that a foodservice operation have a separate position for a receiving clerk. The size and complexity of the operation will dictate this. What is necessary is that personnel are trained to do the receiving. Who they are is not important. So long as they are competent, an owner-manager, chef, cook, porter, or even dishwasher could do it. To discuss the situation, though, we will assume that there is an employee classification known as a receiving clerk. As with any other personnel, success begins with hiring a suitable person and then teaching that person exactly what to do and how best to do it. If someone is hired who is physically, intellectually, or psychologically unqualified for the job, no amount of training will result in a satisfactory performance. What are the qualities suitable candidates should have? To begin with, they should be physically fit for there is a lot of pure manual labor to this job. Even with trucks, lifts, and other mechanical aids, there is a lot of lifting and stacking to do. If the operation purchases flour in 100-pound bags, the clerk will have to be able to handle 100 pounds, and some people are simply incapable of doing that. With regard to education and training, they must be able to read and write. It would be highly desirable if the person has been trained in food evaluation, although this skill could be taught in the operation. The job demands considerable intelligence, for there are many products in addition to food to learn about; there are reports and records to be kept; there is considerable organization of time and activities required. Foods are perishable and have to be very carefully handled. Shelf life of various products, rotation of stock, dating of stock, proper temperatures, good sanitation practices—all these are areas that the receiving clerk must know something about. Suitable candidates should also possess some aggressiveness, or else they will be dominated by both the delivery agents and the foodservice employees. Drivers usually want to get the delivery made as quickly as possible and will pressure, if they can get away with it, the receiver to hurry and shortcut the inspection. If the purveyor and/or the drivers are unscrupulous, they can quickly identify those accounts that have weak receiving personnel, the ones they can push around and cheat. Receiving clerks must be responsible people, able to work under pressure. Of course, they must be totally honest.

Virtually all these qualities, with the exception of product knowledge, are qualities you hire, not teach. You cannot teach employees to be able to perform tasks they are physically incapable of doing. You could teach them to read and write, but practically speaking, you hire this capability, not teach it. You cannot teach a person who is basically dishonest to stop cheating and stealing on the job. You do not teach a nonaggressive person to suddenly become strong and assertive on the job. Thus the first step towards having competent receiving personnel is to hire individuals who are physically, intellectually, and psychologically qualified to handle the work. In this industry, we too often hire people who are not capable of standard performance. Whose fault is it then when they fail to produce?

Once a qualified individual is available, the next requirement is to give that individual the necessary training. Even very experienced people need training in the policies and procedures of the particular organization and in the product specifications (specs). It is not sufficient, for example, that the individual possesses good knowledge of meats. He or she must still know exactly what you expect. If your spec for a New York strip steak was top choice, 12 ounce, maximum fat cover of 3/4 inch, maximum tail length of 2 inches, and the clerk was not aware of this, perfectly acceptable products could be rejected. Perhaps the clerk has worked in an operation where they handled only prime steaks or only 1/2 inch of fat cover was acceptable or 1 1/2 inch tails. In this case, the steaks would not be accepted. The training is obviously much easier when the employee has food knowledge, but training is still absolutely necessary. When this knowledge is not available, it must be developed. Training then becomes critical.

Receiving is so important that many owner-operators and managers do their own receiving with products such as meat, seafood, and poultry and often with produce as well. If not directly involved themselves, they will insist that the chef do it. It should be recognized, however, that doing it themselves or assigning it to the chef is

also an admission that they have not trained anyone for the job, that there are no others competent enough to do it.

The heart of the receiving clerk's training would be the specifications, but this is not the only employee classification that requires specification training. Every single employee in a foodservice operation should have some familiarity with the specifications. The receiving clerk cannot fulfill the job requirements without such knowledge, so it is provided. The other workers can perform without the specs and so training is overlooked. To do so is a mistake since one of the concepts that ought to be taught to all employees is the existence and importance of organizational standards. Showing employees exactly what the various foods should be like can be a very effective way of demonstrating that there are standards and that they must be adhered to.

Another benefit of widespread awareness of food standards is that mistakes are more likely to be caught and less likely to affect the guests. For example, if the supplier made a mistake and delivered an off-spec steak, a competent receiving clerk would reject it. There would be some disorganization, especially if the entire delivery were substandard, but the important thing is that there is no possibility of an unacceptable product being served to a guest. If the receiving clerk accepts them and puts them into storage, a second mistake has been made, but if the cook were aware of the specs, the steak would not be cooked. Perhaps the steaks could be returned, perhaps not. At least they would not be served to anyone. Extend the chain of mistakes even further, and assume the cook prepared one of the steaks. If the waitress or waiter is aware of the specifications and realizes management is serious about standards, the steak will not be served. There is no longer any possibility of returning the steak, and there is an actual economic loss, but the guest is still unaffected. The worst possible scenario would be if the steak were actually served, but even here, a trained employee can salvage something. If the dish-machine operator were aware of the specifications, he or she could possibly recognize the problem from the leftover or uneaten steak portion on the dirty plates. Informing management will not do anything for that particular customer. Most people will not complain, they just don't come back. Management, however, was not even aware of the problem, and now at least they would be. They would also be in a position to assure that the same thing did not happen again. For these reasons, knowledge of specifications should be given to all employees, whether or not they would use that knowledge as part of their primary job. Achieving total guest satisfaction is the ultimate job of everyone, and knowledge of specifications and standards is essential to that goal.

Facilities and Equipment

Adequate facilities and proper equipment are required for effective receiving. The needed facilities are not complicated: adequate space adjacent or proximate to the storage areas, constructed so it can be easily cleaned. Space is necessary to physically handle the incoming goods. The amount required depends on the volume of incoming goods and the frequency of deliveries. For security purposes, the receiving area should not also be the employee entrance or exit. In general, employees should not be allowed to arrive or leave via the receiving area. If that is not feasible—and it may not be—management should know that a serious potential security problem exists and should take steps to counter it. Assuming that this is not the case, the receiving area should be kept locked except when goods are being received and trash is being removed from the operation. Trash removal should be scheduled and supervised to prevent pilferage, theft, and accidental discarding of linen, silverware, and other items that often get mixed in with the garbage and trash.

The one essential piece of equipment is a receiving scale. An operation with an annual food sales volume of $500,000.00 and a food cost percentage of 40 percent would be purchasing and receiving $200,000.00 worth of food yearly. Much of this food would be priced by the pound. It is lunacy not to have a proper scale or, having

one, not to use it. Some of the nonfood products will be paid for by the pound, too. Even in a moderately large operation, there could be several hundred thousand dollars paid for products charged by the pound. In really large foodservice operations, the numbers can be staggering. Some hotels in Las Vegas do $20 to $30 million dollars or more in food sales, and some have cost percentages in excess of 50 percent. This means millions of dollars of food needs to be weighed accurately. An adequate receiving scale should be heavy-duty and accurate; in general, the platform models are best. The accuracy should be tested regularly on an informal basis within the organization and formally by outside agencies such as the Bureau of Weights and Measures. This service must be paid for, but it is a justifiable expense. Informal spot checks can be made by management using products of known weight. Management should also test and record the empty weights of typical packaging cartons so the net weights of incoming goods can be ascertained. We refer here to lettuce cartons, portion-cut steak boxes, and so forth. Weights of kitchen pans commonly used to hold or package prepared foods should also be recorded so the net weights of stews, sauces, soups, salads, and other foods can be figured.

In addition to accurate scales, many other pieces of equipment are useful in receiving. Food cannot be allowed to stay on the receiving dock. For sanitation, quality, and security reasons, it should be immediately moved to either a storage or production area. A cart of some sort is useful for this. In particular, frozen foods cannot be allowed to remain at nonfreezing temperatures. If they should thaw, there could be contamination problems. If they move into a higher frozen range (10 to 30 degrees F.), there could be significant loss of quality. A calculator would also be useful to check invoice price extensions and totals as well as to check the weights or counts on large orders. If the receiving clerk has to record the product cost on the package (sometimes done with canned goods, for example), a marking pen would be required. A marker is also necessary for dating incoming foods, a highly recommended practice. Some cartons will have to be opened, if not for inspection, then for storage. A cutting tool is needed for this.

Thermometers are tools that can be considered in the same category as scales, absolutely necessary. The specifications should include acceptable delivered temperatures since food quality, shelf life, and contamination are all closely related to specific temperatures. As pointed out, frozen foods that have thawed are potentially hazardous from a food-safety standpoint and certainly would show quality loss too. Temperatures over 45 degrees F. and under 140 degrees F. permit the multiplication of dangerous microorganisms, primarily bacteria, and no perishable foods should ever be accepted in this temperature range. This should be clearly stated in the specifications. An investment of about $15.00 for a pocket probe thermometer assures that the receiver can check the temperature of perishable foods. It is management's duty, with the receiving clerk as well as all other employees, to determine exactly and specifically the duties required and then to provide the proper tools, facilities, and organizational support necessary to perform those duties.

Receiving Reports and Records

The most important record kept by the receiving department is the daily receiving report (see Exhibit 4.1). Control is not possible without information, and the following list covers the information management requires from the receiving function.

1. What was delivered?
2. When was it delivered?
3. Who did it come from?
4. What did it cost?
5. Where was it sent or stored?

The daily report therefore must list all goods received. A record indicating that $675.00 of meat was delivered on the tenth is next to worthless. The report should list each product individually: strip steaks, hamburger, lettuce, 6-gallon milk cartons, 1/2-pint milk cartons, and

so on. This provides a permanent, easily accessible record to compare with the purchase orders to see whether all the goods ordered were delivered and whether there were overages or shortages. Control is a comparison process. Management is constantly comparing what has occurred with what should have occurred. The purchase order is the basis for what should have happened, and the receiving report details what did happen. Any discrepancies must be noted, investigated, and explained. The availability of purchase orders and receiving reports does not provide control. Comparison and follow-up do.

The date of delivery is required; even the time of delivery may be useful, especially when there are agreed-upon delivery periods. The name of the purveyor is necessary so management can check to see that only authorized suppliers are being used. Costs are needed to check against purchase orders and to provide information for inventories. The product costs can be taken from the invoices, but they will not be retained and their format is not standardized. The receiving report provides a permanent, constantly accessible record.

Finally, management needs to know what happened to the food. Even in a small operation, it could go either to the storage areas or directly into production. In a large, complex foodservice operation, it would go to one of several storage areas and/or kitchens. A hotel, for example, may have a main production kitchen as well as separate kitchens for two or more restaurants. Each of these kitchens would probably have its own storage facilities, freezers, refrigerators, and dry storage. Food control is basically product control. If the movement of the goods can be tracked at all times from delivery to consumption, any control problem is unlikely. To use a simplified example: 100 steaks were delivered and put into storage with 50 others. Total steaks in storage equal 150. Thirty steaks are issued to the broiler station. Total steaks in storage (120) plus the broiler (30) equals 150. At the end of the evening, 4 steaks remain at the broiler station. There should have been 26 steaks sold, and this figure is compared to the dining room sales figures. If it shows 26, all steaks have been

Exhibit 4.1 Form for Receiving Clerk's Daily Report

SCA-251 PRINTED IN U.S.A.

RECEIVING CLERK'S DAILY REPORT

NO. _____

DATE _____

Purveyor	QUAN.	UNIT	DESCRIPTION	√	UNIT PRICE	AMOUNT	TOTAL AMOUNT	PURCHASE JOURNAL DISTRIBUTION		
								FOOD DIRECT	FOOD STORES	SUNDRIES

SIGNATURE _____

accounted for. There are 120 in storage, 4 in process, and 26 were sold for a total of 150. It obviously becomes more complicated with multiple storage, production, and service areas, but the concept is the same. Management is documenting the movement and location of all foods. As long as they can do so, they have the potential for control. Otherwise, they do not.

The receiving report can be as detailed as is felt necessary. The most basic format will separate the distribution into two categories:

1. Direct purchases. Those foods sent directly to production. These will be charged to production.
2. Storeroom purchases. Those foods sent to the storage areas. They will be charged to the storeroom; production will not be charged until the goods are requisitioned.

Goods that are delivered nearly every day, such as dairy products, may go into storage but be charged directly to production. In this case, the implication is that these foods will be consumed daily, at a more or less constant rate, and requisitions are not necessary. Other foods, such as meats, seafood, poultry, and dry stores, are delivered less frequently. Usages vary, and they are more expensive, so removals from inventory should be accompanied by requisitions, and the appropriate charges to production should be made.

Other types of receiving reports will have columns separating the deliveries into product categories: meat, seafood, poultry, dairy, produce, and so forth. See Exhibit 4.2A. This gives management daily and running totals on the dollar value of purchases by category. It is possible to break it down even further (see Exhibit 4.2B), although this would probably be unnecessary except for the largest operations. Meats could be classified by type: beef, lamb, pork, veal. Finally, each type could be broken into specific items: steamship rounds, butt steaks,

Exhibit 4.2. Variations on Daily Receiving Report

A. Food Category

Date	Purveyor	Meat	Fish	Poultry	Dairy	Produce	Bakery	Grocery		Total
Total										

B. Food Category - Meat

Date	Purveyor	Beef	Lamb	Pork	Veal					Total
Total										

C. Food Category - Beef

Date	Purveyor	Steamship Round	Butt Steak	Liver	Tenders	Ground Sirloin			Total
Total									

liver, tenderloins, ground sirloin. See Exhibit 4.2C. Whichever format is used, the person doing the receiving should sign the report so that management can fix responsibility and check that the receiving is being done by authorized personnel.

In addition to receiving sheets or reports, it may be desirable to use receiving stamps. Each invoice accompanying a delivery would be marked with a receiving stamp containing the following types of information:

1. Date
2. Accuracy of delivery:
   weight
   count
   quality
   price
3. Who received the delivery
4. Okay for payment

This is not only an additional control on the receiving clerk, but it formally provides a means for management to approve payment of each invoice, which has to be done in some manner.

Since there will be deliveries that are over or short, goods incorrectly priced and/or extended, there should be a system for recording mistakes: a credit memo. The information required is:

1. Name of operation
2. Name of purveyor
3. Date
4. Invoice number
5. Items corrected
6. Reasons corrected
   price
   goods not received
   shortage
   overage
   returned for quality or specification reasons
   other
7. Total value of correction
8. Revised invoice total (the amount that will be paid)
9. Signature of receiving clerk
10. Signature of delivery agent

This report should be prepared in duplicate, one copy of which is attached to the invoice for routing through the operation; the other is attached to the purveyor's copy of the invoice.

Receiving Systems

Most foods, as well as other products, are received by the *invoice system*. This simply means that an invoice accompanies the delivery, and the responsibility of the receiving clerk is to check the invoice both against the delivery and against the purchase order. The order is checked and either accepted or rejected in part or in whole. If accepted, the clerk will sign the invoice and either store the items or deliver them to the appropriate production area. If they are direct-issued to production, there must be some sort of record to document and verify that they were, in fact, received by the production department. This aids management in monitoring the flow of physical goods, as previously discussed, and enables food charges to be made accurately.

A system that is not often used, at least for food, but which is interesting from a control perspective, is *blind receiving*. In its purest form it implies that the receiver has no knowledge of what is to be delivered (no access to the purchase order) and the delivery is accompanied by a blank invoice (no products, quantities, or prices). The receiving clerk fills out the invoice according to the goods delivered. This invoice is signed by both the delivery agent and the receiving clerk. The purveyor, of course, does have a record of what was shipped, and this will be sent separately to the foodservice operation where it can be compared by the accounting office with the actual receiving invoice. If the delivery agent or the receiving clerk removed some products or if there were any mistakes, these would show up quickly. Another and perhaps more valuable control is that under this system the receiving clerk has to count and check every item; it is more difficult to short-cut and give a cursory receiving inspection. The main drawback is that it is very time consuming, often unnecessarily so.

A third receiving method is what is known as *standing order*. In practice, this can be handled in a couple of ways. In the most common, there is a regular order quantity, called a standing order, and the invoice will accompany the delivery, as usual. This would typically be done with foods, such as milk for example, which is delivered daily and is consumed more or less evenly throughout the week. It would not be as feasible with products delivered less frequently, such as weekly. It would not be feasible at all with products where consumption and/or usage varies widely, such as meats and produce.

The second type is not technically a "standing order," but there are sufficient similarities to group it with the standing orders. Certain products will have a predetermined par stock. When delivery is made, a count or inventory will be taken of the amount on hand, and the difference between that amount and the par will equal the delivery. Under this system, the purveyor does not know exactly how much product will be sold, so there is no preprepared invoice; the delivery agent makes it out at the time of delivery. This is similar to a standing order because the products involved generally move evenly, are delivered daily, and the purveyor can estimate the order size with some accuracy.

The policy that should be followed by all foodservice operations is not to allow any alterations of the invoice. When delivery agents and/or receiving clerks have the authority to change invoices, the potential for fraud is much too high to be risked.

The method of reimbursement can vary, and this is a policy that has to be worked out between the purveyors and the foodservice establishment. Probably the most common approach is to pay the adjusted invoice total. In other words, if a particular meat invoice totaled $684.75 and was accompanied by a credit memo of $16.95, the foodservice accounting office would pay $667.80. Another way would be for the supplier to credit the next delivery. It is also possible that the invoice will be paid in full but only after a check for the adjustment amount has been received from the supplier. This method is uncommon, however.

Receiving Frauds

There are many ways an operator can be cheated by an unethical purveyor, driver, or receiving clerk or by an honest supplier mistake combined with receiving-department ignorance. Some of the things to look out for are:

1. *Downgrading specifications*: If the suppliers can leave more fat on the roast or a larger tail on the strip steak, their yield (and profit) will increase. Even if prime steaks were specified, the purveyor could supply prime and still cheat on the specifications. Downgrading of specifications does not necessarily imply lower quality (grade) but is often a size, trim, or fabrication problem. The best way to control this is to allow only highly trained personnel to receive foods. Assure that they know both food quality in general and the specifications in particular.

2. *Shipment is incomplete*: You are presented with a full invoice and told the missing items will be delivered at a later time. The obvious control for this is to use a credit memorandum system, even if the missing goods are guaranteed to be delivered that afternoon. Tell the supplier to send them out with a new invoice, and prepare a credit memo on all missing goods. If it was a mistake, they will be more careful in the future. If it was deliberate, they will not attempt it again.

3. *Watering produce*: All produce should be weighed, for there are weight standards and these standards should be part of the specifications. A garden hose can make a case of lettuce appear quite a bit heavier than it really is. Control is achieved by examining the cases for signs of water stains and checking the produce itself to see if it seems to be waterlogged.

4. *Excessive use of packing ice*: Some fresh products, such as chickens, may be packed in crates with crushed ice. If the receivers are careless, some of the chickens could be replaced with ice. The only way to control this is to weigh the chickens without the ice. If the chickens are specified by weight and count, as is likely, they would have to be counted as well. Few suppliers want their drivers standing around while a receiving clerk shakes ice off the chickens and

counts and weighs them, so it is necessary to establish an agreement as to the accepted procedure. There are, from the foodservice operator's position, only two options. Either the purveyor takes the operator's word that an order was short when counted at a later time, or the count is made when delivered, and the driver verifies it. No other option should be acceptable to the operator.

5. *Short weights*: This is the easiest way to defraud many foodservice operations because either they do not have scales or they do not use them. It is easier, after all, not to deliver a product than to deliver it. A purveyor could readily increase the invoice face value by 5 percent or more just by increasing the weights of selected items. There is only one control, so obvious that it should not require mentioning. Experience suggests, though, that it does indeed need to be brought up. Use scales, weigh all products that are paid for by weight, and assure that the scales are accurate.

6. *Better quality on the top row or layer*: Tomatoes, portion-cut meats, and other foods are packed in cartons in two or more layers. A cursory examination may consist merely of opening a box or two and looking at the product. In this case, it would pay the purveyor to pack a lower quality or off-spec product on the bottom layer(s). The recommended receiving procedure is to examine all of the carton. Another method is to routinely open some cartons from the bottom, and thus examine the bottom, not top, layer. One word of caution: Do not always open all boxes from the bottom, for then the temptation will be to pack inferior goods on the top!

7. *Inaccurate dating*: Some products will have dates stamped on the cartons. These could be shelf-life expiration dates or processing dates. In either case, the specifications could designate acceptable time parameters. By changing the date, an unacceptable food would suddenly become acceptable. If an unscrupulous purveyor wanted to do this, it would be very difficult to detect, for a judgment decision must be made. It is not like weighing a product or comparing a top-row item to a bottom-row one. The way to control dating fraud is with competent personnel who are capable of making such decisions. Unless they know food quality, they cannot accurately determine whether the stamped dates are realistic or not.

8. *Repacking*: Many foods today are prepacked into cartons stamped with not only the date but also the count, weight, and often the quality code. When a foodservice operation's receiver is observed comparing the weights and grades and counts listed on the box to the invoice, it tempts the supplier to repack the box with less weight, short counts, or lower quality products. Again the control is competent personnel and proper receiving procedures. The receiver must be required to verify all carton statements. This includes commercially processed and packed goods, such as 5-pound boxes of frozen breaded shrimp, which the supplier merely warehouses and passes on to the foodservice buyer.

9. *Increasing prices*: Some operators feel it is no one's business what they pay for foods. If, however, the receiving clerk does not know what prices have been agreed upon, he or she cannot verify at that time that correct prices have been charged. The qualifying phrase "at that time" is critical, for delivery is the very best time to catch such mistakes. It is foolish to assume that a later check of the invoices will uncover pricing errors. They may, but the closest inspection the invoice will ever receive is when those goods are sitting in front of the receiving clerk, and that person should have a full and complete purchase order. If the prices are wrong, a credit memorandum must be prepared immediately and signed by the driver. Honest mistakes happen, even today when invoices are apt to be prepared by computers (perhaps even because they are prepared by computers). When mistakes are caught immediately, they are less likely to occur again. When the pricing error is deliberate, an immediate correction should prevent future attempts. It happens that purveyors may try to "test" an operation to see what they can get away with.

10. *High counts*: Here the supplier is attempting to "pad" the order. The foodservice operators are not being cheated in the sense that they are paying for inferior goods or for products not delivered, but they will pay for unneeded items. This, at best, will only result in large inventories, which will cost the operator money. At worst, the excessive stocks could spoil or be stolen or wasted. Control is achieved by making a purchase order available to receiving clerks so they are aware of exactly what to expect. Unordered merchandise can be returned, and the invoice adjusted by a credit memorandum. If it is a mistake and has not happened before, the purchasing agent (if informed promptly) may wish to call the supplier and work out some deal. The supplier would certainly prefer the goods not be returned and may be willing to offer some inducement to the buyer to accept them.

11. *Charging for boneless meats and delivering bone-in*: This is an activity that should be easy to detect. Someone has to inspect and evaluate the meat, but this is not always done.

12. *Bulk weighing*: This is a practice urged on the receiving clerk by impatient and/or unscrupulous drivers. The meat invoice, for example, has a total weight of 425 pounds, spread over various types of products: two or three different steaks, rib roasts, ground beef, stew meat, and so forth. The receiving clerk is urged to weigh all the products quickly in order to determine the total weight. If it is 425 pounds, the invoice is obviously okay, and the driver can be on his way. The problem is that the $5.00 per pound steaks could be 15 pounds short and the $1.50 per pound ground beef could be 15 pounds over, yet the total weight would still be correct.

13. *Unqualified receivers*: A delivery agent may attempt to get a randomly selected employee to sign for the order for two reasons. One, the person is not qualified and so can be cheated quite easily. Two, the inspection, if any, will be brief, and the driver can be back on the road in a fraction of the normal time. The control is to inform the purveyor, in writing, who the authorized receivers are and that the foodservice operation will not be responsible for deliveries accepted by any other individuals. It is then the responsibility of management to assure that the authorized employees are always available during designated receiving periods.

14. *Direct deliveries to storage and/or production areas*: The delivery agent appears helpful and offers to carry the foods directly to the storeroom or walk-ins and even to unload it. The problem with this is that proper inspection of the goods is generally not done; it may even be eliminated completely. This is avoided by insisting that all deliveries, regardless of the production urgency, must be inspected properly by an authorized person. In general, delivery personnel should not be allowed in either storage or production areas. One exception to this rule would be when a par stock ordering system is being used. Some foodservice establishments will allow the driver to count the stock on hand and then prepare the order. There is nothing wrong with this if the completed order and invoice are presented to the receiving clerk for evaluation. It can save time for the receiving clerk. It would be preferable, however, for the receiving person to check the inventory at a more convenient, earlier time and then present the order to the driver when he/she appears.

15. *Delivery at peak and/or nonspecified time periods*: The potential control problem here is similar to the previous one. If the delivery is not expected, the authorized personnel may not be available. If they are, the inspection may be performed hastily and sloppily. Authorized receiving hours should be part of the agreement between suppliers and foodservice operators. A driver attempting to deliver during lunch time may not be up to anything more sinister than trying to finish the day a little early, but the operation that accommodates this practice runs a high risk.

16. *Changing or altering invoices*: The control for this has been discussed. No one should have the authority to alter an invoice. If there are any problems with either the merchandise or invoice, a credit memorandum should be prepared.

Receiving Policies and Techniques

The following list reviews receiving practices that should be followed in all types of foodservice operations, regardless of size. Sometimes deviations or shortcuts can be used safely, and they will be discussed where appropriate.

1. *Weigh all items*: In general, it is recommended to weigh the entire order, but there are occasions when prepackaged boxes, cases, and cartons can be randomly weighed. This should not be a consistent practice, and the selection of cartons should truly be random. If the receiving clerk has an established pattern, such as always weighing the top two cartons, it would be easy to get away with light weights in the other cartons. Products such as preportioned steaks and other similarly valuable items should be weighed outside of the carton. At the prices per pound for steaks and lobster tails, the operation should be assured they are paying only for those products, not a heavy box.

2. *Count items*: Many products are purchased by count. When this is so, they must be counted. If, for example, the filet mignon specification was for 8-ounce steaks, an order of 100 steaks should weigh 50 pounds. It is not sufficient that the steaks weigh 50 pounds. The count must also be 100, otherwise the operation will accept either more or fewer steaks than ordered. If they are evaluating usage by product count, as they should be, an improper delivery count would make it impossible to account for all products. Size specifications should include acceptable deviations or tolerances. An 8-ounce steak may be specified as 8 ounces plus or minus 1/4 ounce, which means they are acceptable as long as they range between 7.75 and 8.25 ounces. The specification, however, should require that the *average* weight of a delivery be 8 ounces. This means that 100 steaks must weigh a total of 50 pounds. The supplier should be informed, prior to any deliveries, that weights in excess of the average will either not be paid for or not accepted. If 100 8-ounce filets weighed 51 pounds, the receiving clerk could either prepare a credit memorandum for 1 pound or reject the delivery. If the 100 steaks weighed less than 50

pounds, the order should probably be rejected, for some (or all) of the steaks are smaller than usual. This in turn could cause customer satisfaction problems, and that is a risk which cannot be justified under any circumstances. The suppliers are, of course, free not to bid on any specification they do not feel capable of fulfilling. Operators, on the other hand, must have the freedom of establishing their own standards and specifications.

3. *Check temperatures*: The specifications should include acceptable temperature ranges for all perishable foods. It is difficult to establish a temperature on frozen foods, so the requirement there should be that they are hard-frozen, that the receiver cannot dent the product when it is pressed with a finger. The receiver should spot check chilled temperatures at random. It is not necessary to check every item, although both bulky products, such as roasts, and smaller items, such as steaks or chops, should be tested. Perishable foods delivered at higher-than-desired temperatures will have a reduced shelf life and possibly reduced quality, and they could have high microorganism counts as well.

4. *Check for excessive water*: As pointed out, this could be a problem with fresh produce, especially greens.

5. *Check all rows and layers*: This is also a procedure that can be done randomly. It should not be necessary to open every box and examine every layer. If it is, the operation should not be dealing with that supplier. The receiving clerk is looking for consistency, which is the purpose of having specifications.

6. *Assure that specifications are met*: The receiver must be totally familiar with the organization's specifications and, when not met, should reject the order. It is also recommended that management or the purchasing agent be immediately informed. Depending on the degree of deviation, it may be worthwhile to call the purveyor and find out whether they are willing to compensate the establishment for accepting the order. There is also a potential shortage problem if the delivery is refused, as the products may be badly needed. In that case, the operator wants to know whether the supplier can replace

the order with acceptable products and how quickly. Whatever the answer, the foodservice operator can make a more informed decision as to whether to keep all or part of the order or return it.

7. *Establish a credit memorandum system*: This has been adequately discussed. Such a system must be in effect.

8. *How to handle shortages*: As with deviations from specifications, someone should be informed. Products—particularly perishable foods—are not normally ordered unless they are needed, and management must know when certain goods will not be available. Since no purveyor can possibly guarantee 100 percent delivery of all orders (any more than the foodservice establishment can guarantee all guests that they will never run out of any menu item), the question of acceptable substitutions should be a matter of purchasing policy. In other words, the purveyor and purchasing agent should carefully review the entire product line and attempt to establish which types of products are most apt to be shorted and establish standard substitutions for those items. Then if a shortage does occur, the purveyor can substitute an acceptable alternate product, and the foodservice operation will not be subject to production disruptions. Another possibly concurrent policy would be to have the purveyor inform the purchasing agent *prior* to shipment that certain parts of the order cannot be filled at that time. The purveyor should also state when, if ever, the order can be filled. In the absence of any policy on substitutions, the purveyor can also suggest some. With this information, the purchasing agent can make rational decisions based upon what is best for the operation.

9. *All deliveries must be inspected by an authorized receiver, and all receiving procedures must be followed*: This is specifically in reference to attempts to deliver directly to storage areas. This should normally not be allowed, but if it is, the normal receiving routine must be followed.

10. *Allow no bulk weighing*: This procedure should be discouraged in general but particularly with meats.

11. *Date all foods*: All foods have a finite storage life, with some, such as frozen or canned foods, it is just longer. No foods are improved by storage. The minimum consequence of excessive storage will be quality loss; the maximum consequence would be spoilage with a potential health hazard. It is therefore necessary to assure that all foods are properly rotated. This means that when newly delivered foods are placed into storage, they will be put under or behind the stock already there. In this way when stock is removed, the oldest will be removed first. The best way to assure that this is properly done is to date all foods at time of delivery. Then a casual inspection of the storage areas will quickly show whether the stock has been rotated. If the chef goes into the produce walk-in and sees that the top case of lettuce has today's date and knows there were two cases on hand, it is obvious that the stock was not rotated. Of course, if no one bothers to follow up and check the dates, this is a useless procedure. The dating can be done with stamps, or even easier, with a marking pen. The advantage of the latter is that of simplicity and the fact that the date can probably be displayed more boldly and prominently than with a stamp. One nice aspect of this practice is that it takes practically no time.

12. *Check all deliveries against a purchase order*.

13. *Record all deliveries on a receiving sheet*.

14. *Price merchandise*: This is optional, but many operators require the receiving clerk to calculate unit prices (if they are not on the invoice) and mark the goods. Like the dating, this is probably easiest with a marking pen. When issues are costed, having the cost marked on each unit saves time and increases the costing accuracy, especially when prices change frequently. It also helps make employees more aware of the value of the foods they routinely work with. It is a time-consuming procedure, and management must decide whether the benefits balance out the time and effort. A variation of this practice would be to price only the expensive, portioned products such as steaks, crab legs, shrimp, lobster tail, and so on. This is highly recommended.

Finally, with receiving, as with purchasing,

there must be adequate separation of responsibilities. In very large operations, the functions of receiving and storekeeping may be separated, but in most hospitality establishments, they would be combined.

Storage and Inventory

Objectives of Storage

For our purposes, storage can be defined as that period between the delivery and the usage of various products. In the case of foods especially, the storage period cannot improve the product and only results in deterioration. The rate of deterioration can be very slow, as in the case of canned goods and frozen foods, but it is steady and inevitable. These two product lines, canned and frozen, will not spoil in the sense that they are not subject to microbiological contamination if properly processed and stored, but they are subject to quality deterioration.

Most other foods, however, can become health hazards as well as just deteriorating. In addition to loss through quality deterioration and contamination, the products can be lost through theft and pilferage. The objectives of storage are thus simple: to protect the food against contamination, quality deterioration, and theft. These objectives are achieved by keeping the storage time as short as possible, by maintaining efficient and adequate storage facilities, and by providing whatever security measures are necessary to prevent theft and pilferage.

Food cost problems arise from many causes, one of the most important being spoilage of the food. The term *spoilage* is meant here to include both loss of product due to quality reasons and actual contamination. The result of either is the same: the products cannot be used. The single most common cause of food spoilage is excessive storage time. Food is simply kept too long. Therefore, while we will discuss security controls, we will emphasize stock movement. Spoilage will generally not be a problem when the products are used quickly. There are also financial reasons for turning the stock over rapidly since excessive inventories reduce the operation's profitability.

Storage Requirements

The most important factor for the shelf-life and the health safety of stored foods is temperature. The danger zone for microorganisms is 45 to 140 degrees F. Within this temperature range is the very hazardous range of 60 to 120 degrees F. A general rule of thumb is that perishable foods—those requiring refrigerated or frozen storage—should not, during the preprep, preparation, holding, and serving, spend more than a total of four hours between 45 and 140 degrees F. This means that a rib roast that was removed from the refrigerator one hour prior to cooking and held two hours in the kitchen after cooking before being served would probably be safe (unless it were contaminated by an unclean worker or equipment). It would be dangerous, however, to hold it two hours before cooking, two hours after cooking, serve half of it, and hold the remaining half for another two hours prior to refrigerating it. The total time in the danger zone would be six hours.

Frozen Storage. Frozen storage is misunderstood by many foodservice employees, including management. Foods do deteriorate in freezers. Fats can oxidize (butter can become rancid), proteins denature (shrimp can become tough), and starches retrograde (sauces and gravies can "break"). These are chemical reactions, and they occur in a freezer. Fats can be protected by proper packaging and reduction of storage periods. Proteins can also be protected by reduced storage times as well as lower storage temperatures. Products thickened by starches can be protected by either using chemically modified starches or by using nontraditional starches (that is, not wheat flour or cornstarch). In general, lowering a freezing temperature by 18 degrees F. (10 degrees C.) will result in a reduction of the rate of chemical activity by some 2.5 times. Frozen foods are also subject to various types of physical changes. Mayonnaise (and other emulsions) will break, yeast cells will lose their vitality, and raw bread dough will not rise as well after thawing. Batters leavened with baking powder will not produce normal amounts of carbon dioxide after thawing; ice cream will become "grainy" due to enlargement of sugar crystals; soufflés and angel cakes (uncooked) will lose volume and so forth. The solutions to these problems are similar to the chemical changes: keep the storage temperatures low, watch the storage times, and package the products properly. The recommended frozen storage temperature is 0 degrees F. (-18 degrees C.) for nearly all foods. Ice cream is an exception. Because of the high sugar content, which lowers the freezing temperature, it should be stored at a lower temperature, minus 10 degrees F. or less (-23 degrees C.). For this reason, ice cream products are often kept in separate storage cabinets (sometimes provided by the purveyor).

Not only is it important to keep freezers at 0 degrees F., but it is just as important to maintain consistent temperatures. The types of changes described will occur more readily and faster at fluctuating temperatures than at constant ones. If, for example, the freezer temperature was 0 degrees F. in the morning after being closed all night but rises during the day to 15 degrees F. at closing time, the temperature of the food stored in it would constantly be fluctuating. The potential storage life would be reduced, sometimes dramatically. To cite an extreme example, one researcher reported the following time-temperature relationships for frozen white sauce thickened with waxy rice flour.

Time for Product Stability	Storage Temperature (F.)
3 years	Constant -10°
1 year	Constant 0°
2 months	-10° to + 10°
3 weeks	Constant +10°

Few foods would show this degree of variation, but nearly all foods will deteriorate at an accelerated rate when temperatures swing up and down.

Freezers can be either the walk-in or reach-in type. One advantage of the reach-in is that it often maintains more consistent temperatures. This is because it can recover faster when the

temperature does increase. Opening the door and loading or unloading will result in a sharp temperature rise, probably well above that experienced in a walk-in; but after closing it will quickly drop. It is unlikely, under normal operating conditions, that the temperature of the food will change. In a walk-in, the temperature changes are gradual and long lasting, inevitably leading to rises in the product temperature.

To meet the objective of protecting frozen food against quality loss (remember there is no danger of microbiological growth in a freezer), the following procedures are recommended:

1. *Wrap the foods properly.* Frozen foods should be wrapped with a moisture-vapor proof material. This is a material that will prevent moisture from leaving the food (leading to dehydration and/or freezer-burn) and oxygen from entering the food (leading to oxidation of fats among other problems). Plastic film is not moisture-vapor proof. Aluminum foil is and has the added advantage that it can be wrapped very tightly about the food, excluding most of the air. There is no sense in protecting a product against oxygen entry if you package a considerable amount of air with the product. The drawbacks of a foil wrap are that it is expensive and tears easily. Freezer paper is moisture-vapor proof, inexpensive, does not tear readily, and it is easy to mark the package contents, weight, cost, and date. One drawback is that it will not wrap as tightly as foil, and some air will be packaged as well. Heavy plastic bags (be sure you use bags identified as suitable for freezing) are moisture-vapor proof, reusable, readily labeled, transparent so the contents can be seen, and can be wrapped fairly tightly to exclude air.

2. *Maintain low and consistent temperatures.* This is an equipment problem, and the operator's responsibility is to purchase and maintain adequate freezers, both walk-in and reach-in. From a control standpoint, thermometers are essential. Most equipment sold today has built-in temperature gauges that can be viewed from the outside, but these should not be relied upon entirely. They could become defective, and there are always hot and cold spots

within the freezer. Reach-ins will tend to have reasonably consistent internal temperatures, while large walk-ins could show significant variances depending on where the reading is taken. At any rate, use separate thermometers in both types. One would be sufficient in a reach-in, while two or more should be placed in walk-ins. This will not be an effective control, however, unless someone looks at them! Management and the chef—in fact everyone who has access to the freezer—should make it a habit to check the temperatures every time they go into the freezer. This would have the added benefit of making employees more aware than they typically are of keeping the doors closed. Anyone who has even limited experience in commercial kitchens is aware of how careless employees are about this.

3. *Avoid excessive storage time.* Frozen food can be classified into three general shelf-life categories:

Short (up to a maximum of six months at 0 degrees F.)

Medium (six to eight months at 0 degrees F.)

Long (up to a year or longer at 0 degrees F.)

The following list shows the types of foods that would be found in the short category, and the reason for their instability.

Canadian Bacon—Cured products do not have long-term frozen stability

Ice cream—texture problem, as mentioned

Batters: gingerbread and spice—The batter itself is fairly unstable since it is leavened with baking powder, and highly spiced foods are quite unstable

Baking powder biscuits (uncooked)—Loss of leavening power

Bologna, franks (luncheon meats in general)—cured, high-fat content, and often highly spiced

Ham, sliced—Cured product

Poultry livers and giblets—Organ meats are generally unstable

Products with medium storage life are:

Batters: devils food and white cake—Although the batter is somewhat unstable, as long as the ingredients are stable, it should last six months or so

Fried chicken

Crab, shrimp, lobster

Fatty fish

Meatloaf, meatballs

Whole baked ham—As pointed out, cured products are not stable, but the larger the product, the more stable it is, thus, the contrast with sliced ham

French fried potatoes

Many sandwiches

Many soups

Chicken, meat pies

Fruit pies (unbaked)

Products with a long storage life are:

Applesauce

Baked apples

Bread (baked)

Blackberries, blueberries, cherries, plums

Fruitcake

Product thickened with modified starches

Cookies (baked)

Cookie dough

Lean fish

Peanuts, pecans

Beef stew

Waffles (baked)

As these lists show, the types of products that account for most of a foodservice operation's food costs have a medium shelf life, which means they should be able to be kept six months or more. This is certainly longer than anyone should want to hold such foods. Good financial management alone would preclude tying up substantial sums of money for such a long period. There are a couple of problems here though. One, the operator seldom knows the exact age of the products when they are delivered. Breaded shrimp may have a six-to-seven-month shelf life but not if it is six months old when delivered. Two, the operator does not know the storage history of any of the products. If a product had been held at improper temperatures either in warehousing or shipment, or if it had been thawed and refrozen, the shelf life would be drastically reduced. Three, even if the product is delivered in top condition, unless stored at a consistent 0 degrees F. in the foodservice establishment, it will not last as long as its category would indicate.

A few products are quite unstable and a few can be kept for very long periods, but collectively these types of foods do not have nearly the economic value of the medium-life category. The recommendation, therefore, is to purchase frozen foods from reputable dealers with good warehousing facilities and delivery equipment; then to turn it over at a rate consistent with good financial management. This assures that most foods will not be kept too long. The few very unstable products, such as ice cream, simply have to be turned more frequently—in a matter of weeks instead of months.

4. *Label all products.* Foods stored in a freezer, particularly a walk-in freezer, can easily become lost because no one can tell how long they have been there. Often people cannot even tell what the food is. Identify all freezer foods with the item name, weight, cost, and date. Commercially processed foods will be in packages that have the name and weight, and these also should be dated and priced. Not only will this practice aid in rotating the stock, it will make inventory taking easier, faster, and more accurate.

5. *Maintain a record of freezer contents.* This is especially important for foods packaged and frozen on the premises, such as leftovers. Prepared foods such as soups and stews, meat

trimmings, bones, vegetables, and others are often not carried on the monthly inventory since they are considered to be part of the in-process inventory. In this case, there is no record of what is actually on hand, and it tends to be forgotten and not utilized profitably.

Refrigerated Storage. Refrigerated storage temperatures vary according to the food category. The following temperature ranges are recommended:

Meats, seafood, poultry	30-34° F. (-1 to 1° C.)
Dairy products	34-38° F. (1 to 3° C.)
Fresh produce	36-40° F. (2 to 5° C.)
Leftovers and prepared foods	32-36° F. (0 to 2° C.)

These temperatures provide a reasonable safety margin since the hazardous temperature zone begins at 45 degrees F. Technically, it is safe to store perishable foods at over 40 degrees F., but there is little or no margin for error. Ideally, there should be four separate storage areas, one for each food type. This is seldom done anymore, however, due to construction expense and the value of space. Perishable foods stored at the proper refrigerated temperatures are not subject to pathogenic bacterial growth, but mold and nonpathogenic bacteria can grow at temperatures of below 40 degrees F., and most foods will lose quality fairly quickly due to chemical changes, physical changes, and enzymatic action. Recommendations to prevent food loss due to quality deterioration in refrigerators are:

1. *Reduce storage time.* This is the most important factor. Foodservice personnel must know how long various foods can safely be kept. One of the major problems of food control is that there are so many variances in shelf life that virtually each product has a different expectation, and it is dangerous to generalize. It is beyond the purpose of this text to provide complete information. Specialized food texts should be consulted, but a few examples can be given.

Fresh eggs (refrigerated, kept in packing carton) 1-2 weeks

Fresh eggs (unpacked, unrefrigerated) 1-2 days

Large beef roast (steamship round) 1-2 weeks

Smaller beef roast (standing rib) 1 week

Beef steaks 4-5 days

Ground beef 1-2 days

The only generalization it is safe to make is that all perishable, refrigerated foods should be purchased as close to the anticipated consumption time as possible. If they are not used as rapidly as possible, it would be wise to freeze them (when appropriate, for some foods cannot be frozen). Management should design production and menu flexibility into the operation so that they can run specials and prevent food from accumulating.

2. *Control temperatures.* Thermometers should be utilized as described for freezers. There are hot and cold spots in walk-in refrigerators, and two or more thermometers should be used. Determine which areas are the coldest, and store the meats there. Produce can probably be stored nearer the door, where the temperature is usually the highest. As cautioned with freezer thermometers, thermometers are a wasted expense unless they are looked at daily.

3. *Wrap foods properly.* This is not as critical as with frozen foods, which must be wrapped to protect them over long periods. The minimum objective of refrigerator wrapping is to cover the foods and prevent crosscontamination from other foods, shelving, or pans and trays. Air should also be excluded as much as possible. All the materials recommended for freezer wraps are suitable for refrigerated foods, and plastic films can also be used. These recommendations are for foods wrapped in the operation kitchen. The best packages are generally those in which the product is delivered and food should be kept in them if possible.

4. *Rotate foods.* Observe the procedures discussed in the receiving section. All foods should be dated when they arrive and are stored.

They absolutely must be placed so they will be used after any foods already there. Management and supervisors responsible for kitchen operations have to have a daily routine of inspecting the storage areas to assure that this is being done. When not supervised, employees will short-cut when putting food into and removing it from storage.

Dry Storage. The third type of storage is for dry goods, nonperishable, or semiperishable foods. Canned foods, flour, rice, sugar, coffee, dried spices, potatoes, sometimes onions, freeze-dried products, and so forth are all examples of such foods. They do not require refrigeration, but the shelf life is also time-temperature dependent. In other words, while they do not have to be refrigerated, neither should they be kept in warm areas. The quality and nutritive value of canned goods, for example, can be significantly affected in a matter of weeks if stored at 90 to 100 degrees F. (21 degrees C.) or over. This may seem impossibly high, but there are operations that have such storage areas. The recommended temperature is about 70 degrees F. If a dry goods storeroom can be maintained at 70 degrees F., the food should retain its quality as long as it is stored for reasonable periods. It will not retain quality for a year or more, however. It is not difficult to find foods stored that long in many operations. Dating products when they arrive, rotating them when stored, and removing the oldest stock first combined with a rational purchasing program will assure adequate stock movement.

Although temperature is the most important storage factor, proper humidity levels are necessary with certain foods. Fruits and vegetables require the highest, 85 to 95 percent relative humidity, while all other refrigerated areas should be between 75 to 85 percent relative humidity. High moisture levels encourage the growth of microorganisms while low levels will result in dehydration. Since such high levels are required for most foods, it is even more important to package foods properly and watch storage times.

Other physical considerations for storage

facilities are the layout and location. It would be ideal to have the storage areas located between receiving and production so that the food can progress through the operation in a straight line. Although this is not always possible, the designers should avoid locating them in such a way that there is a lot of backtracking. The key to layout of storage areas is maximum space utilization. Space is becoming increasingly valuable, and most foodservice operators want as much as possible to be income producing, that is, to hold tables and chairs as opposed to production and storage areas. In order to do this, there cannot be any wasted space either in the kitchen or in the storage areas. An additional advantage of reach-in freezers and refrigerators is that they are more space efficient than walk-ins. Virtually all the interior of a reach-in can be filled with food, while only a small portion of the cubic feet in a freezer actually contains products. Walk-ins, however, are necessary for most operations. They can and should be better utilized than they normally are. The objective is to use as much of the floor and as much of the vertical space as possible. This means that the floor should be covered with the maximum amount of shelving. There must be aisles so the food can be reached, but open floor space is wasted space and should be kept to a minimum. An operation that needs to use carts in the walk-in for whatever reason will require wider aisles than an operation that does not use carts. A typical layout wastes floor space. See Exhibit 4.3. In addition to arranging the shelving units intelligently, pay attention to the total height of the units and the spacing of the shelves. A lot depends on the form food will be stored in. If frozen vegetables are to be shelved by the case, the shelves will have to be fairly widely spaced. When the packages are removed from the cases, the shelves can be assembled much closer. See Exhibit 4.4. The trouble with the example used is that next to the case of vegetables, which does require wide spacing, there may be smaller packages with a lot of wasted head space. An additional problem with widely spaced shelves is that they encourage piling, and goods on the bottom tend to become lost. Shelving units often

Exhibit 4.3. Typical Storage Layout

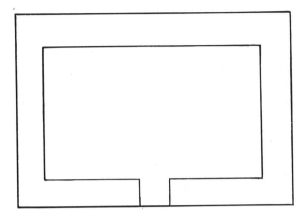

Exhibit 4.4. Shelving Arrangements

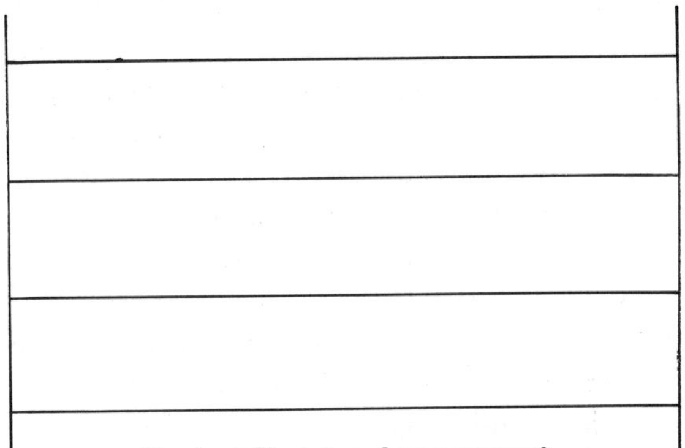

Typical Shelving Arrangement

Improved Shelving Arrangement

do not go high enough, and the upper areas of the freezer or refrigerator are totally wasted when they could be filled with products. In this regard, there are two cautions. One is the strength of the shelving units. The higher they go, the stronger they will have to be. This is not the place to save on investment expense. The second caution is that the total food load stored must not be beyond the refrigeration unit's capacity. This also is not a wise place to reduce investment expense. All the same principles apply to dry storerooms. Floor and vertical space are wasted unnecessarily.

Security

The other objective of storage is to protect the foods from theft and pilferage. The difference between the two is merely a matter of degree and intent. Someone who fills a car or truck with food in the middle of the night is guilty of theft, and realizes full well that he or she is stealing. Employees who take a package or two of 2-ounce portion control coffee and a handful of portion pack catsups and mustards are guilty of pilferage, and they probably do not think of this action as stealing. A thief will break into an establishment, break locks, and pry open doors to get the merchandise. Thieves also know their actions will be quickly discovered and do not really care since they will be gone. An employee guilty of pilferage not only does not regard it as stealing but takes items with the expectation that they will not be missed, that the action will go undetected. It is difficult—not impossible, but difficult—to prevent theft, whereas pilferage can be controlled. To fully protect against theft, however, the establishment would have to be turned into a fortress. This is not realistic, and fortunately theft is not that common, but pilferage is. There are several effective ways in which pilferage can be controlled if not eliminated.

1. *Hire good employees, pay them as well as possible, and treat them fairly.* None of these describes a typical foodservice operation. Selection and hiring of hospitality employees is often done on the "warm-body" theory—any warm body will do, and hiring is done on that

basis. This indicates a basic lack of respect on the part of management for the jobs and, as a result, the employees. Foodservice employees are often paid wages that are as low as the law allows. Finally, foodservice workers are seldom treated in an enlightened manner. Is it any wonder that an underqualified, undertrained, underpaid employee who has little respect for the job or employer, because he or she is treated without respect and regarded as replaceable will grab anything that is not nailed down? Controlling pilferage begins with putting together a stable crew of people who take pride in what they do and in the establishment they work for.

2. *Be aware of what is in stock and where it is.* This is a key factor. Few people will take something, regardless of how insignificant its value is, when they realize that its loss will be not only known, but known quickly. In other words, there must be a high exposure risk. This is achieved by having accurate running counts on foods (a perpetual inventory), especially high-cost foods. With steaks, for example, if the total available supply were stored partially in a locked reach-in and at the broiler station and if the amounts of each were known, a daily reconciliation of the storage amounts with the sales total would quickly show whether any steaks could not be accounted for.

Beginning of Evening Shift:
Reach-in inventory	= 100 steaks
Broiler total	= 23 steaks
Total available	= 123 steaks

End of Shift:
Reach-in inventory	= 100 steaks
Broiler total	= 3 steaks
Sales	= 19 steaks
Total accounted for	= 122 steaks

One steak cannot be accounted for, and its shortage is immediately known. The next thing management wants to know is whether the kitchen or the dining room is responsible, and, if possible, which employee. If it were known that the waitresses ordered only 19 steaks, the missing steak would be the responsibility of the kitchen, specifically, the broiler cook. Note that we use the word "responsibility." The broiler cook may or may not have taken or eaten it, but he or she is responsible for all steaks issued for that shift. Under these circumstances, the broiler cook would not be likely to take any steaks nor knowingly allow anyone else to since the blame would fall back on the broiler cook. Of course, another employee could steal it from the broiler cook, but now the broiler cook has become part of the control system! The major flaw with this system is that, unless someone counts the steaks in the reach-in, there is no control. Twenty or more steaks could be missing, and no one would be aware of it. Pilferage control is achieved only by being able to track items, particularly expensive ones. Most employees will not take goods when they know the loss will be quickly noticed and when they know management will *do* something about the loss. Again, follow-up is important. Even fewer employees will take anything when they are responsible and held accountable.

3. *Restrict access.* This is one way you can assign responsibility and hold personnel accountable. If only one person has access to an area or to specific products, such as lobster tails, you have accountability, and that person becomes part of the control system. Restricting the storage area(s) to one person may not be feasible, but it is not necessary to allow all employees full access to all products either, and this is often done. In that case, even though pilferage were known, who would management hold accountable? There must be an attempt to secure storage areas by authorizing entry to certain employees and restricting that access to specific times.

4. *Document the movement of materials.* There is a record of all incoming goods on the receiving sheet, or failing that, there are the invoices. The receiving sheet documents where the various products were sent. What we are suggesting here is that any further movement of materials also be recorded. This is done with written requisitions; nothing should be able to

leave a storage area or go from one department to the other without a requisition. This aids management both in fixing amounts and locations of all products, and in determining responsibilities for those products.

Access is restricted and areas are made secure by having locks and assigning keys to specific individuals. The function of locks is often misunderstood. A lock is not intended to make it impossible for nonauthorized people to gain entry. That would be impossible; after all, even bank vaults can be broken into, and they use superior materials and vastly more sophisticated locks than would ever be found in a foodservice operation. If you have a thief working for you or if a thief gets into your operation, you cannot totally secure any area. A thief will break a lock, kick down a door, whatever is necessary to gain entry. Fortunately, this is seldom a problem; it does occur but infrequently. Since this type of total security is impossible and probably unnecessary anyway, what type of security is reasonable? It is recommended to use locks on all storage areas. It is not necessary to purchase massive, expensive locks. Any type of lock will discourage basically honest people, but no lock will protect against a thief. Since the objective is to restrict access to authorized personnel, the use of ordinary locks will suffice.

To make the locks effective, management must do two things. One, they should be scrupulously careful about who has the keys. A person who would not dream of breaking into a storeroom, may not hesitate to open a door with a key. Two, the locks should be changed on a frequent but irregular basis. Move the locks around, collect all keys, and redistribute them. Another effective policy is not to allow any keys to leave the establishment at night. Obviously, at least one person must have a key to open the operation each day, but beyond that there really is no need for anyone else to take keys home. Regardless of how this is handled, management should inventory all keys on an irregular basis. This is a procedure whereby all personnel who are authorized keys must show that they have them in their possession at that time. These key inventories should be unannounced and irregular so the employees have no way of knowing when they might have to show possession.

It is also recommended that locks not be mastered to a single key. Having a master key is easier than carrying a huge ring of keys, but it also makes it easier to gain unauthorized entry. Stealing or getting hold of that one key results in access to virtually every locked room or area. Combination locks probably provide less security than keyed locks since a combination can be passed from person to person much more readily than a key can. It would also not be possible to inventory combinations as can be done with keys. Use of combination locks also makes it very difficult to move locks around, since everyone would soon be able to get into all locked areas.

Inventories

An inventory is a status count, a listing of the merchandise on hand. Inventory information is critical to an operation for several reasons, the most important of which are:

1. Food cannot be ordered effectively without knowing what is on hand at the time the order is placed.
2. Food cost cannot be determined without an inventory

In ordering or resupplying, the purchasing agent needs to know how much is required and how much is on hand. The order will be the difference. Without an accurate, current inventory status report, a buyer would be shooting from the hip, and stock levels would probably increase unnecessarily.

Accurate costs cannot be calculated (for any product, not only food) without knowing what was on hand at the beginning and end of the costing period. Costs are determined with the formula:

OI plus Purchases minus EI equals COG
Where: OI = opening inventory
EI = ending inventory
COG = cost of goods

Opening inventory is the total stock on hand at the beginning of the period. That plus purchases

equals the total goods available for sale. This is the maximum number of products that could be used or consumed during the period. Deducting the ending inventory, goods still on hand at the end of the period, yields the number of products used or the cost of those products. This—as pointed out in the analysis section—is not necessarily cost of sales but is actually the cost of goods used for all purposes. Some of the food would have been used for employee meals, some may have been used for promotional purposes, and some could have been sent to the bar. It would also be incomplete because the food department probably used alcoholic beverages that would normally appear on the bar purchases and thus have been calculated in the beverage cost of goods consumed. Formal adjustments may or may not be made for income statement purposes, but management must be aware of the true cost of goods sold so they can compare the cost from period to period. Were these adjustments not tracked, an establishment would not know whether an apparent cost problem was due to lack of control or other causes, such as excessive (higher than expected) employee meals, promotional expenses, or food used by the bar.

Physical Inventory. The accepted way to obtain opening and closing inventories is to take an actual count of all products on hand; this is called a physical inventory. It is necessary to take a physical inventory only when operating statements are prepared. This is typically done each month, so the minimum frequency of physical inventories is monthly. It may be taken more often—biweekly, weekly, daily—but it must be taken for operating statements.

The frequency of a physical inventory is determined by management's need to obtain accurate cost information. Any other method of cost determination is an estimation, and may or may not be accurate. If management feels that they have to have an actual food cost in the middle of each month or each week, they generally will have to take a physical inventory. The problem with physical inventories is that they are time consuming and often inaccurate. The following recommendations on how to take a physical inventory, therefore, will focus on accuracy and speed.

1. Have a minimum of two people to take a physical inventory. This is for both speed and accuracy. There are two functions that have to be performed during an inventory: the products must be counted, and the count must be recorded. One person should count and another record. To make the count as accurate, fast, and efficient as possible, it is desirable to have someone do the count who is familiar with the storage area and the stock. An inventory can take forever when an inexperienced person does the counting. Also a lot of mistakes occur because products may be misidentified or overlooked. Thus the counter should be someone who has daily contact with the stock. It could be the receiving or storeroom clerk, the chef, a cook, anyone who knows where everything is and what it is. This satisfies the need for efficient and fast counting of stock. The other objective, honesty and final accuracy, is achieved by assigning someone from outside the department to write or record the counts. In many operations, this would be the manager or assistant manager. It could also be someone from the accounting department. The key, regardless of who it is, is that it be someone with no direct cost responsibility—in other words, an individual who cannot profit from an incorrect count. The reason for this is that whoever controls the inventory, controls the cost. For example: assume a situation where the actual cost is $550.00 high in April:

April—	OI	$ 5,010.00
	+ Purchases	21,000.00
	Goods available	26,010.00
	- EI	5,200.00
	COG	$20,810.00

Sales = $54,750.00
Actual cost % = 38.0%
Standard cost % = 37.0%
Standard $ cost = $20,257.50

The difference between $20,257.50 (standard)

and $20,810.00 (actual) is the cost overage. If the person responsible for maintaining a 38 percent cost were also in charge of the inventory, it would be an easy matter to "pad" the ending inventory by $550.00. In that case, the calculation would look like this:

OI	$ 5,010.00
+ Purchases	21,000.00
Available	26,010.00
- EI	5,750.00
COG	$20,260.00

Sales = $54,750.00
"Actual" cost % = 37.0%

There is now no apparent cost problem. It does not matter what the cost problem was. The food could have been stolen, wasted, not delivered but paid for, spoiled, and so on. It would not make any difference, management still would not be aware of the existence of a problem, and it could continue. When the inventory "padding" is done to cover up mistakes, the reasoning generally is that the problem will be identified and solved and that the $550.00 can be "made up" the following month. Let us assume the problem is identified and solved immediately. The following month the beginning inventory would be $550.00 short, which would add $550.00 to the cost:

	Operating Statement Calculation	What It Actually Is
May—OI	$ 5,750.00	$ 5,200.00
+ Purchases	22,000.00	22,000.00
Available	$27,750.00	$27,200.00
- EI	5,000.00	5,000.00
	$22,750.00	$22,200.00
	(37.9%)	(37%)

Sales = $60,000.00

The cost overage from April has now been transferred to May, and unless the ending inventory is again adjusted, it will show up on the operating statement. Unscrupulous individuals can use the inventory not only to cover up past mistakes or frauds but intended ones as well. If the operation, for whatever reason, had a very good month, and the cost was 36 percent rather than the standard 37 percent, the ending inventory could be reduced:

April—	OI	$ 5,010.00
	+ Purchases	20,500.00
	Available	25,510.00
	- EI	5,800.00
	COG	$19,710.00

Sales = $54,750.00
Cost % = 36.0%

April (revised)—	OI	$ 5,010.00
	+ Purchases	20,500.00
	Available	25,510.00
	- EI	5,252.00
	COG	$20,258.00

Sales = $54,750.00
Cost % = 37.0%

Although the beginning inventory for May will be recorded as $5,252.00, there is actually $5,800.00 worth of food on hand, or $548.00 more than recorded. In May, if the operation recorded a standard cost of 37 percent, the true cost would be:

May	Operating Statement Calculation	What It Actually Is
—OI	$ 5,252.00	$ 5,800.00
+ Purchases	22,000.00	22,000.00
Available	$27,252.00	$27,800.00
- EI	5,052.00	5,052.00
	$22,200.00	$22,748.00
	(37%)	(37.9%)

Sales = $60,000.00

This means that in May the employee(s) manipulating the inventory could take $548.00 in food and still maintain the standard cost of 37 percent. If, on the other hand, the true cost were 37 percent, the comparison would look like this:

	Operating Statement Calculation	What It Actually Is
May—OI	$ 5,252.00	$ 5,800.00
+ Purchases	22,000.00	22,000.00
Available	$27,252.00	$27,800.00
- EI	5,600.00	5,600.00
	$21,652.00	$22,200.00
	(36.1%)	(37%)

Sales = $60,000.00

In this case, the extra inventory was not taken out, and the ending inventory could again be reduced to show a standard cost of 37 percent. The EI would be $5,052.00, a reduction of $548.00. These two latter cases are known as "reverse padding." The objective of the first of these two methods is to take products (to steal); while with the second method, the employee is "putting something away for a rainy day." Then it can either be removed in the future, or it can be used to cover future mistakes—something like a bank where you deposit food instead of money.

2. Organize the stock in the dry storeroom and use prepared inventory sheets that are in the same sequence as the stock. It is, unfortunately, not unheard of for an inventory to be taken on a blank, ruled, legal pad. When this technique is combined with a typically disorganized storage area, the result is chaos. The inventory will be time consuming and probably inaccurate as well.

3. Price the items on the inventory sheets prior to taking the inventory. If you use the LIFO method (last in, first out—the usual inventory method) the accounting office or the food and beverage controller should keep the inventory sheets and record any changes on a daily basis so that when the inventory is taken, the sheets will reflect the last prices. A common mistake is to

take an inventory, then go back through the receiving or purchase records to find the prices. This again is time consuming and leads to mistakes.

4. The walk-ins and reach-ins cannot be as well organized as the storeroom can, but an attempt should be made, particularly in the freezer, to have standard locations for each type of food.

5. All foods in the freezer(s) should have the cost, weight, date, and type of food clearly marked. One of the difficulties in inventorying a freezer is that there are many packages wrapped in foil, freezer paper, or plastic bags, and it is sometimes impossible even to ascertain what it is, much less what it weighs or is worth. Commercial packages are not always clearly marked; if not, they should be labeled. Random spot checks should of course be made to ensure no one is tampering with the stock. Weights could be increased to cover other pilferage. This would be an easy way to pad the inventory without actually having anything to do with it. Aside from these considerations, though, this procedure will really speed up the inventory process and make it much more accurate.

6. Have the same people take the inventory. They will get better at it and it will go faster.

7. Use the inventory as a training tool. As long as the inventory must be taken on a regular basis, why not assign new people to assist? When they finish they will know much more about the importance of stock rotation, the value of food, where various products can be found, what is available, and the importance of neatness and organization.

8. Consider using thirteen four-week accounting periods during the year instead of the twelve months. The advantage is that each period always ends on the same day, which makes the inventory scheduling much easier. It also increases the consistency of the stock level. The use of a twelve-month operating cycle requires taking the inventory on a variety of days. For example, in 1982, the ending inventory would be taken on:

January—Sunday

February—Sunday

March—Wednesday

April—Friday

May—Monday

June—Wednesday

July—Saturday

August—Tuesday

September—Thursday

October—Sunday

November—Tuesday

December—Friday

This causes problems in scheduling because of the variances. If the operation is closed on a Sunday, it may not be possible to take the inventory then. If it ends on a Saturday, and Saturday evening is the peak period of the week, it may be difficult to schedule an inventory, and so forth. It is more efficient to do it on the same day at the same time. As an example, many operations take a weekly inventory, say on Saturday morning, and they invariably find it is a lot easier than the month-end inventory, which is always done on a different day. The other disadvantage of a calendar year is the inventory size. It is usual to have no deliveries on Sunday and common to have few, if any, on Saturday, which means that the Friday purchases are substantial. An inventory taken one month on Friday evening and the next month on Sunday evening would show considerable variance, and this complicates the inventory turnover analysis. This is ultimately an accounting decision; we want only to point out some of the operating advantages.

Perpetual Inventory. The other type of inventory is called *perpetual inventory*. This is used to provide the same information as a physical inventory but without actually counting any of it. In theory, it is simple. In practice, it can be quite difficult to maintain with accuracy. A perpetual inventory is not intended to replace a physical one at the end of an accounting period. The information for a financial statement should come from a physical inventory or else the validity of the statement is open to question. The perpetual inventory is used to provide information on stock levels so orders can be placed without taking the time to count goods on hand. Cost estimates can be made on a weekly, biweekly, or even daily basis, again without having to physically count the stock. The procedure is to record all additions to and withdrawals from storage. These are the only requirements, but unless management is assured that all additions and withdrawals can be recorded with accuracy, this system not only will not work but could be dangerous. The danger is that decisions will be based on the information provided. Orders will be placed with purveyors, and if the stock level is wrong, the orders will either be over or under what is actually required. If inaccurate costs are calculated due to faulty inventory data, management could make disastrous judgment mistakes—clamping down when no problem exists, or doing nothing when, in fact, there could be a serious problem.

The first requirement—that of recording all additions to storage—is simple to meet. All goods, or nearly all, are documented on an invoice. These items merely have to be posted to the perpetual. It is the second requirement, documentation of all *removals* from storage, that poses the difficulty. The usual procedure is to record all inventory deletions on a requisition, but this seldom works properly. Here are a few guidelines that indicate whether or not a requisition system will work:

1. *Central storage.* If all the foods are stored in one central area, traffic may be able to be controlled. If, as is common, they are scattered, it is nearly impossible to control. Foodservice operations were at one time designed with a separate central storage area that contained the dry goods storeroom and storage (not production) walk-ins and reach-ins. This is not often seen today because it is very space consuming, and most operators would rather have maximum space devoted to seats and tables, which makes sense. Sales come from people sitting in chairs.

The more seats available, the greater the potential sales level, and the higher the sales-per-square-foot, which is a critical financial factor. Today, production and storage freezers and refrigerators are side by side; sometimes they are even one and the same!

2. *Limited accessibility to stock.* The key to a perpetual inventory is that whoever uses products must record that usage before the products can be removed from the inventory. If only one person has access to the stock, the chances of the procedure being followed are good. If many employees have access, the probability of keeping an accurate record is reduced significantly. In many operations, where virtually every employee can go into all storage areas, the question becomes what is the probability that everyone will write down everything taken? The answer is obvious—it is quite low.

3. *Limited time of access.* If the storage areas were accessible for only an hour or two each day, it would be feasible to implement a workable requisition system. When the storage areas are available from opening to closing of the operation, it is nearly impossible to enforce a requisition system.

If, as is often the case, there is no central storage area and all employees have free access at all hours of the day, how could one expect a perpetual inventory to be accurate? Under these conditions, it probably would not work. A perpetual inventory system, therefore, while potentially a valuable control tool, is not recommended for the majority of foodservice operations. We refer here to a total perpetual system, one that encompasses the entire food inventory.

It is entirely feasible, however, to install a partial perpetual inventory, covering high-cost, portion-controlled items such as steaks, lobster tails, and similar products. We *strongly* recommend that this be done. If the guidelines are followed, it will work. Take the steak example previously cited as an illustration: if all steaks (assume they are frozen) are stored in one reach-in freezer with a lock and if only the chef and management have keys, and if the box is opened only when deliveries are made and once each afternoon to issue steaks to the broiler station, and if these issues are faithfully and accurately recorded, a perpetual inventory system has been established. The purpose of a perpetual inventory is to provide day-to-day stock level information. When the issues and deliveries are posted daily, the inventory reflects the current number of steaks located in the reach-in. Note that all the guidelines have been followed: there is one central storage area; there is very limited accessibility to that area; and there are only a few periods when even those authorized people need to have access. Emergencies do, of course, arise and there will be occasions when steaks will have to be issued during the meal period. As long as this happens infrequently, and the issues are made by an authorized person, and they are recorded, there will be no problems. If an operation has no suitable reach-in equipment, they can successfully improvise by having a lockable fixed cabinet in the walk-in. One establishment used a mobile cart with a lock that was stored in the freezer.

The drawback was the possibility that someone could steal the entire cart, but this is the work of a thief and, as pointed out, is not normally a problem. At any rate, that system worked quite well.

There are two basic methods used to maintain a perpetual inventory. One consists of grouping many foods on one record (see Exhibit 4.5) while the other has only one product per sheet (see Exhibit 4.6). There are a variety of ways to enter the data; both figures show one method. There is a box (□) for each entry, divided in half (◨). The top portion shows the balance as of the beginning of that day while the bottom half shows the requisition or issue total. Thus, a box showing indicates that there were forty units or pounds on hand at the beginning of the day and ten were issued or requisitioned during the day. The balance for the next day is thirty and would be depicted. When an order is received, the box would look like this, which means that at the beginning of the day there were ten units or pounds on hand. Fifty units or pounds were received, and

Exhibit 4.5. Food Groups

Category: Steaks

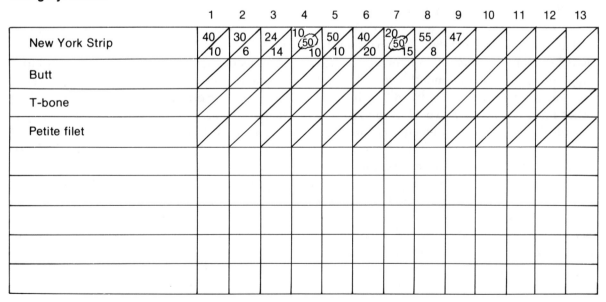

	1	2	3	4	5	6	7	8	9	10	11	12	13
New York Strip	40 / 10	30 / 6	24 / 14	10 (50) / 10	50 / 10	40 / 20	20 (50) / 15	55 / 8	47				
Butt													
T-bone													
Petite filet													

Exhibit 4.6. Single Food

New York Strip

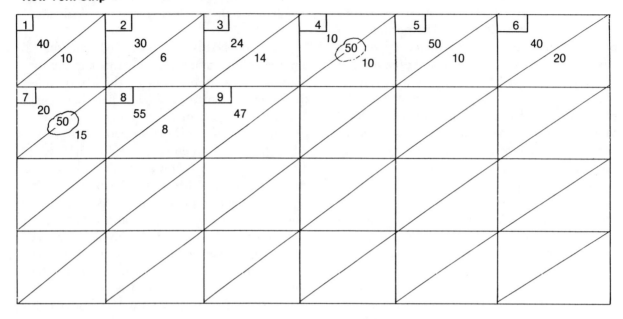

ten were issued. In this case, the beginning balance for the next day would be fifty (10 + 50 - 10 = 50), and the box would show⌐50⌐. Exhibit 4.5 lists only steaks, but it could be for meats, or it could be a consecutive listing of all foods in inventory. Exhibit 4.6 shows only one steak. The advantage of the form shown in Exhibit 4.6 is that only in and out transactions are shown. Many products will not be used on a daily basis and in such cases, the Exhibit 4.6 format could be used for a longer period. If an item were issued only once per week, one month's record would require only four boxes (Exhibit 4.6), while the other form (Exhibit 4.5) would have to have a record of each day, even though there were no transactions.

When perpetual inventories are used, they must be checked for accuracy. The most obvious time to do this is when a complete physical inventory is taken, but if this is done only once per month, missing stock would probably be discovered too late to determine what had happened. The recommendation is to spot check at random between physical inventories. For example, the receiving clerk, or any others whose job requires them to work with the stock, should be instructed to check a few items at random each day. By the end of the month, nearly all product counts would have been compared with the perpetual. If any variances are found, it may be necessary to take a complete physical inventory to determine the extent of the problem.

An inventory classification—not an inventory method—is called an in-process inventory. This consists of foods in production, all foods either withdrawn from inventory or issued directly to the kitchen from the receiving area. One of the many distinctions between foodservice businesses and manufacturing industries is the relative size of in-process inventories. They are quite small in foodservice operations. In-process inventories are usually ignored when taking inventories regardless of whether they are for costing or ordering purposes. The theory is that in-process inventories will be used that day and that they nearly always are the same. If they are the same, they would have no effect upon the cost and can safely be ignored. This theory in practice generally holds up and is sound.

Issuing

Issuing of food may or may not be a formal function. If the only authority for release of food from storage to production is a written requisition, it is an operating function. If employees can get goods from storage with no record of the removal, there is no issuing function. It is desirable from a control standpoint to record all issues, but often it is not feasible to do this. When it can be done, management can realize several control advantages:

1. Issues can be costed to obtain daily dollar cost information to divide into sales. The cost percentage can be compared to the percentage standard, and the dollar cost can be compared to the standard.

2. Requisitions can be compared to production forecasts to see whether the cooks are drawing the proper amount of foods.

3. Requisitions can be posted to a perpetual inventory. Spot comparisons between the perpetual inventory and a physical inventory will show whether the requisition system is working.

4. Requiring all employees to prepare requisitions should improve their production efficiency. It is common for a cook to make dozens of trips to the various storage areas during the day. By requiring a requisition, management is saying to the employee, "Sit down and organize your workload, figure out your total food needs for the entire shift, prepare a requisition and make one trip to procure everything." It is unlikely that this degree of efficiency will be achieved, but it is guaranteed to improve production efficiency, usually by a substantial margin.

Requisitions can be done on single-copy paper, but are more useful when there are one or more duplicates. It is recommended to have at least two copies. The distribution would be: one to the accounting office (or whoever costs them and maintains the cost records), and one to be kept in the storage department. The perpetual can be kept by the storeroom person or by the accounting office. Whoever keeps it, the information should be distributed to several people. The storeroom person needs it to compare with the physical counts; the purchasing agent needs it to prepare orders.

An actual example illustrates the difficulty in establishing an accurate issuing system. A large manufacturing plant operated their own employee feeding operations. This consisted of a cafeteria and an executive dining room. The total daily guest count exceeded 2,000. Since the plant had extensive computer capacity, the foodservice inventory was placed on computer. The way it worked was this: there were computer cards for each product in storage, one card for each individual storage unit. When a can, box, package, or so on was removed from the storeroom, a card was also removed from a rack adjacent to the product, one card for each unit. For example, if two #10 cans of green beans were taken, the person would take two cards, if three cans, then three cards, and so forth. The cards were simply dropped into a slotted box. At the end of the day, the cards were run through the computer, which maintained a perpetual inventory. The print-out of the entire inventory was available the next morning. This appears to be foolproof. The employees are not required to fill out any requisitions; they merely take a card or two when getting food and drop the cards into a box on the way out. Foolproof or not, the system did not work, partly because the employees were not forced to do it properly. There was no management follow-up. Management thought that because it was a very sophisticated system they did not have to concern themselves with such humdrum details as paying attention to what the employees were doing. Technology should be a great benefit to management, but sometimes all it does is make them lazy and complacent. The proof that the system was not effective showed when the physical inventory was taken at the end of each month, and wide variances from the perpetual came up. Management had designed an excellent, simple system that was worthless. The employees thought it was a joke. Other mistakes management made were not limiting access to the storage area and not establishing issuing periods.

When establishing a formal issuing system, management must make some decisions. One would be: how should the issue be costed? There are several ways to do this, and consistency of costing is more important than what method is used. The FIFO (first in, first out) is one: the cost per unit in effect at the beginning of the period is used to determine the value of the food sent to production. Few accountants like this method since prices generally go up, and issues may be undervalued as a result. Chefs, on the other hand, may like it since it could give them a lower cost during the month! The LIFO method (last in, first out) is more common. The last price paid is used to determine the value of the requisition. Some feel that neither method is truly accurate and prefer to cost the issues based on what was paid for each unit. This requires each unit to be priced in receiving (as previously described); and when this is done, it is a simple matter to cost the requisitions. Yet another system, fairly uncommon, is to use the average cost per unit, although the inventory must be on the computer for this to be feasible. The advantage of this procedure, when it can be used, is that the daily cost does not fluctuate up or down whenever the prices change, and some will change almost daily. A disadvantage is that over an extended period the average cost may not accurately reflect the actual costs. The LIFO method is probably the best since it comes closest to the current value of the food being consumed.

To summarize issuing: We cannot make a blanket recommendation that it be a formal function in all operations. It simply will not work in many. Where it can be effectively installed, however, it is recommended without reservation because of its control potential and because of the costing information it yields. Even in operations where it is not feasible, it is still recommended to have all employees (service personnel as well as the production staff) complete requisitions for all goods used. These will not necessarily be used for costing purposes, but it is a good way to force employees to organize their activities better. Management should recognize that by not having an issuing system they are sacrificing a powerful control tool. This is okay so long as

they attempt to maintain control in other ways. The requisitions are one way; designating authorized people for access to storage areas is another. Do not simply allow everyone to go get whatever they want. The storage areas should not be open all day either. Designate specific periods during each shift if necessary, when employees are expected to get all their necessary foods and materials. When an unauthorized person is observed in a storage area, management must question that person as to why he or she is there. In other words, follow up and enforce the rules. When employees request access to storage areas other than at the designated periods, management must determine why. If the reason is that they did not plan properly or forgot something or never got around to getting the goods during the issuing period, they must be cautioned not to let this happen again. Make them accountable, and it is unlikely that these practices will continue to be a problem. If management simply opens the door or gives the employee the keys (both of which are much easier than confronting the employee), there is no control, and management might as well just remove the doors from the storage areas.

Production

Inadequate production control is the primary cause of waste in a foodservice operation. Waste is one of the factors most responsible for excessive food costs. The others are spoilage due to excessive storage times and pilferage. Production control therefore has maximum efficiency in the utilization of food as its primary objective. Waste occurs in many ways. When ten products are sold but fifteen were prepared, there is waste. When an overcooked roast serves twenty people and was expected to serve twenty-five, there is waste. When 5 pounds of vegetables were supposed to yield twenty portions, and only 16 were obtained, there is waste. When 10 pounds of stew meat are specified in a recipe and 12 pounds are used, there is waste. When a product is improperly prepared and sent back by the guest, there is waste. When a product is properly prepared but poorly handled during holding, there is waste. There are many other examples, but these will illustrate how waste can reduce profits. Production control concentrates on controlling these factors. Yields, portion control, cooking control, forecasting, recipes, production scheduling, and food handling procedures are all part of production control.

Production Functions

There are at least three separate production functions in a kitchen, and there are wide differences among them. They are: *preprep, preparation,* and *finish cooking.* Preprep is involved with getting foods ready for cooking. Before making a stew, for example, the meat will have to be trimmed and cut to the proper size, and the potatoes, carrots, and onions will have to be peeled and cut. Once these tasks are completed, the cook can begin preparing the stew. Yields are of great importance in the preprep function, and losses can be significant. There is a high waste potential in preprep.

Typical activities in the preprep function are: dicing, cutting, chopping, preportioning, shaping, weighing, trimming, blanching, and so forth. Proper equipment is necessary for efficient performance of these tasks. Knives, boards, food processors, graters, food cutters and choppers, and scales are necessary. This function no longer exists in many kitchens for it can be moved back in the processing-supply chain, and foods can be purchased already preprepared. The advantage of doing this should be obvious. Yield losses are reduced or eliminated, and less equipment, time, and personnel are required. The kitchen becomes more predictable, and this also increases control.

The second function, preparation, may also not exist in some kitchens today because it is entirely possible to purchase all the menu requirements fully prepared. This is not common, but there are many examples of establishments that do this. In general, they are noncommercial or institutional food services, hospitals in particular. Typical activities performed during preparation are roasting, baking, braising, stewing, steaming, soup or sauce making, boiling, and so forth. Preparation equipment includes ovens, steamers, braising kettles, steam-jacketed kettles, ranges, stock pots, sauce pans, and mixers.

The final function, finish cooking, is a part of every foodservice operation. Even convenience kitchens have to fry, broil, grill, steam, microwave, poach, or sauté foods, either to cook them or to heat them to proper eating temperatures. The types of equipment needed are: steamers, microwave ovens, broilers, steam-jacketed kettles, grills or griddles, ranges, sauté pans, deep-fat fryers, and a hot-water bath (or steam table).

When setting up a kitchen, it is necessary to know exactly what functions will be performed in the kitchen since most of the equipment is primarily used for one function. It would waste money to purchase unnecessary equipment, yet this is done all the time. Review the discussion of each function, and note the equipment required. If, for example, preprep was not done, there may not be any need for cutters, dicers, peelers, graters, or food processors, though knives and boards would still be needed. We have seen kitchens that do no baking yet have a proof box, operations that purchase portioned steaks and meats and yet have a meat saw taking up valuable space. There are many such obvious examples. Some equipment is not specific to any particular function. Steamers are both production equipment (preparation) and finish cooking (service line). The difference is in the size. A steamer used for basic production is large and will take full-size pans, while a service-line pressure steamer usually handles only 1/6 size pans. A steam-jacketed kettle used for production purposes will be floor mounted, and the capacity will be 40, 60, or even 90 or more gallons while the corresponding service-line equipment will be counter-mounted with a capacity of about a gallon.

Ranges can also be used either for production or for service, although it is probably a waste of money and space to put a range in the production area. Anything a range can be used for, another piece of equipment will do at least equally well and with less energy expenditure. Ranges are designed for counter-top, direct heat cooking. This type of heat source need be provided only on the service line where products must be pan fried or sautéed. Other than this, there is no need for a range in any kitchen. Virtually all service lines have ranges, yet relatively few actually do any sautéing or pan frying. If they do not, the range sits there—an expensive piece of equipment that is not needed and if used, is not used efficiently. A range is generally a superfluous piece of equipment in the preparation area. Soups, sauces, and braised products can be prepared equally well in other types of equipment, such as braising kettles or steam-jacketed kettles.

Ovens are basically production equipment and have limited utility on a service line. There are a variety of ovens, and there are yield, efficiency, and control differences among them. A standard oven heats by convection; that is, there are warm currents of air moving slowly within the cooking chamber. The convection currents move according to the following diagram:

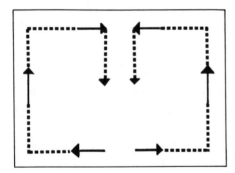

The higher the temperature, the faster the movement. Cooking time is affected by the temperature and the heat transfer coefficient. The heat transfer coefficient is better at higher temperatures since the air currents move faster. A forced-air convection oven (often called a convection oven, which is technically incorrect since all ovens heat by convection) has a fan in it that forces the air to move around the cooking chamber at a high velocity, much higher than would normally be attained. Cooking times are thus reduced, and cooking temperatures may

often be reduced as well due to the increase in the heat transfer efficiency. There are studies that show higher meat cooking losses with forced-air convection ovens, but much of this increased loss is in fat; the servable meat is not affected. In other words, the fat tends to burn off more readily in a forced-air oven. Since fat is often trimmed prior to carving, the meat available to be served is not affected. At any rate, most foods cook as well if not better in a forced-air oven. The increased speed and potential energy savings (lower temperatures) make this type of equipment very attractive. A very versatile oven is one in which the fan can be activated or not, depending upon what is being cooked. This oven is actually two in one: both a conventional and a forced-air convection oven.

A third type of oven that is extremely useful from a control viewpoint is the slow-cooking oven. This is a very specialized piece of equipment that will maintain very low cooking temperatures. It is not feasible to cook at temperatures lower than 225 to 250 degrees F. in most ovens (both conventional and forced-air) because they will not maintain steady temperatures at below those temperatures. They are designed to cook at 300 to 400 degrees F. The slow-cooking oven will maintain temperatures of under 200 degrees F. with minimum variances. Since cooking yields are primarily a factor of heat, the advantage of cooking at a very low temperature should be obvious: substantially increased yield. In addition, these ovens may be mobile, making them ideal for banquets as well as dining-room production, and they can be set to automatically convert to a holding oven when the roast cycle is completed. In the hold cycle, it is possible to maintain a rib roast at 140 to 145 degrees F. (rare to medium rare) for hours if desired. There will be no increase in internal temperature, no weight loss, and no dehydration. When the internal temperature has stabilized following the end of roasting (there is always an increase in internal temperature after cooking is completed, the amount of the rise being dependent upon the cooking temperature and the size of the product being cooked), the roast can be held without any changes in the product standard. The drawbacks are that the cooking time is increased, and that a separate piece of equipment is needed. These are countered more than adequately by the increase in servable product. As an example, assume that the gross profit from an order of prime rib were $6.00 and that the cost of such an oven were $3,500.00 (both figures are currently realistic). The oven would pay for itself when it produced some 583 extra orders. Volume is obviously important, but few operations that had high prime rib sales could fail to pay for the oven in a matter of months. An added benefit is that they would probably be serving a better product as well. Some manufacturers of conventional and convection ovens are offering a "cook and hold" option, which is a slow-cooking and holding feature. These do not have the mobility advantage but this could be compensated for by the versatility of having three ovens in one: a conventional oven (without the fan), a forced-air convection oven (by activating the fan), and the slow-cooking and holding oven.

Production Scheduling and Forecasting

There are two key elements here: one is being able to prepare an accurate forecast of the demand for each menu item, and the other is being able to get these foods prepared as efficiently as possible. Forecasting is the first step, and it is critically important. Unless the forecast is accurate, no degree of production control will prevent waste and inefficiency. A production forecast should be based upon past sales. A new operation is seriously hampered by the lack of such information. An establishment that has been in business for several years and has accumulated no sales records is similarly hampered, but they have no excuse. It is amazing to realize that businesses exist that do not know exactly what they sell, but thousands of foodservice operations fall into this category. Methods of obtaining sales records have been discussed, and this is one of the most important uses this information can be put to. While the entire historical sales pattern is of interest, the recent past is the most important. When forecasting the sales for lunch on Wednesday,

the operator should look at the Wednesday lunch sales totals for the past three or four weeks and modify them according to any unusual circumstances, if any occurred. For example, these are the sales and circumstances over the past four weeks for one menu item:

	Sales	Circumstances
One week ago	45	None
Two weeks ago	42	None
Three weeks ago	21	Snowstorm
Four weeks ago	46	None

It would be reasonable to discard the snowstorm sales and concentrate on the other three. The appropriate forecast would be about forty-five. This would be modified if there were any extenuating circumstances expected. If another snowstorm was forecast, the sales would be expected to drop. If a tour bus was scheduled, the sales would probably be higher than usual. In this case, you would check the sales records to see what has happened in the past when a tour bus stopped. There could be a convention in town, or the weather may be unusually hot or whatever. The point is that management (or whoever has this responsibility) first attempts to determine the most rational level of expected sales per item and then modifies those figures if the circumstances warrant it. When this process is completed, the result is a production forecast. If it has been perfectly done, there will be nothing left over, and the kitchen will not run out of anything. This is unlikely, but a good forecast will result in a minimum of leftovers and a minimum or run-outs.

One of the reasons that banquets are as profitable as they typically are is that forecasting is accurate. The number of guests is known, and the foods they will eat are also known. It is easy to accurately forecast production for a group of one hundred who will be eating stuffed cornish hen. This degree of forecasting precision is not possible in the dining room; however, management must attempt to get it as accurate as possible. It is appalling how many foodservice operators completely ignore their responsibility in this vital matter and allow the employees to decide how much to prepare. Production employees do not know how much is sold from day to day (although they often think they do). They certainly have a feel for the sales pattern, but without actual sales records, it is nearly impossible to accurately determine the likely sales mix for any given day. One point should be made clear here: Many foodservice operators feel it is the responsibility of the chef to do this. There is no objection to this so long as the chef has access to the sales records. Otherwise, he or she is not qualified to make production forecasting decisions. A true chef is a manager in the kitchen, and as such, should have this responsibility; but it is then management's responsibility to provide the necessary information. Without it, the task cannot be adequately performed; if it is not, it is management's fault, *not* the chef's! It is the job of management to establish standards, enforce them, hire and train competent personnel, and provide them with the tools, facilities, equipment, information, and environment necessary to perform at the expected level. Much nonstandard performance is the fault of management, not the employees. Production forecasts should be prepared for all production items and distributed both to the kitchen and the purchasing department. This becomes the basis for which foods and how many foods will be ordered and then prepared.

Once the forecast is made, the next step is to insure that the foods are prepared as efficiently as possible. There is a detailed discussion of production scheduling in the labor control section. The focus of that discussion is on the best utilization of *personnel*, one of the five factors of production. The other four are: *space, equipment, time,* and *products*. Some guidelines on production scheduling are:

Evaluate all recipes and menu items to determine whether the products can be preprepared in any way. An ideal towards which the production planner heads is to have a product preprepped enough so it can be finished very quickly after being ordered but if not sold that evening will not lose quality by holding. Not all products lend themselves to this, but many do, and the advantages should be obvious. Foods can

be prepared quickly, thereby possibly increasing turnover in the dining room. When forecasting mistakes are made, there will not be any quality loss due to leftovers. A rib roast can be preprepped by roasting it, then cooling it quickly. It is held cold and cut to order and then warmed to eating temperature. Vegetables can be blanched and cooled in an ice-water bath, which will also stabilize green colors, and held cold. When ordered, they can be brought up to eating temperature in a matter of seconds by dipping into boiling water (in a small, counter-type fryer filled with boiling water or in a small steam-jacketed kettle). Or they can be sautéed to order, again very quickly, on the range, perhaps with a seasoned or herb butter.

Pastas can be precooked to the al dente stage, cooled, oiled, and portioned. They are heated in a bath of simmering water similar to the vegetables. Fried chicken can be blanched and cooled during preprep. When ordered, they are dredged in seasoned flour or quickly breaded and then deep fried much more quickly than if left raw. Steaks, especially for banquets, can be seared to simulate grill markings, chilled and held until needed, at which time they can be cooked (preferably on a rack elevated over the pan) in a forced-air convection oven. Tenderloin tips are usually fully prepared and held on a steam table, but if the meat were portioned and wrapped in plastic film and the sauce made separately, it would be easy to prepare them to order. When needed, the sauté cook would remove one of the packages of tip meat from the refrigerator (located on the line), sauté them quickly in clarified butter (also available), add the designated amount of sauce, simmer for a few seconds, and serve. The product would be superior, it would take only marginally longer, and the portion control would be better. These are just a few examples of what can be done. Even recipes that do not lend themselves to these practices can be interrupted at some point. Bread dough can be mixed, proofed, shaped, and refrigerated one day. Final proofing and baking can then be done the next. Lasagna can be completely panned one day and baked the next day or, if frozen, next week or next month.

Certain types of hors d'oeuvres and appetizers can be prepared, frozen, and stored by the hundreds in heavy plastic bags in the freezer for use weeks from the time of preparation. Then they are available "on demand."

Evaluate every product made and determine the most efficient way to handle it. To repeat, the objectives are to be able to produce the finished item as quickly as possible and to maintain holding quality. None of this is possible without extensive food knowledge. Some people are under the impression that is no longer necessary to know food; that it is all numbers and marketing today. The answer of course is that you are primarily marketing food—not entirely, but it is still the primary and most expensive product. Another answer is that is far easier to keep the numbers in line if you know your products than if you don't. Finally, how can one possibly schedule production properly without food knowledge? The reply is that management does not do it; they turn the job over to the kitchen to handle. A qualified chef is the best person to take on this job, but such individuals are scarce, and the foodservice establishments in the United States that operate without a qualified chef number in the hundred of thousands. In the majority of foodservice units, therefore, management must take the lead in this critical area. If they are not qualified or interested, they are strongly advised to get qualified and interested!

Production Sheets

The use of a production sheet to transmit the forecast to the kitchen on a daily basis is strongly recommended. The example in Exhibit 4.7 is not the only way to do it, but it contains the necessary elements. It is important that management realize the purpose of this document: It is to inform the kitchen what and how much to prepare. That is its primary purpose. It is not intended to be a vehicle for the kitchen to inform management about what they are doing. The latter is only a secondary purpose of the production sheet, though management can indeed obtain valuable information, as we shall see.

We will examine each of the elements in the production sheet (Exhibit 4.7):

1. *Item.* The source for this is usually a fixed menu, but it could also be from a catering function. In the case where there are daily specials, the source is generally the kitchen so they should make up the menu far enough in advance so that whoever does the production planning can work them into the overall schedule. Daily specials are sometimes prepared according to a fixed cycle, and this would then be handled no differently from the regular menu.

2. *Portion cost/sales price.* These are optional but can be useful. Their use will be discussed at the end of this section.

3. *Forecast.* This is the reason for a production sheet; the source should be management or a managing chef. We have discussed the mechanics of determining how much of each item to prepare.

4. *Original preparation.* Here the kitchen begins to feed information back to management. This is the total produced during preparation, and normally it will be the same as the forecast. There are a couple of deviations here so we will look at each menu item individually. The *stew* forecast was 3 gallons. This is not the type of product that could be readily supplemented during meal service, so if 3 gallons will be needed, 3 gallons would have to be prepared. This was done. The *chefs salad* could probably be supplemented during the meal (especially if all the ingredients were preprepared and ready to go), so it would not be unusual for the kitchen not to prepare the entire forecast. In this case, however, they did. The *hamburger* forecast was forty-six, and the original preparation was fifty. The hamburgers are not really prepared as yet; they will be cooked to order, so what this means is that fifty hamburgers were removed from the freezer and issued to the line. Why fifty rather than forty-six? If the hamburgers were sized at five to a pound, a standard 10-pound box would contain fifty. Perhaps when the forecast is that close to an entire case, it is acceptable to issue a whole carton. Depending on the policy, this deviation may or may not be a problem. The original preparation for *omelette* was fifteen,

Exhibit 4.7. Production Forecast

MEAL _____   DAY _____   DATE _____

Item	Portion Cost	Sales Price	Forecast	Orig. Prep.	Add. Prep.	Total Prep.	Leftover	Used	Actual Sold	Plus Or Minus	$ Short Cost	Sales
Beef stew	.55	1.75	3 gal. (21)	3 gal. 21		3 gal. 21	1/2 gal.	17	15	-2	1.10	3.50
Chefs bowl	.40	1.55	30	30	5	35	2	33	33			
Hamburger	.35	1.10	46	50		50	9	41	40	-1	.35	1.10
Omelette	.25	1.25	20	15	2	17		17	18	+1	(.25)	(1.25)
Hash	.45	1.50	20	20		20		20	18	-2	.90	3.00
											$2.10	$6.35

while the forecast was twenty. Here, as with the hamburger, the omelettes have not yet been prepared; eggs have simply been issued to the line. If we assume the procedure is to use two eggs per order and not to crack them until the order is received (excellent portion control), there is really no problem here. The chef or cook simply puts thirty eggs (fifteen orders) on the line instead of forty eggs (twenty orders), probably figuring that if the forecast was correct, there would be ample opportunity to get ten additional eggs. If the forecast turns out a little high, the unused eggs are better off stored in their original carton than loose at the work station. The *hash* is similar to the stew. Whatever is needed will have to be prepared ahead of time, so the original preparation is the same as the forecast.

5. *Additional preparation.* The source is again the kitchen. They are informing management of any products prepared after the basic production or during the meal. On this day, there were five more chefs bowls made up, and two additional orders of eggs (four eggs) were obtained from storage.

6. *Total preparation.* This is arrived at by adding the two previous columns together. It represents the total amount of food available for sale. This figure should be verified by management; otherwise there is no control. Verification is done when management checks and tastes the food, which should be a regular procedure at the beginning of each meal period. The additional preparation will probably not be known at this time, but management can ascertain it later by checking the usage. Whether or not additional prep was accurately recorded will quickly become apparent.

7. *Leftover.* This is also verified by management. They should physically count the foods remaining after the meal period.

8. *Used.* This is calculated by subtracting the leftovers from the total available for sale. This is the number of each menu item that was used or consumed during the meal period.

9. *Actual sales.* The above total, *used* (#8) is not the same as items actually sold. The source for this information is the sales record, kept either by the dining room or a prechecking system. The usage must be compared to the sales.

10. *Plus or minus.* This column represents the difference (if any) between the usage and sales totals. Management can tell a great deal about what is going on in the kitchen by carefully evaluating this column. The stew was two orders short. Does that mean that someone stole two orders of stew? Should the locker room and the employee cars be searched? Of course not. Stew is served by dishing it up from a pan on the steam table, and it is obvious that it was overportioned. Management must then be prepared to follow up and discuss proper portion sizes and portioning techniques with the line cooks. On the other hand, it may not be their fault. The reply may be, "I told you last week we had no more stew serving ladles, and so we are trying to do our best to estimate the proper portion. Get us the right equipment, and we will do it properly." Sound familiar? The chefs bowl count was right on target, and it should be. These are individual products and could not be overportioned, although the ingredients could certainly be. If the count were off, there was either a mistake made or the product could have been sold without the sale being recorded (also without the money being turned in!). The hamburger count showed one short, and here there is no questions of overportioning. We are actually missing a product. It is unlikely, however, that anyone stole a single hamburger. What is likely is that someone either ate it or the grill cook burned one up. Follow-up is again important. The kitchen should know management will not overlook even a single hamburger patty and that they will be asked to account for what happened. Employees tend to be far more careful about what they do when they are held accountable for their actions. The omelette is strange. There is one order over! What happened? Did the cook generously donate two eggs? The answer lies in the omelette preparation policy. The eggs are to be cracked only when an order is received, but if the cook got careless or in a hurry, she or he might crack many eggs into a bowl, mix them and ladle them out as needed. This is probably exactly what happened, and the orders were

underportioned. Follow-up would consist of reviewing the proper procedure and reemphasizing the importance of standard portion sizes. The hash was short and this is again a case of overportioning.

11. *Dollar shortage.* (optional) The reason the portion cost and selling price may be kept on the production sheet is so any shortages can be expressed in terms of increased cost and lost sales. On this day, the operation realized food losses of $2.10, which could have been sold for $6.35. Many managers would probably prefer to use the larger figure (the sales) when discussing the impact of the various mistakes with the employees.

In summary, the production sheet is a management tool, the primary purpose of which is to control what and how much is made each day. It can also provide useful information as to what is going on in the kitchen, however. A formal production sheet, though recommended, is optional; the necessity for management to control production is *not* optional. It absolutely must be done and the production sheet is the best control device.

Standard Recipes

Standard recipes are a necessity in a professional kitchen. Without them, there is no assurance that consistent products will be served at standard costs. Control is whatever is done to assure this, and the most basic control is a recipe. If the recipe is used properly, the product will always be prepared with the same types of ingredients, with the same amount of ingredients, and in the same way. The product will be consistent from day to day, and the cost will also be consistent, barring purchase price changes, of course. There are many acceptable formats for standard recipes. The one we will discuss is as good as any and better than most by far. (See Exhibit 4.8 for an example.) There are four distinct elements to this recipe form. We will present the recommended guidelines for each.

1. Heading
2. Ingredients
3. Quantity
4. Method

Exhibit 4.8. Standard Recipe Form

NAME: **YIELD**:

Pan Size: **Portion Size**:

Temperature: **Cooking Time**:

Ingredients	*Quantity*	*Method*

Heading

1. *The name of the product obviously must be given.* Make sure it can be understood. If a foreign term is used, translate it so there is no possibility of a mistake. Do not assume people know what various foreign food terms mean.

2. *Yield.* This is critical. A recipe is useless unless it clearly indicates how much it will make. The yield is best given in volume or weight. It should not normally be given in numbers of portions. For example, a soup recipe that states it serves forty-two portions, then identifies the portion size as six ounces is technically correct. It would be much more useful, however, to give the yield as 2 gallons, then the portion size as 6 ounces with a notation that there will be forty-two such portions. The reason for this is that when the soup is finished, the cook can easily check the yield to see whether it came out right. Two gallons can be easily checked; checking forty-two portions is more difficult. Another reason is that servings of other portion sizes can more readily be determined. The cook may have to prepare sixty-four 8-ounce portions, and knowing the total yield to be 2 gallons, he or she would double the recipe (64 x 8 = 512 ounces or 4 gallons).

The yield of a stew would be best expressed in gallons, bread dough in pounds, tossed salad by weight, pasta by weight, rice by volume, sauces by volume, tuna (shrimp, egg, and so on) salad by weight. Some yields, on the other hand, are best given in numbers of servings. All individual portions should be given by number, such as when a recipe is for a single steak to be broiled to order, or an order of chicken, salmon fillet, or whatever. A swiss steak recipe yield would be expressed as a specific number of portions, as would deviled eggs and similar items.

3. *Portion size.* This also is necessary in all recipes. It should be given in weight wherever possible, but many foods are more easily measured by volume: soup is one, cooked rice is another. A single portion should be avoided whenever possible. An example would be one cut, one piece, or one whatever. One of the most accurate ways to give portion sizes is to specify the number of cuts (and how to cut them) in a container. For example: a lasagna recipe should give the yield in total product weight (uncooked) as well as the exact dimensions and numbers of pans. The portion size would be 6 x 4 = 24, which means the pan will be cut into twenty-four pieces, six cuts the long way and four cuts the short way.

4. *Cooking time.* This is optional since not all recipes will actually be cooked. Even with those foods, however, record the expected preparation time. To schedule production properly, the approximate time for each task must be known. If it is known, why not put it on the recipe as a standard? This provides a guideline for the employee and gives management an evaluation yardstick. If a product should be completed in half an hour, and 45 minutes later it is still not finished, something is wrong, and management should find out what it is.

5. *Pan size.* This can refer either to the cooking pan or to any piece of equipment used. Murphy's Law applies here—as it does to nearly all aspects of foodservice operation—in that if there are five pans the product can be prepared in, the employee will invariably pick the least suitable one! Therefore, the recipe should state which utensil(s) and pan(s) are best suited, after this has been determined by the head cook or chef. Remember, one purpose of the recipe is to produce standard products; equipment and preparation time may affect the quality. If they do, standardize them.

6. *Temperature.* This is also optional. If the product is cooked, it will require a temperature; some noncooked products may also have a specific temperature—a cold soup for example. Many foods, however, do not require any specific temperatures. A problem arises when two or more temperatures are needed. The temperature section of the heading is most useful for preheating an oven prior to the cooking. It saves space in the recipe itself and saves time by not having to search for it. When two or three temperatures are used, put the one used first in the heading and the others in the recipe where appropriate.

Ingredients

1. Products should be listed in the order they are used. They should also be grouped together if they are used together in a single step.

2. The descriptions of the ingredients should be consistent. The recommended format is to list the food first, followed by any qualifying information. For example:

Onions, chopped (not chopped onions)

Eggs, fresh, medium (not medium eggs)

Shrimp, peeled and deveined (not peeled and deveined shrimp)

The reason is that it is easier to find the ingredients when they are always first than if they were scattered at random.

3. The ingredients should always be listed in the form they are to be used. For example:

Onion, sliced—Rather than giving onion as an ingredient and instructing the cook, in the method section, to slice it.

Green pepper, diced—Rather than a separate section directing the cook to dice it.

Chicken breast, boned and cut into 1/2-inch pieces—Rather than giving a chicken breast as an ingredient and later instructing it be boned and cut into 1/2-inch pieces.

There are two important advantages to this method. One is that the recipe is less wordy and complex and so it is easier to follow. Using the onion as a further example, in the method section we have the direction to "sauté the onion." If the onion is not listed properly as an ingredient, the method section must read "dice the onion, and sauté." This may not seem like much, but when one recipe has chicken, onion, and green pepper plus celery and tomatoes, all needing special preparing, the cooking instructions can get quite involved—unnecesarily so. Keep it simple if you want consistency.

The other reason for using this nomenclature system is that it makes production scheduling easier. Say for example you wanted to have one person do all the vegetable preprep rather than have each cook duplicate the efforts of the others. There is no sense in having three different people chop two onions each when it would be more efficient to have one person chop six onions and separate them into three portions. With many recipes, it would be difficult to determine at a glance exactly what must be done. By following the system described above, however, all the ingredient forms are listed together and are easy to understand. The cooking is done more quickly, more efficiently, and with greater consistency when all the ingredients are in a ready-to-use form. Even if there is no preprep system, it aids each cook in prepping her or his ingredients prior to starting.

Quantity

1. The quantity should be given by weight whenever possible. Volumes should be used only with products where weight and volume are consistent or with those ingredients used in amounts too small to weigh accurately. A surprisingly wide range of foods are consistent in both weight and volume. With water, milk, wine, and liquid in general, you can use 1 pint or 1 pound for they are the same. One pint equals 2 cups or 16 ounces, and 1 pound equals 16 ounces. Two cups of rice equals 1 pound. Two cups of oil or butter equals 1 pound. Two cups of salt or sugar equals 1 pound. Two cups of flour does not equal one pound, nor do two cups of raisins, chopped parsley, diced carrots, sliced tomatoes, bay leaves, corn starch, and so on.

There are two objectives in designating the quantity. It must produce the same product each time, and it must be able to be costed with consistency. If five people measure 1 quart of flour, you are likely to have five different weights depending on how much they packed the flour and whether or not they sifted it. Five persons weighing a pound of flour would all come up with a pound. In this case, there is consistency in weight but not in measure. Five cooks instructed to prepare 1 cup of diced onions would probably come up with five different onion weights, depending on exactly how coarse or fine the dice were. A pound of diced onions, however, is a pound of diced onions. It would be even better to give the dice size as well; for example, onions, diced 1/4-inch—1 pound. Again, consistency is the goal. Therefore, the rules are: when only weight will assure consistent quantities, weights must be used. When both weights and volumes will give consistent quantities, use the one that is the easiest and fastest for the cook. With water, it would probably be cups, quarts, or gallons; but with butter it would be pounds. The third category, very small-quantity ingredients, are probably measured most accurately by volume. Therefore, most spices would be given in teaspoons or tablespoons. Following these rules should achieve good consistency in the ingredients over time.

The other objective, costing accuracy, is also assured by most of the examples. Onions are purchased by the pound, and specifying quantity in pounds makes it easy to cost that ingredient. When specifying quantity, try to use purchase-price units where possible but not at the risk of complicating the recipe. Cucumbers may be purchased in a basket so there would be no cost per pound, only a cost per basket. Yet it would not be feasible to put a quarter basket in a recipe. In this case, the weight in the recipes must be used. They could be sliced, diced, peeled, grated, whatever—but the weights should be used for product consistency. The costing will be difficult, but in this case it cannot be helped. Recipe costing is covered in detail in a later section. The point here is that the way recipes are written makes them easy or difficult to cost. Not only is 1 cup of diced bacon an inconsistent measure, but how does one cost it? In summary, use weights except where volumes are equally consistent or where it is not practical to weigh.

2. The quantity should be given in the volume measure or weight easiest to use. In order to do this, it is necessary to know the basic conversion units. These are:

3 teaspoons = 1 tablespoon

16 tablespoons = 1 cup

2 cups = 1 pint

4 cups = 1 quart

4 quarts = 1 gallon

1 gallon = 128 ounces

1 quart = 32 ounces

1 pint = 16 ounces

1 cup = 8 ounces

1 tablespoon = 1/2 ounce

Some examples of common mistakes and the corrected measure are:

Recipe Reads	Should Read
3 teaspoons	1 tablespoon
16 cups	1 gallon
4 tablespoons	1/4 cup
1.5 teaspoons	1/2 tablespoon
2 cups	1 pint
6 cups	1.5 quarts
4 cups	1 quart
24 ounces	1.5 pounds

Sometimes you will find something really ridiculous such as "1 gallon plus 1 quart plus 1 cup plus 1 tablespoon plus 1 teaspoon plus a pinch." This is exaggerated a bit, of course, but it is common to find mixed measures. They should be avoided whenever possible. Most quantity recipes will have the ingredients rounded off to a more convenient measure. A measure of 15.5 cups can probably be rounded up to 1 gallon. Likewise 4.25 tablespoons can be called 1/4 cup and so forth. The objective is simplicity. It is easier and faster to measure 1/4 cup once than to measure a tablespoon four times. It is surprising how often these rules are broken.

3. Avoid imprecise measures. We refer here to terms such as *pinch, handful, season to taste* and so forth. The only time such imprecision should exist is when the recipe is being developed. At that point, you really do not know exactly how much salt and pepper, spices, and so on will be used. The purpose of testing, however, is to find out. When the specific amounts are determined, they should be standardized. The only exception to this statement is that with

some products, the taste may vary. Ham is an example; its saltiness will not always be consistent. The same would be true with parmesan cheese. In these cases, you still test and still determine the proper amount. Because inconsistencies are expected here, you specify a slightly smaller amount than is normally used, and then instruct the cook that it will be necessary to taste and perhaps make an adjustment. For example, if in testing a soup, you find that the salt requirement ranges from 1/4 cup (4 tablespoons) to 5 tablespoons, the recipe should give 1/4 cup and then appropriate directions for adjustment. Management should also designate whose taste will be used, for people vary widely in their taste thresholds. Someone with a high salt threshold will oversalt the product if allowed to "salt to taste," even if there are salting guidelines.

Method

1. The directions should be divided into sections, each section numbered and separated from the others by a line. The directions within a section should be paired with the ingredient(s) to be used.

2. The directions should be complete but as simple as possible. There must not be any instructions or terms that can be interpreted in two or more ways. For example, if you want some mushrooms to be sautéed, say "sauté"; do not say "cook." Be specific.

3. Do not give preprep instructions in this section. As explained previously, they are to be given with the ingredients themselves. We should add here that it is then necessary to have separate instructions for preprepping since the techniques will not be covered anywhere on the recipes. This is not a problem. In fact, it is a better way to do it. Then you would have in one source complete directions (with photos or drawings if possible) on how to clean, peel, dice, julienne, chop, slice all vegetables; how to bone and cut up a chicken; how to cut the brochette meat; and so forth. Whatever preprep activities are performed should be covered.

4. Provide as much handling information as is necessary. This includes storage of products not served right away. Such information includes: which specific type of container to store it in, how to cover it, where to store it, what temperature it must be cooled to for safe storage, how to cool it, and any other information necessary to assure quality maintenance and product safety.

5. There should often be garnishing and service information in this section. The basic rule is that if there is a specific way the food should be garnished, plated, and served, it should be standardized and put on the recipe. An accompanying rule is that if there are no such standards, there should be!

6. Use graphics wherever appropriate. It is much more effective to have a picture or drawing of a properly assembled brochette than to try to describe how to put it together. This is true with many products. A polaroid camera can be quite useful for this.

7. The recipe *must* include the product standards. This is one of the most important aspects to a standard recipe, yet also one of the most commonly ignored. How can you produce a standard product without providing a description of the standard? How can the cook tell whether the product is properly prepared or not? Product standards can be described in terms of color, texture, flavor, odor, and temperature. A recipe with instructions to "roast at 350 degrees F. for 1 hour" will not necessarily produce a standard product. All ovens are different. The thermostat may or may not be working properly. The oven may be opened eight times during cooking one day and only once another day. The roast(s) may go in at refrigerator temperature one day and at room temperature the next. In order to assure a standard product, directions similar to the following should be provided: "roast at 350 degrees F. for about one hour. The product is done when it is well-browned all over, the skin is crisp, and the internal temperature is 170 degrees F." If these conditions do not exist at the end of an hour, it is not done and should remain in the oven. If they exist after 50 minutes, the product should be removed from the oven. All

directions such as cook for 5 minutes, boil for 3 minutes, sauté over high heat until cooked, are nonsense. The use of drawings or photos, as recommended, is an excellent way to describe standards. Some terms and phrases that are useful are:

Color

dark brown	yellow-gold
light brown	lemon colored
bright green	translucent
lightly colored	clear

Texture

crisp	flakes easily
not limp	firm to the touch
fork tender	al dente

Taste

salty	hot (taste, not
sweet	temperature)
peppermint	bland (not
spicy	seasoned)

Odor. This is difficult to describe, but food has many more odors than it has tastes (hundreds of odors, only four tastes), and you should make an attempt if the food is supposed to have a distinctive odor.

lime	rich beef
lemon	clam
spice—dill	wine
tarragon	brandy—bourbon, rum,
oregano	so forth
and so on	

Temperature. Steaks should always be described both by color and temperature. The guest may not agree with the house description of rare,

medium rare, and so forth, but if steaks are always prepared to the house standard and the service crew knows what it is, there should be no problem. Roasts should have two temperatures: the temperature at which it should be removed from the oven and the temperature to which it is expected to rise after sitting half an hour or so. Temperature standards are the most precise and should be used as much as possible. They are quantitative, and the other standards are qualitative and thus subject to error. What is brown? What is tender? But 150 degrees F. is 150 degrees F. and should not be misinterpreted. Pictures are the next most precise way of describing product quality standards.

Exhibits 4.9 and 4.10 are examples of standard recipes. Exhibit 4.9 is badly flawed, and the criticisms appear following the recipe. Exhibit 4.10 shows a recipe which is correct in format.

Yield Testing

Yield testing is something that has to be done because without it, you cannot accurately determine what the unit costs are. An exception to this statement would be a totally convenience and portion-controlled operation, but such foodservice units are quite rare. Any operation that even so much as peels onions or carrots must make yield determinations. Most operations do considerably more than that. Although it is true that in-house preprep is decreasing, it is still performed on a significant scale as far as the total industry is concerned.

As stated, yield testing is done to determine what it costs to serve a product. If there is any loss in the product between the times it is received and served, the yield is less than 100 percent and must be known. It is very poor management not to know what it actually costs to set various products in front of the guests. Yield testing is not the only procedure to follow, but it is the first one.

Everything that does not have a 100 percent yield should be tested. Portioned products and prepared foods may have a 100 percent yield, but little else does. Let us look at a list of common

Exhibit 4.9 Incorrect Standard Recipe with Recipe Critique

NAME: Diced Chicken with Pepper   **YIELD:** 18 platters ①

Pan Size: ②   **Portion Size:** ③
                                        12 ounce/platter

Temperature: ④   **Cooking Time:** ⑤

Ingredients	Quantity	Method
Chicken breasts ⑥	20 each ⑨	1. Bone and dice into 1/2" cubes. ⑭
Green pepper ⑦ Red pepper Bamboo shoots	10 medium 18 medium ⑩ 5 cups	2. Wash green and red peppers. Cut ⑮ out top and discard. Slice in half and remove seeds. Dice peppers and bamboo shoots into 1/2" cubes.
Cornstarch Water	1/2 cup 1 3/4 cup	3. Mix until free of lumps. Should have a smooth consistency.
Salt Soy sauce White wine ⑧ Sugar	3 tsp. ⑪ 1/2 cup + 2 tbl. 6 tbl. 3 tsp.	4. Mix these ingredients and add to ⑯ step 3. Place chicken cubes in this mixture and let sit.
Egg white	1 ⑫	5. Beat and then mix with step 4.
Peanut oil	4 tbl. ⑬	6. Put oil in wok, heat until sizzling. ⑰ Place chicken in wok and stir fry until done. Remove chicken and set aside. Drain oil.
		7. Place pepper in wok and stir fry ⑱ until done. Put chicken back into wok and stir fry for one minute. ⑲

Exhibit 4.9 Recipe Critique

1. The yield is given incorrectly. For a wet item such as this is, it would be appropriate to give the yield by either weight or volume. Which one would depend on how the product was to be portioned. If the portion was determined by weight, the recipe yield should be given by pounds. If the item was portioned by volume, the yield should be given in quarts or gallons. We would recommend volume for both portioning and yield.

2. No pan or cooking utensil is recommended. With many recipes it would not make any difference what was used for preparation, but in this case it does. The recipe indicates that a wok is to be used. This should be made clear in the heading. The size of the wok should also be indicated.

3. The portion size is inappropriate unless the product is to be served only family style. Even in that case, we would recommend volume measurement rather than weight. It would be just as accurate but would be easier and faster than weighing. Normally the portion size is given for individual portions.

4. No temperature is given in the heading although several temperatures are of interest. What temperature should the wok be at when the cooking begins? What temperature should the product be when finished? What temperature should the product be when served?

5. How long will this product take to cook? Surely there is a standard, and if there is not, there should be.

6. The chicken breast is not listed correctly as an ingredient. It should be given in the form in which it will be cooked or used. In this case, the method section instructs us to bone and dice the breast into one-half inch cubes. The correct listing would be: Chicken, breast, boneless—diced 1/2 inch.

7. These ingredients, green and red pepper, and bamboo shoots are also incorrectly written. They should be given as follows:

Green pepper—diced 1/2 inch

Red pepper—diced 1/2 inch

Bamboo shoots—diced 1/2 inch

8. White wine is not specific enough. The purpose of a recipe is to produce a standard product. This would not be possible if an ingredient description allows the employees to select from a variety of different products. White wine should be specified as dry (lack of sugar) or sweet. Otherwise a nonstandard product could result.

9. Twenty chicken breasts will not produce a standard product at a standard cost. When the breasts are described properly as explained in number 6, the correct quantity would be a weight. Then the recipe would instruct the cook to use a specific number of pounds of boneless chicken breasts, diced into 1/2 inch pieces. This would produce a standard product.

10. The quantities for the peppers and bamboo shoots should not be given by units or cups. What is a medium-sized pepper? It would probably vary depending on who is making the decision. The final product would also vary, both in cost and quality. The bamboo shoots violate two of the guidelines. Five cups should be given as 1 1/4 quarts. They are the same thing, but it is easier and faster to measure one and one-quarter quarts than 5 cups. The other mistake is in using a volume measure. Weight would be more accurate, and should be used.

11. Three teaspoons equal 1 tablespoon. Measuring a tablespoon requires one measuring action; measuring three teaspoons requires three actions. Use the larger unit of measure whenever possible.

12. What is the measuring unit for the egg white? Most people would correctly assume that it is "each," but the recipes should not allow any assumptions. If you want the white from one egg to be used, write it as: one each. It could just as easily be one cup, one dozen, one pound, and so forth.

13. Four tablespoons equal 1/4 cup. The larger measure should be used.

14. Preprep instructions are given for the chicken breasts. If the breasts had been listed properly, this would not be necessary. It complicates the directions.

15. The same comment applies to the peppers and bamboo shoots.

16. The ingredients for steps three and four can be combined with the diced chicken breasts, and the method can be rewritten. In that case the instructions would describe how to blend together the cornstarch, water, salt, soy sauce, white wine, and sugar to prepare a marinade to pour over the diced breasts. How long should the breasts marinate? The recipe instructs the cook to "let sit," which is not very specific.

17. These instructions are incomplete and confusing. "Heat (oil) until sizzling" How hot is *sizzling*? "Place chicken in wok and stir fry until done." What does *done* mean? "Remove chicken and set aside." Remove with a slotted spoon so the chicken will not be oily?

18. The cook is instructed to stir-fry the pepper until done and then to add the chicken pieces and cook for one minute longer. The same comment made in number 17 about the word *done* applies here. Also, what happened to the bamboo shoots? We were given elaborate instructions on how to prepare them, but now we apparently do not use them for anything.

19. The various steps and ingredients should be clearly separated with lines. It would make the recipe easier to follow. The most serious mistake on this recipe is the total lack of product standards. There should be standards given on some of the steps, and the recipe must end with a complete description of the finished product. Color, texture, and temperature can all be used to describe a standard dish, and they should be.

Exhibit 4.10 Correct Standard Recipe

NAME: Polynesian Chicken in Orange Sauce   **YIELD**: 58 servings

Pan Size: 2 large sheet pans   **Portion Size**: 1/2 breast

Temperature: 300° F. in   **Cooking Time**: 25 minutes
Forced Convection Oven

Ingredients	Quantity		Method
Chicken breasts, bone in, split, 4 oz. each Butter, melted Orange liqueur	58 pieces 1.25 lbs. 5.0 oz.	1.	Blend together the butter and orange liqueur and brush the chicken with the mixture.
Flour, seasoned Eggs, slightly beaten Bread crumbs Margerine, melted	1.5 lbs. 1.5 doz. 2.0 lbs. 2.0 lbs.	2.	Roll chicken in seasoned flour, shake off excess. Dip in the egg and roll in the bread crumbs. Place on greased sheet pans. Place 29 breasts on each pan. Drizzle the margarine over the breasts. Bake for 10 minutes at 300° F.
Orange juice Tarragon Orange peel, grated Ginger root, fresh, grated Salt	1.0 gallon 3.0 tbl. 3 tbl. 0.5 tbl. 1.0 tbl.	3.	Mix together in a saucepan and bring to a simmer over medium heat.
Cornstarch Water, cold	6.0 oz. 0.75 cup	4.	Dissolve cornstarch in water and add to the orange mixture (step 3). Simmer, stirring constantly until the sauce reaches a medium-thick consistency. Remove from the heat. Spoon 1/2 of the sauce over the chicken breasts, and reserve the remaining half. Cover each pan with foil and bake another 15 minutes or until the breasts reach an internal temperature of 180° F. Remove from oven and spoon over the remaining sauce.
Coconut flakes, toasted	0.5 lb.	5.	Sprinkle over the chicken immediately prior to service.

foods and see whether there are any yield variances:

Coffee, ground: No. (There may certainly be waste, but this is very different from yield.)

Onions: If purchased peeled, no. If purchased unpeeled, yes.

Potatoes: Same as onions.

Green peppers: Yes.

Roasts (beef, lamb, pork, veal): Yes.

Steaks: If purchased portioned, no; otherwise, yes.

Lettuce: Yes (unless purchased salad-ready).

Carrots: Yes (unless purchased peeled).

Eggs, shell (fresh): Yes.

Lobster tail, frozen: No.

Crab legs, frozen: No.

Shrimp, green headless: If served peeled, yes; if served in shell, no.

Tomatoes: Yes.

Canned whole tomatoes: Yes.

Canned crushed tomatoes: No.

Canned pear halves: Yes.

Canned fruit cocktail: Yes and no, depending upon whether the juice is used with the fruit pieces. In general, yes.

Milk, cream, ice cream: No.

Flour, sugar, salt: No.

We could go on, but it is not necessary. The following generalizations can be made:

1. Most nonportion-controlled meats have yield variances.
2. All meats to be cut and/or roasted have yield variances.
3. Most fresh fruits and vegetables have yield variances.
4. Many canned goods have yield variances.
5. Many staples (except canned goods) do not have yield variances.
6. Most dairy products do not have yield variances

As with most forms, there are a variety of yield test formats that could be used. Exhibit 4.11 illustrates one such chart. The purpose of a yield test is to determine what the actual cost of serving a product is. This is called the edible portion cost (or the EP cost). The cost of buying the product is called the as purchased cost (the AP cost). The reason portion-controlled foods are attractive from a control standpoint is that the AP and EP are the same. In other words, a steak that costs $4.50 when delivered costs $4.50 when served.

Management must know what their products cost them to serve. Many, if not most, of the products they handle suffer losses; therefore they should become involved in yield testing. The logic of a yield test is that you begin with a product that has a weight and cost. It can be any product: meat, seafood, poultry, carrots, onions, canned goods, and so on. What you have to know is how much there is to start with and what the dollar value is. The second step is to begin removing weight or product, as in trimming off fat, removing bones, using part of the meat for other purposes, draining the syrup or juice from canned goods, and so forth. When this process is completed, the product remaining is what is available to be served, the EP. Much of the difference between this and the starting or purchased weight is discarded or has no value. Bones, fat, syrup, peelings, skin, and so on are all examples of this. A good foodservice operator would not throw these away. They would be used for stocks and in cooking to add flavor, but they have no economic value. The operator would not pay anything for them. Some of the product removed would have economic value. Meat trimmings that can be ground and used in hamburgers, tenderloin meat from a short loin, and cap meat (swiss steak) from a rib roast are examples of this. In this and similar cases, not only is the weight removed from the purchase weight, but the dollar value (determined by what would be paid if purchased) is deducted from the total value. When the process is finished, the result will be X amount of product remaining, which is worth Y amount of dollars. The EP cost can then be calculated either by portion or by pound.

Some Examples:

Product: Short Loin - 23 pounds at $1.95/lb.

Total value = $44.85

End product = boneless strip steaks

Intermediate Products and Value (if any)

Bones: 4 pounds at $0.00 = $0.00

Fat: 6.25 pounds at $0.00 = $0.00

Hamburger: 4.25 pounds at $1.65/pound = $7.01

Tenderloin: 1.50 pounds at $4.25/pound = $6.38

There would be 7 pounds of strip steak remaining (23 pounds minus [4 + 6.25 + 4.25 + 1.50]). This 7 pounds would be worth $31.46 ($44.85 - [$7.01 + $6.38]). The strip steak,

therefore, has an EP cost or serving cost of $4.49 per pound. ($31.46 ÷ 7 pounds), which is considerably higher than the AP (purchase) cost of $1.95/pound!

———————

Product: Whole Tenderloin - 8 pounds at $2.75/pound

Total value = $22.00

End product = filet mignon steaks

Intermediate Products and Value (if any)

Fat: 2.5 pounds at $0.00 = $0.00

Tenderloin tips: 0.5 pound at $3.50/pound = $1.75

Brochette meat: 1.0 pound at $3.62/pound = $3.62

There would be 4 pounds of filet mignon meat remaining (8 pounds -[2.5 + 0.5 + 1.0]), worth $16.63 ($22.00 - [$1.75 + $3.62]). The EP cost per pound is $4.16 ($16.63 ÷ 4 pounds).

Exhibit 4.11. Yield Test Chart

[handwritten: PRACTICE COST FACTOR = 2.30]

Item: _SHORT LOIN_   Date: _____

AP Price $_1.95/LB_   Weight: _23_   Total Cost: $_44.85_

[handwritten margin: MIDTERM]

Breakdown Product	Weight (lb.)	Value (lb.)	Total Value $	Cost (EP) lb.	Portion Size	Cost
BONES	4	—	–			
FAT	6.25	—	–			
HAMBURGER	4.25	1.65	7.01			
TENDERLOIN	1.50	4.25	6.38			
	16		13.39	.84		
STRIP STEAK	7		31.46	4.49		
	23		44.85			

Product: Whole Carrots (tops included) - 12 pounds at $0.27/pound

Total value = $3.24

End product = peeled, topped carrots

Intermediate Products and Value (if any)

Peelings: 1.0 pound at $0.00 = $0.00

Tops: .75 pound at $0.00 = $0.00

There would be 10.25 pounds of carrots remaining (12 pounds - [1.0 + .75]) worth $3.24. The EP cost per pound would be $.32 per pound $3.24 ÷ 10.25 pounds, rounding off.

Product: Whole Beef Rib (untrimmed) - 30 pounds at $2.00/pound

Total value = $60.00

End product = cooked meat, no bone

Intermediate Products and Value (if any)

gat: 4.5 pounds at $0.00 = $0.00

Bones: 6.5 pounds at $0.00 = $0.00

Cap meat (swiss steak): 2.0 pounds at $1.75/pound = $3.50

Ground beef: 0.75 pound at $1.65/pound = $1.24

Cooking loss: 4.75 pounds at $0.00 = $0.00

There would be 11.5 pounds of servable boneless rib roast after trimming and cooking (30 pounds - [4.5 + 6.5 + 2.0 + .75 + 4.75]) worth $55.26, ($60.00 - [$3.50 + $1.24]). The EP cost per pound is $4.81.

To use the yield chart shown in Exhibit 4.11, fill in the heading with the product, AP cost per pound, weight, and total item cost. Then list the various breakdown products in column 1 with their weight and economic value (if any). The last product listed will be the desired end product. Its weight is determined by subtracting the weights of all the breakdown products from the starting weight. Its value is calculated by subtracting the value, (if any) of each of the breakdown products from the total cost. The EP cost per pound is calculated by dividing the total EP cost by the total EP pounds. The last two columns provide space for determining the EP portion cost. As shown, this process can and should be used with any type of product. It can be used to calculate the effect of cooking losses as well.

Yield testing is not a precise process. Food is a natural product, and even with apparently similar items, there are apt to be variances that will result in different yields. If the foods tested are well specified and if the test is performed several times, the average yield can be used. That will be sufficiently accurate. It is recommended to check the yields from time to time to assure their accuracy. In fact, all foodservice operations should have an ongoing testing program so that all products will be retested over an extended period—such as once a year.

Precosting

Once yield testing has been done, the operator is in a position to precost the menu. Precosting is what must be done to produce the information we used in the menu profit analysis section. We took a menu and, using the selling price, serving cost, and number sold of each item on the menu, performed a series of analyses. Precosting is the process that we use to get the total serving cost of each product. Yield testing is a preliminary step to precosting.

A menu item cost consists of three elements:

1. *Cost of the product itself*. This is a cost unique to this item.
2. *Cost of the garnish*. This may or may not be unique to each menu item. It is possible for all foods to have the same garnish, and it is possible for each food to be garnished differently.
3. *Cost of supplementary items*. This may or may not be a cost unique to each menu item. In a strictly table d' hote menu, all entrees are served with the same accompaniments. For example: roll, butter, salad, vegetable or potato, dessert, and

beverage. It would be more usual to have different accompanying items depending on what was ordered. At any rate, this cost category would include all foods served with the entree.

We will look at how each category is calculated.

Product Cost. To obtain this cost, the recipe has to be costed. A product cost analysis sheet (Exhibit 4.12) is used for this purpose. There should be one for each recipe used in the operation. There will be more recipes than menu items since some menu items use a variety of foods. For example: a stuffed tomato recipe could give the option of stuffing the tomato with 3 ounces of chicken salad, tuna salad, or shrimp salad. There would then have to be separate recipes for each of these salads and separate cost sheets for each. The recipe provides the information for the first and third columns in Exhibit 4.12: the ingredients and the amounts used. The source for the second column, the unit price, is the purchase records. Problems arise

when recipes direct the use of foods in units different from the purchase units. In some cases, it is unavoidable, and the purchase unit price has to be changed to accommodate the usage unit. In most cases, however, this is simply sloppy recipe writing. A recipe that cannot be costed accurately will probably not be produced consistently either. As pointed out in the recipe section, 1 cup of diced onions will not produce a consistent product. In costing, we would also have difficulties since onions are purchased by the pound, and the weight of a cup of diced onions will vary considerably. When recipe quantities are given in weight, the costing is much easier and more accurate. Most liquid products are purchased by volume—milk, oil, sour cream, juices, and so on. These are usually also specified on a recipe by volume, so costing is easy and accurate. There are some occasions where differences between pricing units and usage units are necessary. We will list a variety of foods, covering all three categories, and discuss the costing of each.

Exhibit 4.12. Product Cost Analysis

Product _____

Ingredient	Unit Price	Amount Used	Ingredient Cost

Total Product Cost _____ Selling Price _____

Yield _____ Food Cost % _____

Cost per Portion _____ Gross Profit _____

1. *Shrimp* - $7.00 per pound - 6 each per serving: This cannot be costed unless the shrimp are purchased by count (as they should be). Then it would be simple: shrimp 16 to 20 - $7.00 per pound - 6 each per serving. This indicates that the shrimp, which cost $7.00 per pound, are sized so that each pound contains 16 to 20 individual shrimp. For costing purposes, use an average count, an average of 18 per pound or a cost of $.39 for each shrimp.

2. *Tabasco* - $.80 per 5 ounces - 1 teaspoon (a 5-ounce jar costs $.80): This can be costed accurately since tabasco sauce is a liquid, and there are 2 tablespoons of liquid measure per liquid ounce. We know that 3 teaspoons equals 1 tablespoon, so 1 teaspoon equals 1/6 ounce. Therefore the cost is 2.7 cents or 3 cents rounded off.

3. *Mayonnaise* - $18.00, 4/1 - 1 cup: This means that mayonnaise is packed in 1 gallon jars, four to a case (4/1). Therefore, 1 gallon costs $4.50, and 1 cup (1/16 gallon) costs $0.28.

4. *Dill weed* - $3.50 per pound - 0.25 cup: Spices and herbs are very difficult to cost. Dill weed, as given, cannot be costed without further information. If we know how much volume 1 pound of dill weed occupies, it could be accurately costed. Spices and herbs are in the third category, products that have to be handled differently. In this case, someone must take a pound of dill weed (or thyme, or dry mustard, or marjoram, or rosemary, or tarragon) and measure and record the volume. This has to be done only once, but it does have to be done. If it was found that one pound of dill weed was equal to 3.5 cups, the cost sheet would have: Dill Weed = $3.50 per pound (3.5 cups) - 0.25 cup. The dill weed cost would be $1.00 per cup, and the recipe cost would be $0.25. Most spices and herbs can be accurately costed by this method.

5. *Sugar* - .30 per pound - 1.5 pounds: This is easy, but what if the amount was given as 3 cups? It happens that sugar is one of those products similar to water, 2 cups equals 1 pound. Therefore, 1.5 pounds and 3 cups are the same, and sugar could be costed equally accurately with volumes or weights. So could salt, rice, oil, butter, shortening, milk, sour cream, yogurt, stock, wine, distilled spirits, or beer.

6. *Garlic* - $0.25 per bulb - 2 cloves or 1 teaspoon: Here you simply have to make an estimation. Garlic is purchased by the bulb, and the cloves can be counted. In this case it would be written: Garlic - $.25 per bulb (20/1) - 2 cloves, which means there are twenty cloves per bulb, and the cost for two cloves would be 2.5 cents or 3 cents rounded off. Garlic may also be given in volume, which would probably be more accurate since the cloves vary in size. In this case, a few bulbs of garlic have to be chopped or minced to determine how many tablespoons will be yielded per bulb. The recipe then can be costed with some accuracy.

7. *Eggs* - $.62 per dozen - 6 each: No problem here. Six eggs are half a dozen, and the recipe cost is $.31. In professional quantity recipes, however, the egg will probably be given in weight. The reason is that baking (if that is what the eggs are used for) is much more precise and scientific than cooking is. Specifying eggs by number, even if you add medium or large, is simply not precise enough. The eggs must be weighed for optimum results. There are two options. One is to purchase frozen eggs by weight, which can be used and costed accurately, or to crack a quantity of eggs and weigh them. We strongly recommend the former. Not only will it provide increased costing accuracy and product consistency, but it will be less expensive.

8. *Flour* - $.18 per pound - .25 pound: This can be accurately costed, whereas flour - .18 per pound - 10 cups cannot. There are about 4 cups of flour per pound, which can

be used as a ballpark estimate, but it will not yield accurate costs. Therefore, flours should always be weighed.

9. *Olive oil* - $20.75 per case (4/1) - 1 quart: The olive oil costs $20.75 for a 4-gallon case (4/1) or $5.19 per gallon or $1.30 per quart. Therefore it can be accurately costed. Much of the confusion surrounding costing comes from the nomenclature. For example, why does 4/1 mean a case of 4 one-gallon containers, yet 6/1 means a case of 6 number-10 cans? The answer is that this is why food control is difficult; there are incredible inconsistencies. One simply must have experience and knowledge of how the various foods are packaged and what the packing nomenclature is. Distilled spirits, by way of contrast, are much easier. All products come in cases, each of which contains twelve bottles, and virtually all bottles inventoried are the same size. Food, unfortunately, is not so consistent.

10. *Tomato* - $12.00 per 50 - 4 slices (a box of tomatoes costs $12.00 and contains fifty): This cannot be costed without knowing how many slices should be obtained from a tomato; in other words, having a standard. It should be written: tomato, sliced 8/1 - $12.00/50 - four slices. The cost for four slices or half a tomato would be $.12.

11. *Tomato* -$12.00 per lug - 1 each: This cannot be costed. If it was written as: tomato - $12.00/50 - 1 each, which means there are fifty tomatoes (two layers of five rows of five each or 5 x 5), and they cost $12.00, the cost per tomato could be determined. It is $.24.

12. *Lettuce liner* - $10.95 per case - 1.5 ounces: Lettuce is normally purchased in standard cases of twenty-four heads. The weight of the cases will vary, as will the yield. The only way to cost this is to determine a conversion factor based on yield testing over a period of time. The serving size could also be written as two leaves of lettuce, and this requires testing too.

13. *Celery* - $26.00 per case - 1.25 pounds: Unless celery is purchased in 100 percent usable cleaned and trimmed stalks, which can be done, it cannot be costed, even if the case weight is given. The unit cost here should be the EP cost per pound determined by a yield test. In that case, it would read: celery, trimmed—$.40 per pound - 1.25 pounds. This can be costed accurately. The same process applies to onions, carrots, green peppers, broccoli—any fresh fruits or vegetables that do not have 100 percent yield.

14. *Olives, stuffed* - $21.00 per case (4/1) - 3 each: This is a common way to write the recipe. The olives should be portion controlled by count, but the cost cannot be known unless one knows how many olives there are in a gallon jar. The supplier may have this information, and it should probably be on your specification. If it isn't—count them. It has to be done only a couple of times, the second time with a different order.

15. *Bacon, sliced* - $1.67 per pound - 2 slices: This cannot be costed without knowing the number of slices per pound. This should be part of the specification. It would then be written: Bacon, sliced 24/1 - $1.67 per pound - 2 slices. There are twenty-four slices per pound, each one costs $.07, and the recipe cost is $.14.

These then are the procedures for precosting the recipe itself.

Garnish Cost

The second cost element to be calculated is the cost of the garnish. This always causes difficulties, mostly because so few operations have standards. When management cannot predict exactly how or what the plates will be garnished with, it is impossible to cost with accuracy. The first step, therefore, is to standardize all garnishes and plate presentations. There are two ways the cost can be determined. One involves costing an individual garnish just as we were costing individual recipes. The other uses an estimation technique. In the first, you simply prepare a recipe for each garnish used and cost it out. In the case of items like parsley, watercress, and fruits, you will have to do some yield testing. For example, how many plates can you reasonably expect one bunch of parsley to garnish? There will be some loss, and you want to have some idea of how much. Garnishing usually results in considerable waste, so you should be realistic and liberal when calculating losses. The estimation method can be quite accurate. You have to be able to isolate the total costs of all garnish ingredients. The objective is to come up with a grand total of all garnish costs over a period of a few weeks or a month. Yields are not important; you calculate only the actual dollars spent. Say parsley is used only for garnishing, for example, and at the beginning of the month there were six bunches on hand. During the month you purchased seventy-four bunches and had three left at the end. The calculations would look like this:

OI	6		
Purchases	74		
Available	80		
EI	3		
Used	77	at $.27 =	$20.79

This cost would be added to the other garnish costs (if any). The total dollar cost would be divided by the total guest count. If you served 1,800 people, and your total garnishing expense was $72.00, the average cost per guest would be $.04. It would be both fair and accurate to assign a garnish cost of $.04 to each portion cost. This is a useful method for calculating other costs as well. It can be used for the spices in recipes. Instead of attempting to figure the the cost of teaspoons and tablespoons of the many spices and herbs inventoried, the operator will simply take the opening inventory, add the purchases, and subtract the ending inventory of all spices and herbs to get a total period cost. This will then be

divided by the total entree sales count. If the result were $.02, then when costing, the operator would add $.02 to each portion to cover all spices. Some would be a little higher, others a little lower, but the average meal would contain $.02 worth of spices. The important thing is that the cost is adequately covered in the precosting process. This method can be used for table catsup, mustard, steak sauces, table butter pats, coffee cream, table salt and pepper, and other such foods.

Supplementary Cost

In this category we have the cost of serving whatever else is served with the entree. Even if the menu is strictly à la carte, there are additional costs. The guests will use salt, pepper, and other table items. They will probably be given rolls and butter or a cracker basket. The costing technique for these types of foods has just been described. Most menus today, however, are a mixture of à la carte and table d'hote, and there will be a variety of foods accompanying the entrees. Here, as with garnish cost, it is best to determine an average cost. Example: Each guest gets a choice of potato or vegetable. We must cost each possible choice and must have the number of each chosen. When this information is available, we can easily determine the cost of offering this meal option to our guests.

Item	Cost	Number Ordered	Total Cost
Potatoes: Baked	.18	96	$17.28
French fried	.08	64	5.12
Whipped	.06	17	1.02
Vegetables: (all frozen - use an average cost per 3-ounce portion)	.12	72	8.64
TOTAL		249	$32.06

$$\text{Average cost per guest} = \frac{\$32.06}{249} = \underline{\$.13}$$

Therefore you add $.13 to the recipe and garnish costs. The list of supplementary items can be very short or very long, but whatever it is, the total cost of serving the food must be accounted for.

Precosting Summary. The objective of precosting is to predetermine ahead of time how much each item on the menu should cost if everything is done properly. In the analysis section, we discussed several ways of using this information. It is essential information, and therefore it must be accurate to work. A cost consists of the cost of the main product itself (called the recipe cost), the garnish cost, and the supplementary cost. All must be calculated carefully. Naturally, these costs will fluctuate due to changing food purchase prices, and it is recommended that the cost record be updated at least two times yearly—more often if possible. There are computer systems available that can update the product costs daily. All they need is someone to put in price changes, and a report can be generated in minutes, either printed, on a screen, or both. We discuss computers and their control applications for foodservice operations in Chapter 13.

Portion Control

Portion control is whatever action management takes to assure that standard portions are prepared and served. The most sophisticated computerized system is useless if someone puts three egg wedges on the plate instead of two. There are three levels at which portion control can be imposed. The foods can be purchased portioned. This is the best method. If the purpose of portion control is to assure that a standard portion will be served, how could this be better done than by purchasing a standard portion? Preportioned foods give total consistency because there are no yields to be tested and no portioning mistakes to be made. If any portion mistakes are made, they will be made by the processor or supplier and, hopefully, rejected when sent to the foodservice unit.

The second level of portion control consists of preportioning the products within the operation. Examples are: cutting steaks, dishing ice cream in the freezer prior to the meal, preportioning and dishing salads for a banquet, portioning and individually bagging meat for cooked-to-order items, precooking and portioning pasta, preslicing sandwich meat and cheese. There are lots of these preportioning activities that can be performed.

A general guideline to follow is: Do not portion anything at the point of service if it can possibly be avoided. Much better control potential exists when portioning is done during preprep or preparation. These activities are easier to supervise since they are not being performed under meal pressure. Mistakes made prior to a meal can often be reversed, but mistakes made during a meal period nearly always result in problems.

The third, and least desirable portioning level is when it is done at the point of service. There is less control at this level. Mistakes are more likely to occur, and they are less easily reversed. It is unavoidable that some foods must be portioned when served, but management should carefully evaluate every single product from a portioning standpoint and assign each one the best level possible. With steaks, it would be level one, preportioned. In food products where preportioned purchases are not feasible or possible, attempt to portion prior to service. The only products that should end up being portioned on the line are those which cannot be accommodated by the other levels. In other words, they are not designated for level-three portioning but end up there by necessity. Examples of foods that generally must be portioned when ordered are: all steam table items that have to be dished from a pan, such as stew, vegetables, soups, chop suey, breaded shrimp and scallops, and french-fried potatoes.

We will examine a typical luncheon and dinner menu and assign the portioning level to each menu item.

The main concern is for those products that have to be portioned when ordered. We will go

	Menu Item	Portioning Level
Lunch	Soup	III—Must be portioned when ordered.
Menu	Chef Steak	I—Can be purchased portioned.
	Stuffed Tomato	II—Should be prepared ahead of time. If forecast is low, they will be assembled to order, and there there will probably be portioning inconsistencies.
	Chopped Steak	I or II—Can be purchased portioned or portioned in the operation.
	Quiche Lorraine	III—For quality purposes, should not be cut ahead of time.
	Spinach Pie	III—Same reasoning as quiche.
	Sandwiches— various	II and III—Some can be assembled ahead of time.
	Hamburger, Cheeseburger	I—Purchase portioned (including cheese, or portion cheese yourself).
	Stew	III
	Daily Specials	II or III—Depending on the type of product.
Dinner	King Crab Legs	III—Purchased frozen but generally portioned at point of service.
Menu	Filet Mignon	I—Purchase portioned.
	New York Strip	I—Purchase portioned.
	Top Sirloin	I—Purchase portioned.
	Sautéed Shrimp	II or III—Can be preportioned and bagged, otherwise portion when ordered.
	Scallops, sautéed	II or III—Same as shrimp.
	Broiled Pork Chops	I—Purchase portioned.
	Salmon Steak	I or II—Best control if purchased portioned, otherwise portion ahead of meal.
	Fried Chicken	II—Cut and portion ahead and bag.
	Stuffed Trout	I and II—Purchase portioned trout and stuff with preportioned dressing prior to meal.
	Beef Brochette	II—Marinate cubes of meat and assemble skewers ahead. Broil to order.
	Beef Liver	I—Purchase portioned.
	Prime Rib	III—Must be sliced to order.

back through both menus and make portioning recommendations for those specific items.

Lunch

Soup: One of the most effective methods of controlling a portion size is with the serving dish, bowl, or glass. A soup cup has an 8-ounce capacity, but you cannot put 8 ounces in it without spilling and making a mess. It will hold 6 ounces comfortably and neatly. Therefore, set the soup portion at 6 ounces and use 8-ounce soup cups. Bowls of soup follow the same principle. Set the portion according to the reasonable bowl capacity. Sized ladles are useful but not necessary.

Quiche Lorraine. This is usually baked in a pie shell. Control the portion size by number of slices per pie plate. Even numbers are easier and will yield more consistent slices; that is, four, six, or eight slices rather than five, seven, or nine. If a six-slice portion is too large, use a smaller pie shell rather than cutting it into seven slices. Pie markers are useful, but not essential.

Spinach Pie. This is most often baked in square or rectangular pans. Like the pies, they should be portioned by count, so many pieces per pan. Establish standard counts and cutting methods; that is, "cut 3 x 4 or twelve orders."

Sandwiches. If they cannot be assembled ahead, the components (meat, cheese, bacon slices, tomato slices, and so on) should all be preportioned.

Stew. This must be dished as ordered. Like the soup, the serving bowl can be a useful control tool. Standard portioning tools should be used. A scale can also provide accurate portions. Use a scale that can be tared for the bowl: when the bowl is on the platform, the scale registers 0. Then add stew until the desired weight is attained. The best method though is to control through the bowl size because it is faster. A useful portioning technique for banquets is to divide the product evenly among several pans. For example, if you were serving stew (or vegetables, or any dish-up item) to one hundred persons, do not put one pan with all one hundred portions on the serving line. Divide it into four

pans of twenty-five each. When the first pan is replaced, take a quick count to see whether 25 orders have been dished. If not, adjust the portion size. The alternative, as anyone who has ever worked on a banquet line knows, is to risk having ten orders remaining in the pan and twenty plates yet to be filled!

Daily Specials. If a dish-up item (also called a "wet" item), handle as described under stew.

Dinner Menu

King Crab Legs. Purchase as uniformly as possible and portion by count. Weight portions lead to inconsistencies in counts when the legs are not uniform. Inconsistent counts will result in guest dissatisfaction, especially when two or more orders are served at the same table. It is not only as or more accurate to count as to weigh, but it is also faster. Avoid using scales on the serving line. They can slow service and are not necessarily any more accurate for many items.

Sautéed Shrimp. Purchase uniform shrimp and portion by count.

Scallops. They will not usually be as uniform as the shrimp and are probably best portioned by weight. In this case you would either have to use a scale on the line or preweigh and bag the anticipated number of orders. The latter is recommended.

Prime Rib. Portion by count. A standing rib has seven rib bones. If the cooks are instructed to cut one slice with the bone, one without, one with and so forth, there will be a yield of fourteen orders. The yield and cost will be consistent, and it will be faster than weighing. This is a reasonable portion size. A typical rib specification is an NAMP #109, which from a medium-weight steer, will be about 22 pounds. Normal yield in cooked, servable meat (without bone) is about 50 percent. Thus, 22.0 pounds x .50 = 11.0 pounds, 11 pounds x 16 ounces = 176 ounces; 176 ounces ÷ fourteen orders = 12.5 ounces per order, and this is a normal portion size in a dinner house. When portioning meats for banquets, always use counts. Consider the following example:

Given: Entree: roast sirloin
Guest count: 250
Desired portion size (cooked): 6 ounces
Estimated cooking, carving loss = 30 percent
Therefore: 135 pounds of sirloin are required.
(135 x 70 percent yield = 94.5 pounds cooked meat;
94.5 x 16 = 1,512 ounces; 1,512 ÷ 250 guests = 6.05 ounces per portion)

If the cooking is done properly, there will be nearly 95 pounds of servable meat. The portioning could be done by weight, but it would be faster to predetermine how many slices each plate will get. If it was 2, then 500 slices will be needed to serve the 250 people. Divide 500 by the number of roasts to determine the number of slices that must be obtained from each roast. The roasts may be cut in half for easier machine or hand slicing, but this changes only the number of roasts being used in the calculation. If there were 14 pieces of meat, the count per piece would be 36. If each of the 14 pieces yielded 36 slices, there would be a total of 504, and the group could be served. This is much faster than attempting to weigh the orders. What if the cooking loss is higher than anticipated? It doesn't make any difference in the count; you still need 500 slices to serve 250 guests. If, however, you were portioning by weight, you would have to calculate a new portion size because there is now not enough meat for 250 6-ounce portions. Therefore, regardless of the cooking loss you need 500 slices, but with weights you are constantly adjusting the portion size. The recommendation would be to test one or two pieces a few minutes prior to dish-up to determine the proper machine setting to get thirty-six slices per piece, and put those neatly in a pan. While they are being plated, the others can be sliced. Skilled cooks can easily maintain the required pace so the line does not run out. The meat is being sliced practically to order. There is excellent portion control, virtually no chance of running out, little chance of underportioning, and it is fast and simple. When you use a portion scale on a banquet serving line, you slow the line down, unless you carve it well ahead of time, but then there are quality problems. Also the portion scale will not increase the control at all.

Service

The key concept in service control is that finished goods are changing departments, and there must be adequate documentation of the transfers. If other industries ran their business the way many food services do, the people responsible for selling finished goods would come to the factory and, based only on verbal orders, would take whatever they wanted. The organization would determine their sales by counting the money turned in at the end of the period. This sounds like an insane way to do business. It is, however, exactly what is done in many restaurants when waiters and/or waitresses go to the kitchen, call out orders, pick them up, and take them to the dining room where they not only serve the food, but also prepare the checks and collect the money as well. The sales are whatever these people decide to turn in! One of the main objectives of service control, therefore, is to document what foods left the kitchen, when they left, and who took them. When this information is available, comparisons can be made between kitchen counts and dining room counts. Without this control, it is impossible to assign responsibility when cost problems or shortages arise. If the kitchen used forty steaks and the steak sales count was thirty-eight, management would not know whether it is a production or service problem. When there is a record of forty steaks actually having been ordered and picked up, it is obviously a service control breakdown.

Basic Information-Gathering Methods

There are three basic methods of gathering this information:

1. Food checker
2. Kitchen prechecking machine
3. Computerized integrated prechecking system

Food Checker. This is the classic and time-tested method. It consists of assigning an individual to physically check and record all foods prior to removal to the dining room. The recording could take several forms. The checker can merely keep a tally of the various foods, or else collect check duplicates or else ring the checks up on a machine. These are the checks that will be presented to the guests. An additional benefit with this system is that the food checker can check the plate appearance of the meals, assuring that only standard products are being served. It is thus a quality control method as much as a cost control one. There are some drawbacks that prevent it from being widely used today. For one, it is expensive since it requires an additional employee. This is not an inexpensive employee either for she or he will have to be as familiar with the food standards as anyone else in the operation, including the chef. It also will have to be someone with both actual and implied authority, or else the service personnel will either ignore or dominate the checker. When an order is rejected by the checker, the servers will have a delay in their service and will not be happy about that. The cook will have to prepare the item again and will definitely not be happy about that! Unless a strong person backed by management, the checker will hesitate to antagonize either the servers or cooks, both of whom are typically strong willed and short tempered. The other drawback is that space must be provided for the checking station, and space has become more and more valuable. The result is less space available in kitchens as operators attempt to maximize public area space, that is, dining rooms and lounges. In spite of the potential control benefits, this system is fading from use.

Prechecking Machines. The initial attempt to replace food checkers (smart operators did not want to eliminate the function, just the person) was with prechecking machines. These were registers located in the kitchen. Orders were written on standardized guest checks, and the checks had to be rung on the register prior to presentation at the cooking station. The only authorization for an order to be prepared was a properly registered guest check. Each service person had their own code number, so at the end of a meal period the register could be "read." It would show the sales value of all food that left the kitchen as well as how much each person was responsible for. This enabled management to compare dollars of food prepared with dollars of food collected and to compare total counts as well as individual counts. In other words, if there was a $20.00 variance one evening, it could be traced to the specific individual(s) responsible. This system also has drawbacks:

1. The cooks are responsible for checking the prices to ascertain that they are accurate. Cooks normally do not have to pay much attention to prices, they often forget them, and they are frequently working under stress. The result is that mistakes and oversights are frequent.

2. The machines kept only dollar totals. There were no records of specific menu items. It is fine to know that a $20.00 variance occurred, but what the operator really wants to know is which specific foods were missing.

3. A waiter or waitress wishing to circumvent the system does not have to ring the wrong price or avoid ringing the order at all. They merely use someone else's key and the shortage(s) would be traced to another person. Or they could simply use a variety of keys, thereby spreading the shortage.

4. Mistakes will be made from time to time. When this occurs, the mistakes have to be "voided," or removed from the machine. If the operation is sloppy in handling voids, the service personnel can claim legitimate transactions as mistakes, get them voided, and keep the money when collected.

5. There would typically be only one prechecking machine. In a busy restaurant, there could be tie-ups at the register. This delays production and keeps service personnel in the

kitchen instead of in the dining room where they belong.

6. The service personnel are making pricing decisions. They are required to ring all prices. The fact that controls must be established to check that correct prices are used indicates a control weakness. This is something that cannot be avoided with this equipment. In fact, it is an even worse problem when checks are being handwritten. There are systems available, however, which remove price setting as an employee responsibility.

7. There is a potential problem with nonentree items since the check duplicate is normally given to the hot station. What is the authorization for salads, appetizers, and desserts? One solution is to have additional duplicates, but this is expensive, and can make the check writing more awkward. The machine can be designed to produce a receipt (much as any register produces receipts from a roll of register tape). The duplicate receipt is then used as the authorization for all additional items. It is always available since each time a transaction is recorded, a receipt will be produced. The usual procedure is to circle the desired product and present the receipt to the appropriate station. For example, in ringing an order, the check would look like this:

Baked Chicken	$ 5.95
Butt Steak	7.25
Sole	6.15
Shrimp Cocktail	1.75
	$21.10

The duplicate would be presented to the steam table where the entrees would be prepared. The shrimp cocktail would be ignored. The server would then take the receipt and circle the $1.75 for shrimp cocktail, perhaps even write it in, and present it to the pantry.

$ 5.95
7.25
6.15
(1.75)Shrimp Cocktail

$21.10

It is important that these receipts then be kept and secured by the pantry personnel. Otherwise they could be used over and over again, and there would be no record in the machine beyond the first one. Desserts would be handled in the same way.

Computerized, Integrated Prechecking System. This is very similar to the one just described, but with some very significant differences: (Note: not all systems will have all of the following features.)

1. There are usually several prechecking machines available, and they are more apt to be located in the dining room than in the kitchen. There is less chance of tie-ups at the register, and the service personnel do not have to go to the kitchen to ring the checks. They could take an order, ring it up, get some drinks for a second table, take the order on a third table, ring that up, and then take all checks to the kitchen.

2. The machines are equipped with preset keys. The personnel do not ring prices, but press specific food keys, one key for each menu item. The machine will automatically print the item along with the predetermined price. The employees are no longer responsible for setting prices. They have no control over the prices, and mistakes (premeditated or otherwise) are eliminated.

3. There is a record not only of dollars but also specific items sold. There are other ways in which to gather this information, but this is the easiest and most accurate.

4. All the registers can be electronically connected with one another or to a CPU (central processing unit). This means that a "reading" need be taken from only one machine. In some cases, it can be taken from any of them.

5. Guest check control can be provided. When a new check is started, the computer will assign a number to it. This number must be used for all subsequent transactions including payment. Management can extract information at the end of the meal about which (if any) checks are still outstanding, which employees are responsible for them, what the items involved are, and the sales value of the check.

6. There is the same problem of limited check

duplicates so register receipts are used for appetizers and desserts (and alcoholic beverages if they are registered on the same machine and on the food checks).

7. If the computer has a clock, the checks can be timed, which can be very useful to management.

8. Kitchen printers can be provided as part of the system. When the orders are rung on the prechecking machines in the dining room, the order will be printed on a machine in the kitchen. The service person thus does not have to go to the kitchen to turn in orders, only to pick up food. This can be very useful and should increase the portion of the time the servers spend in the dining room. A potential drawback is that if the kitchen gets a little behind, they cannot slow the orders down as they can when the orders are brought in personally. There is, in fact, the danger of a frustrated cook unplugging the printer. You can imagine the chaos that would cause! Some operators claim another disadvantage is that there is no opportunity to clarify confusing orders. The answer to that is that it is the responsibility of management to standardize all check writing procedures so there will not be any misunderstandings. When a waiter or waitress must constantly interpret the check before it can be prepared, there is something wrong.

"Dupe" System. Another system, long used for documenting removal of food from the kitchen, is the "dupe" system. With this system, the check duplicates are retained and audited. The only authorization for a cook to prepare any food is a guest check duplicate, and these should then provide a record of all foods that have been ordered. The duplicates, as in the case of register receipts, must be secured to prevent their being reused. Auditing—or counting the orders, and totaling the money—must be done to make the system useful. It can be tedious, time consuming, and prone to errors. Another drawback is that this system either requires several duplicates, so appetizers and desserts can be controlled, or else it will ignore these types of products and control only entrees. The former is expensive, the latter provides poor control.

There are many sophisticated point-of-sale (POS) systems available today. Foodservice operators should investigate and evaluate them carefully to determine which is best suited to their needs. It is not reasonable to ignore this technology on the grounds that it is too expensive or that it is not needed, although many operators do just that. These operators are under the impression that all they have to do is control costs. Cost control is the most important part of food control, but sales must be controlled as well. If not, there can be a substantial decrease in profits. These systems offer potentially high levels of control. To ignore them because of personal feeling or prejudice could be very costly.

Guest Check Control

This is a basic and necessary part of any effective food-control system. It begins with numbered checks, although that in and of itself does not assure control. Virtually all operations have numbered guest checks, but few have true control. There is no real control unless every single check can be accounted for, each night, week, month, and year. The importance of check control lies in the fact that without it service personnel can sell food, throw away or destroy the check, and keep the money. Control, therefore, is simply designed to track all checks. If any check(s) were discarded, this fact would show up. As pointed out earlier, people will not do something like throw away a check when they are assured the missing check will be noted. Checks will still be missing from time to time. Mistakes will happen, and customer frauds unfortunately happen too. A good guest-check control system will only pinpoint the fact of a missing check; how management follows up will determine the ultimate effectiveness of the control.

The following are a series of steps that, if followed, should assure that all checks will be documented:

1. Purchase checks in large batches, all consecutively numbered. Some operators attempt to save money by purchasing odd lots of numbers. This makes it very difficult to keep track of the numbers because there are so many

legitimate sequences. We will assume that a batch of 25,000 checks has been purchased; the number sequence being 1 to 25,000.

2. These checks must be provided maximum security. The office safe is probably the single most secure location in the operation, but it is unlikely that it could hold 25,000 checks. In many units, the second most secure area is the liquor storeroom (or it should be). Therefore, we will put the 25,000 checks in the liquor room. We will have a perpetual inventory on the checks, by location. At this point the inventory looks like this:

Location	Check Numbers
Storeroom	1 - 25,000

3. A working supply will be issued to the office, perhaps 1,000 checks. They should be issued on the authority of a requisition. The requisition will be posted to the perpetual. The inventory is now:

Location	Check Numbers
Storeroom	1001 - 25,000
Office (safe)	1 - 1,000

4. The cashier will requisition checks from the office. This requisition will also be posted to the perpetual. If the request was for 500 checks, the inventory would be:

Location	Check Numbers
Storeroom	1001 - 25,000
Office (safe)	501 - 1,000
Cashier Station	1 - 500

5. The cashier will issue checks to the service personnel. There are two ways this is typically done. One is to issue a block of checks to each person. These checks are usually bound in pads of fifty. The checks not used during a shift are returned to the cashier. A guest check control sheet will be used to record these transactions. It is important that someone audit these sheets daily to assure that the starting number corresponds to the closing number of the day before. For example, if this were not done, Joan could tear two checks off the pad when checking in the next day, and sign out checks number 26 - 50. She could keep the sales from check numbers 24 and 25 and her count would balance at the end of the shift. It is not necessary to count the checks of each individual server. In fact, this can be difficult since the checks paid are not generally filed by service persons but according to the type of transaction: cash or charge—American Express, MasterCharge, house account, and so on. In this case what the cashier should do is compare the total number of checks used with the total counted. If they balance, it is unnecessary to count each server's checks. Where there is guest check control, it will balance nearly all the time. When there are shortages, each individual's checks will have to be counted. This is done to determine who was short and also which specific check(s) are missing.

The second method is to issue the checks one

Name	Out	Check Initials	Numbers In	Initials	Checks Used	Checks Counted	Checks Missing
Joan	1 - 50	*Jm*	24 - 50	*Jm*	23	22	#21
Al	51 - 100	*AJ*	73 - 100	*AJ*	22	22	-
Mary	101 - 150	*ms*	130 - 150	*ms*	29	29	-
Sid	151 - 200	*sc*	170 - 200	*sc*	19	19	-
Bonnie	201 - 250	*BH*	229 - 250	*BH*	28	28	-
TOTALS					121	120	1

by one. The guest check control sheet will look something like this:

Check	Out	In	Comments
125	SD	SD	
126	BB	BB	
127	SD	SD	
128	BB	BB	
129	MJ	MJ	
130	SD	SD	
131	BB	BB	
132	AP	AP	
133	MJ	MJ	
134	AP	AP	
135	SD	*	Guest walked out with check
136	JL	JL	
137	JL	JL	
Totals	**13**	**12**	

This type of system would be fine in a high-check-average–low-guest-turnover establishment. In the previous example, there are so many checks being used that the servers would be spending too much time signing checks in and out.

With both systems, it is important to identify the missing checks and what was served and then to find out what happened. The kitchen should have a duplicate of each check, so if the check was actually used, there would be a record of what was served. Management then knows which foods and how much money is involved. The table number, time of order (if available), and items served will probably enable the server to recall the customers, which could help determine what happened. It could be that the guest is known and perhaps was preoccupied and forgot to pay, or possibly the guest had been acting suspiciously. Maybe the cashier remembers the guest saying she or he had paid the waiter. Our assumption here is that our employees have not tried to cheat us but that there has been a breakdown somewhere. We want to understand it so it is less likely to occur again. If a guest could walk out, either the server or the cashier, or both were negligent. Perhaps the guest was quite

dissatisfied and just decided to walk out rather than complain and cause a scene. Maybe the guest got impatient and angry when he or she could not get a check and just got up and left. There are many things that could have happened, and management must determine which it was.

Of course, it could be a case of employee fraud. That is the easiest one for management to handle if they can determine that is what actually happened. Some operators equate punishment with control. Their policy is to charge service employees for missing checks. The charge may be arbitrarily determined, or it may represent the sales average of each check. This does not, however, provide control. If the standard charge were $20.00 per check, anyone would be willing to throw away a check with a $40.00 sale, pay the fine, and keep the $20.00 difference. Control is achieved by identifying the specific check(s), determining what went wrong, and then doing something about it. The minimum follow-up would involve reviewing with the personnel involved (or perhaps with all personnel) the proper procedures and how to spot guests who are likely to cause trouble. It could even be necessary to discipline someone or let someone go. This depends upon the circumstances revealed by the investigation. Employees must be held accountable for all their actions. They must be made to understand that they are responsible for the checks they are issued—not fiscally responsible but responsible nonetheless.

The used checks, along with the guest-check control sheets, will be returned to the office, where they can be posted to the perpetual inventory. It would then show the following:

Location	Check Numbers
Storeroom	1001 - 25,000
Office (safe)	501 - 1,000
Cashier Stand	261 - 500
Used check file	1 - 260 (less #26, 59, 143, 217)

If all these checks are actually in these locations and if management has investigated each missing check, there is adequate guest check control. Otherwise, there is not. One can now readily appreciate the difficulty in tracking several number sequences, which is what occurs when checks are purchased in small odd lots.

Employee Meals and Other Such Foods

Since documentation of all foods leaving the kitchen is an objective of service control, it follows that all foods must be recorded on checks. This specifically includes employee meals. Many operations have two policies: one is that all food ordered must be on a check, and the other is that employee meals can be ordered verbally. Dual (opposing) policies seldom work satisfactorily, and this one is no exception to that rule. The problem is that management has created a situation in which, if they watched a cook responding to a verbal order, they would not know whether it was a legitimate transaction or not. It could be, and it could not be. The policy should permit no exceptions: the only authorization for any food to be prepared for any reason is a properly preregistered check. If this were the policy, any deviation would be improper. It is poor control to have exceptions to rules, and it must be avoided whenever possible. An added advantage of requiring all employee meals to be processed through the prechecking system is

that there would be a record of food consumed by employees. If all the foods had been precosted, the employee meal expense could be very accurately calculated. Another way to calculate employee meal cost is to use the standard percentage cost and multiply it by the sales. The key figure in this case is the total sales value of employee meals. This information is yielded by the checks. If the employees consumed food that would normally sell for $2,165.00 and if the standard cost were 37.5 percent, the employee meal expense would be $812.00 (2165 x .375)

Employees should not be allowed to consume unrecorded food. Aside from the potential control problem, it creates difficulties in matching food usages with sales. In some types of operations these policies would not apply. Many very large operations (such as a hotel for example) may have an employee feeding facility, generally a cafeteria. It is still recommended to track individual consumption by requiring each employee to sign the register receipt after their order has been rung up. Another example would be where there is an employee meal, prepared specifically for that purpose. In that case, there should be records of who ate and the value of the food. Still another example is a food service that follows the European tradition of having the whole crew eat at one time, shortly before opening to the public. The food may be off the regular menu, it could be something the chef is experimenting with, or something prepared just for the employee meal. From an accounting standpoint, the requirement here is for an accurate assessment of the food cost.

Another type of food prepared and served with the expectation that it will not be paid for is promotional meals. There may be a two-for-one promotion, or a discount could be offered to guests who arrive and place their orders early in the meal period, or a complimentary meal may be made available for whatever reason. In all of these cases, the food should be written on a check and preregistered prior to preparation and service. It is a simple matter at the end of the meal period to reconcile the kitchen and dining room, both as to total sales dollars and item sales mix.

Expeditor System

There are several systems that can be employed for turning in and picking up food orders. We shall discuss one that seems to be gaining in favor with foodservice operators, the expeditor system. Several variations of it exist but the basic steps are as follows:

1. When the order is taken from the guest(s) it can either be submitted to a supervisor or runner in the dining room or taken to the kitchen and given directly to the expeditor. When the order is received in the dining room, it is that person's responsibility to get it to the expeditor. It is even possible, as is done in a few operations, to send the order to the kitchen via pneumatic tube, although this would be rather exotic and overly expensive for most units. The advantage of the service person not having to go to the kitchen should be obvious: an increased portion of the total time can be spent in the dining room. When the service persons turn in the orders in the kitchen, they pick up their own starters (appetizers, salads). Otherwise the system allows for these items to be sent to them.

2. However the expeditor gets the order, the next step is to call it. If the starters have to be sent to the dining room, they will be called first. When assembled, they will be placed on a cart or tray and delivered to the appropriate station in the dining room. One way to do this is to have a separate dining-room job classification, that of runner. The most common modification is to have the order delivered by whoever is going to the dining room next: busperson, waiter, waitress, supervisor, or manager. When the service personnel pick up their own starters, the expeditor will handle only the entrees and other hot items. They will be delivered when ready by the same system as the starters were.

3. When the foods (starters and appetizers) arrive at the station, they must be served immediately. The expectation is that the person who wrote the order would be on hand. If for some reason he or she were not, someone else has to serve the foods. This requires that the checks be written in a specific manner and that the crew be trained to work together. The system for writing the checks calls for each table in the dining room to have a number 1 chair. Generally it is the one closest to the entrance, hostess, or captain's stand. The other chairs at the table are numbered either clockwise or counterclockwise from the first. The foods on the check must correspond to this numbering system. For example, lets look at a four-top, a table seating four persons.

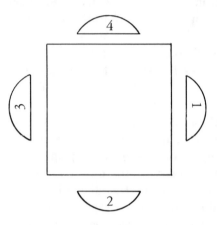

Three people have been seated, at positions 1, 3, 4. The person in position 1 orders a filet, 3 a lobster tail, and 4 the veal scallopini. The order should be written as follows:

Filet
Lobster Tail
Veal Scallopini

If this is done, anyone who can read and can identify the food can serve the right orders to the correct persons. A table of ten could easily be served ten different entrees with no mistakes. This is such a simple concept that one wonders why waiters and waitresses often cannot remember who gets what, even when there are only two guests involved!

The other key to this system is a cooperative crew. If the primary service person happens not to be there, the food must be served by anyone available. It could be the runner-busperson, another service person, a hostess, floor supervisor, or manager. It does not matter who actually does it, so long as it gets done. Some operators claim that it is not possible to get a service crew to cooperate and give assistance on each other's station. This is nonsense, for there are literally thousands of examples to the contrary. It is desirable, however, that the person who wrote the order serve it, and this requires a well-trained, professional crew in both the kitchen and dining room. If the kitchen cannot produce foods on a consistent timetable, the service personnel will have no idea as to when the foods will arrive. If the service personnel cannot organize their stations and workload adequately, they will not be available to serve the food when it is ready. Both crews, therefore, must be highly skilled. When turning in an order, a waiter or waitress must know how long it will take. All items on the menu should have standard preparation times, and everyone should know what they are. When these times can be achieved with consistency, the dining room can time its activities. There will, of course, be delays, but in a well-organized kitchen, they should occur infrequently. When they do occur, it should be a simple matter to inform the dining room to add five minutes or ten minutes to all preparation times. Consistency in preparation times is important regardless of the service system used. An enormous amount of time is wasted by servers making seemingly endless trips to the kitchen to find out whether or not their orders are ready.

One of the advantages of this system—that servers stay in the dining room—is of critical importance. In the kitchen, the server can do nothing that directly affects the satisfaction of the guest. Servers normally go to the kitchen to turn in and pick up orders and, as pointed out, may make several trips to pick up one order.

Both these tasks can be performed by others, providing an opportunity for a higher level of service. There are two options for management in this regard. They can assign larger stations and save on payroll costs, or they can establish higher service standards. This would hopefully result in increased check averages, guest counts, and dining-room turnover.

Another advantage to this system is that foods are served when ready. They do not sit for interminable periods under heat lamps waiting for someone to pick them up. Food, all food, is at its best when freshly plated. It cannot improve while waiting. On the contrary, it can only deteriorate in quality. It therefore makes sense to serve the food as soon as possible and to establish a system to accomplish this.

Still another advantage is that someone is in charge of the kitchen during the service period, coordinating all activities and acting as a buffer between the production and service crews. The expeditor holds an important position which can be adequately filled only by a responsible, highly trained person. This person must be totally familiar with both back of the house and front of the house operations. Ideally, it would also be someone with authority, such as a member of management or the chef or kitchen manager. The expeditor also serves as a quality control checker, evaluating all the plates and trays prior to releasing them to be served. He or she can pace the production as well, assuring that orders flow out on schedule. The system has cost control attributes, too, since a responsible member of the staff will be receiving all checks and can assure that they are properly recorded prior to being accepted for preparation.

An expeditor should be used regardless of whether the food runner system is used. In other words, when the servers turn in and pick up their own orders, they should also work through an expeditor. This assures consistency in order calling, provides a supervisor in the kitchen, and keeps interaction and communication between cooks and service personnel to a minimum. This latter function can be critical for there is great potential for miscommunication or even hostility at this point.

Timing of Orders

It is useful to time orders in and out, and management can use this information in a variety of ways. For example, if a guest complains that he or she has been waiting forever for the food, management can check the order and determine whether it is a kitchen or dining-room problem. If the item has a fifteen-minute preparation time and was submitted only ten minutes earlier, there is no production hang-up. There are two possibilities at this point. Either the guest is exaggerating the time, or the waiter or waitress carried the order around for a long period before turning it in. Restaurant patrons, especially if in a hurry or impatient, can lose their ability to estimate a time span. It really does not matter what the reason is at this point. There is a dissatisfied guest, and the manager must do whatever is possible to turn the situation around. The most important thing to do is get the food served and to do so quickly. As soon as you know the status of the order, return to the customer, either with the food or with assurances that it is on its way.

Following this, management must find out what happened so they can prevent it from happening again. If it was a production delay, they must determine why it occurred. It may not necessarily be the cook's fault. Preprep may not have been done properly; the operation may be extremely busy; the mix of foods prepared could be significantly different than normal (resulting in an unusual demand for items with a long preparation time); there could be equipment problems. The problem could also be the cooks themselves. In any case, management has to know so they can take the appropriate actions. If the delay was due to the order not being turned in promptly, management must determine whether the employee was at fault, or whether other circumstances caused the problem. The individual could have been assigned a heavy station to cover for another person. The station could have been filled all at one time, which generally leads to problems. Or the server may be forced to spend an unusual amount of time servicing the tables for a variety of reasons. As with the

kitchen, once management knows why the delay occurred, they can take action to prevent it from happening again.

The third possibility is that the customer was mistaken; the order was promptly turned in and was being prepared on schedule. In this case, neither the kitchen nor the dining room staffs were at fault. Management should then decide whether the problem warrants being discussed in a training session. If it occurs with some regularity, the servers should be trained in how to spot these types of guests and how to handle them. They could be taught to suggest foods that can be served fast—prime rib for example—and to pay extra attention to such guests. They must be aware that certain types of people expect and demand more attention than others. This is another example of how control works. It depends, first, on accurate and timely information as to what is really going on and, second, on management follow-up. Management can also review timed orders to see whether the various menu items are being prepared within the standard time frame. They can evaluate the preparation pattern over the entire meal period. If, for example, management noted that the preparation times invariably lengthened as the meal period progressed, they should review the prep and preprep policies as well as the equipment. The purpose is to see whether changes can be made to speed up the service preparation time, especially during peak periods. Cooking time for fried chicken (deep fried or pan fried) can be decreased by blanching the chicken beforehand. Certain types of dishes, particularly those with sauces, can be partially or entirely cooked ahead, chilled, and then dished up in an individual casserole. When the order is received, the casseroles would be placed in an oven, preferably a forced-air convection oven, and heated to eating temperature. Crepe dishes, shrimp or lobster Newburgh, eggplant parmigiana, and many other foods could be handled like this. The menu should also be reviewed. A few items, which may not be relatively profitable, could be causing the tie-up.

The first step is to get the information. This is generally done by the servers (or expeditor) who write the time on the duplicate when they submit the order and then when they pick it up. Some of the POS systems have clocks and will time stamp the checks when they are processed. in this case, the finish time would still have to be handwritten. With this system, a shortcut would be to note the finish time only on orders that took longer than expected or desired. Any checks not so marked would have been prepared on schedule. This could save the expeditor time. When the checks have to be timed by hand, the expeditor system gives better results because only one person has to do the job properly rather than an entire crew. The servers also have many other things to do and are literally running from one end of the operation to the other. They can easily forget to mark the checks. One innovative method was implemented by a manager who, on opening a new unit, found he had an extra time clock. It was placed in the kitchen, next to the prechecking register, and all check duplicates were stamped in and out. This provided an accurate and easily obtained record of service preparation times. However the information is gained, it can be useful. We recommend having standard prep times and establishing some system of checking them.

Standardization

Standardization, as pointed out, is necessary for consistency, which in turn leads to predictability. Without predictability, there can be no control. It is in the operation's best interests, therefore, to standardize as much of the activity as possible. In the service function, this would include the following:

1. *Seating*. Establish not only a standard method for seating but also a standard time frame. Determine the maximum time a guest may be kept waiting before being approached by a host, hostess, maître d, or so on.

2. *Service personnel approach to table*. There appear to be two extremes in the way this is typically done. On the one hand, in some establishments the service personnel "freelance," saying anything that comes into their heads. Although this is considered upbeat and casual, it leads to inconsistencies among a service crew and even with one person from table to table. Management can never be sure just what is being conveyed to the guests. The other approach is to prepare a "canned" speech for the waiters and/or waitresses. "Hello! My name is _____. I'll be your server this evening," and so on. The advantage of this approach is that is is consistent. Also management controls the message that presumably conveys to the guests exactly what management wants them to know or be aware of. The disadvantage is that it is frequently overrehearsed and sounds like a recording.

The best approach is to recognize that management has certain messages they want to convey and to assure that the employees know them but then to allow employees to interpret the information in their own manner and words. The types of things that should be made clear are: drink requests, the availability of wine, any specials, the name of the server, pleasure that the guest has selected this restaurant, and some indication that the guest is regarded as important and will be taken care of. Everything that occurs while the guest is there will have an impact, but one of the critical moments is when and how the guest is first greeted by the server.

It is also recommended to have a time standard here as well. Establish the maximum number of minutes that can pass before the guests are approached. Regardless of how busy the operation is, servers cannot allow people to be seated and then ignored. If the server does nothing more than approach the table, explain there will be a short delay, apologize and promise to return, this is far better than ignoring the guest(s). It also would be far better not to seat anyone unless you are prepared to service them immediately. Guests typically will endure a reasonable delay while waiting for a table but become quite impatient when seated, as well they should. A three to five minute wait after being seated can seem interminable to most people.

3. *Order taking and writing*. We refer here to standardized abbreviations for menu items and standardized placement of the various foods on the checks. Anyone who has ever worked at a

broiler, steam table, or sauté station will attest to the difficulty of interpreting checks written in a nonstandardized manner. We are not talking about handwriting, which is a different type of problem. If an operation served three types of strip steaks, a 14-ounce, 10-ounce, and steak sandwich, what would a check written NY mean? Or if there were six types of steak on the menu, what is the cook to prepare when the check requests a *steak-med. rare?* Does *potatoes* refer to french fried, baked, or whipped? Does *chicken* mean the fried or baked chicken. Does *broc* mean broccoli or brochette? Every item on the menu should be written one way and one way only. It really doesn't matter how it is written, so long as it is always done the same way. It also is not necessary for management to come up with the standard abbreviations. The service crew can be assigned that task. Since they will be the ones writing the checks, it probably makes sense to have them do it. But, once they come up with them, *standardize* them. POS equipment that prints the product name as well as the price is highly advantageous since it prevents misunderstandings as to what is being ordered and, in addition, avoids the handwriting problem.

The second aspect to check writing is more subtle and often overlooked: where to position each meal component (entree, vegetable, salad, and so on). One company solved this problem by using a very specialized check:

Appetizer	Temp.	Pot./Veg.
Salad	Entree	Bev.
Shrimp C.	mr	Sr. Beans
Bleu	Filet	Coffee
Paté	—	Asp.
Ital.	Dover Sole	Tea
	Total food	
	Total bev	
	Subtotal	
	tax	
	Total	

There was a location for each type of food, as shown by the top row. The second and third rows show how the check was completed with an actual order. One guest ordered a filet (medium rare), shrimp cocktail for an appetizer, tossed salad with bleu cheese dressing, green beans as a vegetable, and coffee. The other ordered dover sole, paté, Italian dressing on the salad, asparagus, and tea. The advantage here to the kitchen is that they don't have to examine the entire check to find which items to cook. Cooks responsible for entrees check only the middle column because that is where the entrees appear, and so forth. With conventional checks, it can often be difficult to find all the foods. When this happens, mistakes occur; products are not prepared that ought to have been. Even where there are no problems, the process takes longer and slows production. Many foodservice operations cannot afford custom-designed checks (although they should at least look into it), but everyone can pay some attention to placing the foods on the check in some sort of standardized manner. With POS equipment that prints the items, service people should be instructed to enter the foods in a specific order, for example: entree first, followed by vegetables and/or potatoes, then appetizers, salads, and so on. Again, how it is done is not important. That it is always done the same way is the important point.

4. *Submitting the order to the kitchen.* It is foolish to allow an entire crew, perhaps ten or more people, to turn in orders in any way they please—although that is frequently what happens. Management must determine the most efficient, least confusing, and fastest method. Then they must standardize it. The cooks and servers should, of course, be consulted in the decision. After all, they are the people most involved and will be the most affected by whatever system management works out. It is to their mutual advantage to devise an efficient system.

The same applies to how the orders are picked up when ready. We have already described the expeditor system and its advantages. Without using runners to send the food out, the operation must rely on servers coming to the kitchen to get the food. This is the most common method and also the worst. Servers can be delayed for all kinds of reasons, and the food just sits there. On the one hand, we have guests in the dining room waiting for their food. On the other, we have the food ready and waiting in the kitchen. Many operations use some sort of a paging system to inform individuals that an order of theirs is about to come up. There could be a number board that lights up a specific individual's number, or the servers could even carry beepers. These are fine and work as long as the server is available to pick up. If the server is unavailable, however, the food still sits under a heat lamp. A runner system is recommended, at least to supplement the regular system. In other words, if the server has not arrived to pick up within a standard period, the food will be sent out by a runner.

5. *Clearing tables and stacking trays.* Failure to standardize these activities will result in a delay in clearing in the dining room and double-handling in the dish room. The buspersons should be trained in how to clear a table and stack a tray. When employees are put to work without adequate training, they take excessive time to clear, and the trays will be a mess. Each piece of china, glassware, and flatware must be individually handled by the busperson in clearing the table. If the tray is improperly stacked and organized, the dish-room personnel must handle each piece again. The recommended way to stack a tray is as shown at the bottom of this page. When this is done, and the various plates are scraped free of debris, the tray can be handled in the dish room with a minimum of handling. Management should establish a time standard for cleaning a typical table and a standard appearance for the tray when it arrives in the dish room.

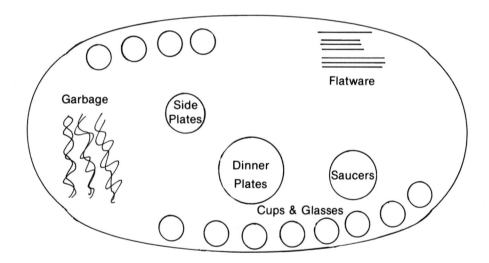

Summary: Food Operations Management

In discussing food operations management, we have taken the approach that the student must first understand the many factors that have an impact on food quality and cost consistency. Next it is necessary to understand how to analyze food systems. The purpose of analysis is to find out what the true situation really is in the operation. The great difficulty in this business is not in solving problems; it is in identifying them. Analysis, if properly done, will identify what the problems are, where they are, when they are occurring, and even which personnel are involved. Finally, with an understanding of the cost and quality factors and the analytical techniques, we can approach the specific ways that the food system can be controlled.

An interesting way of looking at control is that it is really an attempt by management to protect the standards. In other words, whatever management does to assure that the organization's quality and cost standards are met is control. This implies that there are standards to begin with, and so an important management function is to establish rational standards. Without them there is nothing to control.

We shall take this approach with both alcoholic beverage and labor management. First we shall look at the cost and quality factors, then we will study the analytical techniques, and finally go through the various control procedures. In all of these areas, the importance of standards will be emphasized.

Section III

Alcoholic Beverage Operations Management

5 Factors Affecting Alcoholic Beverage Costs

Standards and Controls

As in the case of foods, it is important to have standards for alcoholic beverages—standards for the products themselves and for the product costs. Standards are much easier to establish with alcoholic beverages than they are for foods because there are few problems with quality variance, and the production (mixing) is really simple compared with food production. Standards are nonetheless essential since they assure that bar personnel always serve the same drink, one that looks the same and tastes the same. Without quality standards, products cannot be made with any consistency, and the cost will not be consistent either.

The purpose of controls can be set forth very simply: they assure that the products, when served, meet both the *quality* and *cost* standards. If this sounds easy, it is not. Attempting to establish control in order to assure that all standards are met is a complex, time-consuming, and unending task.

Personnel

Alcoholic beverage control, unlike food control, is primarily personnel oriented as opposed to being product oriented. As a product, beverages are far easier to control than are most foods. The problem with food is that there are many inconsistencies and variances that inevitably result in a lack of predictability. This makes food control more time consuming and less efficient. Compare alcoholic beverages with food to illustrate this point:

Quality consistency: Most alcoholic beverages are very consistent in quality. In a sense, they are manufactured products, and the foodservice operator can expect the same product delivery after delivery. This is particularly true with distilled spirits. We are not suggesting that there are no quality differences between brands, only that any specific brand will always be the same. A bottle of Jack Daniels purchased this week will be exactly the same product as that bought last

153

week, last month, last year, or next month. Cordials and liqueurs, based on distilled spirits and manufactured under rigorous quality control, are also consistent in quality. When produced, beers are also consistent, but since beer is probably the most perishable of the alcoholic beverages, there may be variances in quality, if not when delivered, then when served. Wine, like food, should be regarded as an inconsistent product, and its quality must be evaluated constantly. Due to the often significant differences in growing conditions from one year to the next, wine will change from year to year. This is especially true of vintage-dated wines. Blended wines (such as the bulk-produced house wines) will be much more consistent, but the buyer can still expect variances. Wine is also perishable; and storage, delivery, and handling can result in further quality variances.

Packaging: Alcoholic beverages are characterized by standard packaging, unlike foods, which come in every type of package conceivable. Wines and distilled spirits typically are packed in the same sized bottles, 750 milliliter (ml.) (25.4 ounces), twelve to a case. Beer comes in 12-ounce bottles, twenty-four to a case.

Storage requirements: Wines, especially fine wines, require specialized storage conditions. Even they, however, do not require refrigeration as do many foods. Beer also does not require refrigeration, although as with wine cool temperatures are desirable and warm temperatures must be avoided. Distilled spirits and cordials are very undemanding as to storage temperature requirements. Alcoholic beverages are also likely to be stored in a very few areas, often only one storeroom. Food can be found in refrigerators and freezers (both reach-in and walk-in), in dry storerooms, and in the kitchen as well. The point here is that while nearly all employees have access to food stores, it is much easier to secure alcoholic beverages.

Shelf life: Beer, as pointed out, is very perishable. Wine is too, but compared to beer, it can be successfully kept for a longer period, often many years in the case of some fine wines. Distilled spirits and cordials have a virtually unlimited

shelf life for they are basically inert products. The problem with food is that the shelf life ranges from a day or two to many months, and the foodservice operator has the challenge of attempting to control a product line that has dozens of different storage times.

Cost stability: Alcoholic beverage costs will increase over time, as will virtually all products, but compared with food the price structure is much more stable. Costs of beverages can therefore be predicted with greater accuracy. Prices of some foods, such as fresh produce and meats or fish or poultry, can go up and down like a yo-yo, which makes cost standardization difficult if not impossible. Alcoholic beverage costs, at least in the short run, can readily be standardized.

Yield variances: Alcoholic beverages are all sold by liquid measure, so, theoretically at least, the yield is a consistent 100 percent. In practice, the yield is seldom 100 percent, but this clearly points out the difference between food and alcoholic beverages. Beverage yields fall short of the potential 100 percent due to improper personnel practices while, with many foods, the potential yield is well short of 100 percent under the best conditions, and it is never consistent. The main problem with food is that the products themselves cause much of the inconsistency. In beverage systems, the employees are nearly the sole cause of yield variances while in a food system, employees only add to an already difficult control situation.

Access to stored products: Alcoholic beverages typically have reduced (relative to foods) access on two levels. One is the number of people, and the other is the time. It is entirely possible to set up a beverage storage area so that only two or three people are authorized entry, and those two or three persons normally do so only when deliveries are received and when the daily issue to the bar is made. Food storage areas, on the other hand, are typically accessed by all or nearly all of the employees constantly throughout the day. This obviously increases the degree of difficulty.

Beverage systems are therefore best controlled by monitoring the activities of personnel. We are not suggesting that personnel be ignored in a food system or that product control be ignored in a beverage system but that management should have a primary interest in one or the other. A way of illustrating this principle is that, were a case of frozen shrimp left unattended in the receiving area, the only statement that could be made with certainty is that it *would* spoil. It also could, of course, be stolen, but that would not be certain. If a case of liquor were left unattended, it would not spoil, but it *would* be stolen!

Sales Mix

The specific sales mix can have a significant effect on the beverage cost structure.

Beer, Wine, Spirits

Each of these types of products has a different potential percentage cost, and the overall cost will depend upon the sales mix. For example, assume that the potential (ideal) costs are as follows:

Beer (bottled)	35 percent
Wine	50 percent
Spirits or Cordials	20 percent

The costs and profits of operations A and B would be (see Exhibit 5.1): The cost percentage for operation A is 33.1 percent while for B it is 24.7 percent, and the profit difference is $675.00. Operation B is not necessarily better managed; in fact it could be poorly managed and still produce as much profit as or more profit than would A (see Exhibit 5.2). Restaurant A is being managed better (it attains the potential cost in all three categories), while restaurant B is operated less efficiently (the actual cost exceeds the potential in all categories); yet restaurant B is still making a greater profit. This example could

Exhibit 5.1 Sales Mix by Type of Product-A

PRODUCT	A			B		
	Sales	Costs	Profit	Sales	Costs	Profit
Beer	$ 4,000	$ 1,400	$ 2,600	$ 1,500	$ 525	$ 975
Wine	1,500	750	750	500	250	250
Spirits	2,500	500	2,000	6,000	1,200	4,800
TOTAL	$8,000	$2,650	$5,350	$8,000	$1,975	$6,025

Exhibit 5.2 Sales Mix by Type of Product-B

PRODUCT	A			B		
	Sales	Costs	Profit	Sales	Costs	Profit
Beer	$ 4,000	$1,400(35%)	$2,600	$1,500	$600(40%)	$ 900
Wine	1,500	750(50%)	750	500	275(55%)	225
Spirits	2,500	500(20%)	2,000	6,000	1,500(25%)	4,500
TOTAL	$8,000	$2,650(33.1%)	$5,350	$8,000	$2,375(29.7%)	$5,625

be further complicated if draught beer were served because the potential cost is closer to spirits than it is to bottled beer. Thus, the beverage cost is dependent on the sales mix of products that are sold under different pricing and cost structures.

Lounge or Banquet or Dining Room

The same thing is true for considering the various beverage sales outlets when they have varying price-cost structures, as they typically do. Assume these standard or potential costs:

Lounge	22 percent
Banquet	33 percent
Dining room	25 percent

These would vary primarily because of the product mix in each department and marketing policies as well. The lounge would consist mainly of spirit and beer sales, the dining room would have most of the wine sales, and the banquet department would probably have many functions where the products were priced by the bottle rather than by the drink. Operations A and B would look like this (see Exhibit 5.3). Again, there is a profitability variance that has nothing to do with the relative difference in operating efficiency. The potential cost is a factor of the sales mix by departments. The eventual actual profits are, of course, a factor of both the sales mix and the effectiveness of control.

The sales mix therefore can have a significant effect upon beverage cost percentages and profits. The same mix can affect costs and profits when alcoholic beverages are sold under varying price structures, as are beers, wines, and spirits or when various departments in the foodservice operation sell more of one type of alcoholic beverage than the other, for example, the lounge and dining room(s), or when one department (catering) has a price structure that differs from the others.

Market Consumption Trends

Historically, the typical beverage sales mix in the United States has been tilted towards spirits with beer second and wine a poor third. Current and projected trends, however, show that wine is rapidly gaining in popularity. In fact, in 1980, the total gallon volume of wine shipped in the United States (domestic and imported) exceeded that of distilled spirits for the first time in our history. As the example on sales mixes clearly shows (see Exhibit 5.1), the highest percentage cost alcoholic beverage, by far, is wine. The traditional use for wine has been as a food accompaniment. As such, the operator could justify the high percentage cost because it was essentially an "extra" sale. In other words, whether wine was ordered or not had no effect on the sale of other alcoholic beverages before or after the meal. The gross profit from wine sales, although lower (in percentage) than beers and spirits, was an "extra" profit, and so the percentage was not important. Exhibit 5.4 shows why. Here it is obviously more profitable to sell wine than not to sell it, even though the overall

Exhibit 5.3 Sales Mix by Department

	A			B		
	Sales	Costs	Profit	Sales	Costs	Profit
Lounge	$4,000	$880(22%)	$3,120	$3,000	$660(22%)	$2,340
D.R.	3,000	750(25%)	2,250	2,500	625(25%)	1,875
Banquet	1,000	333(33%)	667	2,500	825(33%)	1,675
TOTAL	$8,000	$1,963(24.5%)	$6,037	$8,000	$2,110(26.4%)	$5,890

Exhibit 5.4 Wine Profitability as an Extra Sale

	No Wine Sales			With Wine Sales		
	Sales	Costs	Profit	Sales	Costs	Profit
Beer	$1,000	$333(33%)	$ 667	$1,000	$333(33%)	$ 667
Spirits	4,000	800(20%)	3,200	4,000	800(20%)	3,200
Wine	-	-	-	1,000	500(50%)	500
TOTAL	$5,000	$1,133(22.7%)	$3,867	$6,000	$1,633(27.2%)	$4,367

cost percentage increases from 22.7 percent to 27.2 percent, an increase that conventional wisdom would consider intolerable.

Some of the recent nationwide increase in wine consumption, however, has come through nontraditional usage, *replacing* other beverages—particularly spirits—as a before dinner drink, as a social beverage, and as a cocktail party beverage. When this occurs, the *profitability* as well as the percentage can be negatively affected. Consider the example in Exhibit 5.5. Increases in wine consumption, when achieved *at the expense of spirits*, will decrease overall profitability. This is exactly what has been occurring steadily since the late 1970s.

Another trend that affects beverage costs is the increase in popularity of the so-called super-premium beverages. Dom Perignon champagne, despite its formidable price, is in short supply. In fact, it is allocated to distributors. Other examples of such products are Chivas Regal Scotch, Jack Daniels bourbon (Tennessee bourbon), Crown Royal Canadian whiskey, cognacs, various gins and vodkas, and especially cordials and liqueurs. The effect of increased sales of these products is to increase profits for they are typically priced to produce higher dollar gross profits. There are similar consumption trends with beer. The new category of domestic super-premiums as well as imports are particularly strong on the market, and like their wine and liquor counterparts, they can be sold for higher dollar profit margins.

Seasonal Sales Variations

Most operations are subject to some variance in sales mix over the year, and this can frequently be significant enough to alter the overall cost

Exhibit 5.5 Wine Profitability as a Replacement Sale

	Unit A			Unit B		
	Sales	Costs	Profit	Sales	Costs	Profit
Beer	$1,000	$ 333(33.3%)	$ 667	$ 800	$ 266(33.3%)	$ 534
Spirits	4,000	800(20%)	3,200	3,500	700(20%)	2,800
Wine	1,000	500(50%)	500	1,700	850(50%)	850
TOTAL	$6,000	$1,633(27.2%)	$4,367	$6,000	$1,816(30.3%)	$4,184

percentages. Beer sales can be expected to take a larger than normal market share during hot weather; spirits will do the same during very cold weather. The holiday season is generally accompanied by increases in consumption of sparkling wines, premium wines, and the super-premium spirits and cordials.

Selling Prices

The prices products are sold at affect the cost percentages (they have nothing, however, to do with the actual dollar beverage cost). Management has a great deal of control over the beverage cost percentage. The three elements used to calculate what the cost should be or should have been (the standard or potential cost) are:

- the number of each product sold (sales mix)

- the cost of each product

- the selling price of each product

As mentioned in the food section, knowledge of all three is essential to establish a cost percentage that the actual percentage can be compared to. The operator generally has some control over the sales mix (if she or he cares to exercise it), but this control is limited, probably more so than with food since beverage consumers tend to be more specific about what they order. Operators do not have as much control over beverage *product costs* as they do over food costs either. Not only are the AP prices they pay for alcoholic beverages less variable and controllable by the operator, but the recipes for drinks are not subject to the same degree of interpretation as food recipes are. Finally, the portions served tend to be more uniform in beverages than in foods. All these add up to decreased management control over product costs. *Selling prices,* however, are an area over which management policies can exercise much influence. Moreover, the selling price is one of the stronger influences on sales mix. It is common to price as many drinks the same as possible. This is done partly to facilitate

management analysis of sales and costs and partly because most bars still ring drinks by hand; the more prices there are to remember, the greater the likelihood of pricing errors. When the pricing decision is taken away from bar and service personnel, as with a programmed computer system, management can literally have a different price for every drink sold. The advantages in menu pricing flexibility should be obvious.

Volume

Increases or decreases in sales volume should not affect the beverage cost percentages. The dollar *gross profit* will increase or decrease with sales, but the *profit percentage* should remain the same. The only variances that should affect the cost percentage are the sales mix, the drink costs, and the selling prices. In theory, then, if no changes occur in these factors, increases or decreases—even substantial ones—in sales would not change the expected percentages. Most operators, though, expect their cost percentage to drop when sales increase. The fact that they often do is usually an indication that they are not operating at optimum efficiency prior to the increase. For example, if three or four bottles of whiskey per week were being wasted, stolen, or sold (without reporting the sales) prior to the sales increase and if the same losses were occurring after the increase, the cost percentage would drop even though there were no changes in sales mix, drink costs, or prices. The reverse is obviously true when sales drop. Not all losses can be blamed on fraud, cheating, stealing, and so on. Bars are operated by people, and people will make mistakes, the effect upon profits often being a function of the sales level. Volume therefore can affect cost and profit percentages.

Layout and Design

These can affect a beverage operation's profitability in several ways. A bar requires a certain amount of space. If too much is allocated, the return per square foot is likely to be reduced. If too little is available, the sales potential may not be attained. The objective should be to utilize the available space as efficiently as possible, considering the square feet, shape, locations of entrances and exits, relationships of the bar to other operating facilities (other bars, dining room(s), kitchen(s)), traffic patterns, and volumes.

There are many ways in which space can be wasted or utilized inefficiently. The most important area is the bar itself, and the design should enable the bartender(s) to put out a high volume of drinks with the least amount of effort and movement. A layout that requires the bartender to continuously walk back and forth to get drink materials will result in a lot of wasted energy, time, and reduced drink output. Equipment is also critically important behind the bar. A bartender working a well-equipped and well-designed station can put out many more drinks (and with less drink variance) than the same person could in a less well-equipped station. For example, the bartender gets an order for a Scotch and water, bourbon and water, and a whiskey and soda. He or she will ice three glasses, pick up a bottle of Scotch from the speed rack and pour it, replace the bottle, and get a bottle of bourbon, then a bottle of blended whiskey. Each of the mixes (water and soda) would then have to be obtained and poured. Following this, the drinks would be garnished and served. The bar could, however, be set up so that when the order is received, the three glasses are iced as before, but then the bartender, holding the bourbon and Scotch glasses in one hand and the blended whiskey glass in the other, reaches toward a row of levers placed in the underbar. The glasses are pressed against the lever and a premeasured quantity of the desired spirit is issued. The bartender then reaches towards another row of levers above the first where the water and soda are added. Then the glasses are placed on the bar and garnished. This bartender has the potential of serving many more drinks than does the first one and probably uses less energy in the process. Or, alternatively,

flex hose guns could be used for both the well spirits and mixes. In that case, the bartender would ice three glasses, put the liquor in with one gun and the mixes in with the other. The efficiency is not as great when spirits are ordered that are not in the automatic dispensing systems used. An example would be if the orders were for J & B Scotch and Jim Beam bourbon. In that case, the bartender would probably have to pour from the bottles and may have to move a few steps to get them. Another example is when drinks are ordered that require several spirit and nonspirit ingredients, such as lemon mix, cream, various fruit juices, and cordials. A bar serving a high percentage of these types of drinks or the call drinks may not have its pouring efficiency significantly increased by the automatic dispensing systems described, but there are other systems available that could handle these types of situations.

Another design and equipment feature that affects the operation of the bar is the ice-handling system. The ideal situation would be to have an ice maker behind the bar; when ice has to be delivered, it takes extra labor hours, and there is the risk of running out and temporarily being unable to pour. The way in which the glasses are washed and stored can affect the operating efficiency as well. The main penalty assigned to the operation by improper design of the pouring, washing, and ice systems is reduced drink-pouring capability, but there will also be pouring variances, which generally lead to cost problems.

Security

All products stored in foodservice operations have some value to employees (and others), and they must be protected from theft and pilferage. With alcoholic beverages, this is true to an extreme degree. In fact, aside from cash, there is nothing more attractive than alcoholic beverages.

We will discuss stock security thoroughly in the section on storage control. The point here is that high costs and lost profits are sometimes due to lost products. When one considers what a typical bottle of spirits could be sold for and what the potential profit from each bottle is, it is clear that lack of security can be very costly. Basically, security is achieved by an adequate information system so that management is immediately aware of the theft and then is quickly willing to do something about it. It is unfortunately true that theft often occurs because employees know it will go undetected at least long enough so that identification of those involved will be impossible. Sometimes it is never detected.

Poor Cash Control

Here, we are specifically referring to cases in which drinks are sold and cash is collected but not turned in. This is the primary objective of most fraudulent activities on bars. Products can be, and are, stolen. Drinks can be overpoured, underpoured, given away, and so on, but the biggest single control challenge facing most bar operators is to collect the money from all drinks sold. The fact that this is not done is probably the number one reason for high cost percentages and reduced profits. We will discuss this aspect extensively in the sections or bar personnel frauds and cash control.

Receiving Procedures

Receiving of alcoholic beverages is considerably less complex than is that of receiving foods, but it must still be given proper attention by management. The most obvious problem is that of paying for products never received, but several others come to mind. Products could be delivered but never find their way to secure storage areas. Substitutions could be made; higher than agreed upon prices could be paid; damaged or deteriorating goods could be accepted.

Suppliers

As with any other product, who the products are purchased from can have an impact on the costs, either positive or negative. If the buyer is purchasing from the wrong supplier, for whatever reason, optimum serving costs are not likely to be obtained. The biggest direct influence the supplier has on costs is the prices charged. There are other influences, but they have an indirect effect. These would be delivery, breadth of product line, warehousing facilities and distribution equipment, policies for payment, minimum order quantities and dollar values, and so forth. One point made with food is worth repeating here: purchasing from the right supplier will not necessarily save any money. The right supplier is one who can provide the desired specific products at the lowest cost. The assumption here is that this is the supplier from whom the buyer should be purchasing. Dealing with any other supplier will only increase the cost of operating. There is, therefore, no money to be saved, but there is vast potential for spending more than is necessary by not dealing with the right purveyor.

Stock Levels and Inventory Turnover

When excessive stocks are maintained, specific costs can result. While some of these do not apply to alcoholic beverages, others do. Inventory levels higher than necessary reduce the organization's return on assets. High inventories tie up cash that might more profitably be utilized elsewhere. There is increased risk of theft and pilferage. There is often increased risk of spoilage and quality deterioration, although this does not apply to all alcoholic beverages. Beers and some wines can certainly lose quality if held too long, but distilled spirits and cordials do not change after being bottled. Large or excessive stocks invite waste because employees tend to become careless with products when they see that there is an ample supply; although this is probably less true with alcoholic beverages than with food and, particularly, supplies.

A high beverage inventory can be a real problem in many foodservice operations because of the need to maintain materials for lounge, dining room, and banquet consumption. In hotel foodservice operations, there may be several lounge and dining room outlets as well as room service. The critical point differentiating beverage operations is that normally there is one food production facility in most operations, and it serves both the dining room and banquet rooms. Even when there is more than one dining area (a coffee shop for example), they often are serviced by one kitchen. Alcoholic beverages, on the other hand, typically require multiple production outlets. There could be a main bar, service bar (for the dining room) and, on any given night, one, two, or more banquet bars in use. The result is that beverage operations require more inventory duplication than do food operations, and the inventory levels can easily get out of hand.

There is also a distinct tendency, unique to beverage systems, to stock multiple examples of the same basic product. Most operations would only carry one strip steak, one kind of aluminum foil, one kind of bar picks, and so on, but the same establishment might have eight Scotches, seven bourbons, six gins. There are marketing justifications for this to a degree, but it is generally overdone. The result is excessive numbers of brands stocked and excessive inventory levels.

Marketing Policies

The policies pursued by management in marketing their operations will have a profound effect on the beverage costs and the beverage profits. Most important from a cost viewpoint is the pricing structure. It is common to have at least two-tiered pricing: regular prices and the so-called happy-hour prices, which are lower. Three-tiered pricing is also quite prevalent. There will be three separate prices for the same products: regular (or normal) prices, "happy-hour" prices (lower), and entertainment prices (higher). The decision to utilize variable pricing will probably result in a percentage cost variance from the normal or regular one. It also results in management frequently not knowing what the beverage cost should be, and severe problems arise from this. Cost analysis is basically a comparison process, and in this case management is not able to determine what cost the

actual cost should be compared to. This quite obviously leaves them in a very vulnerable position.

Other discounts, due primarily to promotions, will have the same effect. They change the standard or expected cost and make it even more difficult to determine what the standard cost should be. Without a reasonably accurate frame of reference, management cannot determine whether the operating performance is legitimate or not.

State and Local Regulations

Alcoholic beverages are subjected to a vast and bewildering array of regulations. To begin with, there are federal regulations, and one must remember that this is the same federal government that once completely banned the production and sale of alcoholic beverages (except for medicinal and religious purposes) for over ten years! The federal laws and regulations are, therefore, at best restrictive. Compounding the problem is the fact that many states (and counties within states) do not even today, more than fifty years after the repeal of prohibition, allow alcoholic beverages to be bought and sold like other products. Alcoholic beverages can be sold in all fifty states, but in eighteen of them (known as control states), the retailer must purchase from state-operated facilities. The retailer can be a retail store, bar, restaurant, or hotel. The other thirty-two states (known as license states), plus Washington D.C., allow the retailer to purchase from wholesale distributors. In other words, in these states liquor can be bought like other products, from a sales organization that is responsive to the needs of the customer. This is decidedly not the case in the control states. Within the license states, however, individual counties may still restrict the sale of alcoholic beverages. There are also variances between laws regulating distilled spirits and those for beers and wines. The net effect of these various regulations is to reduce profits in some areas and to increase the operating difficulty in all areas.

6 Analysis of Alcoholic Beverage Costs

Percentage Analysis

Percentage analysis for beverage systems has the same uses and limitations as discussed in food analysis. Percentages are best used as monitoring tools to determine whether the system is operating properly or not. An advantage to using percentages is that they can be compared from period to period, whereas dollar costs often cannot. A beverage cost of $6,000 one month and $8,000 the next would not necessarily be meaningful, while a percentage cost comparison of 20.5 percent to 21.9 percent could be. Unless, however, standard percentages are being used, false conclusions can be drawn. A standard beverage percentage is based on three factors: *sales mix, product costs,* and *product selling prices.* Exhibit 6.1 shows a simplified standard percentage cost calculation. The result, 21.3 percent, becomes the frame of reference against which the actual cost is measured. One does not, incidentally, have to use only the actual cost. That would be determined by a physical inventory, but management may use one of several estimating systems to come up with costs to compare. This would not be done at the end of the accounting period but can be very useful on a weekly basis.

One of the problems with percentage analysis is that while it can indicate a variance, it does not necessarily indicate that a control problem exists. Even when the variance is determined to be due to lack of control, it is difficult using percentage analysis to pinpoint the problem

Example: If the cost were 24 percent (actual or true cost) and the standard were 21.3 percent, there would be a cost variance. This variance, however, could be due to a change in the sales mix. If beer sales had accounted for a greater share of the guest count, the standard cost would no longer be 21.3 percent. In fact, it could be 24 percent. In such a case, there is no control problem, although there could be a profit problem. If the increase in beer sales came at the expense of the sale of spirits (same number of drinks sold), the profits would be down. If the increase in beer sales were due to *additional* sales (increase in total number of drinks), the profit would be up, and the change in percentage would be no problem (although the profits could have been increased even more if the extra sales had been in spirit drinks rather than beer).

Exhibit 6.1. Standard Beverage Percentage

Item	Sales	Cost	Selling Price	Total Cost	Total Sales
Bourbon	400	$.35	$1.75	$ 140.00	$ 700.00
Scotch	600	.41	1.95	246.00	1,170.00
Vodka	800	.31	1.75	248.00	1,400.00
Gin	350	.32	1.75	112.00	612.50
Beer	900	.29	.95	261.00	855.00
Total	3,050			$1,007.00	$4,737.50

$$\frac{\text{Total cost}}{\text{Total sales}} \times 100 = \text{Standard percentage}$$

$$\frac{\$1,007.00}{\$4,737.50} = .213 \times 100 = \underline{21.3\%}$$

The variance could also be due to a change in the pricing structure. This would also require an investigation. Management would, of course, be aware of pricing changes, but they are frequently not aware of their true impact on cost percentages. If it is determined that neither the sales mix nor the pricing has changed, then the variance must have been caused by the third factor—the product cost (in dollars). Even in that case, there may not be a control problem. A control problem exists when the costs are higher than they should be. If the dollar costs are up because the operation was paying higher prices for alcoholic beverages, there would be a new standard percentage, and it could show there is no variance from the actual.

To summarize this point: variance between actual and standard percentages indicates a control problem only when the standard is calculated accurately, so the first thing management should do is make sure none of the three factors has changed. Once a control problem has been indicated as the probable cause of the variance, the percentage is not very useful in identifying where the breakdown has occurred.

The use of a standard percentage for comparison purposes is made more difficult by a fact already discussed; the sales mix between departments will affect it. Thus, the best use of a standard percentage is generally to monitor each department or sales area. There often is no overall standard percentage unless there is some stability in the departmental sales mix.

Standard Cost Analysis

The procedure here (see Exhibit 6.2) is similar to the standard percentage calculation but with one important difference: the sales are ignored; only the projected dollar cost is needed. In Exhibit 6.2 this cost is $4,649.92 (Box I). The cost is calculated using two of the factors from the percentage calculation. Information must be available on the number of drinks sold and the cost of each drink. This is provided in column B (number sold) and in column D (item cost). Multiplying the number sold of each drink by the cost of that drink yields the total projected cost for that drink. This is shown in column G (menu costs). The total of column G (shown in box I) is the overall projected total cost. This is what we refer to as the *standard cost*. It is the cost that *should be* attained if everything is done properly. Analysis consists of calculating the actual beverage cost (by taking a physical inventory) and comparing it to the standard to see whether there is any variance. It would not be reasonable to expect 100 percent agreement between the two. In fact, such a result would cause most beverage managers to suspect someone of tampering with the data. It is reasonable, however, to suggest that each operation have a target variance. Exceeding this would be regarded as unacceptable. This would tend to be different from firm to firm. One operation could be quite simple and sell nearly all drinks as shots straight from the bottle. It would be easy for them to maintain accurate cost information. In this case, the reasonable expectation would be for nearly 100 percent agreement between standard and actual costs. Another bar establishment might sell a lot of mixed drinks, and the cost information would be an estimate if they do not have the equipment to accurately track the sales mix. In this case, the standard cost is recognized to be less than totally accurate, and it would be foolish as well as unreasonable to expect full agreement. Management should still have an acceptable range of variation however. It could, for example, be 10 percent, and so long as the variance does not exceed that, the results will be regarded as satisfactory.

If the standard cost is not at all accurate but is developed by estimating both sales mix and costs, the procedure is not even worth doing. This characterizes many beverage operations, for they do not know what they sell or what it costs them. It must be pointed out, though, that not only can they not use this system to evaluate their performance, but they cannot use a percentage for comparison either because it depends on the same information. Thus we would not argue with operators who criticize this analytical technique (standard cost) as being too complicated and requiring too much information. Our only reply is that without this information they absolutely cannot evaluate performance and have no way of knowing whether or not optimum profits are being attained. Yet these same operators persist in computing their PC (percentage cost) with a nearly religious fervor!

Up to this point, the standard cost system has yielded little more information than has the standard percentage system. Its advantage is that

we are working with dollar figures and not only can evaluate the total costs, but if there are variances, we can evaluate product by product. In Exhibit 6.2, the total cost should have been $4,649.92. Let us assume the actual cost was $4,950.00, which is a variance of $300.00 (rounded) or 6.5 percent. Management expects a variance of no more than 1 to 2 percent. Knowing how much the actual dollar cost is off is far more useful than saying the percentage is up so many points. In this case, an actual cost of $4,950.00 would give a bar cost percentage of 19.5 percent (on sales of $25,391). This is 1.2 percent over the standard of 18.3 percent. What exactly does 1.2 percent mean? It means nothing until it is transformed into a dollar amount. When we find that we spent about $300.00 more to sell our products than we should have, we are beginning to obtain some meaningful information to base decisions on. The $300.00 variance in itself does not tell us enough however. Since we have, in Exhibit 6.2, the projected costs by category of spirit, we can examine each category independently.

Exhibit 6.3 shows the results of this. There are two categories that account for $277, or 92 percent, of the $300 variance. These are Scotch and vodka. Of the two, the Scotch is obviously the more important. In two categories, bourbon and rum, there was less liquor used than there should have been, probably due to underpouring. This is often a serious problem, but in this case it appears to be minor. Scotch has to be the number one priority for further investigation and action, with vodka number two. Everything else can safely be put on the back burner for the time being. Exhibit 6.4 shows the specific product-by-product analysis of Scotch and vodka. It is quite apparent there are some strange things going on with both:

Scotch: The three premium or "call" brands, J & B, Cutty Sark, and Dewars, all *appear* to be okay, showing minimal variance in each case. The super-premium, Chivas Regal, and the well (or house) brand, Lauders, account for nearly all the scotch cost problems. At this point, the bar manager wants to know the probable cause of these cost overages. One likely explanation could

Exhibit 6.2. Beverage Profitability Work Sheet

Restaurant: _____

Date: _____

Period: _____

(A) Menu Item Name	(B) Number Sold (MM)	(C) Menu Mix %	(D) Item Cost	(E) Item Selling Price	(F) Item CM (E-D)	(G) Menu Costs (D*B)	(H) Menu Revenues (E*B)	(L) Menu CM (F*B)	(P) CM Category	(R) MM% Category	(S) Menu Item Classification	(T) Profit Factor
SCOTCH												
J & B	450	2.65	0.30	1.75	1.45	135.00	787.50	652.50	H	H	Star	.98
Cutty Sark	400	2.36	0.31	1.75	1.44	124.00	700.00	576.00	H	H	Star	.86
Chivas Regal	219	1.29	0.53	2.50	1.97	116.07	547.50	431.43	H	L	Puzzle	.64
Dewars	400	2.36	0.29	1.75	1.46	116.00	700.00	584.00	H	H	Star	.87
Lauders	500	2.95	0.23	1.50	1.27	115.00	750.00	635.00	H	H	Star	.95
Scotch Total	1,969				1.46	606.07	3,485.00	2,878.93				
CANADIAN												
V O	837	4.93	0.34	1.50	1.16	284.58	1,255.50	970.92	L	H	Plow Horse	1.45
C C	838	4.94	0.34	1.50	1.16	284.92	1,257.00	972.08	L	H	Plow Horse	1.45
Crown Royal	231	1.36	0.50	2.00	1.50	115.50	462.00	346.50	H	L	Puzzle	.52
Windsor Supreme	250	1.47	0.22	1.25	1.03	55.00	312.50	257.50	L	L	Dog	.39
Canadian Total	2,156				1.18	740.00	3,287.00	2,547.00				
Column Totals:	N					I	J	M				

K = I/J   O = M/N   Q = (100/Items)(70%)

Additional Computations:

Exhibit 6.2, continued

Restaurant: _____

Date: _____

Period: _____

(A) Menu Item Name	(B) Number Sold (MM)	(C) Menu Mix %	(D) Item Cost	(E) Item Selling Price	(F) Item CM (E-D)	(G) Menu Costs (D*B)	(H) Menu Revenues (E*B)	(L) Menu CM (F*B)	(P) CM Category	(R) MM% Category	(S) Menu Item Classification	(T) Profit Factor
BLENDED WHISKEY												
Imperial	288	1.70	0.18	1.25	1.07	51.84	360.00	308.16	L	L	Dog	.46
7 Crown	1,400	8.25	0.20	1.25	1.05	280.00	1,750.00	1,470.00	L	H	Plow Horse	2.20
Blended Total	1,688				1.05	331.84	2,110.00	1,778.16				
BOURBON												
Jim Beam	675	3.98	0.24	1.25	1.01	162.00	843.75	681.75	L	H	Plow Horse	1.02
Jack Daniels	494	2.91	0.34	2.00	1.66	167.96	988.00	820.04	H	H	Star	1.23
Early Times	625	3.68	0.25	1.50	1.25	156.25	937.50	781.25	H	H	Star	1.17
Wild Turkey	250	1.47	0.36	2.00	1.64	90.00	500.00	410.00	H	L	Puzzle	.61
Ten High	675	3.98	0.23	1.25	1.02	155.25	843.75	688.50	L	H	Plow Horse	1.03
Bourbon Total	2,719				1.24	731.46	4,113.00	3,381.54				
Column Totals:	N					I	J	M				

Additional Computations:

K = I/J   O = M/N   Q = (100 Items)(70%)

Exhibit 6.2, continued

Restaurant: _____

Date: _____

Period: _____

(A) Menu Item Name	(B) Number Sold (MM)	(C) Menu Mix %	(D) Item Cost	(E) Item Selling Price	(F) Item CM (E-D)	(G) Menu Costs (D*B)	(H) Menu Revenues (E*B)	(L) Menu CM (F*B)	(P) CM Category	(R) MM% Category	(S) Menu Item Classification	(T) Profit Factor
GIN												
Seagrams	450	2.65	0.20	1.25	1.05	90.00	562.50	472.50	L	H	Plow Horse	.71
Gordons	450	2.65	0.19	1.25	1.06	85.50	562.50	477.00	L	H	Plow Horse	.71
Beefeater	625	3.68	0.34	1.75	1.41	212.50	1,093.75	881.25	H	H	Star	1.32
Tanqueray	256	1.51	0.35	1.75	1.40	89.60	448.00	358.40	H	L	Puzzle	.54
Gin Total	1,781				1.23	477.60	2,666.75	2,189.15				
VODKA												
Smirnoff	1,313	7.74	0.28	1.50	1.22	367.64	1,969.50	1,601.86	H	H	Star	2.39
Popov	1,425	8.40	0.17	1.25	1.08	242.25	1,781.25	1,539.00	L	H	Plow Horse	2.30
Gordons	1,200	7.07	0.16	1.25	1.09	192.00	1,500.00	1,308.00	L	H	Plow Horse	1.95
Vodka Total	3,938				1.13	801.89	5,250.75	4,448.86				
Column Totals:	N					I	J	M				

Additional Computations:

K = I/J   O = M/N   Q = (100/Items)(70%)

Exhibit 6.2, continued

Restaurant: _____

Date: _____

Period: _____

(A) Menu Item Name	(B) Number Sold (MM)	(C) Menu Mix %	(D) Item Cost	(E) Item Selling Price	(F) Item CM (E-D)	(G) Menu Costs (D*B)	(H) Menu Revenues (E*B)	(L) Menu CM (F*B)	(P) CM Category	(R) MM% Category	(S) Menu Item Classification	(T) Profit Factor
RUM Bacardi	900	5.30	0.26	1.50	1.24	234.00	1,350.00	1,116.00	H	H	Star	1.67
Ron Rico	300	1.77	0.18	1.25	1.07	54.00	375.00	321.00	L	L	Dog	.48
Castillo	300	1.77	0.20	1.25	1.05	60.00	375.00	315.00	L	L	Dog	.47
Rum Total	1,500				1.17	348.00	2,100.00	1,752.00				
TEQUILA Jose Cuervo	250	1.47	0.26	1.25	0.99	65.00	312.50	247.50	L	L	Dog	.37
Two Fingers	125	0.74	0.22	1.25	1.03	27.50	156.25	128.75	L	L	Dog	.19
Tequila Total	375				1.00	92.50	468.75	376.25				
BRANDY Christian Brothers	200	1.18	0.22	1.50	1.28	44.00	300.00	256.00	H	L	Puzzle	.38
Courvoisier	269	1.59	0.74	2.50	1.76	199.06	672.50	473.44	H	L	Puzzle	.71
Hennessy	375	2.21	0.74	2.50	1.76	277.50	937.50	660.00	H	L	Puzzle	.99
Brandy Total	844				1.65	520.56	1,910.00	1,389.44				
Column Totals:	N 16,970					I 4,649.92	J 25,391.25	M 20,741.33				

Additional Computations:

$$K = I/J = \frac{4,649.92}{25,391.25} = 18.3\%$$

$$O = M/N = \frac{20,741.33}{16,970} = \$1.22$$

$$Q = (100/Items)(70\%) \quad \frac{100\%}{31} = 3.23 \quad 3.23 \times .7 = 2.25\%$$

Exhibit 6.3. Variance Breakdown

Category	Standard Cost (from Exhibit 6.2)	Actual Cost (from physical inventory)	Variance ($)
Scotch	$606	$810	$204
Canadian	740	743	3
Blend	332	345	13
Bourbon	731	724	(7)
Gin	478	480	2
Vodka	802	875	73
Rum	348	345	(3)
Tequila	93	95	2
Brandy	520	533	13
Total	$4,650	$4,950	$300

Exhibit 6.4. Variance: Scotch and Vodka

Category	Standard Cost (from Exhibit 6.2)	Actual Cost (from physical inventory)	Variance ($)
SCOTCH			
J & B	$135	$140	$5
Cutty Sark	124	127	3
Chivas Regal	116	175	59
Dewars	116	123	7
Lauders	115	245	130
Scotch Total	$606	$810	$204
VODKA			
Smirnoff	$368	$310	$(58)
Popov	242	370	128
Gordons	192	195	3
Vodka Total	$802	$875	$73

be that the bartenders are substituting Lauders, which sells for less, for Dewars, Cutty Sark, and J & B. When the money is collected, they keep the difference. For example, a guest orders J & B; the bartender pours Lauders, and collects $1.75 but deposits only $1.50, the amount expected from a sales of Lauders. Wait a minute, you might ask, if this occurs, why is the cost for J & B, Cutty, and Dewars not lower than it should be? The bartender is not pouring these brands when ordered, so the usage and cost should be lower. If the bartender(s) are "giving" these drinks away (selling them, but not recording the sales), this would account for the difference. For instance, if there had been a whole bottle of Dewars accumulated by substituting Lauders whenever Dewars were ordered, the bartender then could sell the entire bottle and keep the money. This is money on top of the 25¢ made each time the substitution occurs! What about the Chivas Regal? Here possible answers are that this brand is either being sold without depositing the money, or the bartender is pouring heavy. People who drink Chivas Regal can reasonably be expected to show their gratitude for a healthy overpour!

Vodka: The vodka pattern is similar. There is a huge shortage on the Popov (probably the well stock), which could have occurred by substituting Popov for the higher priced Smirnoff. The Smirnoff cost is well under what it should be, indicating that it probably had been substituted for on a frequent basis.

These are merely examples of an analysis. It was made easier than it sometimes is because a couple of categories were so much out of line. This may appear to be an overly simplistic example, but when people are stealing or cheating, the data will usually show unusual patterns. A different type of problem occurs when nothing sticks out. In other words, the $300.00 cost variance is evenly distributed among all the categories and brands. There are thirty-one brands listed in Exhibit 6.2. If each one was off by $10.00, the entire variance would be accounted for. In such a case, it is possible that each brand is being manipulated equally, but that is unlikely. A more rational explanation is that the bar operation is generally sloppy, and overpouring or other waste occurs on every-thing. One thing to watch for is a lower-than-standard cost (the actual cost is $300.00 *below* the standard) with the variance spread evenly. That could well indicate general *underpouring*. The danger there is that a bottle that is underpoured has more potential drinks in it, hence greater potential sales value. Sooner or later (probably sooner), the extra sales will not be deposited.

Standard cost analysis is ideally suited to food systems because they are product oriented. If a problem occurs, it is most likely to show itself in an analysis of the costs. Beverage systems should be primarily personnel oriented, and thus there are other perhaps more useful ways to analyze a beverage operation.

Ounce or Inventory Analysis

This is an extremely accurate but very time-consuming analytical method. Like the others, it is a comparison process. In this case, the actual usage is obtained by taking daily physical inventories to determine how many ounces of liquor were used. This can be given as one overall total, but the discussion on standard cost should make it clear that it would be much more useful to have data on each spirit category and each brand stocked. The *standard usage* is calculated by multiplying the sales from each drink by the ounces of liquor that should have been served for each. Totaling these will result in the amount of liquor that should have been poured for those drinks sold. Again it is recommended to break the figures down by category and brand. When variances exist, they must be evaluated and explained.

This type of system is difficult to implement because it requires a daily (or very frequent) physical inventory, and in addition, unless some sort of mechanical or electronic drink-counting system is used, it is nearly impossible to get sales information accurate enough to be useful. A related problem occurs from daily inventories; unless there is sufficient volume, minor inventory mistakes can have a major impact on the results. For example, consider the effect of one missing bottle (750 ml or 25.4 oz.) as shown in Exhibit 6.5.

The missing bottle, if added to the ending inventory, would reduce the liquor used by some 25 ounces in each case. In the first unit, this is

Exhibit 6.5 Effect of Inventory Error

	Unit #1	Unit #2
Opening inventory (oz.)	1,905	3,048
Issues to bar (oz.)	203	1,245
Liquor available for sale (oz.)	2,108	4,293
Ending inventory (oz.)	1,873	3,004
Total ounces used	235	1,289

over 10 percent of the calculated usage. In bar 2, the effect is to overstate the actual usage by less than 2 percent, a rather significant difference. This is why small-volume establishments so often obtain widely fluctuating costs when they take inventories daily.

Note that this analysis is not dependent on a percentage. The cost percentage could vary significantly from day to day, but as long as the ounce comparison was in line, the percentage variance should not cause any concern. This system, like the standard cost system, is product oriented and therefore not entirely suited to the needs of a beverage operation.

Standard Sales Analysis

This is also called the *potential sales system* because it gives management information as to what sales should have been if everything had been done properly. Note that in this system, the cost percentage again is not the important factor. It is one measure of profitability and an excellent monitoring tool, but it has nothing to do with establishing or maintaining control. If the profitability, as measured by the percentage, is inadequate, then pricing and portioning policies should be reevaluated. The purpose of control is to assure that potential profitability is attained. It has nothing to do with what that level of profitability is, should be, or could be.

The standard sales system cannot be successfully implemented unless the operation has some basic controls and standards in use. These are:

1. Standard portion sizes
2. Standard prices
3. Standard glassware
4. Standard measures
5. Standard procedures for drink accountability

The system can be used in absence of these standards but not as a *control* system, merely as an analytical tool to measure the efficiency of a beverage system.

The procedures are fairly simple and are as follows:

1. Establish the *potential* or *standard* sales value of each brand and bottle size in the inventory.
2. Determine the exact usage of each brand during the appropriate period.
3. Multiply the bottle sales value by the total usage. Total all brands, and the result is the sales that should be generated during the period.
4. *Compare* the actual sales with the potential or standard sales.

Establishing the bottle sales value (step 1) is simple to do in most cases, but for some items the sales mix will have to be known. If a bottle is used only for one sized drink, and all the drinks are sold for the same price, the calculation is as shown in Exhibit 6.6. The standard sales value of this particular brand is $45.68 per bottle. If ten bottles are used, the sales should be $456.80. If, however, a bottle is used for drinks that vary in portion sizes and/or selling prices, the calculation is a little more complicated. Here it is necessary to know how many of each drink is sold, and the sales value is an *average* sales value. For example: you want to calculate the sales value of a bottle of well gin that is used to make martinis and a variety of other drinks. Each martini will have 2.5 ounces of gin, while all other gin drinks have a portion size of 1.0 ounce. Martinis sell for $2.50, and all the other gin drinks sell for $1.15. To establish the bottle sales value, you need to know only the sales mix. This could be obtained with great accuracy from a computerized beverage system, or it could come with varying degrees of accuracy from check

Exhibit 6.6 Standard Sales Value—Single Use Bottle

Calculation when a brand is nearly or entirely poured as one drink

Brand:	Jack Daniels
Bottle size:	750 ML (25.4 oz.)
Drink size:	1.25 oz.
Number of drinks per bottle:	25.4 / 1.25 oz. = 20.3
Drink price:	$2.25
Bottle sales value:	20.3 drinks per bottle x $2.25/drink = $45.68

abstracting, spot checking, estimating, and so on. We will assume, for our example, that a known sales ratio of 65 percent martinis to 35 percent other gin drinks exists. This means that, of every 100 gin drinks, 65 will be martinis and 35 will be other gin-mixed drinks. The calculation is shown in Exhibit 6.7. *Column A* lists the drinks made from this gin. There are only two, but there could be three, four, or even more. *Column B* gives the sales mix, *Column C* the drink portion size, and *column D* the total liquor used. In this case 197.5 ounces is used for every 100 drinks. This figure is obtained by multiplying column B (number sold) by column C (portion size in ounces). *Column E* is the percent of the total liquor that each drink accounts for. It is obtained by dividing each individual total (from column D) into the overall total. With martinis, 162.5 ounces divided by 197.5 ounces equals 82.3 percent. The other drinks are 35 ounces divided by 197.5 ounces, or 17.7 percent. Each of these percentages is multiplied by the total ounces in the bottle. This is *column F*, the ounce share each drink has of a 750 ml bottle (25.4 ounces). For example, martinis have 82.3 percent of 25.4 ounces or 20.9 ounces (you can, of course, round off), and the other drinks have 17.7 percent of 25.4 ounces, or 4.5 ounces. *Column G* is arrived at by dividing

the number of ounces available for each drink type (F) by the drink size (C) for the total number of drinks available per bottle. If there are 20.9 ounces of gin available for the purpose of making martinis, and each martini is supposed to contain 2.5 ounces, there are 8.3 martinis available for sale in each 750 ml bottle. Don't get confused by the 3/10 of a martini; this is an average for each 100 total drinks. There are similarly 4.5 other gin drinks available.

Column H is the drink selling prices, and *column I* is the total sales that can be expected from each drink type. It is obtained by multiplying the number sold (from column G) by the price per drink (H). Thus martinis should yield $20.75 and other gin drinks $6.75. The grand total is the bottle standard sales value, $27.50 ($20.75 plus $6.75). What this means is that if each drink contains the proper portion, if each drink is sold and sold at the proper price (and all the money is turned in), if there are 65 martinis sold for every 35 other gin drinks, the sales per bottle should be $27.50. If they are not, either the sales mix is wrong, or the selling prices are not being followed, or the portions are off, or some combination of all three. The standard sales value from a one-drink-one-price bottle will be accurate. The standard sales value

Exhibit 6.7 Standard Sales Value—Multiple Use Bottle

Calculation when a brand is used for several drinks with different portion sizes and selling prices

Product Gin   **Date** 10/82

A	B	C	D	E	F	G	H	I
Drink	**Drinks Sold**	**Portion Size**	**Total Liquor Used**	**% of Total Liquor Used**	**Ounce Share of Each 750 ml Bottle**	**Drinks Per Bottle**	**Price Per Drink**	**Sales**
Martini	~~100~~ ~~65~~ 1.5	~~2.5~~ oz.	162.5 oz. 150 oz	82.3 % 63%	20.9 oz. 16 oz	8.3 10.6	$2.50 2.00	$20.75 21.20
Other	~~50~~ ~~35~~ 1.75	~~1.0~~ oz.	35oz. 87.5	17.7 % 37%	4.5 oz. 9.4	4.5 5.4	$1.50 7.50	$ 6.75 13.50
Total	~~100~~ 150		~~197.5~~ oz. 237.507	100.0 % 100.	25.4 oz.			$27.50

34.70

of a multiple-use-multiple-price bottle will not be very accurate unless you know what your sales are.

A common reaction to this is that since the sales mix information is not available, the standard sales system is not really worth serious consideration. It is, according to many operators, too "theoretical" and therefore of little use. The truth is that without accurate sales information, not only this system, but any other as well is doomed to failure. If you want to use the cost percentage—how can you determine what it *should* be without the sales mix? You cannot. You must know the sales mix even to do simple percentage analysis. If you don't, the percentage is merely a hypothetical or financially desirable figure.

Step 2 in the standard sales system is to determine the total beverage usage during the period. This is easily obtained by taking a physical inventory.

Brand: Well Gin

Opening inventory	6.5 bottles
Plus: issues to bar	16.4 bottles
Total available for use	22.9 bottles
Less: ending inventory	5.7 bottles
Total used	17.2 bottles

Ending inventories are often taken only to yield dollar values, but they can be as valuable when used to yield usage totals for each brand.

The third step is to multiply the bottle sales value by the bottle usage. In our well-gin example, this would be:

Bottle sales value	$ 27.50
Bottle usage	17.2
Total bottle sales	$473.00

This figure, $473.00, represents the sales that should have been generated as a result of using 17.2 bottles of well gin.

The final step is to compare the standard or potential sales with the actual sales, keeping in mind the predetermined variance allowance. It would be unreasonable to expect no variance at all, even if you are using very accurate drink sales mix figures. Each operation has to determine how accurate their bottles sales value calculations are and set a variance percentage that they can agree is realistic and acceptable. It may be only 1 to 2 percent or it could be 10 percent. Each operation is different.

It is probably safe to say that virtually any unit that does not use this system would find their variance to be startlingly high the first time they calculate it. Two actual accounts illustrate this. A consultant was doing some management training seminars for a fifteen-unit table service chain, and the discussion came around to bar control systems. The standard sales system was outlined, and the executive management was asked whether they had ever used it. The reply, from the comptroller, was that a year or so before they had decided to test it on their largest and most profitable beverage operation. What, the consultant inquired, was the variance between potential sales and actual sales, if any? The reply was nearly 20 percent. Actual sales were only a little more than 80 percent of the potential! The comptroller said, however, that the manager thought the system was a lot of work and that the figures couldn't possibly be correct, so they never did anything else with it. The other example concerned a hotel and restaurant school student project. The student was interested in running an analysis on an actual operation as an independent study. A restaurant was found that was willing to provide the necessary information. The problem was that they had no drink sales records, so management estimated them. The student also reported to the professor that the standard portions that were given him by the management were not used by the bartenders. At any rate, the student persevered and worked out the sales value of each brand poured and came up with a total potential sales. It was both his and the professor's opinion that the validity of the figure would be fairly low since the calculations were based on so many estimations. They felt that the variance could possibly be as high as 20 percent without meaning anything. The variance turned out to be 40 percent! The actual sales were only 60 percent of the calculated potential! The report was submitted to the manager who promptly disregarded it as preposterous. The point here is not that the variance was actually 40 percent, but that there was a high probability that it was substantial and certainly warranted investigation. One would think that the manager would at least have attempted to make the estimations more accurate and recalculate the standard sales to see whether the figures could possibly be somewhat accurate.

The standard sales can be calculated on a modified inventory work sheet as shown in Exhibit 6.8 (called a *standard sales work sheet*).

A *Brand*: These would be arranged by category (Scotch, bourbon, Canadian, rum, wines, beers, and so forth).

B *Opening inventory*: This is the ending inventory of the previous period. It is given in bottles. Note that in order to determine the standard sales, it is not necessary to inventory the storeroom along with the bar. The bar is where the products are used, and you need only the usage from that area. When using inventories for determining what the actual costs are for an operating statement, however, it *is* necessary to have opening and closing inventories on *all* stock.

C *Period issues*: These are the totals of the daily requisitions during the period (the issues to the bar from the storeroom). These are given in whole bottles unless partial bottles are sent to the bar, and this is not recommended.

D *Total available*: The number of bottles that were available for usage during the period.

E *Ending inventory*: This is taken by management as described in Chapter 7. Here we show the technique of estimating the partial bottles by tenths.

F *Bottle cost*: Taken either from inventory or purchase records.

G *Extended ending inventory*: This would be the purpose of a standard *inventory* work sheet. It provides information on the value of the stock remaining at the end of the period. We want to show that this is not the only information that can be obtained from an inventory.

H *Bottle usage*: This information is typically not generated by an inventory, but it should be for it is of critical importance. Aside from its use in the standard sales calculation, management should constantly be aware of the movement of each brand during each period. There should be expected or standard patterns of activity, and these ought to be compared to the actual movement.

I *Bottle standard sales value*: Calculated as described.

J *Total standard sales*: This is the "what it ought to be" figure. It is compared to the actual sales. In our example, we have isolated two categories of spirits: Scotch and bourbon. We give the sales expected from each category as a whole, and this as a minimum should be compared to the category sales. Most registers will ring Scotch on a different key than bourbon. The degree of control is greatly enhanced, however, when we can compare each brand. This can certainly be done, although some sort of computerized point-of-sale equipment is probably necessary.

K *Actual sales*: Taken from the register totals.

L *Variance (plus or minus)*: Exhibit 6.8 shows that the Scotch sales were $96.50 short of what they could have been, while the bourbon sales were only $11.50 short. If these were the only two kinds of spirits sold, the focus of attention would be easy to determine. The Scotch would be a high priority for investigation, while the bourbon could wait until the Scotch is straightened around. Having the brand-by-brand analysis, as we do here, provides the information really needed to determine what is actually occurring and where the problems are. For example: with Scotch, all the brands except Chivas Regal, the super-premium brand, show a sales shortage. The Chivas actually has taken in

Exhibit 6.8. Standard Sales Work Sheet

	A	B	C	D	E	F	G	H	I	J	K	L
Brand		Opening Inventory (bottles)	Period Issues (bottles)	Total Available (bottles)	Ending Inventory (bottles)	Bottle Cost ($)	Extended Inventory ($)	Bottle Usage	Bottle Standard Sales Value($)	Total Standard Sales ($)	Actual Sales ($)	= or (-) ($/%)
SCOTCH												
J & B		4.5	12	16.5	4.9	8.16	$ 39.98	11.6	35.00	$406.00	$386.50	(19.50)
Cutty Sark		2.5	7	9.5	2.8	8.21	22.99	6.7	35.00	234.50	191.50	(43.00)
Chivas Regal		2.4	4	6.4	2.1	12.37	25.98	4.3	50.00	215.00	238.00	23.00
Dewars		3.7	4	7.7	3.3	7.84	25.87	4.4	35.00	154.00	138.00	(16.00)
Lauders		6.4	16	22.4	6.7	6.25	41.88	15.7	30.00	471.00	430.00	(41.00)
Scotch Total		19.5	43	62.5	19.8		$156.70	42.7		$1,480.50	$1,384.00	(96.50)
												(6.5%)
BOURBON												
Jim Beam		3.8	4	7.8	3.2	6.75	21.60	4.6	30.00	138.00	128.00	(10.00)
Jack Daniels		3.5	8	11.5	3.8	9.15	34.77	7.7	40.00	308.00	320.00	12.00
Early Times		3.4	3	6.4	3.9	6.20	24.18	2.5	30.00	75.00	64.00	(11.00)
Wild Turkey		1.1	2	3.1	1.6	9.05	14.48	1.5	40.00	60.00	75.00	15.00
10 High		5.6	13	18.6	5.3	5.21	27.61	13.3	25.00	332.50	315.00	(17.50)
Bourbon Total		17.4	30	47.40	17.8		$122.64	29.60		$913.50	$902.00	(11.50)
												(1.3%)
							$279.34			$2,394.00	$2,286.00	(108.00)
												(4.5%)

more money than it should have. One possible explanation for this is that the bartenders have been pouring the other brands when Chivas was ordered. In this case they did not keep enough of the additional income generated! If Chivas was ordered but not poured, the usage for Chivas would be less than what would be expected from the sales. The usage for the brands actually poured would be higher than the sales indicate. When management has detailed information on the usage and sales for each brand on the bar, it is very difficult for bar personnel to juggle the data; there are simply too many variables for them to consider. The same thing appears to be happening with the bourbon, but it is on a smaller scale and is better balanced.

This then is the standard sales control system. It does work, and when management has the equipment to provide the necessary information, it would be foolish not to use it. It also puts the control emphasis where it belongs, on the sales, not on the cost.

Gross Profit Analysis

This is the same concept that we introduced in the section on food analysis as menu engineering. Here we are applying it, with some modifications, to an alcoholic beverage system. The key is that each product sold has a total profit potential that is based on the number of drinks sold and the profit from each drink. It is expected that the rational manager would want to increase profits and that this would take precedence over the percentage or even the sales level. Percentages do not have any consistent relationship with profitability. Often sales do not either, which brings to mind an old story:

Question: "How can you sell those drinks at that price? I don't see how you can make any money!"

Answer: "I lose 5¢ on each drink, but I make it up in volume!"

The point is that volume and percentage combine to yield a certain level of profit, and it is that profit which ought to receive the most attention. Brand decisions, inventory levels, merchandising and promotion, pricing, bar layout, bottle placement, pouring system design—all these decisions and more should be made based upon their impact on profitability. The objective is to increase gross profit. First, however, management must have full and complete data of the profit structure. This is the importance of menu engineering. It provides the necessary information as well as strategies for improvement.

Exhibit 6.2 was used both in the percentage analysis and standard cost analysis discussions. Its most important use, however, is for profit analysis. Each drink is compared to a profitability and popularity standard. Each drink will be categorized as either high or low in profitability and either high or low in popularity. The calculations are made as they are with the food menu. The standard for popularity (the menu mix percentage) is 2.25 percent (100 percent divided by 31 menu items times 70 percent equals 2.25 percent). Any drinks that have a sales percentage of 2.25 or over are considered to be more popular than the standard. Drinks that account for less than 2.25 percent will be ranked below the standard.

The profit standard is $1.22 ($20,741 total profit divided by 16,970 drinks sold equals $1.22 per drink). All drinks that produce a gross profit of $1.22 or higher are considered highly profitable. Profits below $1.22 result in the ranking of a drink (or brand) as low profit. The rankings of each brand are shown in columns P and R. As with a food menu, there are four possible ways the brand can be classified:

High profit plus high popularity = stars

High profit plus low popularity = puzzles

Low profit plus high popularity = plow horses

Low profit plus low popularity = dogs

The classification of all these brands appears in column S. Finally, there is the profit factor. This, you will recall, is a figure indicating the relative total profitability of each brand or menu item. It is calculated by dividing the total gross profit

($20,741.33) by the number of brands sold (31) for an average profit of $669 per brand. The total profit from each individual brand is then divided by the average. When the profit from a product is the same as the average, the profit factor will be 1.00 ($669 divided by $669 equals 1.00). When a brand's profits exceed the average, the profit factor will be more than 1.00 ($800 divided by $669 equals 1.20). When the profit from any particular product is less than the average, the profit factor will be less than 1.00 ($500 divided by $669 equals .75). The profit factor is therefore an indication of where each brand stands relative to average profitability. A menu is considered well balanced when most of the items are near 1.00. The problem with very high numbers is that they must be counterbalanced by one or more very low ones, which means there will be unprofitable brands on the bar. It is difficult to justify purchasing, receiving, storing, inventorying, issuing, pouring, and controlling products that do not produce reasonable profits. The profit factors are given in column T.

Here is an example of how the analysis would proceed:

Scotch: This category looks fine. J & B, Cutty Sark, and Dewars all produce profits near the average. Chivas Regal has a fairly low profit factor, .65, but this is an example of a type of product frequently found in alcoholic beverage systems that probably would not be in a food system. We could call them "super puzzles." These are products that will never be big sellers, but they are very profitable to sell. They tend to be high quality, expensive, status items. Not to carry them in a quality establishment would be unthinkable; it would not be consistent with the image of the operation. Another reason for having them available is that guests can "trade-up" if they desire. In our example, if there were no Chivas Regal available, over 200 Scotch drinks would be switched to one of the other brands—all of which produce a much lower gross profit. Unless the total profit from these super puzzles is very low (indicating virtually no demand), their availability can usually be justified. The term given in the beverage trade to

these brands is super-premium brands. Other examples are:

Scotch -Johnnie Walker

　　　　Royal Salute

Canadian - Crown Royal

Bourbon -　Jack Daniels

　　　　Wild Turkey

Orange Liqueur - Grand Marnier

Champagne - Dom Perignon

There are many others, of course, but these serve to illustrate the point. At any rate, even though Chivas Regal is a puzzle and it is not as profitable as the other Scotches, there would never be any serious thought of eliminating it from the menu as might be the case with a food item. The remaining Scotch, Lauders, does quite well and is in fact the second most profitable Scotch brand.

Another way in which beverage analysis differs from food analysis is that each category must be evaluated on its own. Compare the tequila category to the Scotch. It is awful from a profitability viewpoint. In a food menu, if tequila were a category such as sandwiches, steaks, salads, and seafood, the entire category would be quickly dropped. In a bar, however, *all* categories must be represented, but the number of brands and the pricing policies are subject to modification.

Beverages must also be analyzed according to their market positioning status. In general, there are three positioning categories. The first is the standard products, which are typically stocked as well or house brands. There would seldom be a necessity for more than one in each liquor type. A second category is premium. These are the call brands, the ones guests request by specific brand name (not Scotch and water but Johnnie Walker Red and water, for example). Most operations would want more than one brand represented in this category. The total number would really depend on the spirit type. There are a lot of Scotches that will be requested but not many blended whiskies. Actually, this is an easy decision for management to make for they should let the guests make it. If something moves, stock it; if it does not, don't. It is as simple as that. Most operations tend to stock too many brands under the mistaken assumption that they "have to carry them in case someone asks for them". We prefer to stock only those brands that *are* actually requested and not to speculate on what might be requested.

The third category is the previously discussed super-premiums. They need not move as well as the premiums, but they should show reasonable turnover or else there is no demand. Bar operators should be very cautious about stocking too many brands from this category. In many cases one would be sufficient. Strategies for profit improvement are similar to those discussed for food. With Scotch we would probably be satisfied with the profits of all items except Chivas. This being a puzzle, we would normally want to increase the sales (its weak point, number of drinks sold), but since it is a super puzzle, it is never going to be a high-selling product. It may be, though, that due to its image and status, we could charge a higher price and increase the profit that way. Perhaps the consumer who drinks Chivas does not care what it costs. If this is the case, and it often is, then it is foolish not to charge more. Not to do so is to unnecessarily limit the profits.

The Canadian category is quite different from Scotch. There is a lot of variance in the profit factors, indicating that VO and CC are highly profitable, while Crown Royal is only half as profitable as the average product, and Windsor Supreme is very low. In addition, it is worthwhile looking at the average profit per Canadian drink.

It is $1.18 (Canadian total, column F) while the Scotch average was $1.46. These profits should be roughly comparable, and the fact that they are not is probably due to pricing errors. VO and CC are underpriced relative to the Scotches. The very low sales for Windsor Supreme could be due to two factors. VO and CC are the premium brands, and Windsor Supreme is the well brand. Either there is little demand for a house or well brand (most Canadian whiskey requests are for a specific brand), or the low VO and CC prices have unnaturally skewed the demand away from the well liquor. One strategy could be to increase the selling price of both VO and CC, hoping that the demand would not change appreciably. If the demand stayed about the same, a follow-up strategy would be to drop the Windsor Supreme since there would clearly be little demand for a house Canadian. If the sales of Windsor Supreme increased, its retention would be justified on the grounds that a normal relationship between call and well brands now existed. Crown Royal, like Chivas Regal, is a super-premium. It is a super-puzzle in that the sales probably cannot be increased significantly, but the profit can. The strategy would therefore be to raise the price of Crown Royal. If all these changes were implemented, the profit could be projected as follows (see Exhibit 6.9):

Windsor Supreme has been dropped, and the prices of VO and CC and Crown Royal have all been increased. The result is an improvement in profit of $571.16 ($3,118.16 minus $2,547.00). Crown Royal sales have stayed the same, and VO and CC have absorbed the sales that previously went to Windsor Supreme. VO and CC are served both when requested by name and when a

Exhibit 6.9 Canadian Category Profitability after Revision

Brand	Sales	Cost	Selling Price	CM	Total CM
V O	963	$.34	$1.75	$1.41	$1,357.83
C C	963	$.34	$1.75	$1.41	$1,357.83
Crown Royal	230	$.50	$2.25	$1.75	$402.50
Total	2,156			$1.45	$3,118.16

Canadian whiskey is requested. This bar thus has no well brand, but the prior sales pattern indicated none was necessary.

The Scotch situation was quite different. There clearly was a demand for a house brand (Lauders). The average profit margin (CM) from Canadian drinks has risen to $1.45 from $1.18! With a food menu, such a projection could be wishful thinking for the guests may well trade down, and the total category sales would decline. With alcoholic beverages this may not necessarily happen. The Canadian drinkers would still prefer to consume Canadian whiskey and normally would not switch to another spirit category. Knowledge of the market and consumers is necessary to planning profitable strategies. If, for example, the Canadian market was price conscious and simply stopped patronizing the establishment due to price increases, this strategy would be foolish because profits would be lost. Menu decisions must be made with the assumption that the guest count will not change, or if it does, it will increase. Any changes that result in a decrease in patronage will simply reduce profits. In our bar example (Figure 6.2), every drink lost would cost the operation $1.22 (the average CM) in lost profits, and this loss would probably go directly to the bottom line.

One important point about strategies has been brought out. Objectives must be clearly identified. The objectives here are to sell the same number of Canadian drinks, to maintain sales of Crown Royal at a higher price, to increase sales of VO and CC also at a higher price, and to increase the total CM to $3,118.16 and the average CM to $1.45. Having these goals in a quantitative form makes it easy to later evaluate whether or not the revisions were successful. These goals also provide guidance for promotion and merchandising. It is obvious that the operation should be prepared to face criticism and resistance to the price increases, especially for the VO and CC. They may develop a promotion emphasizing the quality of VO and CC (well known and accepted), and the fact that these are now, in effect, their house brands. In other words, they will attempt to defuse

potential criticism ahead of time by making the change appear advantageous to the customers.

The *blended whiskey* category is interesting. One, Imperial, yields a poor profit (profit factor = .46) while the other, 7 Crown, is the third most profitable product and over twice as profitable as the average, with a profit factor of 2.20. There are only two marketing positions with blended whiskey, premium and standard, with no super-premium products. This is also pretty much a one-product category. Seven Crown, for years the top selling spirits brand in the United States, is still number three and has today an even larger percentage share of the blend market. The operator's strategy here could be to eliminate the Imperial, which is used as a well blend, and pour 7 Crown for all blend drinks. There is little demand for a blended whiskey other than 7 Crown; the sales totals show this. If this were done, there would be a decrease in profit because the Imperial produces $.02 more than does the 7 Crown. The profit decrease will be $5.76, which is only one-third of 1 percent. Our approach is that it is worth more than $5.76 to be able to eliminate a brand from the inventory because there is one less product to purchase, receive, store, issue, inventory, maintain on a perpetual inventory, track the sales of, and so forth.

Tequila: There are two tequila brands in stock and both are dogs. They both are unpopular and produce a poor profit. There would undoubtedly be a temptation to remove both, but this is another instance where alcoholic beverage menus differ dramatically from food menus. If this were a food menu, two items as unpopular and unprofitable as these would be dropped quickly. Most operators would agree, however, that tequila must be carried on the bar. It would be expected by guests, and certain drinks cannot be made without tequila. Whether or not to carry tequila is not, therefore, a decision controlled by management. How many tequilas to stock and how much to charge is, however, a decision management has much control over. In this case (Exhibit 6.2) the reasoning is:

—We must stock tequila, but there is no reason to have two.

—As long as we must have tequila, we might as well make at least the average profit on it. Therefore, we should increase the price to $1.50. If people stop buying tequila we really don't care.

—The brand to keep would be the more popular one. The sales here show that Jose Cuervo is more popular than Two Fingers, so it would be the one to keep.

—There are no clear-cut differences between well and call qualities as is the case with most other spirits. As a result, there are not the distinct market positions of standard, premium, and super-premium as with many other spirit categories.

The revised tequila category could look like this:

Brand	Sales	Cost	Selling Price	CM	Total CM
Jose Cuervo	375	$.26	$1.50	$1.24	$465.00

The sales would be projected to remain the same, and the increased selling price would result in a profit increase of $88.75 ($465.00 minus $376.25). Tequila is not easily substituted for; it is too unique. So the sales would probably be about the same even with a price increase.

Using this approach, the operator would go through the entire beverage menu looking at each spirit category independently and evaluating each individual product. The key evaluation criterion is total brand profitability; but, as pointed out, this is not the sole criterion. Other analytical factors are: market positioning, product image or status, type of product, pricing structure, number of products stocked, and call versus well brands. The ultimate objective is to increase the total profit, but changes that result in fewer brands stocked are nearly as desirable for they will decrease the inventory investment and improve the operating efficiency.

7 Control of Alcoholic Beverage Costs

Profit Potential of Alcoholic Beverages

Most operators want to optimize their sales of alcoholic beverages since they have such a high profit potential. In fact, the overall profitability of a firm could depend upon the food-alcoholic beverage sales mix. Failure to attain a projected sales mix could have disastrous consequences as the example in Exhibit 7.1 shows. The only mistake here is that the beverage sales did not account for 25 percent of total sales, as anticipated. All the other factors, generally regarded as the critical ones, are in line. These would be: total sales, percentage cost of foods sold, and percentage cost of beverages sold. Yet because the sales mix was not correctly anticipated, the profit is $1,035 less than expected. When total sales and all cost percentages are on target, the operation would have to be regarded as well managed; profits, however, are lower than expected.

The point of this example is that alcoholic beverages are more profitable than food because they have a lower product cost. This means that the bar operator can mark up his or her selling prices higher than can the food operator. This fact is well known, but what is not fully appreciated by some managers is that alcoholic beverages should be more profitable throughout the operating statement. The cost of labor is less, for the bar operator pays personnel only to sell and serve products, while the food operator must pay for the processing and production of various goods. Thus, food is at a disadvantage due to requiring extra people for an extra task. It also is a fact that production people are higher paid than are service people (who generally receive tips). The result is that in a beverage operation we have fewer employees earning lower wages relative to food systems.

Operating costs are also lower with alcoholic beverages. The cost of china and flatware would be nearly nonexistent, although glassware costs would be high. Ware washing expenses are likely to be reduced, as would linen, cleaning, maintenance, supplies, and especially energy expenses. This reduction in expenses makes sense because beverage operations are less

Exhibit 7.1. Effect of Food/Beverage Sales Mix

Projection					
	Sales		**Cost**		**CM or**
	($)	**(%)**	**($)**	**(%)**	**Gross Profit**
Food	56,250	75.0	22,500	40.0	$33,750.00
Beverage	18,750	25.0	4,125	22.0	14,625.00
Total	$75,000	100.0%	$26,625	35.5%	$48,375.00
Actual					
Food	62,000	82.7	24,800	40.0	37,200.00
Beverage	13,000	17.3	2,860	22.0	10,140.00
Total	$75,000	100.0%	$27,660	36.9%	$47,340.00

complex than food operations are. They require less space, equipment, and general support.

Beverage operations will also cost less to develop so investment expense will be lower. Foodservice operations with high ratios of beverage sales can generally expect an improved return on investment. Finally, not only do beverage systems offer potentially higher bottom-line profits, but attainment of those profits should be easier than with a food system. Alcoholic beverage systems are significantly less complex than are food systems and should be easier to control. In practice, however, this often does not hold true. It is probable that the industry loses a higher percentage of potential beverage profits than food profits, although it really should be the reverse.

Standards

One of the most important tasks of management is to establish the operational standards. This is no less critical with beverages than with food, although it is certainly easier with beverages. Standards assure that everything is done the same way—always. Consistency is the goal, and consistency leads to predictability.

With standards, management is in a position to predict cost of products served and quality of products served. When that occurs, management has the basis for control. We say the basis because control will not result without management follow-up. Without standards, however, there would be no consistency in either cost or quality, and management would be unable to achieve control under such conditions regardless of how hard they work or how much experience they have.

What should be standardized in a beverage operation?

Glassware. One of the best ways to attain portion control is to use standardized serviceware, especially glassware. Standardized glassware can also be an important part of the marketing effort.

Measuring devices. These are one of the most effective portion control methods. Unless, however, bar personnel are using jiggers and shot glasses specified by the operation, there is no effective control.

Pouring procedures and techniques. Again, these are for portion control.

Garnishing. This is for marketing as well as for cost control purposes.

Pricing. There is no sense in even attempting to control a bar operation without prior assurance that standard and proper prices will be charged. This is one of the easiest ways to defraud an operation, but even in the absence of such attempts, mistakes are made. This is especially the case when several people have the authority to ring drinks and assign charges, a common practice.

Ordering and calling. These procedures must be standardized to insure maximum speed, maximum sales, profit attainment, and reduction (if not elimination) of mistakes.

Check writing. Established for sales control and elimination of mistakes.

Drink formulas. For cost control, quality control, and guest satisfaction.

Station setup. For efficiency, speed, and reduction of waste.

Cash handling. For sales and cash control.

Register procedures. For sales, cash control, and speed.

Replenishment of bar stock. For inventory control, cost control, and sales control.

Ordering stock for the storeroom. For inventory control, and improved asset management.

Bottle arrangement in bars and storage areas. For speed (and accuracy) in order preparation and inventory taking.

This is not a totally complete list, but it answers the question of what should be standardized. The answer is *everything*! The more aspects of the bar operation that are effectively standardized, the greater the control.

Bar Frauds and Improper Practices

A point made earlier is that beverage control is primarily personnel and sales control. For this reason, prior to discussing purchasing, receiving,

inventory, and so forth, which are oriented to product control, we will discuss the many ways that unscrupulous or poorly trained and sloppy beverage employees can cause low profits. In many cases, we will give examples that have actually occurred in various operations.

Credit Cards

Virtually all establishments now handle some type of credit card. Some do most of their business on a charge basis. When hundreds of thousands of dollars pass through a foodservice unit via credit cards, it is obvious that there is a lot of money for someone to take advantage of, especially if management is not vigilant. The following is one example of the type of things that can happen. A bartender came into the possession of a credit card. How isn't important. It could have been left accidentally by a guest, or it could have been stolen from a guest, or it could have been purchased by the bartender from someone who specializes in maintaining a large and diverse inventory of credit cards. It is what he did with it that is important. He would collect checks that were paid in cash (both collected on the bar from his guests and from the lounge guests by the cocktail waitress), and set them to the side. Instead of cashing them out at the end of the shift, he sent the waitress home and ran all the checks through the register as a charge, using the credit card and keeping the cash. He would handle $50.00 to $75.00 in this manner, about three times per week. In addition, since any customer spending that much money would be expected to tip, the bartender put a $20.00 to $30.00 tip on the check and took that as well.

This is the type of activity that is not generally a problem because the employee involved is a thief. Few people will take something when they know its disappearance will be noted; a thief will. In this case, there was no way the bartender could get away with these actions over an extended period since the credit card company would inform management of the problem and probably get involved in the investigation. When that time came, however, the bartender had not been seen for a few days and was never seen again. This is an example of what we refer to as theft. Most employees would take something, products and/or cash, if they felt that its loss would not be noted. Or if it were, that it would be so long after the incident happened that it would be nearly impossible to implicate any particular individual(s). This is termed *pilferage*, and it is a great problem in the foodservice industry. By the time this credit card scam was discovered, the bar was out nearly $2,000.00, none of which was ever recovered.

The operation made several fundamental errors that enabled this to happen. The first and most critical was that it was a new unit, and the corporation decided to save money for a few months by not having an assistant manager. This meant that the bartender was left to close alone most of the time. Another error was in not adequately training the bookkeeper. Although an experienced bookkeeper and office manager, she had never worked in a restaurant and did not realize that it was unusual for one person to keep coming back and spending such amounts. The overall charge sales were also higher than this company normally experienced in the lounge. These mistakes were compounded by the lack of an adequate credit card policy. The booklet distributed by the credit card company to show invalid cards was not made available to any of the cash handlers or the office. The bartender, of course, would have paid no attention since he knew the card was no good, but the bookkeeper would have caught it if she had been trained to check all large charges or repeat charges. In this particular operation there was no reason for the bartender to have access to the charge machine. The food and beverage facilities were in a hotel and were managed on contract. All bar charges could have been rung by the cocktail waitresses at the food cashier station, and after that closed, at the hotel front desk. Afterwards, an assistant manager was hired and close the operation, and the bookkeeper became a veritable bloodhound in sniffing out suspicious activities. The current validity of cards used for all charges over $25.00 had to be checked (by phone) before honoring the charge, and the charge machine was removed from the bar. But this all occurred after almost $2,000.00 in sales had been written off.

Substitutions

The preliminary step to fraudulent activities in the bar is to somehow create a reservoir of undocumented liquor. The next step is to sell it and keep the money. Many bars are so poorly managed, however, that the first step is not even necessary, for the management does not really know what they are using or what the sales should be. One way to create extra, unaccounted-for liquor on the bar is to substitute. This can be done either by brand to the customers or by the bottle. In the first case, the bartender will pour from the well when a call drink is ordered. She or he would, for example, pour Lauders Scotch when Cutty Sark is ordered (or pour Cutty Sark when Chivas Regal is ordered, but this would be more difficult to get away with). The advantage is that the call drink is more expensive. If the bartender has poured Lauders and is expected to collect $1.50 when $1.95 is actually collected, he or she is free to keep the difference. In fact, if the operation uses the standard sales analysis, the bartender would have to pocket it, otherwise the sales would be higher than expected!

Substitution by the bottle is more blatant. An empty call brand is filled with the well brand and the substitute brands can be poured with no fear that someone would notice that the wrong bottle was being used. The payoff is higher as well. Assuming the entire bottle could be poured in one shift, and that 1 1/4-ounce drinks were being poured, the figures would look like this:

Bottle size   = 750 ml (25.4 ounces)

Number of drinks   = 20 (25.4 ounces ÷ 1.25 ounces - rounded)

Call brand   = $1.95 x 20 = $39.00

Well brand   = $1.50 x 20 = $30.00

The difference, $9.00, belongs to the bartender. One obvious problem with substituting is that the guests may notice the difference, but a skilled bartender can easily avoid this. With some spirits, there is little difference between brands. Vodka is an example. With many vodkas, the main differentiating factor among them is proof.

The objective in processing vodka is to remove as many of the distinctive characteristics as possible so that a neutral product will result. Another factor is the manner in which the drink is ordered. If one guest requests a spirit "neat" (no ice, no water, no mix), as would normally be done with fine brandies and cordials, it would be quite risky to substitute. A drink ordered mixed with Coca-Cola, however, could easily be substituted since the strong, distinctive flavor and odor of the mix would mask any subtle differences in the spirits. A skilled barperson could also take advantage of the circumstances under which the drinks were consumed. An individual who appears to be paying attention to and savoring the drink would not be a good candidate for substitution. In bars, however, many patrons pay little attention to what they are consuming and maximum attention to sports, business discussions, the other sex, and so forth. There are obviously opportunities for switching brands with little risk of discovery.

In addition to the lost profits, there is the problem of loss of customer goodwill. Inevitably some guests will notice the switch, which may lead to negative word-of-mouth advertising. An operation's reputation for integrity is too valuable an asset to risk in this manner. Of course, the bar personnel typically do not care; they merely get another job.

There are several ways to control this type of activity. One is to place the bartender under as much observation as possible. Substitutions are not likely to be attempted when someone is watching. It is impossible to watch all the time, but if management combines frequent, irregular visits to the bar with an effective spotter program, this can act as a deterrent. Management can and should use the customers as well. It is good public relations to get to know the guests, and a lot of valuable information can be gained as well. Bottles can also be removed for evaluation from time to time. A food manager will presumably be able to differentiate among beef, veal, and chicken, between sirloin and tenderloin, between frozen and fresh green beans so why not a bar manager among the various products on the bar? In actual practice, however,

few operators ever evaluate or taste alcoholic beverages. In tasting spirits, the products should be mixed with equal parts of distilled water, and the product should not be swallowed. Every manager who has responsibility for an alcoholic beverage operation should be familiar with the smell and taste of each brand carried on the bar. The water is added to dilute the alcohol, which tends to make taste evaluation less difficult, while the reason for not swallowing should be apparent.

Underpouring

This is one of the single most serious bar problems and is a much more profitable activity for the bartender than overpouring is. Underpouring results in the availability of surplus liquor, the main objective of bar frauds. For example: pouring 1 1/4-ounce drinks from a 750 ml (25.4 ounce) bottle will yield twenty drinks, but if 1-ounce drinks are poured, twenty-five drinks will result. If each drink can be sold for $2.00, the bartender could keep $10.00 from the sales of each bottle. Percentage analysis would not come close to revealing the loss, nor would sales analysis. The sales would appear in line, for the bottle would yield the expected twenty drinks at $2.00 each, or $40.00. What management is not aware of is that the sales potential is much higher. There should have been more liquor used and more sales recorded. Underpouring is an easy thing to do on a bar and nearly impossible to trace. The best control is to require that all drinks be recorded prior to being served. If this were done, the money for all twenty-five drinks would have to be turned in, or a cash shortage would result. As we have seen with food control, documentation is of critical importance. Sales analysis in this case would show that insufficient product was poured relative to the sales, and what was occurring would be obvious. Measuring devices can also be helpful. A lined shot glass is excellent because one can readily observe whether a full measure was poured. Two cautions apply here: someone must actually look at the glasses, and the correct glass must be used. Spirit brands are not the only things that can be substituted! The two-sided metal jigger is not effective as a control for underpouring. It is easy to fill the jigger to just below the rim and quickly dump it into the drink glass. Because most of the volume is at the top of the cone-shaped jigger, a very slight underpour could be significant.

Mechanical or electronic measuring systems are excellent, but they too can be circumvented. Consider a system in which the bartender pushes a button or lever and gets an exactly measured 1 1/4-ounce drink, which is also recorded. All the barperson has to do is to draw off fifteen drinks in a single container. There are now nearly 19 ounces of liquor available for sales. If the bartender can sell more than fifteen drinks from it, the difference can be pocketed. A drawback here is that these drinks must be hand poured, but most (not all) automatic systems must be combined with some hand pouring, so this should not be a problem for the bartender. The requirement for documentation of all sales is effective here as well. In our example, any drinks drawn from the system would automatically be recorded, but the bartender would be required to manually record all hand poured drinks. If this were enforced, he or she would end up donating money to the operation. Consider: fifteen drinks withdrawn in bulk, recorded, and expected to yield $30.00. The bartender then pours them manually, getting eighteen drinks, each of which must again be recorded. The expected sales now total $66.00 ($30.00 plus [18 times $2.00]). The bartender can collect only the $36.00 (18 times $2.00), so must come up with $30.00 or be short. Two things should be obvious here. One is that under such circumstances the bartender would never attempt this fraud. The other is that unless someone watches constantly, the cross-checking circumstances will not occur. A policy stating that all drinks must be recorded will not control the bar. Management observation combined with effective use of spotters and selection of the proper bar system can control the bar.

Similar to underpouring is the practice of shorting cocktails consisting of a variety of spirits and cordials. Drinks such as the Harvey Wallbanger, Pink Squirrel, Mai-Tai, and so forth can be adequately prepared by a skilled barperson with smaller than specified portions of the several components. Cream, ice, lemon, egg white can all be used to add volume, and the use of these products is seldom, if ever, evaluated. Some bars will sell a large amount of such drinks, making this practice potentially quite profitable. It is becoming popular to install a soft ice-cream machine in the bar for the preparation of alcoholic ice-cream drink specialties. Ice cream is a lot cheaper than cordials and spirits, and tracking the usage of only the cordials and spirits can be costly to the bar operator.

Bringing in Bottle(s)

This is an old, classic fraud, one nearly every bar manager knows about, but it is probably still widely practiced. Since a bottle of liquor can normally be sold for four to five times its cost, it makes good business sense for the bartender to do it, if possible. If this is done, it will not show up in the percentage nor in the sales analysis for reasons outlined earlier. There are two commonly used controls for this type of activity: par stock and bottle tagging.

Par Stock. Management determines the optimal number of bottles for each brand that will be carried at the bar. This is the par stock. If any bottles were brought in by the bar personnel, there would be one or more extra bottles on hand. This can be an effective control but only if someone counts the bottles. Again, a policy is not effective control. Not only must the bottles be counted and the count compared to the par, but the count must be done randomly. In other words, if the par is checked only on Saturday morning when the weekly inventory is taken, no discrepancies will appear. Management should check it then, of course, but also make it a practice to take random counts. The expectation of the bar personnel should be that management will frequently check the par stock. Sometimes the entire stock will be checked, more often a few brands at a time, and there is no way of predicting when or how often. Although this is not the only reason for maintaining a par stock on the bar, it is an important one.

Bottle Tagging. This system calls for the operation to affix some sort of identifying mark on each bottle issued to the bar. The mark could be a numbered or unnumbered sticker, a stamp, generally numbered, and so forth. The idea is that were a bottle to be brought in from the outside, it would not have the required mark and, hence, would be easily identified. This is an excellent control technique but only if someone actually inspects the bottles on the bar to assure that all are okay. This inspection, like the par stock verification, should not be done on a regular basis. It is more effective to check at random intervals.

An actual example will illustrate the fallacy of control by policy alone. An assistant manager, newly assigned to a unit, was given the task of preparing the daily bar issue. The importance of placing the company stamp (in the form of a gummed label) on each bottle was emphasized. He dutifully complied with these instructions. One day, several months later, while going through some storage drawers on the bar, he came across hundreds of the bottle labels! The bartender's explanation was, "Your predecessor was always forgetting to put the labels on the bottles. If anyone from the corporate office ever saw an unmarked bottle, they would go crazy. So I said, give me the labels and I will put them on."

The control is better when numbered stamps or labels are used. In that case, the guidelines for guest checks should be followed. Use a long series of consecutive numbers and maintain a permanent record accounting for every number along with the results of investigations into missing numbers. Look for missing numbers to show on bottles on the bar, perhaps not right away but certainly in the future

Free Pouring

From a conceptual standpoint, the problem if this is allowed is that management is permitting line employees to make basic management decisions. These are decisions that must be made only by management; the responsibility cannot be passed to line employees nor can the authority be delegated. Setting the portion size is such a decision. Letting bar personnel free pour (not using a measure of some sort) is essentially the same as letting them make the basic portion decision and doing so perhaps hundreds of times per day.

Many bartenders claim that they can free pour with nearly total accuracy. With some experienced personnel, there is reason to believe they can be quite accurate, but this is not the point. There must be standard portion sizes, and the drinks must be measured somehow. To claim that standard portions are important and then make no provisions for measuring them is to send a clear signal to the employees that they are not really that important. In fact, standard drink sizes are necessary for quality control as much as for cost control. They assure consistency of product as well as of cost. As such, they are sufficiently important to justify an investment in a measuring system somewhat more sophisticated than a shot glass or jigger, both of which, as shown, can be easily circumvented. This is one of the more important benefits of an automatic (electronic or computerized) bar system.

In summary, free pouring should not be allowed. It violates the principle that basic management decisions should not be delegated. Management is in the uncomfortable position of not really knowing what portions are being poured, even if they watch them being poured. This is a poor way to run a business. It is unlikely that any other businesses could be found where the employees making a product can decide, product by product, what the size ought to be. Our industry may be different, but it is not so different that basic business common sense does not apply. As for the contention that a skilled barperson can free pour accurately, the person may be able to under test conditions, but what about eight o'clock at night when the bar is full and several waitresses are lined up waiting for drinks? Another rationale for free pouring is that it is faster than measuring each drink, and more drinks can be poured, thereby increasing the total profits. This is true. If there is sufficiently high demand, management should certainly investigate some pouring system other than hand pouring. A well-designed electronic or mechanical pouring system can be far faster than hand pouring.

Overpouring

Although less potentially profitable to the bartender than underpouring, this can be a serious problem. The expectation is that the guests who are the recipients of such generosity will be sufficiently grateful that they will shower the bartender with tips. Rest assured that the guest who does not respond accordingly will receive no more overpours. This is one problem with overpouring; the barperson is using an asset that belongs to the company—the beverage stock—for his or her personal gain. This is unethical as well as illegal. Another problem is that product quality control goes out the window. Many drinks are not improved by putting more liquor in them; just the opposite actually. There is also the problem of potential loss of sales. A guest may consume fewer drinks if they are much larger or stronger than normal. This may not affect the bartender's tip, but it certainly affects the establishment's profits. Finally, there is the obvious problem of cost control because there is none. Control is achieved by being able to accurately predict what the cost will be. In this case, it cannot be done for the cost changes at the whim of the barperson.

Controlling overpouring is easier than controlling underpouring. Overpouring is generally obvious, whereas underpouring may not be. The action must, however, be observed. Vigilance at the bar is thus an important control measure. An effective spotter system is useful for this as well. Comparing usage to sales is also a good idea. The standard sales analysis would show insufficient sales relative to the amount of liquor poured. Standard cost analysis would show the discrepancy too. In the latter case, the results would be too much liquor used relative to the drinks poured. If the barpersons are underpouring some drinks or bringing in bottles, though, they can overpour without affecting the cost-to-sales ratio.

Giving Drinks Away

In actuality, no bartender truly believes in free drinks. Bartenders expect to be paid for them, or such drinks will not be provided in the future. There is a legitimate reason for purchasing a drink for a patron—to gain goodwill. In this regard, the expectation of the establishment and the barperson are not dissimilar. The difference is that the employee is attempting to gain personal benefit, while the operation wishes to gain institutional benefit. As such, the authority to purchase drinks for guests must be limited to management. This process of buying the guest a drink is often given too much importance by bar operators as well as bar employees. If the purpose is to obtain goodwill, to develop feelings of gratitude and warmth in the patrons, alcoholic beverages are not generally as effective a tool as are foods. Most guests will respond more positively in the dining room with a complimentary appetizer or dessert. If alcoholic beverages are to be given away, the dining room is also the best place to do it. A glass of wine or an after-dinner drink will normally draw a more enthusiastic response than will giving away a drink in the bar.

Some bar customers seem to feel that it is their "right" to get a free drink now and then. The operation that goes along with such demands either will go out of business or will reprice all its products to cover this practice. In some situations, free drinks could be a good promotional gimmick. One bar did exactly that. Every fifth drink was free (although it could just as well be the third or fourth). Prices were not adjusted. The idea behind the promotion was representative of classic gross-profit theory. The average profit per drink dropped, but so many more drinks were sold that total profits went up.

Serving Unregistered Drinks

We have mentioned the necessity of registering or recording all drinks served. Failure to do this results in a situation whereby when the money for unregistered drinks is collected, it can belong to whomever the bartender feels is most deserving. To be realistic about it, the bartender really cannot turn the money in for it would show up as an overage. Consider: 120 drinks served at $2.00 each, but only 100 were registered. The machine, when read, will indicate that checks paid in the amount of $200.00 should have been collected (100 drinks times $2.00). The bartender, however, actually collected $240.00. She or he obviously will not make a deposit of $240.00 when only $200.00 is expected.

Failure to register every drink sold is therefore potentially very costly in terms of reduced profits. This is how a barperson can most easily dispose of the surplus liquor accumulated via underpouring and so forth. As mentioned, the single most effective bar control is to assure that every single drink sold be permanently recorded. If this is done, there will be no bar control problem unless an employee just decides to take all the cash and run. This is the action of a thief. As explained, this is not the type of person or activity that can be controlled. It is only rarely a problem anyway. Taking undocumented receipts, however, may well be a nightly occurrence in many bar operations.

Merely assure that you have a record of every drink served, and there will be no control problems. If the bartenders take any cash, it will immediately show up as a shortage. That is the good news. Now the bad news: it cannot be done. However, with the proper combination of personnel, equipment, and facility design, you can get close enough. What this means is that if you hire good people, pay and treat them fairly, design and equip your bar for control, and pay attention to it, you *can* expect to control the bar. Control, like any other activity, must be planned. Without proper planning, you could live at the bar twenty-four hours a day and still lose significant profits.

Watering the Bottles

Why should bar personnel risk bringing liquor into the bar or take the trouble to selectively underpour certain products at certain times when all they really need in order to supply surplus liquor is the water faucet? If, for example, a bar sold 200 drinks per day (at 1 1/4-ounces per drink), they would use ten bottles per day or seventy per week. If each bottle had two shots of water added (one shortly after opening, the second when about a third was gone), the bartenders(s) would have 140 extra drinks available each week. If the drinks sold for $2.00 each, this would amount to $280.00 per week! Note that this would not affect the bar cost percentage, the standard cost, or the standard sales. How difficult is it to get away with adding a little water to a bottle of spirits? The color of vodka, gin, and tequila will not be affected. The brown goods (bourbon, Canadian, Scotch, and blended whiskies) could have a dilution of the color hue, but not if a little tea was added as well. In other words, color changes cannot be depended on to reveal watering: What about aroma? Adding a little water will have absolutely no effect. In fact, adding a lot of water will have virtually no discernible effect on the smell of the product. Taste would be expected to suffer, but how many spirits are tasted "neat," straight from the bottle undiluted by ice or mixes? The answer is very few; most spirits are at least served over ice, which quickly becomes water. We can therefore depend upon neither color, odor, nor taste changes to indicate watering.

Water cannot be denied on the bar so an effective control program would concentrate on before and after. *Before*: Hire reliable and trustworthy personnel. It is strongly recommended to avoid personnel with long years of experience at many operations. Train your own people. *After*: Establish a policy of pulling, from time to time and at random, bottles to be submitted for chemical analysis. This is the only sure method for ascertaining whether tampering has occurred. This is also useful for detecting substitutions discussed earlier. Less precise but often effective is random testing of the spirits on the bar with a hydrometer to check the alcoholic content. When water is added, the proof or alcohol content (proof equals two times the alcohol percentage; that is 80 proof equals 40 percent alcohol by weight) will drop. These instruments are not sensitive enough to reveal the addition of a shot or two to the bottle, but the mere fact that there is an ongoing testing program can act as a powerful deterrent. Were the bartenders to get greedy, the watering would show up.

Bar Personnel Check Out Their Own Cash

This is not only a bar problem, it is also a violation of proper cash management. Persons who have cash collection responsibility should never be in a position to know how much they are expected to turn in. The recommended closing procedure is to count and remove the starting bank and deposit the rest. In particular, the bar personnel should not be allowed to take register readings, which would give them the expected cash figures. The reason for these procedures is that if cash were being accumulated fraudulently via any of the ways already discussed, the cash handler needs to know how much can be removed. It is important to note that the money is often in the cash drawer. Bartenders seldom would be so blatant as to put the money collected for a drink in their pockets but will place it in the cash drawer—unrecorded of course.

The Inventory Is Taken by the Bar Personnel

The important point here is that whoever controls the inventory controls the cost. This was explained fully in Chapter 4. Bar personnel should be involved in inventory taking but should not be given the task to do by themselves. When bartenders alone take inventory, there is really no possibility of control.

Purchasing, Receiving, Issuing, and Storing Delegated to the Bar Personnel

Many bartenders seem to regard the purchasing function as theirs by some sort of divine decree. One really cannot blame them since they perform it so often. Purchasing alcoholic beverages is easier and less complex than is food. With food purchasing, the problem of control is no more important and perhaps less so than the problem of quality consistency and availability of goods. With alcoholic beverages, the quality consistency is not a factor and availability is only a minor one. The questions of control, of back-door dealing, of kickbacks, of private deals, and so on are of paramount importance. Management must therefore maintain complete control over beverage purchasing and, especially, over all contacts with sales representatives. Bartenders and other beverage personnel are, if competent, an excellent source of information that management can and should use in making decisions. Purchasing policies should be formulated by, and all decisions made by, management, however. This applies to control of receiving, storing, and issuing as well.

Bar Personnel Working Banquet and Main Bars

This may not be a problem in larger operations, particularly large hotels with well-defined banquet or catering departments, but it will often present problems in small to medium-sized operations. What happens is that the full-time bartenders are used to handle the catering parties. We have already established that an unscrupulous barperson will attempt to create a supply of extra liquor on the bar, which can be sold for personal gain or given away to entice large tips. When these individuals work both banquet and regular bars, they can claim excess usage on the banquet bar and move a bottle or two back to the main bar where it can be used in any manner they please. For example: The XYZ company is having a dinner preceded by a hosted bar (the company picks up the bar tab and is charged by the bottle as opposed to a no-host or cash bar, where the patrons will individually pay for each drink). The actual liquor consumption was as follows:

Scotch	1.5 bottles	Gin	1.75
Bourbon	.75	Vodka	1.5
Canadian	1.25	Rum	1.0
Blended	.50	Brandy	.25
			———
		Total	8.5 bottles

The bartender provides the following usage list to management, and the customer's bill is prepared based upon it.

Scotch	2.0 bottles	Gin	1.75
Bourbon	1.0	Vodka	2.5
Canadian	2.0	Rum	1.5
Blended	.5	Brandy	.25
		Total	11.5 bottles

The bartender now can move three bottles back to the bar and use them there. If the bartender(s) have the freedom to work both areas and to prepare the billing (not at all uncommon), they certainly will not experience any difficulty in getting the excess products back on the main bar.

Control recommendations are to schedule bartenders in one area or the other but not both and for management to issue the stock, to pay attention to the pouring during the banquet, and to take the ending inventory promptly and prepare the billing themselves. With a no-host or cash bar, the biggest attraction is the potential for removing cash, which can readily be done, especially when management is not using a standard sales system to evaluate the results (that is, each bottle is worth $30.00; we therefore expect $30.00 for each bottle poured). When the standard sales technique is used, however, the barperson can merely underpour and take in more than the standard. This can best be controlled by vigilant observation, use of some sort of measuring system, and frequent removals of accumulated cash.

Banquet bars can also be used to confuse the cost calculations. Beverages in the catering department are often sold under a different cost-price structure than they are in the lounge and dining room. In particular, the sales by bottle instead of by drink will create a different, usually higher, percentage cost. It is necessary in all such instances to maintain separate income and cost records. Otherwise a high cost on the bar, for instance, could be blamed on the banquet department.

Ringing the Wrong Price

The bartender registers every drink, but for selected customers she or he would ring up a scotch or other mixed drink as a beer, which is priced considerably lower. The characteristic of the customers that entitles them to this generosity is simply this: *they are willing to pay the full amount.* In other words a particular guest may have four drinks, normally priced at $2.00 each. The bartender rings each drink on the beer key at $.75 each. When the patron cashes out, the check total is $3.00 not $8.00, but $8.00 is paid to the bartender, resulting in a very nice $5.00 tip! This can be done because there is often a surplus supply of liquor available for such uses and because management tends not to pay much attention to beer. In this case, control is achieved by the use of spotters and by using standard sales analysis, comparing the use and sales of each product type—bourbon, Scotch, beer, wine, and so forth. The above described situation actually happened and was very difficult to trace because it was done discreetly, only three to four times a week with four or five individuals. The bartender certainly did not get rich from it but was able to take home an extra $50.00 to $60.00 weekly.

Working Out of an Open Drawer

One of the most basic beverage control policies is that the cash drawer must be kept closed between transactions. When this is done, there is a record on the register tape of every entry-transaction. This is also one of the most commonly violated control policies. Many bartenders like to maintain an open drawer because it speeds cash handling and is, undoubtedly, easier. It also enables untraceable money collected from unregistered drinks to be placed in the cash drawer. Later, at the end of the shift, or whenever is convenient, the money can be removed. If the cash drawer were kept closed, the barperson could open it only by using one of the register keys, and then a record would exist. This is, of course, not an insurmountable obstacle for the bartender, but it does tend to complicate his other activities.

Some knowledgeable people claim there is no such thing as perfect beverage control, that any system can be beat. This goes too far. It is fair to say that if good, reliable people are hired and trained, a system can be set up that, while probably beatable, would require far too much effort on the part of the barpersons relative to the potential gain. It would involve too high a degree of risk of exposure. Quite frankly, an unethical person does not have to work that hard or accept that level of risk; there are simply too many easier places to work!

Control this activity by making it a termination offense to have an open cash drawer between transactions. Follow up with random personal observations, and use spotters. It is also recommended that whenever the register is opened for a "no-sale" reason (change for cigarettes, to break a large bill, and so on), it always be done using one card or check. This can then be evaluated (daily) by management to determine whether the bartenders appear to require excessive access to the cash drawer.

Clearing the Register Early

The register(s) will be cleared (the reading taken and reset to zero) prior to closing. When the establishment closes, the procedure will be repeated. The first "reading" tape will be submitted, the second will be destroyed (after removing the money of course). For example: the bar closes at 2:00 A.M. At midnight, the bartender "reads" the machine and resets it to zero. The tape indicated that there should be $575.00 in cash receipts collected. At 2:00 A.M., the bar closes, and the procedure is repeated. This time the tape shows a total of $46.50 in cash checks paid. The bartender can remove $46.50, and no record exists after the tape is destroyed. The irony of this is that every drink will be registered properly since the bartender is now in business for himself or herself and wants to maintain an accurate record in order to know exactly how much can be removed.

Several control procedures are suggested. Do not allow bar personnel to close the operation. Do not allow bar personnel to take readings (deny them access to the reading keys). As a minimum, have a register system that maintains continuous transaction numbers on the side of the tape. If this were done, there would be a gap between the closing number of night one and the opening number of day two, making it obvious

that the register was operated for a period after the supposed closing. This, however, is not effective unless someone actually checks the transaction numbers and does so on a daily basis. Do not reset the registers to zero when closing, merely read the ending figures. Many operators do not like to do this because over time it results in large, unwieldy totals (for example, the sales for the day are $179,862.14 less $179,155.85 or $746.29). They would rather punch a button and obtain $746.29. It may be easier, but it is also easier to manipulate.

Alteration of Checks Following Payment

The bartender will alter a paid check to reflect a lower total, keeping the difference. Slightly different but similar is when the checks are signed (as in a club). In that case, the check can be altered to show increased consumption (thereby creating surplus liquor or increasing the tip if a percentage is automatically added as a service charge), or the tip itself can be altered.

Control over this requires controlling check alteration and/or machine voids. There must be a strictly adhered to policy prohibiting any employee other than management to change a figure on a guest check, and management should have some sort of a void reporting system. A simple form could be developed that required the bartender (or any other cash-handling person, including service persons) to record and explain all voids. Mistakes will happen. Careful evaluation of the daily voids reports will quickly show management whether the voids are due to legitimate, unavoidable errors, to probable carelessness, or to possible theft. Lack of control over voids can tempt employees to collect money for drinks and then claim the register service ring was a mistake, that the customer walked out without paying, or that the drink was returned for one reason or another. Incidentally, when the latter occurs, the policy should be to ring up the replacement drink just as though it were a new order, and to call in management to void the first transaction. Although this may appear a bit unwieldy, it does two positive things, First, it makes management aware of the error. Second, it is consistent with the policy that every drink served must be preregistered. Once any exceptions are allowed, a loophole is created.

Removing Loose Change from the Bar

The bartender removes change while the guest is in the restroom or making a telephone call. If the guest happens to inquire when he returns, the bartender innocently explains that she thought the person had left and it was a tip. We have even seen certain bold individuals remove the change from in front of a guest, thanking them for their generosity! A truly ingenious method was devised by a waitress in a military club where it was common for a group of members to sit at a table, place their money in the center, and begin ordering. She would dampen the bottom of the tray, lay it on the table while writing the order, and leave with several pieces of paper money sticking to the bottom of the tray.

The Bartender Acts as Food Cashier

The reasoning here is obvious. Since the bartender must handle cash, why not funnel all cash through the bar, thereby saving the expense of a separate cashier? With most operations, this would not be an efficient way to collect food cash, but some establishments could easily do it. Even in such cases, however, it is strongly recommended not to do so. One of the very best bar control procedures is to take the cash collection function away from the bartender (as in a service bar for example), and one of the more foolish things that could be done is to turn the food receipts over to the bartender to go along with all the beverage receipts.

Spillage, Breakage, Evaporation

Bar personnel often claim they are entitled to one to two shots per bottle to cover legitimate spillage, breakage, and evaporation. We have had bartenders inquire, when being interviewed for employment, about how many shots they were expected to get out of a bottle. In one instance it was explained that since a quart contains 32 ounces and since the drink size was one ounce, thirty-two would be expected. The applicant said he expected an allowance of two

shots. It was explained to him that a daily record was to be kept on the bar documenting spills, breakage, and so on, and that the total of drinks poured, plus this record had to equal thirty-two drinks per bottle. The individual promptly removed himself from further consideration for the job! Giving bartenders an allowance of two shots per bottles is just the same as telling them that they can sell two drinks from every bottle and keep the money.

Running "Tabs" for Guests

This occurs when payment is not collected for each round, and the guest is not given a check or register receipt with each round. It escapes us why any bar operator would allow his or her personnel to run an undocumented "tab" for a guest. Often, there simply is no record other than a handwritten one on some note pad kept either by the bartender or the waitress. The opportunities for fraud are many. Either the establishment or the customer or both could be cheated. Running a tab is quite legitimate and even necessary in certain types of places, but everything should be recorded on the register prior to being served, and a check should be presented to the guests and kept with them between rounds. This alone will not prevent fraud, for many guests pay scant attention to the check. A group ordering several rounds could easily have a few extra drinks added to the check without noticing. These drinks could be used to cover drinks that have been sold (and money collected) without being registered. Many operations do not use guest checks. In this case, they should collect each time a drink is served. Using the register receipts (the slips of paper produced by the register for each transaction) to keep track of the drinks sold is totally inadequate.

Draft Beer

Draft or tap beer offers many opportunities for pilferage because it is not often analyzed even as well as are spirits, and we have already established that spirits are frequently inadequately evaluated. When management pays little attention to the ratio of product used to receipts obtained, the situation is similar to when private bottles are brought in. There is a product available to be sold for personal benefit. When management does not know what the income should be from a keg of beer, it is easy for bar personnel to sell beer and keep the money. In a beverage operation selling a lot of draft beer, this could amount to dozens or even hundreds of glasses per week at anywhere from $.50 to $1.00 per glass (or more). There are three things that must be known to calculate the number of servings from a keg. These are:

1. Size (capacity) of glass (mug, stein)
2. Shape of glass
3. Size (depth) of head desired

The glass shape and head depth are both very important. A 9-ounce glass holds 9 ounces only if filled to the rim. Putting a head on it reduces the glass capacity. The larger the head, the smaller the portion. The shape is related in that the effect of altering the head is magnified in glasses that are funnel shaped, larger at the top than at the bottom. The classic beer glass, the pilsner, has this shape. With this type of glass, if the standard head were 1/2 inch, by pouring a 1-inch head the bartender could very significantly increase the number of servings per barrel. These would be extra servings for which income is not expected.

Control procedures would be, first, to know exactly how many standard glasses are expected from each keg and what the total sales should be. Second, maintain a daily (or even shift) count as to barrels used. This involves estimating the contents of partial barrels by tenths, which is not totally accurate but workable. Weighing the partial barrels is quite accurate but could be difficult for many operators. An alternate method is to take a sales count or reading whenever a barrel is changed. This can be very accurate since you know one barrel was used and just have to check the sales resulting from its use. It does not have to be done every time, just frequently and at random. Third, follow up with spotters and random personal observations to assure that extra glasses are not being obtained by increasing the head.

This control is made more difficult when two

or more beers are on tap selling at different prices, such as a premium import and light beer. In this case, it is necessary to separate the sales of each. This can readily be done by using separate register service keys. Use of a counting device to track the glasses poured is also recommended. Another control complication occurs when two or more portion sizes are used, as with a glass and mug, or a glass, mug, and pitcher. It is necessary to have a count indicating how many of each were poured. Without such a count, the usage and sales cannot be compared, and you will not have any control.

Misuse of Promotional Material

If for example, the bar is using two-for-one coupons, the bartender can sell drinks for him- or herself and use the coupons to cover the theft. This can also be done on any other type of giveaway or reduced price promotion. The bartender claims drinks that he collected cash for were actually used for promotional purposes. This is similar to what can be done during the so-called happy hour. During this period, drinks are priced lower than the regular price. The bartender will ring several extra drinks, drinks that have not actually been ordered. When the prices return to normal, this number of drinks will be served without being registered, and the difference between the happy-hour price and the regular price can be kept by the bartender. The same thing can be done when prices are increased, which is frequently done when entertainment is provided. The drinks are registered at the lower price but collected at the higher price.

Controlling promotional materials, such as coupons, is essential. They should be numbered, each one must be accounted for, and an attempt should be made to verify the use of each, perhaps by having the "winner's" name placed on them. Management should have a system to control the disbursement of the coupons, and they definitely should not give this authority to any of the employees. Control of operations that have two-tiered or three-tiered pricing depends on being able to compare usage to sales. If more drinks are registered than are actually served during the cocktail hour, a comparison of liquor poured and drinks registered would show a discrepancy. This comparison would be nearly impossible to make, however. What is feasible is to take a register reading at the close of each pricing period and change the cash drawers. Unless drinks are paid for when served, this will not work either. For this reason, it is recommended to have happy-hour drinks paid for when served. Otherwise, there will always be uncollected drinks outstanding at the time the changeover is made. If this is not feasible, the policy should be to collect all outstanding drinks prior to the changeover. If either of these were done, it would be very difficult for bar personnel to get away with ringing drinks at one price and collecting later at a different price.

This same type of fraud can also be used with guest checks. Commonly ordered drinks will be rung on several blank checks which are then held and used when a guest orders the drinks later at the regular price. Since guests often pay no attention to their checks; this will often be feasible. This can be prevented by regular evaluation of the check sequence numbers to determine whether some appear to have been held for a period. Auditing the transaction sequence numbers will show that a check was registered during one period and used during another. Specially marked guest checks are useful as a control and so would the use of a different guest check for the promotional period. The basic control discussed earlier, requiring that all drinks be documented prior to service, is also a control over this type of activity, for the bartender has to be able to serve unregistered drinks later in order to collect (unless, of course, he has a previously rung check he can present to the guest).

Soft Drinks

In an establishment that has a high demand for soft drinks in the bar, bartenders do not have to risk misuse of spirits, which are watched more closely than other products, or even beer. All they have to do is collect money from the sales of soft drinks, which often will sell at $1.00 or more to discourage the purchase of nonalcoholic beverages. The usage of these products is seldom evaluated, making this a very low-risk activity.

Control procedures are to require these items to be preregistered, to have a separate soft drink key on the register, and to evaluate usage. This latter is difficult, however, particularly since most operations are using some sort of premix or postmix system. The most effective control is to assure that there is a record of a soft drink being served. This means the money must be collected and turned in or else the deposit will be short. Counting and evaluating the soda actually used could, however, provide a psychological deterrent by increasing the apparent risk.

Bar Personnel Set the Bar Cost Percentage

This is so obvious an invitation for fraud that it should not have to be discussed, but our experience is that bar personnel are often allowed to determine what the percentage should be. Obviously, the percentage the bartender establishes could allow considerable use of the beer and spirits for personal gain.

Reusing Guest Checks

This can be done in two ways. The simplest is merely to use a particular check over and over and keep collecting. For example, a guest early in the evening orders a common drink and has a normal number of them (normal for that operation). These drinks are all handled properly until the check is paid. The bartender, realizing that several other guests will order the same type and number of drinks, holds the check and does not ring it out as paid. The next guest who orders these drinks is given the same check. This could be done several times during the shift, the check not being cleared through the checks-paid key until the end.

Slightly different is the following: a guest has eight beers, all properly recorded, pays the check, and leaves. The check is not rung out but is set aside. A later guest has six beers, also all properly recorded. When this guest pays, however, the bartender switches checks and collects for eight beers. Both checks then are rung as paid. The bartender has served 14 beers (8 plus 6), has rung 14 beers as paid, but collected money for 16 beers! This fraud depends on the guest not noticing the extra drinks, but it is common for guests to pay little or no attention to their checks. If the guest does notice it, the bartender merely apologizes for the error and gets the correct check. Few people would pay much attention to this seemingly "innocent" mistake, especially on a busy bar.

Since both these activities depend on the check not being registered as paid until long after they go through the service key, auditing the checks would be a useful control procedure. Specifically, one would look at the transaction sequence number. Checks handled in this manner would generally show a larger than normal spread between drink servicing (especially the last drink served) and collection. A reasonable assumption on the part of management would be that the check was held for some reason. The bartender should then be required to explain and justify any such delays. Even if the bartender could do so satisfactorily, he or she is unlikely to again put himself or herself in the position of having to explain such a variance. As pointed out, bartenders who wish to steal look for low- or no-risk situations, and they are not much interested in attempting something that will alert management. Management need not take the overall attitude that stealing or a crooked activity has taken place when something turns up. Their attitude merely has to be that a problem exists and we want an explanation. An honest person who is making errors can be made aware of them and correct them. A dishonest person is either caught, or made aware that, if continued, such activities will result in job loss due to incompetence, if not for stealing.

Breaking an Empty Bottle

The bartender will break an empty bottle and claim it was full. This is essentially the same as bringing in a bottle: an entire bottle is available to be sold without recording the sales. There really is no control to prevent this occurring once, since accidents will happen. We would recommend the bartender be required to explain,

in detail, how he or she could be so careless, what was being done, why, and at what time. The bartender should also be made aware that the operation cannot afford to employ people who waste products, inadvertently or not. In other words: document and record all mistakes, and make employees responsible for their actions.

Room Service

In many smaller (and some not so small) hotels or motels, the liquor for room service will come from the bar. In such cases, it would be profitable for the bartender to sell a bottle over the bar, collect the money, get rid of the bottle, and ring it up as a full-bottle sale to room service. This is because the full-bottle selling price is generally significantly lower than the sales obtained from using it at the bar. On the bar, for example, the standard sales value may be $40.00 (twenty drinks at $2.00 each), while the room service price may be only $25.00. If this were done, it could not be found out by checking the room records since it would be recorded as a cash sale, not a room charge.

Some degree of control would be established by requiring that all room-service checks be signed by the guest (even when they pay cash) and be initialed by the employee making the delivery. The room number should also be given. This is not foolproof, but it does require collusion with the delivery person(s) and making inquiries at the front desk, which could require further collusion. The more people involved, the more difficult it becomes and the less lucrative it becomes. Detection becomes easier as well.

This is not an attempt to list all the fraudulent types of activities that can take place on a bar, but it does cover most of the common ones and serves to emphasize how easy fraud can be when management does not maintain control. Some good advice would be: do not trust or mistrust any employees. Instead, set up the operation with sufficient control so that the question of trust becomes relatively less important.

Purchasing Alcoholic Beverages

Objectives

The objectives of alcoholic beverage purchasing are the same as for food: obtaining the *right quality* and the *right quantity* at the *right time* and the *right price* from the *right supplier*.

Right Quality. This decision, as with most alcoholic beverage decisions, is easier to make than are food quality decisions. Beverages are more structured as to perceived quality, and there is widespread consumer acceptance of these quality images. Cutty Sark, for example, is regarded as superior to many other Scotches (particularly those bottled in the United States) but as inferior to Chivas Regal and other super-premium brands. The same principles apply to beers and wines as well. It is of little importance that many of these perceived quality distinctions may not stand up in blind tastings. The reason is because they are brand perceptions. An example of a similar phenomenon with food would be Heinz catsup. In selecting a catsup to put on the table, most food operators would select Heinz, which is widely accepted by the consumer as the quality product.

When making quality decisions, the critical aspect for the bar operator is to decide which quality image the establishment projects. Once an overall quality level has been selected, the operator merely has to pick the specific brands that are known to be consistent with that quality level. The distillers, brewers, and wineries spend a great deal on advertising to position their products at a specific quality level, and this makes beverage decision making easier. Once a particular product has been decided on, the delivered quality will be remarkably consistent, which is another advantage beverages have over food. Some wines, of course, are excluded from this last statement. Vintage wines, being the product of one year, will differ from year to year. Yet overall, quality is what the guests perceive it to be. Since broad agreement on quality exists among guests, operators just have to select products whose perceived quality is consistent with the image they want to project.

Right Quantity. The beverage buyer is responsible for maintaining adequate stocks. This means neither too much nor too little. If a bar never runs out, they are carrying too much stock (or else their sales are unusually consistent). There are two quantity decisions to be made. One is for the storage area(s), the backup stock. The other is for the bars themselves. In making these decisions, the operator will have to consider these factors:

Storage space: How much space is available? Where is it? (Space is expensive, as much as $100 or more per square foot in some locations.)

Inventory turnover: The specific turnover of each brand as well as the overall turnover must be known. Obviously, the faster each product moves, the greater the demand for inventory.

Cost of money: Money tied up in inventory cannot be used for other purposes. One company states that rather than tie up $100,000.00 in a wine cellar, they would prefer to open another restaurant. The trend, especially with the high cost of money, is to stock less and increase turnover. This requires skillful purchasing planning and management.

Cost of storage and handling: Storage space must be secured. It often requires cooling, and stock must be inventoried. The greater the stock, the greater the cost of storage and handling.

Security: All storage areas require security to some degree, but those containing alcoholic beverages require it to an extensive degree. The more products stored, the greater the expense and time needed to provide adequate security.

Risk of spoilage: This is not a decision factor with spirits and cordials. Beers are quite perishable, and stock levels must take that into account. Wines, in general, are perishable, but they vary widely. Under proper conditions, some wines exhibit astonishing longevity, but the right conditions are quite expensive to provide.

Flexibility: The stock level may need to be adjusted continually, especially when there is a large fluctuation in sales and/or a sizable catering business (itself generally variable).

Right Time. The proximity to service must be considered. Ideally you would want products to arrive just when needed. A commentator on the PBS (public broadcasting system) once described the Japanese auto industry as being based on the "just in time" principle. When a part is needed for the assembly line, it typically arrives just in time. It is not kept on hand for months, days, or even hours prior to the need. The point he was making was that American factories, for a variety of reasons, hold massive inventories of parts relative to the Japanese. This was identified as an important negative manufacturing cost factor for the American products. The very same principle applies to the bar. The closer the delivery is to the actual need, the more profitable the operation can be so long, of course, as it arrives just in time and not too late, for you cannot sell what you do not have. This is a need-cost relationship that must be balanced. There are other time factors to consider. Proper receiving personnel must be available at the time the delivery is made. The availability of funds is especially important in states that do not allow credit, since the goods must be paid for at time of pickup or delivery.

Right Price. As with food, the ultimate serving cost is the important decision factor. Since, however, alcoholic beverages have a potential for 100 percent yield (theoretically, as we have described many activities that can reduce actual yield), purchase cost (AP) should equal serving cost (EP). The responsibility of the buyer should therefore be to obtain the lowest price for each specific brand. There are several factors that influence alcoholic beverage prices, and the most significant is the state the operation is located in. This will be discussed shortly. Discounting and post-offs are also important. There are too many legal restrictions on the sale of alcoholic beverages to cover here, and they greatly limit or constrain pricing policies.

Most sellers will offer discounts, if this is permitted. The most common discount is based on quantity; the more you purchase, the lower the price. There is obviously a point where the operator cannot financially justify increased cost per case savings due to increased inventory costs, but a smart buyer will take maximum advantage of the seller's discount policies. Sellers also will offer post-offs, which means that they are passing on savings provided them by their suppliers, the distillers or manufacturers of the products. Discounts may also be available because a product is not moving (the supplier has turnover problems), because a new product is being introduced, or because a product is in danger of losing quality (not with spirits or cordials but a possibility with beers and a distinct possiblity with wines). Discounts other than regularly available quantity discounts and post-offs should be carefully calculated, especially since they tend to be available only on certain products and for limited times. A discount for a new product could be a poor deal if the demand for it has yet to be developed. In this case, you might take so long to sell it that the savings would have long since dissipated. A discount for a deteriorating product could never be a good deal. A discount for a promoted product could be favorable. This would depend on the product and the circumstances. A discount on a product the supplier is stuck with will probably not be a good deal because the ultimate consumer of their products is the same as yours—the local market. If nobody is buying it from them, most likely no one will purchase it from you either. One exception to all the above (except poor quality goods) is when the operator can promote or use the product in a unique way. Perhaps a special drink can be developed, or perhaps it could be temporarily poured, at an increased profit, in the well.

These purchasing decisions should be made in the order presented. The most important is the quality decision and specific brand selection. Next is quantities desired. Following that, the timing decisions should be made. Once these have been decided upon, the best price is the lowest price at which specific products can be delivered, in specific quantities, and at particular times. This is where the last objective comes in.

The Right Supplier. The right supplier is the one who can best meet the first three objectives at the lowest price. This is how suppliers should be selected. They are often selected on price alone. While this is not as dangerous a policy with alcoholic beverages as it is with food, it should still be avoided. The other objectives should precede price in order to maximize profit. A low price for the wrong product will not maximize profits; neither will a low price for huge quantities that take forever to sell; neither will a low price for goods that are available either long before you need them, long after you need them, or at an awkward time such as when no one is available to take care of them so they promptly disappear.

Some additional supplier rating factors are:

1. *Do they send salespeople or order takers?* Salespeople have knowledge in two areas. They know, in great detail, their product line. They are qualified to answer any questions the operator may have on the various spirits, beers, cordials, and wines carried by the supplier. The other area they must be knowledgeable in is the operator's specific business. A salesperson who cannot discriminate between one beverage operation and another is worthless to the buyer. What the bar operator wants to know is what is currently going on, what are the trends, what are the specials, what is coming and so on and so forth. Most important is how does it impact on my operation? What is the best thing for me to do now? In order to be of use to this operator, the salesperson must know his products and how he can do the most profitable job for his customer. Using these criteria, most salespersons are merely order takers. The flow of information is one way, from the establishment to the supplier.

2. *Quality of products.* This is not as critical an evaluation factor with alcoholic beverages as it is with foods, but there will still be quality differences in products offered by various distributors. There are two ways that the quality could vary. An example of one is Canadian Club whiskey versus a Canadian whiskey imported into the United States in barrels and bottled here. Nearly all consumers would acknowledge that there is a quality difference between the two. The other type of variance occurs when the product has declined in quality. Spirits and cordials fall into the first category. They normally would not be expected to change, decline, or deteriorate. Beer and wine fall into the second category. They will change with time. Unless storage conditions are satisfactory, they will lose quality. When evaluating distributors of spirits for quality, you should evaluate the brands they carry and pay great attention to the quality perception of the consumers. When evaluating wine merchants, you must pay attention to how they handle the products, what their storage facilities are like, and what their inventory turnover rate is, in addition to the perceived quality level of their product line. In other words, if a spirits purveyor carries quality products, you will receive quality products. With wine, it is more difficult to know this since there is less assurance that high quality goods on inventory will result in high quality goods being delivered.

3. *Delivery schedule.* Other factors being equal, the more willing (or able) a supplier is to accommodate your desired delivery times, the more valuable that supplier is. The operator should seek to negotiate such factors as frequency of delivery, day of week, and time of day.

4. *Delivery attitude.* At any point where disparate personnel interact, there is a possibility of confusion and/or conflict. The delivery agents meeting the foodservice operation's personnel are certainly an example. The delivery inspection-acceptance of the order will not always go smoothly. The operator should be interested in dealing with reasonable, helpful people. Delivery agents are sometimes poor representatives for their organization. They can be impatient, surly, and difficult to get along with when problems arise (such as missing products, extra products, wrong prices, incorrect invoice extensions, and so forth).

5. *Shortages.* The buyer's expectation when placing an order is that those products will be delivered. Unneeded products are not customarily ordered. Therefore, when delivery shortages occur, the establishment could be unable to take care of its guests. Assume, for example, that approximately 20 percent of your bourbon drinkers prefer Jack Daniels, which produces an additional gross profit of $.50 per serving relative to any other bourbon in stock. If there are 150 Jack Daniels drinks sold weekly, the result of being out of Jack Daniels is to lose $75.00 in profit each week. This is not only gross profit, it is net profit as well since all costs are fixed, and the profit will go straight to the bottom line. This is an optimistic scenario since it implies that no customers are lost, that they simply order a different (less profitable) bourbon. There is also the possibility that they might not order at all or order fewer drinks. If either happens, the profit will decline even more. Finally, a product that is not delivered does not represent a good deal regardless what the price is or how good the product is.

6. *Discount policies.* This must obviously be taken into consideration. There will often be some significant differences among distributors, and the buyer must do her homework and find out what they are.

7. *Price increase policies.* Alcoholic beverage prices are not nearly as variable as food prices are, but they will still increase over time. The buyer should track the prices quoted over a year or more. In other words, it is not enough to find out what the current prices are, you need to know what they have been over the past year. In that way the buyer can understand the pricing pattern of the seller. A purveyor whose current prices are not the lowest but whose history shows that they generally are either the lowest or among the lowest should be given fair consideration. This supplier's current prices could be reflecting new or anticipated industry costs that he or she has responded to faster than the competitors. In such a case, it may well be that after everyone else has made the pricing adjustments, this supplier could once again have the best prices.

8. *Emergency orders.* Every operator will sometime or other run out of a product and need it replaced as quickly as possible. A supplier's willingness and ability to respond to these needs is an important selection criterion. A customer who is inept and constantly requesting special deliveries will quickly become a disfavored customer to the purveyor, but the operator should legitimately expect accommodation when emergencies arise. Every organization is different, and their capabilities along this line will differ.

9. *Profitability of supplier.* This concept was discussed in the food section and is no less applicable here. A purveyor in financial trouble will, at best, result in the buyer's wondering about the future source of the products needed to operate. At worst, a financially troubled firm could attempt to stay afloat by cheating its customers. This, fortunately, is difficult to do with alcoholic beverages due to the stability and quality consistency of the products, but it is still a danger. Sales to various establishments at unrealistic (high) prices could possibly be assured with payoffs to bartenders or unscrupulous buyers, for example. A purveyor worth considering is one who makes a fair profit (enough to justify the investment and operating time) by operating efficiently and intelligently. A restaurant that is profitable because it serves good food and takes care of its customers is likely to be a good place to eat; conversely, a restaurant in danger of going under is not likely to be a wise choice. The same principle applies to suppliers.

Purchase Decisions Versus Order Decisions

The principle here is the same as that introduced in food purchasing: management cannot delegate certain purchasing decisions. They must make these decisions themselves. These decisions are:

1. What to buy (specification)
2. How much to buy (stock level)
3. Whom to buy from (supplier)

What to Buy. Management should get input for this decision from a variety of sources. The basic information to look for is what people like.

A bar operator should be very knowledgeable about consumer trends and attitudes. With alcoholic beverages, the consumer actually makes the what-to-purchase decision. A knowledgeable bartender can be a valuable source of information here. Industry sales statistics can be very useful as well. A trade organization called DISCUS (Distilled Spirits Council of the United States) can provide a great deal of sales data. The trade publication *Impact* provides information on beers and wines as well as spirits. With wine, there are many useful magazines and newsletters. The *California Wine Institute* in San Francisco can be a valuable data resource. The point is that management needs to know what people drink, and this information is available. Local and regional trends must, of course, be recognized for few trends will be reflected equally across the United States.

How Much To Buy. Management cannot delegate this because they are ultimately responsible for inventory turnover and for using money and stock as profitably as possible. Some of the factors to consider when making this decision are:

1. *Supplier delivery constraints.* The supplier may be unwilling, unable, or both to deliver as frequently as you would wish. The result is larger than desired stock levels. This could be a result of location. For example, one international hotel company maintains a three-to-four-month liquor supply in most of their Latin American hotels. When questioned as to why, the answer was "If I want a liquor delivery in January, I must order it in October (from the United States). Maybe it will be delivered in January and maybe, for a variety of reasons, it might not arrive until February or March." These hotels maintained what would ordinarily be termed "excessive" stock levels but these were, in their particular case, rational and reasonable inventories. To carry less stock was considered an unacceptably high risk of running out.

2. *Storage space.* Space is very expensive today. Construction costs are estimated to be some $70.00 to $80.00 per square foot, exclusive of equipment, and an operator should naturally wish to have as much of this space as possible reserved for income-producing activities. The larger the storage facilities, the smaller the public space. Thus, there is always pressure on the designer to limit storage space, and it is not unusual for operations to be limited in their storage capacity. The cost of carrying inventories is also a factor. Most operators would not want to tie up capital by filling massive storage areas. Still, there is the need to carry sufficient products and supplies to support the day-to-day operations. With alcoholic beverages, there are two main areas to consider: the storeroom and the bar(s). Of these two, the bar is the critical one. When the bar is quite limited in its storage capacity, a larger backup supply will have to be maintained in the storeroom. One of the decision criteria for automated dispensing systems is that one storage-dispensing station can often service multiple bars, thereby reducing both storage and inventory. The rule of thumb for storage space is as small as possible but as large as necessary. The ideal situation would be to make the design decision after all the other factors were known, but this is not always possible.

Efficient utilization of the available space is as important as the size of the space. Many beverage storage areas, both storeroom and bar, are underutilized. The type of shelving and layout of shelving are important. For example, standard food storage shelving is not efficient for beverage storage. Spirit bottles should be stored upright (to keep the corks, if they have corks, away from the highly alcoholic liquid). Standard food shelving results in a lot of empty headspace between the tops of the bottles and the next shelf. Wines should be stored on their sides (to keep the corks moist), and shelving should be more closely spaced. There are specialized wine shelving and storage racks available, and management should be familiar with them so they can select the best combination. Floor space should also be utilized as fully as possible. Often, the shelving is arranged poorly, and there is a lot of wasted floor space. Consider the examples in Exhibits 7.2 and 7.3. In the first one, there is a lot of open floor space relative to the shelf space. In the second example, the shelf depth has been

Exhibit 7.2. Storage Floor Plan One

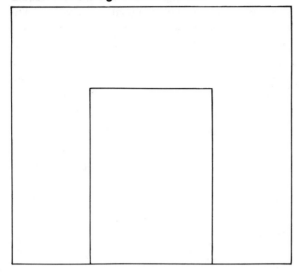

Exhibit 7.3. Storage Floor Plan Two

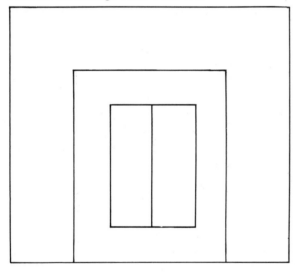

reduced slightly to enable the placement of an island in the middle. A further advantage is that the island can be accessed from both sides, making its area more usable. Shelving that is too deep can result in wasted space in the corners, and at the back, stock can get lost or turn very slowly. Exhibit 7.3 has nearly 10 percent more square feet (floor space) devoted to shelving, which—combined with its greater usability— gives a significant increase in storage capacity.

3. *Value of cash.* The more expensive money

becomes, the less management can justify investing (for that is what they are doing) in inventory. Stock that is being turned rapidly is producing income. Stock that turns slowly is tying up cash which could be used for other purposes.

4. *Brand movement.* The stock level decision ultimately comes down to a brand-by-brand evaluation. Management should set guidelines on total space allocation and total inventory dollars. They should, however, work up to total space and dollar requirements by making a decision on each brand about the optimal stock level. If the total from all these individual decisions exceeds the guidelines or goals, and this could happen, one of two options is available. Reevaluate the brand specification decisions and the stock level decision to assure that all brands are necessary and that the amounts specified are also necessary to support the anticipated business. Then review the sales forecast again. When all this is done, and there is still no appreciable change in the brands and amounts necessary, the organization's guidelines and goals will have to be altered. If that is not feasible or acceptable, some changes will have to be made in the concept and design so the goals can be met. The mistake operators often commit is that they do not make realistic appraisals of what the situation is likely to be under current or normal conditions. If they did this, they would realize that actual situations as planned would often be unacceptable. Knowing this, a creative and imaginative manager or owner could possibly alter the operation to create new operating conditions. This idea has been referred to constantly throughout the text.

5. *Location.* The importance of location is also illustrated by the example of the hotels in Latin America. Some locations will be proximate to a strong and extensive distribution network while others will be far from it. The more expensive it is for the distributor to make a delivery, the less frequent the deliveries will be. Frequent deliveries under difficult conditions will generally result in unacceptably high product costs. The result of less-frequent deliveries is larger than ideal stock levels.

6. *Stock mix or diversity of brands.* The greater the number of brands stocked, the higher the total dollar investment will be. For example, if a beverage operation has a demand for 500 vodka drinks per week and they get 21 drinks per bottle, the minimum inventory necessary is twenty-four bottles a week. If they had only one brand, all they would need to maintain is a par stock of two cases and have a weekly delivery. If they could get delivery two times per week, they could cut the stock to one case. If, however, they had six vodka brands, the par stock would be far higher. The operator would establish pars on each brand sufficient to assure constant availability. Some would move more slowly than others, but the stock would have to be available. The par may also be predicated on the fact that purchases of less than full case lots will be penalized by higher prices. The total number of bottles inventoried will almost certainly exceed twenty-four. Another cost factor is that each brand will be purchased in smaller lots, probably eliminating any quantity discounts available from occasional large purchases. The result is more bottles stocked at a higher per-bottle cost. Every beverage operator should constantly evaluate the numbers of brands carried with the objective of reducing them if possible.

Who to Purchase From. This, the supplier decision, is the third of the basic purchasing decisions that should be made by management. The possibilities for fraud arising from improper delegation of this responsibility are endless. Another reason for management to retain this decision is that, ideally, it should be made only on the basis of which supplier best meets the purchasing objectives. If it is delegated to someone else, who knows what criteria the decision will be based on? Perhaps the salesperson is a nice guy, perhaps he comes into the bar frequently and leaves nice tips for the bartender, perhaps there is a kickback arrangement. In other words, at best the decision is not being made rationally; at worst, it is being made illegally.

Order Decisions. Once the three basic purchase decisions have been made, what remains is to maintain the necessary brands at the desired level. This is ordering, and it can be delegated. Consider this: we wish to serve Popov vodka; the par stock in the storeroom is two cases, and the authorized supplier is Southern Spirits, Inc. If we have also decided to always order in full-case lots to take advantage of the discounts. To prepare the weekly order requires no real decision making. It is merely an arithmetic exercise. We have one case of Popov on hand; we need to build up to two. Therefore we order one case from Southern Spirits. Anyone who can read, count, and use a telephone can handle this adequately. They do not even require access to the storage area(s) since a perpetual inventory, which is feasible with alcoholic beverages, will give the current stock level. One word of caution: This is a perfectly workable ordering concept, but it is sometimes complicated by supplier post-offs, closeouts, and other special deals. When these occur, management may feel it appropriate to purchase products not normally stocked or to purchase regular products in unusual amounts or to purchase from another supplier. In other words, all three basic purchase decisions have been changed. This situation does not often occur with food, but it is not at all unusual with alcoholic beverages. Altering the basic purchase decisions, even temporarily, should be done only after careful evaluation of the total costs, not only in inventory value but in cost control and operating efficiency. Because of this possibility, however, it may be difficult for the beverage operator to delegate all ordering decisions. If it can be done, it is recommended. Management should not make decisions that can be safely made by employees. There are plenty of activities that only management is qualified to do, and they should concentrate on them.

Open Versus Control States

The selection of a suitable supplier is affected not only by the factors we have discussed, but also by some considerable legal constraints. Although the buyer is subject to the laws of cities, townships, and counties, we will consider only the effects of the state alcoholic beverage regulations here. There are two basic types of states: control states (also known as monopoly states), and open states (also called license states) (see Exhibit 7.4). In the control states, the seller of the alcoholic beverages is the state itself, hence, the term *monopoly* since the state is the sole source. In open states, the products are available from licensed wholesalers and retailers. There are many differences in the specific regulations of the various states, but this is the general scheme. One aspect that should be more widely recognized and is not is that management has more control over the beverage system in a monopoly state than in an open one. One of the more time-consuming and difficult tasks management has is to make the three basic purchase decisions. In the case of the supplier in a control state, there is no decision to be made; there is only one. The other two decisions—how

much to stock and what to purchase—are also restricted. While these restrictions do reduce the decision options, there is no doubt that the job is made easier because of them. As regards control, one of the real problems is in preventing or reducing unethical and/or illegal supplier-buyer relationships. This is not really much of a problem in a control state.

Considerations in Control States

1. *One price.* In general, there is only one price for each product. The buyer cannot shop around to reduce the product cost. In the absence of competition, this price is usually higher than it is in an open state. Thus, while management will spend less time controlling the purchasing function, the beverage operation may be less profitable. Beverage percentage costs do tend to be higher in control states.

Exhibit 7.4. Control States and License States

Control States

Alabama	Ohio
Idaho	Oregon
Iowa	Pennsylvania
Maine	Utah
Michigan	Vermont
Mississippi	
(wholesale only)	Virginia
Montana	Washington
New Hampshire	West Virginia
North Carolina	Wyoming (wholesale only)

License States

Alaska	Mississippi (retail only)
Arizona	Missouri
Arkansas	Nebraska
California	Nevada
Colorado	New Jersey
Connecticut	New Mexico
Delaware	New York
Florida	North Dakota
Georgia	Oklahoma
Hawaii	Rhode Island
Illinois	South Carolina
Indiana	South Dakota
Kansas	Tennessee
Kentucky	Texas
Louisiana	Wisconsin
Maryland	Wyoming (retail only)
Massachusetts	District of Columbia
Minnesota	

2. *Reduced brand selection.* This means that in a control state the buyer will not have as many brands to choose among. The reason is that the state monopoly will be inclined to stock only the products that move well in general. If a specific operator had a demand in her bar for a product that did not move well in the state, the chances are that it would not be available. There are two types of exceptions to this general rule. The state may be willing to supply this product to the bar, but only if the buyer agrees to take delivery of a large amount at a time. For example, a buyer may request brand A, which the state does not inventory. The operation has a demand of about four bottles per month, which management feels justifies the addition to their selection. The state agrees to supply the product but only if the buyer will take two cases. In the event the buyer agrees, the state will buy two cases and turn it over to the bar. They still do not maintain an inventory of brand A. The buyer must decide whether the need for this product justifies purchase of a six-month supply at one time. Most operators would not want a turnover of only two times per year for any of their products. The other exception is when the consumers demand a broad range of brands. For example, in Nevada—an open state—enormous amounts of alcoholic beverages are sold due to the demand generated by the casino hotels. The demand, however, is not for large numbers of brands but only for large total volumes. In Michigan, a control state, the demand is generated by the resident population, and the state sells to authorized retailers located all over the state. The result is that the state, in several instances, stocks a larger variety of brands.

3. *Lack of credit.* In control states, the sales are generally made on a cash basis. The operator is not permitted to sign for the liquor, and he or she cannot take possession without cash or a certified check. Business checks are typically not accepted. The state wants assurance that the check will be honored.

4. *Reduced delivery options.* This can sometimes be stated "no delivery options," for the establishment has to make its own arrangements for pickup and delivery. The products are available only from a state outlet. In metropolitan areas, it is possible to hire a delivery service that will pick up orders for several operations and deliver them. There is a charge for this service, of course. In less populous areas, the operator must make the pickup. This avoids the delivery agent cost, but there is obviously a cost to the operator in doing this.

5. *Problems with stock-outs.* A "stock-out" occurs when the requested product is not available. A monopoly can be expected to be less responsive to its customers' needs. If the buyer has other sources for particular products, the seller will make a greater effort not to be short; but when the buyer has no other place to go, the seller may not be as diligent in its efforts.

6. *Reduced order-size options.* A control state may have minimum order amounts. For example, the buyer could be required to purchase in multiples of three. Orders for a specific brand would not be accepted for one bottle or two; the minimum would be three. Nor would the operator be able to order four, five, or seven bottles. Orders must be placed for three, six, nine bottles or for full cases. This could have the effect of reducing the inventory turnover and increasing the stock level, both of which reduce operating efficiency.

7. *Reduced invoice adjustment options.* In general, there are none. When an order is accepted by the buyer, he or she has already paid for it. Returns or swaps are not permitted. In an open state, the seller may be permitted or be willing to make an accommodation to a good customer when a mistake has been made. Again, a competitive seller tends to be responsive to customers' needs, while a monopoly seller may not necessarily be.

Considerations in Open States

1. *Price competition but not on all items.* Although competitive pricing is an element of open or license states, it does not cover all products. There are two factors that tend to reduce the necessity for competitive pricing. One is the granting of exclusive distribution rights for specific brands or lines to a particular purveyor. The result is a situation much like that

in the control states. There is only one source, and anyone wanting the product will have to pay the asking price. The other deterrent to full competition is the reluctance of sellers to compete on the price of products the beverage establishment must stock. We refer to those heavily advertised brands that must be available due to the overall demand. Alcoholic beverages are not selected with the same freedom as foods are. With all alcoholic beverages, beer and wine as well as spirits, the consumer decides which specific brands must be carried. When the buyer is in a position where he must purchase a particular item, and there are two or more potential suppliers, it is not in the suppliers' interest to compete on price. The suppliers' approach generally is to maintain a competitive position on the discretionary products. When they get enough business in general, the other goods will be included in the order. Thus on the top brands, those certain to be purchased, the prices from various suppliers tend to be the same, whereas suppliers will compete vigorously on products management has selection discretion on.

2. *Ordering and Delivery.* This is similar to that of other products. In license states the operator calls an order in, or gives it to a sales representative. The order is then delivered. In other words, the standard order arrangement; but as we have seen, this works much differently in a control state.

3. *Credit.* This is generally available in open states. The buyer can sign for a delivery and pay at a later date, but there are usually some restrictions, particularly on when the payment must be made. The operator will be required to pay the invoice within a specified number of days or by a certain date. If the bill remains unpaid past that date, the supplier is required to inform the authorities. Then the buyer will not be allowed to make any further purchases until payment is made. Since hotels, restaurants, and bars must purchase only from approved sources, this has the effect of putting them out of business until the debt is made good.

4. *Lower prices.* There may not be full competition on all products, but a competitive environment does exist. Prices in general can be expected to be lower than in control states.

5. *Special inducements.* In a competitive situation, sellers will attempt to persuade buyers to preferentially purchase from them. As a result, they will offer a variety of discounts. These are not often, if ever, available in control states.

6. *Increased demands on management time.* Management will spend more time with the purchasing function because there are more decisions to be made, and they will have to deal with salespersons.

Well Stock Versus Call Stock

Call stock, as stated, are spirits ordered by name (Grand Dad and water), while well stock consists of spirits served to guests who do not specify a particular brand (bourbon and water).

Considerations on Call Stock

1. There is limited competition, even in license states, for these types of products. They are marketed by the "pull" technique as opposed to "push." The objective is to create such a high demand with the ultimate consumer that this demand will tend to pull the product into the bars, restaurants, hotels, and retail establishments. Push marketing is generally done when the product has a generic (nondifferentiated) perception among the consumers. In this case, it will not sell without being "pushed." Call brands mostly fall into the pull category. They are stocked because the guests ask specifically for them. If they are not requested, they are not (or should not be) stocked.

2. Management is also limited when it comes to making brand decisions. As pointed out, the customers make these decisions.

3. Quality is not much of a selection factor. The reason for this is that specific brands are being selected in response to consumer demand. Distilled spirits are manufactured products and can be expected to maintain a consistent quality standard. In other words, when a brand such as Smirnoff Vodka is selected, for example, the quality will always be consistent. It is not a selection criterion.

Considerations on Well Stock

1. In open states, there will probably be price competition. The purveyors cannot sell these products unless they push them because the operator does not have to stock any particular brand. The result is that there will be inducements to purchase.

2. There is a rather substantial range of discretionary brand decision making available to management. It can be assumed that all suppliers have potentially satisfactory products, so the buyer has a choice.

3. Quality is a decision criterion with well stock. When, for example, a brandy is selected, a wide variety of qualities are available to choose from. There are expensive French cognacs down to the cheapest grape distillate. The type of establishment and the consumer expectations will provide guidelines to the quality level. There will still be many brands to choose from within quality levels, however, and this puts the buyer in a favorable bargaining position.

When Is a "Good Buy" Favorable?

The operator must always be cautious when considering purchasing larger than normal quantities or brands not currently stocked. The purpose of these beverages is to produce a profit when sold. Until they are sold, there is no profit; and the purchase of a long-term supply could cost the operator money instead of saving money. Although the cost per unit (bottle or case) will be lower on a "deal," the total cost may be higher than usual because of the quantities involved. This additional cash can earn money if invested. Therefore what the operator is doing is considering an investment. If the investment in extra inventory saves $100.00 in beverage costs but could have earned $125.00 if used elsewhere, the establishment loses. Another way of looking at the situation is from the viewpoint that the additional cash is not available and must be obtained. If the cost of borrowing money is 15 percent per year, and the opportunity means purchasing an extra $3,000.00 of goods, which are expected to last four months, the buyer must save $150.00 merely to cover the cost of the money (15 percent per year equals 5 percent for

four months; 5 percent times $3,000.00 equals $150.00). This would not provide coverage of the costs of risk (spoilage, pilferage, theft, waste), storage, handling, or obsolescence (if the operation is stuck with an off-the-wall brand that no one wants). These are the financial considerations, and during inflationary periods they become critically important. During the early 1980s, when interest rates were extremely high, one major foodservice chain instructed its managers not to purchase ahead on alcoholic beverages unless the savings were equal to 2.5 percent per month (or 30 percent a year!). They considered this their current cost of money. It would have to be an extraordinary opportunity to yield savings of this magnitude.

Another consideration when an opportunity is presented is the overall operating stability. There is no justification when the result is to overload storage space or fill the bar up with slow-moving products.

How Many Purchasing Sources Do You Need?

There are two ways to obtain leverage with suppliers. One form of leverage is attained by concentrating the orders with as few suppliers as possible. This creates maximum order sizes and makes the buyer important to the supplier, important because the buyer is contributing larger profits to the supplier. Larger orders mean higher profits; larger orders may also result in fewer orders, which increases the supplier's delivery efficiency. The buyer, in return for this accommodation to the supplier, should expect some accommodations too— lower prices for one, increased supplier services for another. The buyer's attitude should be that some of the increased profits must be put back into servicing the account.

The other form of leverage is that realized when a buyer has several suppliers and forces them to compete constantly for the business. In most cases, the nature of the product will dictate which leveraging method will be the most effective. When purchasing call brands, there will not be any choice when distributors have exclusive representation. When a popular call brand can be purchased from two or more purveyors, the buyer can probably obtain the best deal by attempting to get them to compete with each other. As pointed out, however, suppliers may be reluctant to do this.

With well brands, either strategy could be employed. It is entirely possible to spread the business among all the suppliers since all will have suitable brands. This approach involves making separate deals on each type of spirit: vodka, gin, bourbon, Canadian, Scotch, tequila, rum, blended whiskey, brandy, and so on. The buyer will say "Okay, vodka, who has the best price on 80 proof vodka? Who will deliver when I want it in the amounts I require?" The alternate method would be to purchase all well liquors from one supplier. The objective is to attain the lowest overall cost of purchasing this entire category. This is the recommended procedure, but buyers will often not follow it because they overlook the total cost of using many suppliers and concentrate on the individual costs. For example, let us say a bar is getting all its well spirits from Capitol Liquors. Southern Wines and Spirits wants to get some of the business so they quote a price on a bourbon that is lower than the one being purchased from Capitol. This price is irresistible, and the buyer switches. If this happens with enough other products, Capitol finds that their orders (and profits) are dwindling. They can no longer justify the prices they have been charging for the entire line (and services provided). Prices from Capitol will probably increase, and services may decrease. The buyer is then ordering from several suppliers and may not be getting the lowest overall price.

The recommended approach would be this: "My well stock will account for about 55 percent of the business, or about $3,500.00 per month ($42,000.00 per year). I prefer to deal with one supplier and give him all this business. In order to do this, however, I have to have a package that yields the lowest overall costs. Once I make my decision, I am not interested in any other supplier offering to beat the prices I pay. My attitude will be to question how they can offer a lower price now on a small amount of business

than they previously could on a much larger sales potential. It does not make any sense economically and seems like an attempt to get a foot in the door. I would even suspect low-balling."

In general then, when any alcoholic beverage is unique (is not generic), there will probably not be any choice of supplier. When generic brands are being selected for well spirits or house wines, all suppliers should have equivalent products, once an appropriate quality range has been selected. The best approach seems to be to concentrate the orders. An added benefit, of course, is that fewer orders will be placed, and fewer deliveries will be received. Storage areas will be accessed less frequently, and fewer invoices will be processed. There will also be reduced salesperson traffic. All these factors will reduce the time and effort associated with the purchasing function and so save money.

How Many Brands Should You Stock?

Cost and Operating Advantages of Reducing Brands

1. Inventory investment will be lower.
2. Less time will be required to order, receive, and store beverages
3. Storage space requirements may be reduced.
4. Bar storage will probably be reduced.
5. Inventories will be taken more easily and more quickly.
6. The perpetual inventory can be maintained with less effort and probably greater accuracy.
7. It becomes much easier to evaluate and analyze the beverage system.
8. Forecasting individual brand movement for ordering becomes less complicated.
9. Sales forecasts are easier to prepare.
10. Stock-outs become less of a potential problem. For example, if a bar has fifteen Scotches, it is nearly impossible to correctly anticipate the usage for each. Unless the bar operator wants to carry wildly excessive inventories, most of the fifteen will not be heavily stocked. The bar accepts the risk of frequently being out of a

few brands. If there were only one brand, all that management would have to forecast would be the total Scotch demand, not the demand for each brand. The bar could reduce its dollar investment and at the same time reduce the possibility of running out. The only way they could run out would be to be out of Scotch completely, whereas with multiple brands, they could have thousands of dollars of Scotch on hand and still be out of a specific brand or two.

11. The bartenders' and drink servers' jobs become less complex.

Operating Disadvantages of Reducing Too Much

1. The main disadvantage is the increased risk of not having a product available for sale. The worst thing that could occur would be the loss of a customer. This would not normally happen, but it could. It is more likely that the guest would switch to another brand. Depending on what the guest switches from and to, the profit per drink could be reduced. Imagine a gin drinker switching from a Beefeater martini to one made from the well gin or, even worse, to beer or wine. Once that guest is there and orders, all operating costs are fixed, and the gross profit difference from the drinks will go directly to the bottom line. Even if there is no profit difference, there is a danger of having a less than fully satisfied guest. This generally results in less frequent patronage.

2. The guests' selection is diminished. The dilemma of foodservice operators is that they must always attempt to satisfy two opposing sets of desires. The guests desire to have as wide a choice as possible, while the establishment is better off with a limit of selections. This duality appears in virtually all aspects of the foodservice system. The guests would normally prefer the largest portions of the highest quality products at the lowest prices. This would quite obviously increase their perception of value and maximize their satisfaction. It would also put the firm out of business, so the operator—being bottom-line conscious—would prefer to serve smaller portions and charge higher prices in order to maximize profits. This is not feasible either, so the operator must simultaneously satisfy her profit goals and the guests' value expectations. This is not easy. As a matter of fact, if the industry failure rate means anything, it is not often successfully accomplished. To summarize, there is danger in carrying too few brands if the guest perception is that it results in an inadequate choice.

Beverage Purchasing Trends

Alcoholic beverage purchasing appears to be gaining the prominence that food purchasing has traditionally had. As a result, it is becoming more professional. There are several reasons for this. The first is the cost of money. Beverages account for significant expenditures and inventory dollar investments, and these must be handled as efficiently as possible. Another is the factor of reliable supply. A professional purchasing system is a stable one. The suppliers selected are, quite simply, the ones who are best suited to meet the organization's needs. Unstable relationships between buyers and suppliers result in the buyer constantly switching from one supplier to another. Under such circumstances, it is difficult to assure a consistent, reliable supply of goods.

Some trends of growing importance are:

1. *Smaller inventories.* Most hospitality chains are attempting to reduce the amount of alcoholic beverages stocked and increase the turnover. Without stable supplier relationships, however, this is difficult to do. The operator not only will attempt to decrease the number of brands but also will want to carry less stock, meaning more frequent deliveries. This puts pressure on the supplier.

2. *Greater attention to discounts.* The company wants assurance that it really is in each

operation's best financial interests to take advantage of a discount. Central purchasing by chains can put the buyer in a very favorable position with regards to discounts, especially if the chain has several units within a geographical area serviced by the same distributor. This type of leverage becomes less effective on a national scale due to the great variety of legal restrictions on alcoholic beverages.

3. *Closer contacts between restaurateurs and producers.* This insures reliability of supply, particularly important with wines, especially California wines. California has many small, premium wineries whose wines are very difficult, if not impossible, to obtain using the normal channels of distribution. With these wineries—often called boutique wineries—the buyer should work closely with the producers since they influence the distribution of the limited stocks available.

4. *Changing wine lists more frequently.* This protects against running out without overinvesting in stock. Product offerings are thus changed to accommodate availability. Some foodservice operations are becoming increasingly reluctant to invest in costly wine cellars. The obvious solution is a more flexible wine list.

5. *Direct imports.* This is another way to protect against running out of specialty items, which might not normally be available on a continuous basis.

6. *Buyers working more closely with distributors.* There is a more professional, business-like atmosphere. Distributors are expected to keep the operator informed about such things as post-offs or any free goods promotions offered by distillers to their customers, the distributors. Distributors can also provide brand-selection advice. Distributors are also expected to be experts on consumer purchase attitudes within the marketing area. They can provide advice on the most favorable mix of products, recommendations on order patterns (frequency, amounts, and so forth), and new product information. A very important distributor service is assistance with merchandising. They should be able to come up with ideas for both promotions and merchandising. They may even

be able to provide assistance in implementing the ideas, including props and materials.

A Special Problem: Suppliers' Wine Storage

Wines, particularly fine wines, are very fragile and must be kept properly. The most important storage criterion is temperature. Wines should be kept cool, and they should be kept at a constant or nearly constant temperature. Warm temperatures can ruin an expensive wine and so can fluctuating temperatures. In warm climates, this is of critical importance. In Las Vegas, for example, where the outside summer temperature can be 115 degrees F., noncooled storage areas can become incredibly hot. In this area, it is an absolute necessity for the wine distributor to have refrigerated warehouse facilities. This is an extreme example of heat, but few areas in the country maintain consistent temperatures year round. In those that do, such as San Diego and Hawaii, the mean temperature is too high for wine storage. It is also necessary to keep wine bottles on their sides or upside down to keep the corks moist and airtight. The buyer should inspect the distributors' facilities and observe their handling procedures.

Minimum-Maximum Stock Levels and Reorder Point

The minimum-maximum stock level is an alternative method to a par stock for determining how much you want to carry in the storeroom. The par stock concept is necessary on the bar, but the minimum-maximum concept may be better suited for central storage. Each brand will have a minimum amount below which you would never want to fall. The order will be placed to build up to the maximum. The maximum should be able to handle normal business with a safety margin to protect against running out (except in unusual circumstances).

The reorder point is the time when the order must be placed so that you will receive the order before falling below the minimum stock level. The reorder point will depend upon the lead time needed, the time between placing the order and receiving the goods. If, for example, the minimum level equals one case, the maximum level equals four cases, the lead time is three days, and the estimated usage per day is four bottles, the reorder point would be when the stock level dropped to two cases. During the time it takes for the order to be delivered, you would use one case (three days times four bottles per day) and would have one remaining when it was received. The order would be for three cases since the maximum level is four cases and one would still be on hand at delivery time.

Receiving of Alcoholic Beverages

This is not a difficult function from a technical standpoint, certainly nothing so complex as food receiving. It is, nonetheless, a function that management should either perform themselves or personally supervise. The reason is that alcoholic beverages must be immediately moved to secure storage areas. This implies that whoever does the receiving must have access to the storage, and only management should be authorized to have keys to wine, spirits, and beer storage areas. Delegation of storage access is often done under mistaken assumptions about what a management person is. A head bartender whose primary job is to work behind the bar in a line-employee category is not a management person. A person whose primary function is to hire, train, and supervise bar personnel, who assists in making bar policy decisions, who is assigned cost responsibility (labor and operating costs, not only product cost) is a management person. That person may or may not also work behind the bar. It depends upon the operation, although it would be difficult to adequately carry out all these responsibilities while spending much time working a bartender shift. Most so-called head bartenders are line employees who have been given additional *duties*, not responsibilities. The result is a serious potential control problem along with a probable reduction in bartending efficiency.

What Information Should Be Obtained?

1. *What was received?* There should be records kept, documenting which specific products and what amounts of each were received.

2. *Who received it?* With alcoholic beverages, it could be disastrous for nonauthorized personnel to accept and take possession of the goods.

3. *When was it received?* It is desirable with all deliveries to have them arrive at a time convenient to management, but with alcoholic beverages it is more than merely desirable. It could be critical to the security of the delivered stock. Management (or someone who is authorized) should be available to receive the delivery. To assure that they are available and to avoid valuable personnel being tied up while waiting for a delivery, it is important that beers, wines, and spirits all come when they are expected.

4. *Was it quickly moved to the appropriate storage area(s)?* Alcoholic beverages are, by their alcoholic nature, much more volatile than other liquids and foods. This means that they will evaporate more readily. This can easily be appreciated. The amazing thing is not that the liquid evaporates, but that glass bottles and sometimes cardboard cases disappear as well! Management should be interested in documenting the movement of all such products.

5. *Were the invoices posted to the perpetual inventory?* The perpetual inventory can be a valuable control and operating tool, and management should require documentation that it is up-to-date. This can easily be done by marking the invoices to indicate that they have been posted.

Handling of Invoice Variances

Here, unlike with food, the buyer is not completely free to work out delivery variance adjustments with the supplier. There will probably be legal regulations that limit the buyer's options. Whatever is legal and permitted should be agreed upon between the buyer and seller beforehand. This way there will be no confusion when mistakes occur, and responses will always be made according to a predetermined policy.

What Should Be Done During Receiving?

Receiving of alcoholic beverages requires little specific technical competence which, as pointed out, is in marked contrast to the receiving of food. There are also fewer opportunities for the fraudulent types of activities that often occur when foods are delivered. We refer here to such things as light weight, downgrading on specifications, wrong count, poor trim, and so forth. These practices generally do not apply to alcoholic beverages since they are, more or less, standardized products. There are, however, some possible variances. The following should be checked when receiving:

1. Proofs of spirits should be specified and verified upon delivery. An 80-proof liquor contains less alcohol (and more water) than a 90-proof spirit and is less expensive (assuming the same spirit). When higher than normal proofs are specified, the proof must be checked.

2. Vintage dates on wines should be specified and verified. A vintage-dated wine is the product of a specific year and is a unique product. The same wine from another year is likely to be different because growing conditions are seldom the same for the grapes from one year to the next. Often, the variance can be quite dramatic, so management should specify particular years (after evaluation) and verify these upon receiving the wine.

3. Beer dates should be checked. Beer is quite perishable and loses its freshness fairly quickly. The cases are date-coded, and the beer distributor can tell management how to read the codes. This is not a major problem. Many beer distributors, well aware of the perishability of their products and the seeming inability of bars and restaurants to rotate stock, will have their drivers rotate it themselves; they will also voluntarily remove and replace older stock. The reason they will spend the time and bear the expense is simple. Beer is a branded product. Consumers who drink beer generally drink a specific beer. If a bar customer were to get a bad Budweiser, the chances are that he or she would blame Budweiser, not the establishment. The breweries and distributors cannot take that risk, so they take the necessary steps to assure that the stock is always fresh.

4. If a bottling date on a wine has been specified, it must be checked. Nonvintage wines are generally blended wines. They are not the unique product of one growing season but are blended from two or more vintages, the objective being to produce a standard, unchanging product. This type of wine is often best when young and fresh. The operator (after a sensory evaluation) may decide that the most recent bottling is the preferred one. The cases will be coded, and the receiver will have to be able to interpret the code.

5. Cases should be checked to determine whether any bottles have broken, leaked, or have been capped and sealed empty (this is rare but can happen). The cases can be opened to do this, or they can be weighed. If weighing is used, the standard weights of all full cases must be known and posted in the receiving area.

6. The cases should be visually inspected for signs of damage and/or leakage.

Merchandise Discounting

In some areas, "bottle discounts" are given instead of or in addition to cash discounts. In other words, instead of offering a $5.00 per case discount when purchasing a full case, the distributor will send an extra bottle with the case. If the bottle sells for $5.00, the effective discount is the same for the operator but is less expensive for the distributors because it does not cost them $5.00.

This practice can cause problems, however, since the extra bottles often do not appear on the invoice. A system must be developed to insure that all such bottles are documented and placed on the receiving records. If this is not done, there is the possibility that unrecorded bottles will end up on the bar. Imagine a system in which the bartender did the receiving, and bottle discounts were common. The bartender would not have to bring in his own bottles, they would be delivered! Every unrecorded bottle that makes its way to the bar could be worth as much as $50.00 to $60.00 to the bar personnel.

Another problem is that of costing the merchandise. A case costing $60.00 will be carried on inventory at $5.00 per bottle; but if some cases have thirteen bottles (with the discount), the bottle cost is less. Some system of accurately recording the costs will have to be developed since the invoices will not reflect the true cost.

Blind Receiving

As in the case with food, this is not recommended. Blind receiving, you will recall, is when the receiver gets no written invoice and must record everything on the delivery. This system is more feasible in beverage receiving because the products are easier to count. There should, however, be some sort of written purchase authorization available so that the receiver can compare the delivery with the order. If this is not done, overages and shortages will not be noticed—or else will be found too late. The agreed-upon prices should also be known to the receiver.

Receiving Adjustments

As pointed out, there are fewer options in handling of invoice adjustments with alcoholic beverages relative to foods. In some states, there are virtually none. The operator must develop a policy consistent with the legal regulations and include it in the agreement with the supplier. In general, the invoice should not be tampered with. A credit memorandum should be prepared stating the exact nature of any discrepancy (wrong price, price extension error, goods not delivered, goods refused, goods delivered broken, and so on) and the dollar adjustment. Since it is usually not legally possible to hold a liquor invoice until a credit is received from the purveyor, the best policy would be an agreement with the suppliers that all invoices will be paid net, that is, after deducting the amounts on the credit memos. The supplier should receive a copy of the extended credit memo attached to the

supplier's copy of the invoice. It must be signed by both the supplier's agent and the receiving person.

Storage

Objectives

Storage is a holding phase, and the objectives of storage are:

1. To insure against theft
2. To insure against undocumented issuing
3. To assure proper rotation of stock
4. To provide constant awareness of what stock is on hand
5. To maintain the quality of the products

Security is probably the most important of these objectives. Alcoholic beverages are the most desirable of all the products handled by a foodservice firm. They would rank behind only cash as a target of pilferage or theft.

Stock issued from the storeroom must be recorded so management can determine how many bottles were used on the bar(s) and, more important, what the sales should have been. This record is also necessary to maintain a perpetual inventory. *Stock rotation* is necessary with both beers and wines. It is not with distilled spirits, but it is recommended practice to rotate them as well. *Quality protection* should be a goal with all products and supplies while in storage. With food it is of paramount importance. With wines and beers, it is important for they will deteriorate if not properly cared for. With spirits, which are basically inert, product change is not a concern.

Physical Aspects of Storage

Space. The space requirements can vary widely among establishments and beverage types. Beer frequently demands a lot of space, especially relative to the sales dollars generated. A case of beer and a case of spirits will occupy about the same space, but the sales potential from the beer may be only $24.00 while the spirits could easily generate $500.00. When tap or draft beer is served, the space requirements increase. Wine varies widely according to the type of establishment and whether it sells wine mostly by the bottle or by the decanter or glass. Wine space is frequently wasted by not having properly designed storage racks. Since wine should be stored on its side, it lends itself to space-saving rack designs. Upright storage tends to be less space efficient. Spirits usually require substantial space commitments; cordials much less.

Location. There is no significant difference among the beverage types. All should be convenient to the dispensing area(s). It is preferable that alcoholic beverage storage be located in medium to high traffic areas. You ordinarily would not want liquor storage isolated where unauthorized entry or exit would be unlikely to be noticed.

Equipment. Draft beer needs tapping equipment. Wine requires corkscrews, ice buckets or ice stands, cork retrievers (a small wire implement that removes the cork from a bottle if the cork slips into the bottle when opened), wine serving baskets, funnels, and decanters. Spirits and cordials do not require anything special. For general usage, a case opening knife is needed, and, if wines are packaged in wooden cases, there will have to be something available to pry them open with.

Temperature. Cordials and spirits can safely be stored at any temperature. They do not require refrigeration nor will warm temperatures (within reason) affect them. Draft beer has not been pasteurized and must be held refrigerated (36 degrees F. or 2 degrees C.). Bottled or canned beers are pasteurized and are stable at room temperatures; however, warm storage should be avoided. It is probably best to store these beers in cool (not refrigerated) areas. Wine is temperature sensitive. Ideal wine storage areas should be kept at 55 degrees F. with no temperature variation. Since most establishments will not have specialized wine cellars, the operator should be sure that wherever the wines are stored, the temperature is not over 70 degrees F.

and is as constant as possible. Storing for a few months at more than 70 degrees F. or at widely fluctuating temperatures can cause deterioration.

Humidity. With wines, you should avoid very dry storage due to the possibility of the corks drying out. With other beverages, humidity does not matter except that very humid conditions could affect metal beer cans. They should not, however, be kept long enough for that to be a problem.

Keys and Locks

The most important element of a security system is the key policy. Professional thieves do not need keys to gain access to locked areas. As a general rule, however, foodservice employees who wish to steal do have to have keys. As pointed out, it is difficult if not impossible to secure your facilities from a thief. Fortunately, it is usually not necessary. Management's main security challenge is to prevent pilferage or petty theft by the employees. A rational key and lock policy can be very useful. Some suggestions are:

1. Limit access to the keys. Only persons who receive and issue alcoholic beverages require access to the storage areas, and only they need the keys. This means that in many independent and chain operations, access can be limited to management. Then two things happen, both of which are good. If only management has the keys, only one, two, or three people can get into the liquor storage room. This is good because the fewer who have access, the better. The other is that if only management has the keys, the odds against them giving the keys to anyone else should be increased. This is also good. Line employees might be sloppy about protecting the keys when they have them. In other words, keys are more likely to be "lent" to other employees for a variety of reasons.

2. Avoid master keys. It is tempting to have many (or all) locks mastered to a single key. There is then only one key to carry around as opposed to dozens on a huge ring resembling a horse necklace. The problems are: What if the

one key is misplaced? What if it is given temporarily to an employee who then has a copy made? What if the key is lost? In the first case, that of a misplaced or temporarily lost key, management must risk having someone else find the key and keep it—and perhaps use it. In the second case—giving it to someone—if the person has a key made and several people have access, management will not be aware of the extra key until some stock is missing. The last example, where the key is truly lost, is not any better. Then all the locks have to be changed, because management cannot risk the key being found and used.

3. Emergency key. There is a key available for emergencies, but its use must be recorded. This solves any potential problem arising from restricting possession to one or two people, neither of whom will always be available when emergencies occur. If the bar ran out of well Scotch at 9:30 p.m. and if no one with the keys were there at that time or the assistant manager was tied up in the kitchen, a real crisis would take place. Either the bar would not be resupplied or the assistant manager would give someone the keys. With a key available at the cashier's desk on a sign-out-sign-in basis, the bartender could get more Scotch, and management would have a record of who went into the liquor room, at what time, and what for. They could then follow up to assure that the stock issue was recorded properly and that nothing was missing.

4. The purpose of locks should be to *reduce* accessibility to an area, not to make access impossible, which would be an unworkable situation. It is therefore not necessary for the liquor storeroom (or any other storage area) to simulate a bank vault. Inexpensive locks are generally quite satisfactory. If you have a thief working for you, a lock will not keep him or her out. If the lock gets broken during a theft, you could lose an expensive lock as well as some liquor. We are not suggesting cheap locks. Cheap anything is never a good value, but there are many relatively inexpensive locks available that will do the job satisfactorily and provide good value. It is also recommended to move locks

around occasionally and at random. An unauthorized person could temporarily possess a key, but its value would be limited if the person did not know what it opened.

Tag or Sticker Systems

As described under bar personnel frauds, these are intended to supplement the concept of par stocks on the bar and reduce or prevent personnel from supplying their own stock. They can be a good control procedure and are recommended. It is necessary to completely safeguard the tags or stickers, however. Access to them by bar personnel obviously eliminates even the appearance of control. The control would be enhanced by using consecutively numbered tags or stickers. Management could track them as they would numbered guest checks. If any were used privately by the bartender, numbers would be missing. Even with numbered stickers, however, no control exists unless all the numbers are accounted for. A record of missing numbers must be kept, and bar bottles must be checked to see if these numbers show up.

Full Case Storage

Storage of full, unopened cases does not present any problems (except possibly those associated with excessive inventory). Once opened, cases should be emptied and discarded. In general, retention of cardboard containers can cause sanitation problems. Roaches and insects are often unwittingly delivered to operations with the cases, so getting rid of the containers when they are received is a good practice. The problem with opened, partially filled cases is that the total stock is not visible and is easier to steal. If loose bottles are removed from the shelves it is more noticeable than if they are taken from opened cases.

For better sanitation and better stock control, open cases when received and put all bottles on the shelves. If partial cases must be stored, keep a running balance plainly marked on the case with a bold marking pen. Adjust the balance whenever you remove a bottle, and check the count periodically.

Inventory Controls and Procedures

Perpetual Inventory

Unlike with food, we do recommend use of a perpetual inventory with alcoholic beverages. At any given time, an accurate perpetual inventory will show the amount of merchandise on hand. This can be used to check stock security, to order, and to track and evaluate the usage of specific brands. The usefulness of a perpetual inventory in ordering is of particular importance since orders can be prepared without having access to the stock. That means that persons other than management can prepare the orders—at least partially.

Unless the perpetual is accurate, however, it is likely to be a liability rather than an asset. Potential accuracy is why we recommend its use in a beverage system. The guidelines for accuracy are:

1. All *additions* to stock must be recorded. This is no problem. Merely post the deliveries from the invoices. It is easier than with food for there are far fewer beverage deliveries each week.
2. All *removals* must also be recorded. This is the difficult aspect. Unless management can assure that *all* merchandise removed from storage is posted to the perpetual, they might as well not bother with one.

Alcoholic beverages are often all stored in one area, making it easier to control and reduce access. Authorization for access is typically limited to a few people, making it more likely that issues will be handled properly. Necessity for access is limited (or can be) to one time daily plus deliveries. All these conditions reduce the possibility of unrecorded issues. The perpetual should be spot checked regularly against an actual count, and this must be done between physical inventories. You do not want to wait till the end of the month to find out you are missing some bottles. This is an easy check to do. Since the liquor should be issued daily, the person doing this should make it a practice to check a few brands each day. By the time the month has ended, each brand will have been checked, probably more than once, and it will take only a few extra minutes to do this.

A perpetual inventory can be maintained either on bin cards or sheets. A bin card (Exhibit 7.5) has only one brand and no time limit, whereas a sheet (Exhibit 7.6) has several brands and will have a time limit, perhaps a half month or month. The bin card uses more paper space to record an inventory; it takes longer to post invoices and requisitions; and it is not as convenient to use when you want to check the stock level. On the other hand, when a product moves slowly, one card may well last for a year or two. It is also easier to track the usage of one brand over time. The bin sheet gives a better total picture. It shows the number of bottles issued each day, and it can be set up so each sheet is for a separate beverage category—vodka, gin, beer, wine, cordials, bourbon, and so on. The bin sheet also wastes time and paper space with slow-moving products because there is an entry every day whether or not there were any issues. Both are suitable, and each manager should decide which form best meets his needs.

Physical Inventory

A physical inventory is an actual count of all merchandise on hand. It is necessary for preparation of operating statements. The only way to determine the cost with total accuracy is to have an exact count of what is on hand at the end of the operating period. The cost-of-goods formula depends on inventories:

Opening inventory

Plus: purchases

Equals: goods available for sale or use

Less: ending inventory

Equals: goods sold or used

Operating statements are typically prepared monthly, so a physical inventory must be taken monthly. It may be taken more frequently, as often as management feels they require accurate

Exhibit 7.5. Bin Card

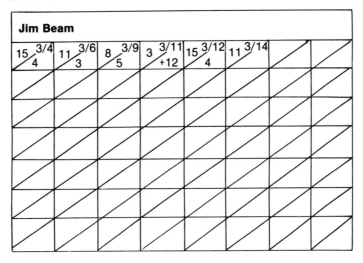

1. On 3/4, there were 15 bottles of Jim Beam in the storeroom.
2. On 3/6, 4 bottles were issued, showing a new balance of 11 bottles.
3. On 3/9, 3 bottles were issued, showing a balance of 8 bottles.
4. On 3/11, 5 bottles were issued, showing a balance of 3 bottles.
5. On 3/12, a case (12 bottles) was delivered, showing a balance of 15 bottles.
6. On 3/14, 4 bottles were issued. The current balance is 11 bottles.

cost information that they cannot get any other way. There are other ways to determine costs, but they are all estimates. It can often be shown that some of the cost-estimation techniques will yield sufficiently accurate information for tracking costs during operating periods. In this case, it may not be necessary to take several physical inventories. Inventories are time consuming and cost money. When the information they yield is no different from what could have been obtained more easily, at less expense, it is foolish to rely on physical inventories.

The guidelines given for food inventories apply to beverages as well. There should be a minimum of two people, one to count, one to write. The counter should be one of the bartenders or someone very familiar with the stock so the inventory will be taken quickly and accurately. The writer or recorder should be a member of management or from the accounting or comptroller's office so the inventory will be honest. The person counting could deliberately alter the counts, of course, but an experienced

person doing the recording would be able to control this. The recorder would ask for some counts to be repeated to check against the original count or would pick products at random and count them along with the bartender and so forth.

There are several physical inventory methods. One thing that should be understood is that nearly all use estimation techniques because many of the bottles are open and only partially full.

Inventory Methods

1. *Weighing.* This is supposed to be the most accurate, but it is probably an estimation method as well. A scale is used to weigh the open bottles. To be completely accurate the scale must be tared (display zero weight with an empty bottle on it) for each bottle type since there are differences between bottles. Spirit and cordial producers often use the bottle as part of the marketing plan, and there are a wide variety of shapes, sizes, and bottle weights. The contents of the bottles

Exhibit 7.6. Bin Sheet

Brand	3/1	3/2	3/3	3/4	3/5	3/6	3/7	3/8	3/9	3/10	3/11	3/12	3/13
Jim Beam	15 / -	15 / -	15 / -	15 / -	15 / -	15 / 4	11 / -	11 / -	11 / 3	8 / -	8 / 5	3 / +12	15 / -
Daily Totals													

can also vary in weight, particularly with cordials. The fact that a drink such as the Pousse Cafe (layered cordials of different colors) can even be made is proof that the specific gravity (and weight) of various cordials show significant variances. Even the bottle proof can affect the weight. Alcohol is lighter than water, so an 80-proof spirit would weigh more than would a 100-proof spirit (80 proof equals 40 percent alcohol plus 60 percent water, whereas 100 proof equals 50 percent alcohol plus 50 percent water). Complete accuracy would therefore require that each bottle gross weight be adjusted by bottle weight, proof, and sugar content (if a cordial) to obtain the net weight.

Aside from this, weighing can be cumbersome since either the scale must be moved as the inventory is counted or the bottles must be taken to the scale. Both would tend to slow the process without appreciably increasing the overall accuracy.

2. *Full-bottle only.* In this method, the partial bottles are ignored and only full and/or unopened bottles are counted. The theory here is that there is always the same approximate amount of liquor available in the opened bottles. If this were true, the inventory would be accurate without the open bottles. For example: if the opened bottles always equal 315 ounces, the cost-of-goods calculation would have the same result regardless of whether the opened bottles were

used or not (see Exhibit 7.7). It is not necessary that the open bottles inventory be exactly the same (which it will not be) but only that it be approximately the same. When the bar volume relative to the open bottle inventory is high, this becomes even more feasible (see Exhibit 7.8).

In both cases, bar number one and number two, the difference in the usage from inventory-ing only the full bottles is 60 ounces. In bar one (high volume), 60 ounces amounts only to about 1/2 a percent, whereas in bar two, it is over 2 percent. In this example, the high-volume operation could possibly disregard the open bottles, while the other could not or should not consider it.

3. *Calibrated tape or stick.* These are devices to measure the bottle contents. The tape is flexible while the stick is typically shaped to fit the bottle. The problem is that there are many bottle shapes, requiring a great variety of measuring sticks. The tape can be used with any bottle, but not with consistent accuracy for dissimilar shaped bottles will read differently.

4. *Calibrated bottles.* Here the bottles themselves are marked and the contents can be quickly and accurately recorded. The drawback is that only a few manufacturers use such bottles. Since the government shows such interest in regulating the alcoholic beverages industry, one wonders why all spirit bottles are not required to be marked in milliliters.

Exhibit 7.7 Effect of Open Bottle Inventory—Low Volume

Opening inventory =	2,540 oz.
Plus: purchases	4,500 oz.
	7,040 oz.
Less: ending inventory	2,495 oz.
Equals: cost of goods	4,545 oz.
Opening inventory =	2,540 + 315 = 2,855 oz.
Plus: purchases	4,500 oz.
	7,355 oz.
Less: ending inventory	2,495 + 315 = 2,810 oz.
Equals: cost of goods	4,545 oz.

5. *Estimation by tenths.* This is the most common method and, properly done, is sufficiently accurate. It does rely on an estimation of the contents of the bottle, but most of the other systems use some degree of estimation too. There are two factors to evaluate when estimating tenths: accuracy and consistency. Of these two, consistency is more important. For example, if a bartender estimates the contents to be 4/10 bottle when it is actually

5/10, but she would *always* call it at 4/10, there is no problem. After two inventories, the differences would be eliminated. If a particular individual would call the same bottle 4/10, 5/10, and 6/10 on three consecutive inventories, the inconsistency would be more of a problem than the lack of accuracy.

This system is also a very quick way to obtain the ending inventory. The caller merely counts the full bottles and calls them (eight) while

Exhibit 7.8 Effect of Open Bottle Inventory—High Volume

Bar Number 1
(with open bottles)

Opening inventory 3,000 oz. + 465 oz.	=3,465 oz.
Plus: purchases	10,000 oz.
	13,465 oz.
Less: ending inventory 2,800 oz. + 405 oz.	=3,205 oz.
Goods used	10,260 oz.

(without open bottles)

Opening inventory	3,000 oz.
Plus: purchases	10,000 oz.
	13,000 oz.
Less: ending inventory	2,800 oz.
Goods used	10,200 oz.

Bar Number 2
(with open bottles)

Opening inventory 1,000 oz. + 465 oz.	=1,465 oz.
Plus: purchases	3,000 oz.
	4,465 oz.
Less: ending inventory 1,100 oz. + 405 oz.	=1,505 oz.
Goods used	2,960 oz.

(without open bottles)

Opening inventory	1,000 oz.
Plus: purchases	3,000 oz.
	4,000 oz.
Less: ending inventory	1,100 oz.
Goods used	2,900 oz.

picking up the opened bottle and adding the estimate (point 5). The writer records 8.5 on that brand, and they go to another. When the stock is properly organized, the inventory can proceed quickly using this system.

The key to which method is best is to balance cost against accuracy. Management should desire the best information at the lowest cost. There would obviously be a point beyond which additional time and expense would not yield a useful increase in accuracy. The reverse is true, too; there is a point where it does not make any sense to even collect the information if it is likely to be highly inaccurate. In this case, any expenditure, no matter how small, is not justified.

Physical Arrangement of Stock

How the stock is arranged is critical for two reasons: speed and accuracy. The inventory should be taken as quickly and easily as possible because time is valuable. Also, if the inventory takes too long, it may not be taken at all. The inventory must be accurate because in a well-run operation it will be the basis for many important decisions.

What Information Should Be Obtained?

1. The dollar value of all merchandise on hand
2. The dollar value of each type (bourbon, Canadian, Scotch) and brand (Jose Cuervo, Schenley gin, and so on) on hand.
3. The dollar value of the stock in each storage area: storeroom(s), bar(s)
4. The total number of bottles on hand broken down by product type, brand, and location. This is needed to determine the bottle usage of each beverage type and brand.

Inventory Turnover

This is calculated just as is food inventory turnover.

$$\frac{\text{Cost of goods consumed or sold}}{\text{Average inventory}} = \text{T/O}$$

It should be calculated on the total beverage inventory as well as on the bar(s) and storeroom(s). To determine a rational turnover figure:

1. Track each brand over time so you know how much will normally be used per day, week, or month.
2. Set a par stock in both the storage area and the bar for each brand. The bar par will depend on the issuing frequency, and the storeroom par will depend upon the delivery frequency. The rule of thumb is to stock 1.5 times the expected usage, although this will vary with some brands. A very slow-moving cordial, for example, may not have any backup in storage. When it gets down to the point where it could run out, a replacement will be ordered. In this case, the usage is so low that 1.5 is not a reasonable figure.
3. The objective is to get the inventory as low as possible *without* running out of stock and *with* taking full advantage of specials, discounts, and post-offs.

Issuing

Par Stock

Issuing may or may not be a formal function in a food system, but it *must* be in an alcoholic beverage system. The first step is to establish the par stock on the bar using the 1.5 times usage rule just discussed. Other guidelines are: the par should not assume that the bar never runs out. If that were the case, there would be too much stock on the bar. It also should not handle those occasional peaks that can be anticipated, such as Mother's Day and New Year's Eve. The par can temporarily be expanded to meet such needs. The par should handle normal business with a reasonable safety margin.

Issues to the bar should be made on a daily basis. These are done by building up to the par stock for each brand on a bottle for bottle replacement. Each empty bottle is replaced by a full one, and so the integrity of the par is maintained.

Requisitions

The only authority for issuing stock should be a written requisition made up at least in duplicate. One copy should stay at the bar to be checked against the order when it arrives. The other should go to the storeroom, where it becomes the basis for the daily issue. A third copy may be desired for the accounting office, particularly when the storeroom copy is retained. The requisition should be signed by the person requesting the stock, by the person filling the order, and by the person accepting delivery to the bar. If there are any shortages, there is a record of what left the storeroom as well as what was received on the bar. It would be easy to pinpoint the individual(s) responsible. These requisitions then become the source for posting stock depletions to the perpetual inventory.

Who Is Qualified to Prepare the Requisition?

Anyone should be able to prepare the daily bar requisition since it is merely a matter of listing all the empty bottles. The closing bartender(s) should be instructed to collect all empty bottles and put them on the bar, or in an empty case, or on a cart, wherever is best. The requisition can be written at that time, or the morning bartender can prepare it. Actually anyone who can read, write, and count can prepare it, from the morning bar porter to any of the bartenders.

How to Fill the Requisition

Whoever does the issuing should fill the requisition brand by brand, for example, taking three empty bottles of well gin off the cart and replacing them with three full ones. When finished, both the full and empty bottles should be counted to assure that both counts are the same. The empty bottles should then be destroyed to prevent any possibility of them being put back on the bar where they could again be exchanged for full bottles. One potential control problem with the full-for-an-empty system is that a bartender would no longer have to bring in a full bottle. He could bring in empties or reuse the empties as described! The second is avoided by breaking all empties and the

first by checking the bar par stock. An extra bottle—empty or full—would show up, but only if the stock is checked frequently and randomly.

Issue Patterns Should Be Observed and Documented

Deviations from normal levels of activity should be questioned, investigated by management, and justified. Variances will occur, but management must assure that they are legitimate. For example, if the normal daily issue for bar rum was three to four bottles, and one day it was seven bottles, management should find out why. There may very well be a logical explanation; in fact, when management routinely follows up on such variances, a logical explanation will almost always be forthcoming. It could be that there was a real run on rum-based drinks the previous evening. Sales records should show this. Management should not accept the bartender's word that this happened. Issues of less than normal amounts should also be investigated since they could be the result of the bartender selling her liquor, which would not require replacement at the end of the day.

A Special Case: Banquet Issues

Banquet beverage issuing can be troublesome for many foodservice operations. Very large hotels will probably have separate banquet storage areas, but most units cannot justify either the extra space (if they even have it) or the added inventory investment. These smaller units have a choice of issuing banquet stock from the storeroom or from the bar. The advantage of storeroom issues is that it separates the bar and bartenders from banquet functions, and this avoids some control problems. The disadvantage is that there are always partial bottles remaining after catering functions, and these would then be returned to the storeroom. One of the guidelines for good storeroom management is to avoid opened bottles. The only opened bottles in the unit should be on a working bar.

The control implications are evident. An additional problem is the disposal of any remaining partial bottles from storage. If these are sent to the bar, the par stock concept will not work. For example: the par is 6 bottles, and at the end of the day there are 4 empty bottles, 1 open bottle (2/10 full), and 1 unopened bottle. An issue of 4 full bottles leaves the bar with 6 bottles containing 5 2/10 bottles of liquor. An issue of 4 opened bottles, each a quarter full, leaves the bar with 6 bottles containing 2.2 bottles of liquor. If the par of 6 bottles is accurate, they will surely run out and probably fairly quickly. It also complicates bar usage and cost-sales calculation. If not used on the bar, the open bottles would have to be reissued to the banquet department. The same problem of insufficient stock could result. There also could be a marketing problem since it is normally recommended to start catering beverage functions with unopened bottles and open them in front of the guests as they are needed. This is especially true on a hosted bar. It also complicates the cost-sales calculations of the banquet.

If not issued from the storeroom, however, the catering stock will have to come from the bar stock. This requires sufficiently large par stocks to handle the additional requirements. The advantage is that opened bottles go back to the bar, where they can most easily be used. The bar may physically not be able to handle the additional storage, however. In that case, we would recommend for banquets that the par stock on the bar be temporarily increased and all leftover (empty, partial, and unopened full) bottles be returned to the bar. The empty bottles turned in the next day should bring the par back to normal. For example: eight bottles is the par for blended well whiskey, and four bottles are needed for a party. The bar requisition is for nine bottles (five for the bar and four for the party). Only five empties accompany the requisition, but it is submitted with a banquet requisition for four bottles. The next day, the bar requisition is for four bottles, and it is accompanied by eight empties. In other words, the bar par stock is always maintained at eight bottles. There is no banquet par. It must be cleared to zero after each party. All banquet issues, regardless of where they are made from, must be authorized by a banquet requisition. This is necessary to maintain the perpetual inventory and, more important, to accurately assign a cost to the department and perhaps even to each function.

Service

Most of the key points of service control were covered in the section on personnel frauds. We will only summarize them here.

Document All Drinks

If there were a record of every drink served, management would have few bar control problems. The best way to do this is to use some sort of electronic or mechanical monitoring system, but this is difficult if the bar personnel are determined to bypass it. If all products served go through the system, the effectiveness can be excellent. Some systems, however, permit a significant amount of hand pouring, and it is easy for the bartenders to serve without ringing the drinks. Spotters are helpful, but they cannot cover the bar continuously. This is not actually necessary since knowing that spotters are used randomly can make unscrupulous bar personnel act very carefully, especially if they also know they will lose their jobs if *ever* observed serving an unregistered drink. Installation of a video system is now a feasible option for management. Video cameras can be programmed to record a certain number of frames per minute on a videotape. This is potentially a nearly foolproof way to place the bar under continuous observation but it, like many other controls, is no good unless someone takes the time to monitor the tapes. This system would also make it easier to deal with unions. A spotter may report that the employee did not follow proper procedures. If the employee denies this, it is the word of one individual against another. Few unions would allow an employee to be terminated under such circumstances. A videotape could provide conclusive evidence. Either the drink was registered on a guest check and the check presented along with the drink, or it was not. The cash drawer is either open or closed. If violation of procedures constitutes grounds for dismissal, and if management reviews the tapes regularly (or has them reviewed; this service could be purchased), the use of a video system could be very effective. Although unions, many employees, and perhaps even activist organizations may object to such surveillance as a violation of privacy, there is ample precedence for such control. Banks have routinely used video cameras for some time, and Las Vegas casinos use them to monitor table-games and dealers.

Use Guest Checks

This works in conjunction with documenting drinks in that it provides a record of the drinks sold. Systems can be installed so that no drinks can be poured without placing a check in the cash register. Guest checks can be audited and all sorts of improper practices can be found in a check audit.

Measure All Drinks

Portion control is very important with products such as alcoholic beverages that are served hundreds—perhaps thousands—of times per day. Requiring the use of measuring devices will not, in and of itself, achieve the desired control, but it helps. Drink measurement is also necessary if management is to impress upon employees the importance of drink consistency for both cost control and quality control. It is recommended, if possible, to deny employees the ability to make portion decisions by using some sort of automated portioning system. Allowing employees to decide the portion size hundreds of times per day is, when you think about it, not a very sound business practice, and food and beverage units should be operated as businesses.

Par Stocks

Not only establish par stocks for each brand, but check the bar frequently and randomly to see whether the counts are in line with the par.

Bottle Stickers or Tags

Some such system can be useful but only if the stickers, tags, stamps, or whatever are totally controlled by management. There is no control at all if the employees can get their own tags or

duplicate them. For this reason, some sort of numbered tag system is recommended, with continuous follow-up to assure that all numbers are accounted for. This should not be too difficult. If, for example, the bottles were marked when requisitioned, the requisition would provide a record of how many bottles were sent to the bar. Then it could be used to update the sticker number record. If numbers 506 to 10,000 were unused, and the requisition was for twenty bottles, numbers 506 to 525 would be removed from the list of available numbers. When management checks par stocks, takes inventory, and so forth, they should also check the numbers, knowing which number sequences are active. This would force employees bent on fraud not only to obtain duplicate tags or stickers but to have specific number sequences as well. One can reach a point on the bar where, while it is not impossible to steal or cheat, it becomes so complicated and troublesome that it is simply not worth the effort. Most bar personnel do not wish to work overtime to gain a few extra dollars per day in a high-risk situation, especially when there are so many places where they can steal hundreds of dollars weekly, with nearly no risk and do so practically in their sleep.

Use Standard Recipes

This is as much for quality control as for cost control. It is poor business practice to let employees decide how a product is to be prepared and served. It is management's job to determine what the house standards ought to be and to assure that they be met with consistency. This does not mean that recipes must be engraved in stone. If a newly hired bartender makes a better Bloody Mary than you presently serve and if its cost is consistent with your present costs, then use his recipe—but *standardize* it. Assure that everyone uses it, and continue to use it unless or until you find a better one.

Credit Cards

Establish sound procedures on the acceptance of credit cards.

Free Drink Policies

Do not give bar personnel the authority to provide free drinks to guests, regardless of the circumstances. Some owners or managers will go even farther and actually pay cash when themselves buying a drink for a guest. This has a double effect. First, it is a more meaningful act to the patron when she or he actually sees cash change hands. Second, it is better control because there is cash expected for *all* drinks poured, with no exceptions even for the boss.

Cash Drawer

Require the drawer to be closed following each transaction and to remain closed between transactions. Require the bartender to use a special card (or one specific guest check) when opening the register for a no-sale reason (change and so forth). This check should be dated, signed, and turned in with the other checks.

Cash Handling

It may not be possible to remove or reduce the bartender's cash-handling responsibility, but if it can be done, do it.

Banquet Control Systems

Many foodservice units do not have adequate control over their banquet or catering operations. We are not referring here to large hotels and similar types of units that have separate, well-defined catering departments and generally have structured control systems designed specifically for those departments. There are thousands of other units for whom catering is an occasional function, and thousands more that have quite a bit of activity but not enough to justify setting up a distinct department. With these operations, the need is to establish a management information system that provides the minimum data necessary for control: separate cost and sales records. This would be necessary even if the catering cost structure were the same as the rest of the operation, for management needs to know exactly what is happening in each area and with each type of activity. Often, though, the potential cost percentage in catering is different, and management must know what it is to be able to interpret the operational data.

A *banquet work sheet* can be useful in providing management the kind of information they require. See Exhibits 7.9, 7.10, and 7.11 for examples of this work sheet. One is uncompleted, and the others show two types of functions. A description of the basic sheet and its components follows Exhibit 7.9.

Column A: Brand. These are whatever specific brands are to be issued to the function bar. Sometimes the group booking the party will specify particular brands; sometimes they will give the instructions "well brands" or "top-shelf," which means that management will stock the bar either with the well stock or with premium brands of each spirit type. The setting up of the bar will probably be delegated, but management should verify that these particular brands were the ones issued. A few prudent switches by the bartenders could give them the opportunity to enhance their earnings.

Column B: Issue. This is the amount to be set up for the function. It could be at the discretion of the bartender (be careful here) or management, or it could be specified by the people booking the party. If it is a cocktail party to be followed by a business meeting, the person in charge may well want to limit the amount of liquor available. This is another entry that must be personally verified by management, for the protection of the group as well as the establishment. This work sheet becomes the requisition authorization and will probably be prepared in duplicate for requisition purposes. As outlined previously, the stock could be issued from a separate banquet inventory (a large hotel for instance), from the storeroom (common but not recommended), or from the stock at the bar. Having this record would make it easy to remove the banquet usage from the main bar total and separate the sales and costs.

Column C: Additional issue. If the booking agreement provides for replenishment of the beverage stock when and if it begins to run out,

Exhibit 7.9. Banquet Work Sheet

Date _____   Group _____

A	B	C	D	E	F	G	H	I	J	K	L
Brand	Issue	Additional Issue	Total Available	Ending Inventory	Usage	Bottle Cost ($)	Standard Bottle Sales Value ($)	Total Cost ($)	Standard Sales ($)	Actual Sales ($)	Variance = OR (-) ($/%)

there must be a record of whatever additional requisitions were made. This is another step that has to be verified by management.

Column D: Total available. This is simply the total of columns B and C.

Column E: Ending inventory. This is critical information, and it must be correct. Both the billing accuracy and management's analysis of the function depend on the ending inventory. It should probably be taken by management themselves.

Column F: Usage. This is obtained by subtracting the ending inventory (column E) from the total available (column D). It is the total amount of product, brand by brand, that was used.

Column G: Bottle costs. This figure comes from the current inventory records. The recommended inventory value to use is the last price paid. This is the LIFO method (last in-first out). Some accountants like to use the average inventory cost, and providing you have some sort of computerized inventory and purchase record, it is feasible. However, you would probably want to put a time parameter on it. An average over the last ten years would not be a meaningful figure.

Column H: Standard bottle sales value. This is calculated as outlined in the discussion of the standard sales control system if the liquor is to be sold by the drink. Banquet liquor is often sold by the bottle (a *hosted* bar, the host picks up the tab). In that case, the bottle sales value is whatever the selling price happens to be for the entire bottle. Hotel room service is handled the same way.

Column I: Total cost. This is obtained by multiplying the bottle cost (column G) by the bottle usage (column F). It gives the total cost of using the primary products but not the auxiliary products such as mixes, garnishes, and so on. How to handle these will be covered in the discussion on using the work sheet for specific groups.

Column J: Standard sales. This will be the total sales, either as calculated by the standard sales method (drinks sold individually) or by the bottle sales price (drinks sold by the bottle).

With a hosted bar, this is the basis for billing the customer.

Column K: Actual sales. With a *hosted* bar, this is exactly the same as the previous column, standard sales. With a *no-host* bar, it reflects the total cash deposit.

Column L: Variance. In the case of a *no-host* bar, there is the possibility of a variance between the standard sales (column J) and the actual sales (column K). Any variance should be given both as a dollar figure (the most important) and as a percentage deviation from the expected figure (the standard or potential sales). Management should have an expectation of what is reasonable for a percentage variance. In other words, they may feel that a 2 percent variance could be explained due to spillage, waste, mistakes, and so forth. As long as the variance does not exceed 2 percent, the results would be satisfactory. A variance of more than 2 percent, however, would result in an investigation. As explained previously, it is not realistic to expect 100 percent sales compliance with the standard when evaluating the total operation. Quite frankly, though, we would recommend it for individual catering functions. In many cases, there is only one portion size poured and one price charged. There is no reason why total accuracy cannot be expected under such circumstances.

This is how the basic work sheet operates. Let us look at its use in both a *no-host* bar and a *hosted* bar. Exhibit 7.10 shows the work sheet as used for a *no-host* function.

A- The brands specified, in this case probably by management, are mostly well brands.

B- The issues should preferably be in whole bottles (1.0, 3.0, 6.0) as shown here.

C- In this case, only two bottles were added during the function: one vodka and one Bacardi rum.

D- The total bottles that were available for use: 2.0 gins, 1.0 blended whiskey, and so forth.

E- The ending inventory is taken in tenths, similar to the main bar inventory. Management should either have taken the inventory themselves or verified it before the bottles are removed from the banquet room.

Exhibit 7.10 Banquet Work Sheet—For a No-Host Bar

Date 3/24   Group Klaxon Corp.

A	B	C	D	E	F	G	H	I	J	K	L
Brand	Issue	Additional Issue	Total Available	Ending Inventory	Usage	Bottle Cost ($)	Standard Bottle Sales Value ($)	Total Cost ($)	Standard Sales ($)	Actual Sales ($)	Variance = OR (-) ($/%)
Well Gin	2.0		2.0	.6	1.4	3.97	30.00	5.56	42.00		
Vodka	3.0	1.0	4.0	1.2	2.8	3.91	30.00	10.95	84.00		
Bourbon	2.0		2.0	1.1	.9	4.52	30.00	4.07	27.00		
Scotch	2.0		2.0	.4	1.6	5.01	30.00	8.02	48.00		
Blend	1.0		1.0	.5	.5	4.10	30.00	2.05	15.00		
C C	2.0		2.0	.9	1.1	8.15	35.00	8.97	38.50		

Jose Cuervo	1.0	1.0	1.0	.3	.7	4.70	30.00	3.29	21.00	
Bacardi	2.0	1.0	3.0	1.0	2.0	4.35	30.00	8.70	60.00	
Budweiser	24.0	---	24.0	6.0	18.0	.19	1.25	3.42	22.50	
Miller Lite	12.0	---	12.0	2.0	10.0	.17	1.00	1.70	10.00	
								$56.73	$368.00	$351.75
										($16.25)
										(4.4%)
Mixes, Garnish, etc. 2% of sales (.02 x $375.00)								7.35		
								$64.08		

Potential % = 17.4%   Actual = 18.2%

Potential G.P. = $303.92 Actual = $287.67

F- Total product used, by brand.

G- Cost of each brand poured.

H- In this type of function, the drinks are paid for individually, so the standard sales calculation is made. As pointed out, it is fairly easy to do for banquet or catering affairs. This may or may *not* be the same sales value as is used in the main bar. The calculation is made by dividing the bottle capacity by the portion size to obtain the number of drinks per bottle and multiplying this by the selling price of the drinks. None of these factors may be the same in banquets. The bottle size is generally the same, but the portion sizes and selling prices usually differ.

I- Total cost.

J- Total standard sales. This is the amount of money that is expected to be available for deposit at the end of the function. It shows the expected income by brand.

K- One of the problems with the banquet bars is that it is very difficult to get sales breakdowns by brand. It can be done but would require some sort of computerized point-of-sale equipment. This may be a wise investment for a large banquet department, but it could not be justified for many operations. The result is as shown here. There is an overall sales total but no brand breakdown. This weakness is not as serious as it may appear, since any shortages are the result of one function at one time in one room and possibly worked by one employee. Under such circumstances, it is easy to focus responsibility, and that is what control is really all about. A recommended policy would be to expect 100 percent compliance with the standard and to evaluate each and every function. Bartenders who meet the standard will be invited back to work again: others will not. One very real danger here should be obvious. If the bartender can pour *more* drinks per bottle and take in *more* than the standard, she could pocket the balance, and management would be satisfied, not knowing that the customers had been cheated. Banquet bars thus demand a lot of supervision. There have to be pouring standards just as on the regular bar(s).

L- The standard sales were not attained in Exhibit 7.10. The amount of $375.00 should have

been taken in; the deposit was only $358.75. Column L shows a variance of $16.25 or 4.3 percent. Management must decide whether this is acceptable. One may be tempted to let it slide; after all, $16.00 is not much, and neither is 4 percent. You should, however, look at it this way. If the bartender was paid $25.00 for the party, the $16.25 he was short means in effect that the labor cost was $41.25, or 65 percent higher than it should have been! Another way to look at it is from a profit standpoint. The profit from this particular function is decreased by $16.25, and we are talking *net* profit, not gross profit. All expenses for this function are fixed when the bartender walks in. If the gross profit goes down, the net is similarly decreased. Still another way to look at it is: would you willingly pay this bartender an additional $16.00 every time he worked a party?

At the bottom of the work sheet are some additional figures. One shows how to handle the mixes and garnishes. You could figure an exact cost the same way that the cost of the basic product is determined. This is time consuming and possibly not a good use of management time. Here it is done by a percentage estimation. We are saying that, on the average, the cost of these types of things is about 2 percent of sales. Since the sales should have been $375.00, the estimated cost is $7.50. This is added to the actual cost of all the spirits and beers ($56.73) for a grand total of $64.23. There are two additional pieces of information: potential and actual percentage cost, and potential and actual gross profit (dollars). The bar cost should have been 17.1 percent; it was 17.9 percent. The profit should have been $310.77, it was $294.52.

The third example of the banquet work sheet, Exhibit 7.11, differs from the one just discussed only in that it is for a *hosted* bar, in this case, a wedding. Note that the bottle sales values are different. They are lower, and this would be typical. Note also that there cannot be any difference between the standard sales and the actual sales. This figure is obtained by multiplying the number of bottles consumed by the selling price for each bottle. It is done at the end of the function. The handling of the mixes and garnishes is the same. There is no potential versus actual cost percentage or profits. There is only the actual percentage cost and the actual gross profit.

At the end of a period, the banquet work sheets are totaled. The sales total should equal the sales as recorded on the daily reports for the period. This is seldom a problem. The information that management usually does not have is the cost data, and these sheets provide that. For example: assume that the banquet stock had been issued from the bar and any partially consumed bottles, as well as unopened bottles, are returned to the bar. When the cost of goods is calculated for the bar, merely subtract the cost of the banquets. The result is the actual cost of sales. You now have cost and sales both for the main bar and for the banquets. Any discrepancies in the overall beverage cost could be traced to one or both of these areas, and at least you would know where your problem was.

Automatic Beverage Control Systems

These systems are becoming increasingly popular today, and the reason is simple. They provide a very powerful management control tool. The companies that manufacture and sell them have an even more simple rationale: most operators do not get the maximum profit available from each bottle. The primary reason for this is that not all the liquor in the bottle is sold. It may be stolen, given away, spilled, lost through breakage, wasted through overportioning, and on and on. Or it may well be sold but by the bartender, who has become an entrepreneur! No one really knows how much is lost due to these and other reasons, but the manufacturers of control systems claim such losses can total four to six drinks per bottle. These systems, are, therefore, *primarily* designed to assure that all the liquor in each bottle is sold.

There are many systems on the market, and they range from simple and inexpensive to complex and expensive. To begin with, let us look at what can be expected from a beverage system. It is unlikely that any one system would have all of the capabilities described here; it is

also unlikely that any operation would require all of them. What the operator needs is to decide which capabilities are important to her specific establishment and then to determine which available system best meets these needs at the lowest price.

Capabilities and Advantages

1. *They will measure a predetermined portion.* This allows management to have a high degree of control over the portion and avoids the normal situation where line personnel are allowed to make a basic management decision—the portion size—and make it perhaps hundreds of times per day. This system should eliminate spillage. It should also eliminate overpouring (although underpouring could still be a problem). If management is interested in accuracy of portion sizes, and they should be, this is an excellent way to achieve it. There should be increased uniformity of drinks prepared. Quality control is as important as cost control, and one of the keys to quality control in a beverage system is to keep the products consistent.

2. *They will record the fact that a particular drink has been served.* The importance of this should be obvious after all the discussion about ways to document the fact that drinks have been served. If a drink cannot be served without going through the system, one of the really critical control objectives has been achieved. Under these circumstances, management would not care if the bartenders brought in their own bottles because the sales would be recorded, and the cash would be expected to be turned in. It is when drinks can be served unrecorded that the cash can be kept.

3. *They will count the drinks sold and categorize them.* This can be of great value to management. Many of the analytical techniques discussed earlier depend upon having accurate information on the sales mix. This record could be as simple as a count of the drinks sold by type (bourbon, Scotch, brandy, and so on), a listing of the number of drinks sold of each brand (Cutty Sark, Smirnoff, Jim Beam), or a complete listing of every different drink likely to be prepared! With this type of information, using the

Exhibit 7.11 Banquet Work Sheet—For a Hosted Bar

Date 5/26   **Group** Jones Wedding

A	B	C	D	E	F	G	H	I	J	K	L
Brand	Issue	Additional Issue	Total Available	Ending Inventory	Usage	Bottle Cost ($)	Standard Bottle Sales Value ($)	Total Cost ($)	Standard Sales ($)	Actual Sales ($)	Variance = OR (-) ($/%)
Well Scotch	4.0	---	4.0	1.8	2.2	5.01	27.50	11.02	60.50	60.50	
Bourbon	2.0	---	2.0	1.0	1.0	4.52	25.00	4.52	25.00	25.00	
Gin	3.0	---	3.0	1.2	1.8	3.97	22.50	7.15	40.50	40.50	
Vodka	4.0	---	4.0	1.9	2.1	3.91	22.50	8.21	47.25	47.25	
Canadian	2.0	---	2.0	1.4	.6	4.94	25.00	2.96	15.00	15.00	
Tequila	1.0	---	1.0	.6	.4	4.05	22.50	1.62	9.00	9.00	
Rum	3.0	1.0	4.0	.3	3.7	4.16	22.50	15.39	83.25	83.25	
Blend	1.0	---	1.0	.4	.6	4.10	22.50	2.46	13.50	13.50	

Brandy	1.0	—	1.0	.5	.5	4.95	25.00	2.48		12.50	12.50
Champagne	24.0		24.0	—	24	2.25	10.00	54.00		$306.50	$306.50
Red Wine	12.0		12.0	3.0	9	3.50	8.00	31.50		240.00	240.00
White Wine	18.0	3.0	21.0	1.0	20	3.50	8.00	70.00		72.00	72.00
										160.00	160.00
								211.31		$778.50	$778.50
											0
Mixes, Garnishes, etc. 2% of spirit sales (.02 x $306.50)								6.13			
								$217.44			
							27.9% cost				
							$561.06 Gross Profit				

standard sales control system is feasible. In many bars, the register sales may not accurately reflect the true sales; but when every drink prepared is recorded, the sales totals can be assumed to be legitimate.

4. *They can update the inventory.* In other words, you have a true perpetual inventory. You are not posting deletions once a day based on requisitions. Instead, every time a drink is poured, the 1.25 or 1.5 ounces or whatever is poured will be removed from the inventory. This is a powerful information tool for management. We are referring here only to the bar inventory, not the storeroom stock. That, of course, could be put on an automated perpetual inventory, but it would take a different system in most cases. Requisitioning to the bar can be very simple when the bottle-for-bottle daily system is used, and these kinds of capabilities can make it even easier. The issue would be equal to the amount poured of each brand. For example: if the ending print-out indicated that the well gin had been depleted by 100 ounces, you would issue four bottles to the bar (4 times 750 ml equals 4 times 25.4 ounces or 101.6 ounces). One potential problem with doing the requisitions this way is that it may be difficult, over time, to maintain a par stock on the bar. The number of bottles of each brand may change from time to time. This would not be too serious as there are other ways to check the integrity of the stock on the bar.

5. *The size of the inventory can be controlled better, and perhaps the inventory turnover could be increased.* This is especially true in establishments where there are multiple sales outlets. In such places, there must ordinarily be an inventory for each bar, and this can lead to a considerable inventory investment. When a common inventory can be used to service multiple bars, the total stock will be reduced relative to the sales. This, in turn, leads to another advantage: larger than normal bottles can be used. The larger the bottle size, the lower the cost per ounce of the product. Not only could the total inventory in ounces be reduced, but by using 1.5 L or 3 L bottles, the average cost per ounce will also be reduced. Larger bottles can be advantageous for yet another reason: there is always a small amount of liquor left in the bottle when hand pouring. The only way to avoid this is by having the bartender (or someone) stand there holding the bottle upside down for a time to assure that all of the liquor is drained out. This is not feasible, but when the bottles are mounted upside down in an automatic pouring system, that is exactly what happens.

6. *There may be better control over the inventory security.* Consider a typical situation, in which the bartenders have full and complete access to whatever is stored at the bar. Because of this we take inventories frequently, use bottle sticker or tag systems, establish par stocks, watch for bartenders bringing in their own bottles, and so on. If the system is set up with a remote, nonaccessible pouring stock, security is greatly enhanced. It is conceivable that there could be three or four bars operating simultaneously without any bartender (or any other employee) having access to a single drop of liquor.

7. *Some systems have the capability of doing complete cocktail mixing.* In other words, they are not limited to mixing scotch and soda, bourbon and water, gin and tonic, and other such drinks. They can make a martini with varying gin-to-vermouth ratios, mix Pink Squirrels, Grasshoppers, Harvey Wallbangers, and other drinks that call for one or more spirits mixed with one or more cordials and assorted cream, soda, and other ingredients.

8. *Draft beer monitoring and pouring can be integrated into some systems or installed as a separate system.* If you recall our discussion on beer management and control, we emphasized the importance of keeping track of how much beer (volume) had been poured and using this to calculate how many glasses, mugs, or pitchers should have been obtained and what the sales should have been. Such a system can also record every time a beer is poured, and this becomes a permanent record that management can use for a variety of purposes.

9. *Cash control will be much more effective.* Cash control in a hand-pouring system consists of comparing the cash in the register drawer to what the register cash total happens to be. When unrecorded sales are made and the proceeds from

those sales removed, there will not be any cash variances. There is also no cash control. If unrecorded sales are eliminated, or at least made quite difficult, the cash total in the register becomes considerably more meaningful.

10. *Pricing decisions are taken away from the employees.* In most beverage (and food) operations, although management sets the prices, the employees actually decide what prices will be charged. One of the most important responsibilities of management is to constantly monitor the dining room and lounge or bar to assure that the correct prices are used. Prices are programmed into these systems and will be used automatically. The employees have no control over prices. In beverage operations, it is fairly common to have several prices for the same drinks. Examples are when reduced prices are used during a portion of the day for the so-called happy hour or when higher prices are used during the evening when the entertainers begin.

This is a problem unique to beverage units; food establishments do not routinely charge different prices for the same products. They certainly have different price structures for different periods of the day (lunch, breakfast, dinner), but they normally have specialized menus for each period. Many of the automated beverage systems have the capability of changing from one price level to another quickly and easily. Engaging this capability, of course, is restricted to management.

In addition to all these capabilities, there are some other advantages. *Training* of bar personnel should be easier, especially when the bartender or waiter or waitress happens to be inexperienced. A full hand-pouring system is not easy to handle, and you will either have to have an experienced person or spend considerable time, effort, and expense to properly prepare an inexperienced employee. It is, of course, entirely possible that using some sort of computerized pouring system could make the bar *more* difficult to work at. This will be discussed in the section on potential disadvantages.

Supervision will certainly be simplified. In fact, management should be able to spend a fraction of the time supervising the bar that they

normally would. Moreover, the effectiveness of that supervision should increase markedly.

It is possible that the total space required by the bar production area (not the guest-service area) could be reduced. Since space costs are exceedingly high today (and going higher), management should be interested in using as much of the space as possible to generate income. This is normally an advantage available only to operations in the planning stage. It would be difficult to modify existing production and/or service areas.

Increasing productivity is always of interest to foodservice management, and a well-designed beverage system could possibly reduce the number of employee hours necessary for operation. Related to this is the very real potential for increased drink production. Many of the systems now available can raise drink output; they are far faster than hand pouring. Productivity is increased by having the same number of drinks produced by fewer employees. It is also increased by having the same number of employees produce more drinks. This latter is the preferable option.

Potential Disadvantages

1. First and foremost, there is the possibility of a breakdown of the system or some part of it. There is no sense in pretending this will not happen because it will, sooner or later. Some of this equipment consists of very complex electronic hardware, which is often mated to mechanical components. This is likely to cause even greater problems. The electronic portions—the computers themselves—do not have many if any moving parts, while the pumps, guns, levers, and so forth do have a lot of moving parts.

Breakdowns can also occur from operating errors. The programs and procedures may seem simple, but when typically computer-shy foodservice employees and management are initially confronted with the machines and procedures, it can really be overwhelming. There can also be other problems over which the operator has no control, such as the weather. Frequent thunderstorms, tornados, and power losses can cause nightmares with lost data, equipment being down, and so forth. There are generally provisions for saving the data, but if a system is designed really well, it may not be possible for the operation to run without it. The liquor may not even be in the same room. Waitresses may not know the prices; even bartenders may not know the prices. Why should they? Such information is not necessary to perform the function they were hired for.

2. The sales volume is not adequate to justify the capital investment. All equipment, whether it is a new slow-cooking oven, a food processor, or a tilting braising kettle, must be justified. In many cases, low-volume operations simply cannot be advised to go heavily into the comprehensive, full-blown systems.

3. Cost of routine maintenance has to be considered. It would generally be included initially under some sort of warranty agreement, but the time will come when the operator will have to assume the responsibility. This is reasonable, but management will have to consider the costs when evaluating the system from a financial viewpoint. Along with routine maintenance, repairing system malfunctions must be considered. The system manufacturer should be able to provide management with some realistic estimates of what these expenses are likely to be over time.

4. There is or may be a problem with customer distrust or dissatisfaction. In general, this is advanced as a tremendous problem by many in the business, but in reality, it is often either a crutch or an excuse for not considering the new technology. A realistic way to look at is that if it would indeed result in patron dissatisfaction, there is no question that the equipment could not be used. Management should make this decision, however, based on empirical evidence that consumer acceptance would be a problem. An opinion by the bartender does not constitute empirical evidence, nor does an opinion by a corporation executive or one vocal customer. Although often exaggerated, customer attitudes can be a problem and must be considered when evaluating the systems. A closely related problem would be the patrons'

reduced ability to identify the brands. When the product is coming out of a bank of bottles lined up against a back wall, there could be some suspicion regarding what was actually being dispensed. This could be even worse when the liquor comes from a totally unseen area.

5. Increased pouring speed was mentioned as one of the positive factors, but you should realize that the wrong system or an improperly installed or designed system (for your operation or needs) could result in reduced service speed. This is not uncommon and is certainly not limited to beverage systems.

6. A real problem from a control standpoint is that *manual mixing* is often not totally eliminated. When this occurs, management is in the unenviable position of having exceptions to its procedures. Take for example the following: "You must run all drinks through the machine, unless, of course, you cannot." Many of the virtues of the systems just described are seriously compromised when some drinks must be mixed manually or when hand pouring is not eliminated. This brings to mind the operation that installed a state-of-the-art bar system in the early 1970s, a very expensive system at the time. It could handle twelve brands. Management was asked how much of their total business they estimated actually went through the system. The reply was about 60 percent. To gain control over 60 percent of their business, they invested an amount equal to some 15 to 20 percent of their yearly annual volume at the time. What made it even worse was the fact that the system was put on the service bar where cash was not handled at all. Removing cash handling from the bartender is possibly the single *most* effective bar control known to the business.

7. It was pointed out that some systems have sophisticated cocktail mixing abilities. Most do not, however, and in an operation with a large demand for special drinks, the inability to handle them could be a significant negative factor.

8. Due to continued technological changes in the capabilities of electronic equipment and systems, caution must be exercised in purchasing registers and dispensing equipment. This is especially true when they are dedicated to each

other (will not work or will not work easily with any other type of equipment).

Training and Implementation

Training with these systems is very different from the typical training situation that exists in most foodservice operations. Training is not something that our industry does very well, though we can often muddle through. If you have ever seen the complete and total havoc that can result when untrained or poorly trained employees get their hands on computer terminals, you would realize that these are not situations in which one can muddle through. A *formal* training program is absolutely necessary. The purchase of any system would result in operational chaos without it. The system representatives will probably provide the initial training, and it will most likely be done competently and professionally. There is a rather large employee turnover in the hospitality industry, however, and who is going to train the new employees? Not the company you purchased the equipment from; if they trained all new employees, it is doubtful they would ever get out of the operation! Training costs are real. They will be continuing, and they must be included in the evaluation of the system costs.

The question of sabotage has to be considered by management. What kind of sabotage techniques could be implemented, and how can the system be safeguarded from them? There are a variety of reasons why employees might wish to sabotage the system, but certainly the desire to cover up theft has to rank near the top. On a scale of 10, we would give that one reason a 9.9.

It would be very helpful if a spare-parts kit could be provided that would allow the establishment's maintenance personnel (or management) to troubleshoot, repair, or replace any part of the system.

Classification of System Types

To simplify the matter, there are four basic types of systems available.

1. Manual pour bottle-top
2. Manual pour bottle-top with remote electronic counter
3. Semiautomatic mechanical dispensers
4. Electronic or automatic systems

Manual Pour Bottle-Top. In this type of system, the bartender pours each bottle manually and individually. One advantage is that all or merely a part of the bar stock can be controlled, whichever management desires. This would include cordials, which are notoriously difficult to control. These systems are nonelectric; there is no concern with a power failure, loss of operating capability or memory, and so on. They are adaptable to varied bottle sizes and shapes. In general, they are the least expensive systems and can be very useful as a supplementary system for room service, the service bar, or in catering.

Manual Pour Bottle-Top with Remote Electronic Counter. This is a logical extension of the previous system type. The bottle-top pouring device is electronically connected to a counting device. The portions are also controlled with greater sophistication.

Semiautomatic Mechanical Dispensers. Here we have such equipment as flex-hoses, touch faucets, and mechanically operated levers. Flex-hoses are particularly interesting since some have the capability of serving from six to twelve different products. If you want to talk about speed, have a bartender pick up a bottle, pour a drink, put the bottle down, and repeat the process for five or six different drinks. Have the same bartender pick up a flex-hose once and pour six, seven, eight different drinks. You do not have to know much about beverage operations to realize how much time can be saved and how many more drinks can be served. This is assuming, of course, that there are customers available to order the additional drinks. Multiple flex-hoses may be interfaced on a single system, and hookup with electronic registers can readily be accomplished. These are more expensive than types one and two but considerably less expensive than type four. Due to the rather extensive reliance upon mechanical components, repairs and maintenance would likely be higher than with other systems.

Electronic or Automatic Systems. Here we are talking about fully automated dispensers interfaced with electronic cash registers. Among the features is the necessity to have a check in the register prior to mixing the drink. There is great potential for control information, such as sales records, inventory, ordering amounts, and so forth. This type of system would be considerably more expensive than the other three.

Analysis and Evaluation

In order to make a rational decision as to whether any of these systems should be installed, an overall operational evaluation will be necessary. Here are some of the things to consider.

What Are Costs Currently Running?. It is not always necessary to reduce the bar percentage cost to justify a control system, but it is one of the first things you would want to look at. You could evaluate in terms of pay-back period: how long it will take you to save enough money to pay back the cost of the system? The first thing to look at in this approach would be the current cost structure.

What Savings Are Likely To Be Obtained? Here the operator looks at what the bar cost is likely to be with the proposed system(s) and what that is going to mean in savings. As with all such estimates, it is probably best to be somewhat conservative. One approach would be to use the standard cost approach: determine what the standard cost would be if everything were done properly. This would be compared to the current costs, and the difference would be the savings. In order to do this, however, it would be necessary to have considerable information, information the operator probably does not have. After all, if the operator had such information, he or she would probably already have some sort of system. At any rate the beverage operator will have to come up with a reasonable projection of what the operating costs would be with the equipment.

How Much Liquor Is Sold Directly to the Customer? In bars where most of the drinks are served by the bartenders directly to the customers seated at the bar, the question of potential guest dissatisfaction becomes very important. This is the type of situation where guests could influence the decision. In a service bar, where the guests never or nearly never see either the bartenders or the drink-mixing process, this would not be very important. The same is true in a lounge establishment where the majority of the drinks are prepared out of sight of the person drinking them. When the patrons cannot see the drink mixing procedure, what difference could it possibly make how they are mixed? With this, as with most decisions management is called on to make, the best advice is to know your operation.

What Is the Impact On the Physical Facilities? A cost analysis alone will not enable management to make the best decision; they have to look at the other factors as well. Some expensive systems have been purchased with no expectation of reducing the beverage cost but rather of increasing the operation's efficiency. The physical facilities are a case in point. If the bar production area can be made smaller, it may be possible to have increased seating or to install an entertainment area. The bar production area could well be made smaller by removing the liquor from the bar and putting it in a separate area.

What About Employee Productivity? Most managers would or should be interested in a system that enables more drinks to be prepared without adding any employees or employee hours. Even if the bar cost percentage does not change, there will obviously be increased profits due to the higher sales. For example, a bar cost percentage of 25.0 percent on $40,000.00 sales would yield a gross profit of $30,000.00. The same bar cost on $46,000.00 sales would result in a gross profit of $34,500.00.

Will Management Become More Productive? How much is management time worth? Would you be interested in a system that would give you the same degree of control you now have but with a significant reduction in the time required to monitor it? It is difficult to put dollar values on these factors, but they must be considered, and they can often be the deciding factors.

How Complete Is the System? It does not make any sense to pay for features you are not going to use; nor does it make any sense to purchase equipment that does a lot of things you are not interested in and does not perform the functions you have identified as necessary or desirable. Make a list of the capabilities you need most and find the equipment that best delivers them at the lowest cost.

How Reliable Are the Equipment and the Manufacturer? The questions to ask are:

1. How many have been sold?
2. Where are they?
3. Can I go see them?
4. What has the performance record been?
5. What will you do when the equipment goes down?
6. How long will it take you to get here?
7. Can most breakdowns be fixed on the spot?
8. Can I troubleshoot breakdowns? How?
9. Do you carry spare parts, or will they have to be ordered from some exotic far eastern country and be shipped by rowboat?

Can Most Drinks Sold Be Placed On the Machine? As mentioned previously, it is desirable to have all drinks poured go through the system. This may not be feasible in some circumstances, however. At any rate, you want the equipment to control as much of your sales as possible. There is a point below which you would not wish to go, and this would have to be determined for each specific operation. One operator may feel that controlling 70 percent of the sales would be adequate, while another would

say at least 90 percent is necessary before a new system would be justified.

Cost Analysis

An interesting study was performed and reported by Hannay in the November 1977 issue of the *Cornell Quarterly* (published four times yearly by the Hotel School at Cornell University). He evaluated the impact of this type of equipment on three cost areas:

1. Labor cost
2. Product cost
3. Liquor loss

His research showed that there was indeed a saving in labor cost due to increased pouring productivity. Product cost could also be decreased due to the purchase of larger-than-normal bottles. Liquor loss was defined as that occurring due to spillage, mistakes, not completely emptying the bottle, and so forth. He found that, unlike the other two cost areas, a difference existed here among the various types of dispensing systems. In other words, labor costs can be reduced, but there is no significant difference among the various systems. Product costs can be reduced, but there is no significant difference among systems either. With liquor losses, though, the dispensing equipment interfaced with electronic cash registers showed the greatest cost reduction. His conclusion, however, was that the additional savings did not justify the considerable increase in purchase cost. This conclusion was based on a break-even analysis showing how many bottles of house brand liquor had to be sold before the savings per bottle equaled or surpassed the cost of the equipment. This is a sound approach and should be considered by operators when making this type of decision.

Summary: Alcoholic Beverage Management

There is one fundamental difference between alcoholic beverage management and food management. With food, the emphasis is on the products themselves; with alcoholic beverages, the emphasize is on personnel. This is due to the variability of the two categories of products. Alcoholic beverages are remarkably consistent and predictable, while foods are not. Management has two basic objectives in food and beverage management. One is to assure that the quality standards are met and the other is to assure that the cost standards are met. With foods, the lack of consistency in products, prices, costs, yields, shelf life, and so forth make attaining the standards difficult and time consuming.

Cost control and quality control are equally important. With alcoholic beverages, cost and quality consistency are assured by the products. If the standards are not met, it is usually due to incompetent or unethical employees, and the problem is likely to be nonstandard costs, not nonstandard product quality. We have therefore not ignored product control but have emphasized the necessity to control the activities of personnel. We have also made the point that, again unlike food, cost problems are really sales problems. This means that the answer to an apparent cost problem is not missing products but missing sales. Beverage control thus concentrates on personnel and sales.

Section IV

Labor Management

Payroll expenses are the highest single cost category in a typical foodservice unit. Of the major cost categories, labor also may be the least controllable. More than any other expense, labor must be carefully planned ahead of time. Once the unit is in operation, management does not have a wide range of effective control measures. Labor cost is, in theory, a semivariable cost. This means that as sales go up, payroll costs will increase but not in the same proportion. The labor cost *percentage* will therefore decrease. When sales decline, payroll costs should decline also but again, not usually by as much. The cost percentage will go up in this case. Many foodservice managers believe, and rightly so, that when you open for business, payroll is a fixed cost. The employees are there in position, ready to go. The dish machine, range, lounge, dining room, and so on are all staffed. The dollar payroll cost is fixed for that particular day. The percentage cost is dependent upon several factors.

1. Management's ability to accurately predict the current number of guests so staffing can be effectively planned.
2. Management's ability to bring, over time, additional guests into the establishment.
3. Management's ability to persuade the guests to purchase a wider range of products, such as appetizers, desserts, alcoholic beverages, as well as to trade up—purchase more expensive products, particularly entrees.

Payroll cost control is very complex and probably less controllable than the other expenses.

Percentage Cost Versus Dollar Cost

We will emphasize dollar payroll cost and will pay little attention to the cost percentage. As explained, the percentage is not consistent. At each level of sales, there would be a different percentage, and it is not realistic to expect the percentage to be held constant. Food and beverage costs, which are true variable costs and as such have a fixed relationship to sales, can and should maintain about the same percentage, regardless of the sales level. This is not the case with labor costs. The labor cost percentage is determined by the payroll dollar cost, the number of guests served, and the check averages. The only one of these three factors that it is appropriate to discuss in a control context is payroll dollar cost, so we will concentrate on that.

8 Factors Affecting Labor Costs

Perhaps more than in other cost categories, payroll control depends upon sound and realistic planning. the operator must be aware of the many factors that affect this cost. Not only awareness but also understanding is necessary to attaining control and keeping it.

Menu

The menu affects the cost in many ways. Contrast for example two menus, one of eight entrees, one of thirty entrees. Assuming the same customer count, the dining-room labor hours necessary to service the guests would probably be no different between the two menus, but there could be a vast difference in the kitchen.

In purchasing, we have already discussed how time consuming the setting of product standards and specifications is when properly done. Now we have created one situation in which the work has nearly been quadrupled over another. Even though the total volume of food being received, stored, and produced may be the same, the fact that so many more types of products are being handled increases the workload. It also decreases the efficiency of production. Foodservice operations typically have low levels of productivity. One reason is the way they produce their products. Assuming a guest count of five hundred per day and assuming that all menu items sell at the same rate (which would not normally occur), production for the eight-item menu would be at a rate of about sixty per product. For the thirty-item menu it would be less than seventeen. The production cost per unit would probably be higher with the lower production figures. Producing many products daily in small amounts is one way to nearly guarantee continued low productivity!

In addition to the numbers of items on a menu, the types of items will significantly affect the workload. A limited menu consisting of steaks, lobster tails, and standing rib would not be nearly as labor intensive as would one that had shrimp Newburgh, beef Stroganoff, two or three specialty sauces, and pâtés. A paradox exists here, however: relying on convenience and/or prepared foods will not necessarily increase productivity, but it will reduce the workload. If, for example, the operator should suddenly begin purchasing the Newburgh, Stroganoff, sauces and pâtés already prepared, the amount of work to be performed would obviously go down but not necessarily the labor hours. The key is the number of kitchen people necessary to serve the meal. If the guest count remained the same, the operator could well be in a position where she or he still needed the same number of kitchen personnel to serve the food, but they now have little to do prior to the meal service period. Dish personnel will be unaffected by the change. Pot washing will be affected in the same manner as production—less work to do, but no personnel reduction is possible for there is typically only one person scheduled per shift. This type of person is referred to as a fixed employee; you need one regardless of the workload. Reducing the workload actually decreases the productivity because it has no effect upon the dollar cost! Dining-room employees are similarly unaffected by any change in purchasing preprepped foods. The paradox is that we normally regard the complexity of production as a critical payroll cost factor, but in an already operating unit, it may not be. Its importance as a cost factor comes mainly in the planning stages. The full potential benefits of convenience or prepared foods are normally realized only when planning an operation. Many operators have been able to reduce total labor costs under already-operating conditions, but it generally involves much more than simply changing the purchase specifications. A major menu revision is probably necessary. Equipment changes, labor changes, and retraining of employees are other areas that must be evaluated.

Guest Turnover

The important aspect of guest count is not the total numbers of patrons but the relationship between available seats and total guests. This is called the seat turnover (also dining room T/O, guest T/O), and it is calculated according to the following formula:

$$T/O = \frac{\text{Number of guests per shift or day}}{\text{Number of seats}}$$

Example: Guest count: Lunch = 215
Dinner = 150
Dining room seats = 100

Calculation:

Lunch T/O = $\frac{215}{100}$ = 2.15

Dinner T/O = $\frac{150}{100}$ = 1.5

In order to illustrate the effect of seat turnover on profits we will make the following assumptions:

Waitress labor cost = \$25.00 per shift
Waitress station = 20 covers (seats)
Check average = \$7.00 per person
Restaurant A has 100 seats
Restaurant B has 220 seats
Guest count (both restaurants) = 200

Restaurant A
Sales = \$1,400.00 (200 x \$7.00)
Number of waitresses = 5 (100 Seats ÷ 5)
Payroll cost (\$) = \$125.0 (5 x \$25.00)

Payroll cost (%) = 8.9% $\left(\dfrac{\$\,125.00}{\$1,400.00}\right)$

Seat T/O = 2.0

Restaurant B
Sales = \$1,400.00 (200 X \$7.00)
Number of waitresses = 11 (220 seats ÷ 20)
Payroll cost (\$) = \$275.00 (11 x \$25.00)

Payroll cost (%) = 19.6% $\left(\dfrac{\$\,275.00}{\$1,400.00}\right)$

Seat T/O = 1.1 .91

Although the above is somewhat simplistic, it does illustrate rather clearly the relationship of turnover to profits. The number of customers is, of course, of great importance; but the size of the operation and its minimum staffing cost are equally important. Put another way, each of these two restaurants, when they open tonight, will have a fixed payroll cost. For restaurant A, it is only $125.00 since the operation is fairly small. Restaurant B, on the other hand, has a much larger investment in payroll. It costs them $275.00 to open tonight. This, then, is the true payroll cost, and it is a dollar cost. Management has some degree of control over this. The cost percent on the other hand is a result of how many guests show up tonight and what they purchase. Management does not have nearly as much control over these factors.

Layout of Physical Facilities

Here again we encounter a payroll factor over which operating management has little control. The way the facilities are planned more or less fixes the general level of staffing required. Before the facilities can be planned and laid out, it is necessary to have a menu, but since this gives only the types of food, it is also necessary to have fairly accurate individual item sales forecasts. If there are steaks on the menu, the kitchen will obviously require a broiler. However, the decision about which model or how many and where to locate them would depend upon how many steaks the operation was expected to sell and when they would be sold. The physical layout can affect the payroll cost in many ways.

Kitchen

If the dish machine is in the wrong place or pointing the wrong way, it increases travel time. In a busy operation, this could result in additional personnel just to move material to and from the dishwashing area. If there is not a good straight-line flow so goods can be received, stored, and moved to production with minimal back-tracking, you could have a lot of unnecessary work. This is not only a matter of needing additional employees, which certainly increases labor costs, but also one of creating extra work. This additional movement reduces the time available for other tasks, which decreases productivity.

The steam table must be located properly so service personnel can get in and out of the kitchen easily, quickly, and with minimal travel. The equipment battery behind the steam table must be laid out so a minimum number of people can put out a maximum number of meals.

If the freezer is not next to the fryer, each time there is an order for french fries, breaded shrimp, or other fried items, the cook has to move out of and then back into the primary work area. He or she simply cannot put out maximum volume that way. Being realistic, we realize that the cook will then stockpile the frozen products next to the fryer, which solves the labor productivity problem but creates other problems such as poor quality and potentially contaminated foods!

Dining Room-Lounge

What happens in a dining room? Guests arrive and are seated, and the service persons assigned to them arrive and depart to order and pick up various foods and beverages. Other personnel—usually, though not always—must bring water and coffee, replace ashtrays, replace linen, and collect and replace the dirty china, glassware, and flatware. Even under optimum conditions, this represents a lot of travel. Moreover large amounts of materials are being transported back and forth. Under less than optimum physical conditions, this creates inefficiency and more work, and could result in additional personnel.

Spatial relationships are very important here. Where is the kitchen in relationship to the dining room? A seemingly little thing such as locating the door to the kitchen improperly or not having two doors can put a great burden on the service staff. Where is the bar? Does the waitress have to go to one end of the operation to order and pick up drinks and then go to the opposite end of the building to do the same with food? Are the side or service stations located for maximum efficiency in restocking from the kitchen as well as providing materials for the tables? Are there enough side stations? How many is enough? Each side station probably occupies space sufficient for a four-top table. What is the customer demand at any one time? Could you handle more guests (increase the turnover) with another table? These are types of questions that must be brought up and answered if a dining room is to be properly designed.

Another important layout factor is the seating mix: how many deuces (two seats) four-tops, six-tops. If a mistake is made here, it can result in increased payroll and/or decreased seat turnover. Both would have a negative effect upon profits. An actual example of this was a hotel that opened in a downtown business section. The majority of the hotel guests were business persons. Nearly all the breakfast trade came from the hotel. The typical patron was either alone or with one other person. The luncheon trade was mixed between hotel guests and local business people. The usual pattern was guests in groups of two. Obviously this dining room had a lot of deuces, right? Wrong. It had 210 seats and only 6 tables were for two people. All the others were for 4 to 6 people. The normal situation was that when the dining room was "full," there were only about 100 to 120 persons being served. If the demand for seats exceeded this, which it usually did, there was a wait. Since there was no shortage of eating alternatives in this location, many left instead of waiting. The kitchen and dining room had to be staffed to handle the maximum potential demand—some 200 people at one time. But the layout and design mistakes prevented this from being achieved very often, even though the potential customers were there. This mistake was eventually rectified but only after nearly a year of lost guests and lost profits and at a large capital expenditure for new tables. Many other examples of the effect of layout on ultimate payroll costs could be given, but these should make the point.

Type and Amount of Equipment

The way the unit is equipped can have a lasting effect on productivity. Do the employees

have to chop and grate by hand, or is there a food processor in the kitchen? Are stocks made on top of the range in large stock pots which then must be strained into other pots, or are they made in floor-mounted steam-jacketed kettles with a strainer and spigot on the bottom? When stocks and soups have to be cooled, does the cook transfer the hot liquids to smaller, shallower containers and put them in ice-water baths, or can he or she merely adjust some controls on the steam-jacketed kettle and circulate ice water in the jacket instead of steam? Is the equipment mobile or wall-hung, so cleaning time can be reduced?

When dishes and glassware come through the machine, are they stacked on shelves? If so, before being removed to the dining room they will have to be restacked on carts. If the proper equipment were available, these materials would be stacked directly on specialized mobile carts when cleaned. These carts can then be rolled to the appropriate area, and double handling is reduced. Dish machines can also be installed in a circular pattern so one worker can load and unload from the same place.

The bar can be equipped so that the bartender must pick up two or three different products to make one drink and may have to take several steps to do this. With certain types of equipment, however, the bartender can mix that and virtually every other drink without moving, even without picking up each spirit or mix separately.

The busperson can take a tray to one table, clean it, and take that tray to the dish area, get an empty tray, return to the dining room and repeat the sequence. With a cart, however, the busperson could reduce the number of trips to the kitchen to one for every four or five tables. Any host, hostess, or dining-room manager who has had to make guests wait because there are empty tables but no clean ones can realize the benefit of this type of equipment.

A common situation for banquet production would be to prepare pans of food to be cooked, put them on a cart, wheel the cart to the refrigerator, and unload the pans. At the proper time, the pans will again be loaded on a cart and taken to the ovens where they will be unloaded again. When cooking is completed, the pans are again loaded on carts and taken to the appropriate dish-up area. With the right equipment, however, the sequence could be to load the pans of prepared food on a special type of cart in which part of the cart, the part with the food, rolls into the oven. The cart is taken to the refrigerator, held and then rolled into the oven, and after cooking, rolled to the dish-up area. There is only one loading and one unloading. The same principle is followed with a cook-and-hold oven. The roasts do not have to be removed when cooking is completed. They are not removed until they are needed.

With equipment, operating management has more control options than they do with layout. It may prove to be impossible to make any significant changes in the layout, while much of the equipment discussed here could be added to an ongoing operation in order to increase employees' efficiency. It is expensive, however, since either you are adding equipment that had not been planned for, or you are replacing equipment that has proven to be inadequate. This latter, in effect, doubles (or more) the total cost of that equipment. Initial equipment decisions are thus of critical importance, and mistakes result in reduced profits if not actual operating losses.

Local Labor Markets

This is a factor that is probably beyond the power of either planning or operating management to regulate except for the control planners have over location, for that is the decisive element. Wage rates can and do differ enough around the country to increase or decrease the payroll several percentage points. In addition to wage rates, significant variances in both the availability of labor and the competence of that labor exist. In some locations, it will be so difficult to find qualified people that management will have constant staffing problems. Many of the people they do hire will require extensive training, and even then productivity can be expected to be low.

In this case the importance from a planning

viewpoint is to recognize that this is the reality of the situation and to design the physical unit and the various operating systems to compensate. The things management should consider anyway—convenience foods, labor-saving devices, and so on—are not only desirable but necessary when they are forced to use labor that is largely unskilled and perhaps underqualified. This factor is not, however, permanent. Training could reverse the situation, but the past record of our industry in this area offers little assurance that this will or can be done.

Type of Service Provided

Most table service food operators in this country use what is logically known as American service. In this system a single service person is assigned to a table, supported by a busperson. The service person takes and serves all food and beverage orders and performs some service maintenance while the guests are there, such as changing ashtrays, filling water glasses, and clearing used dishes and glassware. The bus personnel typically do these types of tasks also as well as the final clearing, resetting, and making sure that the dining room is adequately stocked with the necessary working materials—china, glassware, flatware, linen, and perhaps coffee, water, and ice. Any deviation from this system will have effects upon the utilization of and cost of labor. It could decrease the cost such as when a buffet system is installed in the dining room for lunch. Fewer orders are going into the kitchen, which means the possibility of reducing the dining room staff and perhaps even the production staff as well. You would still need production people to prepare the food; but with the right equipment and layout combination, this may not be as labor intensive.

In the other direction, French or a form of modified French service would almost certainly increase the labor cost. With French service, you must have more dining-room personnel, and they will be paid more as well. The food is not completely prepared and plated in the kitchen and is either prepared or finished at tableside. This requires not only more people and equipment but also more space and time. Reduced seating and lower guest turnover generally result, both of which reduce employee productivity.

There are many other types of service, all of which can have either a positive or negative effect upon payroll costs.

English Service

All food is cooked in the kitchen and carving is done in the dining room by the host who then plates the food for passing around the table. Seldom used in commercial operations, this method would probably reduce payroll costs since it places some of the service burden on the guests.

Russian Service

Food is fully prepared and cut in the kitchen and placed on platters. The food is served from the platters to each guest. This can be an elegant compromise to the full-blown, very formal French type of service and would probably cost less than the French but certainly more than the American.

Cafeteria Service

Very common and labor saving because the guest is taking part in the service process. Another advantage is increased seat turnover. Drawbacks are generally in the form of reduced gross profit margins per guest. The self-service features of both buffets and cafeterias are the main operating impetus behind the proliferation of salad bars, soup and sandwich bars, and other similar concepts, although there are often marketing reasons as well.

Counter Service

Saves labor, space, and time. Although gross margins are reduced, they generally are compensated for by high guest turnover. Where appropriate from a marketing standpoint, this service style is worth considering.

Personnel Hiring, Training, and Supervision

Hiring the wrong person for a job, training that person poorly or not at all, and supervising him or her inadequately describes the existing situation in many foodservice operations. The likely result will be increased labor costs.

Hiring

In order to hire qualified people, management must have a clear, definite idea of what the employee will have to do. It is beyond the scope of this text to go into personnel management in detail. Many of the personnel problems in the hospitality industry, however, are due to a basic lack of management knowledge as to what each employee is expected to do and the physical and psychological qualities required for successful performance. The square-peg-in-a-round-hole theory applies here, and there are a lot of square pegs hired. All the training in the world is unlikely to enable them to fit into the round holes they were hired for. Management should distinguish between qualities you hire and qualities you teach. With a waiter or waitress, for example, it is essential to have a person who smiles readily, can communicate warmth and a feeling that he or she is interested in others. This person should enjoy providing service and making other people happy. These are qualities you hire. Training will not make someone like others if this is not in her or his nature.

Training can, however, develop technical skills. Employees can be taught about the menu, how the products are prepared, how to write orders, how to sell, and how to serve food, clear tables, and organize their work. They can be taught about the bar and the various alcoholic beverages served. To summarize this point: you hire those physical and psychological attributes required by a particular job; then you teach whatever skills are necessary. A common mistake is to hire skills, to look for so-called "experienced" people regardless of their attitudes and personal qualities.

Training

This is one of the most important of all management tasks. There are actually several types of training responsibilities. First and probably most important is the need to teach new employees whatever is necessary to perform their jobs. It could be as simple as working with a newly hired dishwasher who has worked in other restaurants on the identical model machine. In this case you show the new person where the clean dishes are to be stacked, where the soap is stored, and so forth. If the person had never operated a dish machine of any sort before, you would have to give a considerable amount of technical knowledge. He or she would have to be taught how the machine operates; how to interpret the many gauges; the purposes of the various compounds used for cleaning, rinsing, and drying; how to set-up and break down; how to clean. The worker would have to be shown how the dish room fits into the overall operation, the effect on the dining room and lounge if clean materials do not arrive regularly and on time. This then is the first level of training. The objective here is to assure that an employee can perform according to a standard, that he or she can do the job satisfactorily.

The second objective of training is to assure that the employee can continue to perform and at an increasingly higher level. Management should expect performance to improve over time, but they must also accept the responsibility of constantly working with the employees to assure continued growth. This requires two approaches. One is to continually monitor performance to make sure it does not start to drop. The other consists of ongoing training to improve job skills and teach new skills. A dining-room crew, for example, should always be in a state of training. Once they can meet the basic requirements of the job, management should want to work with them to improve their sales abilities or perhaps to teach them more sophisticated service techniques.

The third objective of training should be to provide employees with the skills necessary to move up within the organization. When a waiter is needed, it would not be necessary to go outside to locate and hire one if one of the buspersons had already been trained. Here you would have a person who already knew the physical operation, the standards, the systems, the personnel. Moving such a person up would obviously be less expensive and disruptive than bringing in someone new, who—even if skilled—would have a lot to learn about your specific operation.

Supervision

Poor supervision wastes potentially valuable employees and fails to extract standard performance even from well-trained employees. It is unlikely, however, that the employees will be well-trained since it is the same supervisors who do some of the training. One of the more important management tasks, therefore, is to hire and train competent supervisors. A common mistake here is to qualify a person based on technical skills rather than administrative ones. It is certainly necessary for a dining-room supervisor to understand its operation, but a top waiter or waitress will not necessarily be a good supervisor. The skills required go well beyond those used to wait on tables. A supervisor will have to make out work schedules, train employees, enforce standards, motivate personnel, and be responsible for cost control of both labor and materials. These are areas they will have to be trained in since waiting tables cannot be expected to have developed the necessary knowledge.

Employee Turnover

One of the labor cost factors that makes it nearly impossible to extract even barely adequate productivity from a crew is the huge turnover which is a fact of life in the foodservice industry. It is not unusual to have a yearly turnover figure of over 100 percent, which means that an operation employing eighty people can expect to hire—and train from scratch—over eighty people during that period. Some job categories are more unstable than others. Out of an eight-person production staff, you might lose only one person. The six-person dish crew, though, could be filled by twelve or fifteen different people during the year.

Whenever someone leaves, there is a replacement cost. Estimates of this cost vary, running as high as $800.00 (or more). There is the cost of locating a suitable candidate, which could range from thousands of dollars for a management recruitment program to just a few dollars for an ad in the local paper for a busperson. Then there is the cost in time of interviewing candidates. Perhaps tests will be administered which will cost money as well. Training is expensive, in terms of both time and materials used. Employees, even skilled ones who are well-trained, will not be fully productive for a period. Breakage will be higher on the dish machine; smaller stations will have to be assigned in the dining room; food will be prepared more slowly; mistakes will be made, mistakes which can result in loss of customer goodwill as well as loss of products. It is probably impossible to calculate the total cost from employee turnover, but it seems quite apparent that a stable crew can be more productive and so less expensive to manage over time.

Absenteeism

Absenteeism occurs when an employee is not on the job. This occurs for any number of reasons. Employees are sick; they are sick of working; there is a ball game they want to attend; the car will not start; they don't have clean uniforms; a grandmother dies; it is too cold; it is too hot; a baby-sitter does not show up (absenteeism caused by absenteeism!); and on and on and on. When this occurs, the unit can operate shorthanded, which may decrease the labor cost but probably at the expense of customer satisfaction and operating efficiency. This, like turnover, is difficult to calculate. Over time, however, it will surely cost in terms of lost sales if nothing else. If the missing person is replaced, the labor cost will probably increase since the replacement is likely to be an employee

already there who ends up working overtime or an employee normally not scheduled, also at an overtime rate.

Overtime

Overtime work at higher wage rates has the effect of decreasing productivity since the same amount of work is being done but at higher wages. Managers who cannot control overtime will have severe labor cost problems. It is not difficult to control, but management must have policies and adhere to them. Some overtime is inevitable, as pointed out in the discussion on absenteeism. Much of it, though, comes from employees attempting to pad their wages by working a few extra hours. These are seemingly well-intentioned and loyal employees who will claim that this or that had to be done, that they could not leave because it got busy and so forth. In fact, lack of overtime control inevitably leads to absenteeism for when employees can accumulate a full week's wages in four days, they may feel little need to show up for the fifth day.

Low Employee Productivity

All the factors discussed here have the effect of lowering productivity, down from a relatively low level to begin with. Productivity in the foodservice industry is far lower than in other industries of comparable size. Productivity can be measured in many ways, the simplest being to establish a ratio of hours worked to guests served. Whenever more guests can be served without increasing the hours worked, productivity has increased. Conversely, when there is a drop in guest counts—and this has been happening in many operations—which is not accompanied by comparable reductions in the work force, productivity decreases. Actually, management must continuously increase productivity merely to maintain acceptable cost percentages. Assume, for example, a very stable foodservice operation in which guest counts are steady. Since the wages will probably have to increase over time, unless the employee output is also increased, the labor cost percentage will automatically go up. The operator has the option, of course, of increasing menu prices in order to maintain the percentage, but this is proving to be more and more difficult to do.

Productivity improvement is therefore necessary, and it does not occur when management just encourages everyone to "work harder." It can come about only by making basic changes in the operating systems, particularly the production and service systems. Although the problem of low productivity has been recognized for many years as one of the most serious facing the industry, productivity has still been decreasing in recent years. Suggestions on improving productivity will be discussed in the labor control section.

9 Analysis of Labor Costs

Analysis is basically a comparison process. You are constantly comparing the actual to the desired, or put another way, you compare what is to what should be. Effective analysis thus depends on two factors. One is accurate knowledge of what the true costs are. This is relatively simple, yet in practice some operators do not always realize their true costs. The second factor, however, is the difficult one. This is the establishment of a frame of reference to compare the actual cost to. This is the establishment of the what-should-it-be figure. Analytical procedures must also take into account the need for breaking figures down into meaningful components. It is useful to have some sort of labor standard for the entire operation, but if comparison to the actual results showed that the standard (whatever form it takes) was being exceeded, where does management go from there? For decision making, they would require standards on each of the major departments. They might, for example, have separate standards for the kitchen, dining room, lounge, and banquet departments. The value of this approach is that when the overall standard is exceeded, manage-

ment can determine which specific department is responsible. They could find that only one is out of line or that all are off. The results could show one department to have a major problem or that all departments have minor problems. The purpose of analysis, therefore, is to develop information that informs so that management is in a position to take meaningful action.

In our discussion of analytical techniques and procedures, we will focus on the development of the frame of reference—what the standard should be—and on the logical breakdown. It is just as meaningless to go too far as it is not to go far enough. You may want to break out productivity figures for dish-machine personnel as a separate category. This would probably make sense in most operations, but it would normally not be necessary to have separate standards on personnel who load the machine, those who unload the machine, lunch dishwashers, dinner dishwashers, and so forth. The effort and expense necessary to generate such detailed information cannot be justified by the improvement in decision making.

Percentage Analysis

Analysis based upon an expected percentage is the most common industry approach. As pointed out earlier, however, it is not a recommended method because there is no standard payroll percentage as there is with food and beverage. A standard cost is one that can reasonably be expected to occur. This approach is valid with food and beverage because they are not based upon the number of guests but rather the mix of foods or beverages guests purchase. This mix can change, and when it does, the standard percentage changes. But the mix is reasonably predictable, at least from season to season, or quarter to quarter. The payroll percentage, however, is based upon the following factors:

1. Number of guests
2. Check averages
3. Number of employees
4. Number of hours worked
5. Wage rates

These five factors could be augmented by other considerations, such as lunch versus dinner versus breakfast, overtime, types of employees, and work hours, but these five cover the major payroll cost aspects. We will examine them one-by-one for the degree of predictability and management control, for that determines the potential to establish standards.

1. *Number of guests*. This is very difficult to predict. One reason—probably the main one—that the banquet business is profitable is that it is very predictable. If a party is booked one year in advance, management knows exactly how many people will be coming—or at least, with a guarantee, how many will be paying, which is the same thing. They also know what the sales will be, how many employees will be assigned to work the banquet, how many hours they will work, what the payroll and product cost will be, and hence what the profit will be. In the dining room, however, you never really know, at least with a high degree of accuracy, how many you will be feeding that night.

2. *Check averages*. This is more consistent

than guest count and can be predicted with some accuracy. These two combined (the number of guests times the check average) will yield the sales in dollars.

3, 4, 5. *Number of employees, number of hours worked, wage rates*. These are very predictable and totally under the control of management. All together they yield the payroll in dollars. The ratio of payroll dollars to sales dollars is the payroll percentage. The great difficulty in establishing a standard percentage is that these relationships are constantly changing. Management should base the schedule on the expected guest count. If the guest count forecast is accurate, the labor percentage forecast will also be accurate. As pointed out, however, the guest count is normally quite variable, which means that the employees are scheduled more or less in expectation of some average level of business. You will not often find labor schedules that are much different from day to day within a particular operation. The reasons are both the unpredictability of the guest count and the operational need for some scheduling stability. Most people accept jobs with the expectation that they will be working regularly. Management does not have complete freedom to expand and decrease the work force significantly on a day-to-day basis regardless of whether the sales go up and down. As stated, the result is constant variance between the sales and payroll dollars, making the concept of a standard percentage untenable. Management must have standards for payroll analysis, but they should be based primarily on payroll dollars and hours worked, not percentages.

Percentages are valid as overall operating guidelines. Every operation faces economic and financial realities. The commercial sector must make profits; the noncommercial or institutional sector must confine spending within established limits. The use of percentages is less useful for institutional operators because they often regard sales as a constant rather than variable factor. The important thing for them is to control expense dollars, not to worry about the ratio of expense dollars to sales. Commercial operators, however, faced with variable sales levels, do have to contend with percentages. To illustrate these two ways of thinking we will use an industrial plant employees' cafeteria and a table service restaurant. If the manager of the plant cafeteria maintains a consistent payroll dollar, the percentage will not vary since the sales are constant. If the restaurant manager maintains a fixed-dollar payroll, the percentage can still fluctuate dramatically since the sales are not constant. The plant cafeteria manager can use dollar payroll guidelines and maintain financial stability. The restaurant manager needs a percentage guideline. He or she must know what ratio of payroll dollars is necessary for a profitable operation. Especially important is what the upper limits are, which if exceeded would possibly create losses.

Another way of putting this is that out of each sales dollar, the restaurant can afford to spend $.35 on product cost, $.38 on labor cost, $.15 on operating expenses, and $.07 on fixed expenses. This would yield a profit of $.05 or 5 percent, and this level of profit is what the organization requires to justify its investment. With this information, the restaurant manager knows that when the payroll exceeds 38 percent, the operation will probably not meet its financial goals. Therefore management's responsibility is to make whatever adjustments are necessary to stay under that figure or to change the other figures so that the 5 percent profit can be maintained.

This is the importance of percentages; they provide overall operating guidelines for the commercial sector, and they are less significant for much of the institutional sector. In the planning stage, establishing the relevant percentages is absolutely necessary to assure that the financial objectives can be met. In the operating stage, percentages provide a sort of warning system for management, but they are of limited use in controlling payroll.

Analysis of Sales per Man Hour

This technique is also popular and widely used. The figure is calculated by dividing the total sales by the total number of hours worked.

$$\frac{\$17,850 \text{ (total weekly sales)}}{1,295 \text{ (total weekly payroll hours)}} = \$13.78$$

This figure, $13.78, is the sales per man hour. The way to use it is to calculate it weekly and compare it both to a standard and to previous amounts. The interpretation is generally that when it increases, there has been an improvement in the utilization of labor. When it decreases, productivity has declined. To be most useful, it should be calculated for each department. A sample is shown in Exhibit 9.1. The calculations for each department are as follows.

Kitchen
1. Total sales = total food ($13,388.00)
2. Total hours = 575
3. $\dfrac{\$13,388.00}{575} = \$23.28$
4. Sales per man hour = $23.28

Dining Room
1. Total sales = dining-room food and beverage ($12,513.00)
2. Total hours = 500
3. $\dfrac{\$12,513.00}{500} = \$25.02$
4. Sales per man hour = $25.02

Lounge
1. Total sales = lounge beverage sales plus dining-room beverage sales ($3,662.00)
2. Total hours = 120
3. $\dfrac{\$3,662.00}{120} = \$30.52$
4. Sales per man hour = $30.52

Banquet
1. Total sales = total banquet food and beverage sales ($2,675.00)
2. Total hours = 100
3. $\dfrac{\$2,675.00}{100} = \$26.75$
4. Sales per man hour = $26.75

Using these figures, management could track the performance of each department over time and compare it to a standard. Note that each individual figure is well above the overall operation's sales-per-man-hour figure. This is realistic and is due to the various relationships between producers of food and beverage and the sellers of those products. Bartenders, for example, produce alcoholic beverages that are sold in both the lounge and the dining room. The sales from those locations should therefore be compared with the hours required to produce them. The dining-room service personnel serve both foods and beverages, and both should be used in calculating their productivity.

Use of the total operations sales per man hour ($13.78) is not an accurate benchmark as to what has actually occurred. Consider a situation in which the dining room had a significant decrease due to a drop in both food and beverage sales, yet this sales drop was fully compensated for by an increase in banquet food and beverage sales. The change is a drop in both the dining room and lounge sales per man hour, while the kitchen did not change at all since they are still producing the same food sales. The banquet department could show either an increase in sales per man hour (if

they required little additional help to service the increased sales) or no change. The net effect on total sales per man hour could be none (remain at or near $13.78), but there is definitely a problem in the dining room. This would show up only by comparing each department's figures to the previous ones. This type of analysis would also pinpoint the problem as a sales problem in the dining room but not the lounge. It would show that there are no staffing problems in either the lounge or dining room unless the drop in sales is expected to be permanent. In that case, staffing changes would be necessary.

Although it can a be useful analytical approach, there are drawbacks to the use of this technique, particularly if used exclusively. It ignores a very important, even critical, aspect of operations analysis: sales dollars are ultimately based on guest counts. Menu prices can, and do, increase over time. If the net effect of pricing changes is to increase the check average 8 percent (for example, from $8.75 to $9.45), the sales-per-man-hour would go up. Using the numbers from Exhibit 9.1, the sales per man hour calculation would now be:

Exhibit 9.1. Sales per Man-Hour Data

Sales

Department	Food	Beverage	Total
Dining room	$11,513.00	$1,000.00	$12,513.00
Lounge		2,662.00	2,662.00
Banquet	$ 1,875.00	800.00	2,675.00
Totals	$13,388.00	$4,462.00	$17,850.00

Payroll Hours

Department	Hours
Dining Room	500
Lounge	120
Banquet	100
Kitchen	575
	1,295

1. Sales change = $17,850.00 x .08 = $1,428.00
2. Sales increase = $17,850.00 + $1,428.00
   = $19,278.00
3. Payroll hours = 1,295

4. Sales per man hour $= \dfrac{\$19,278.00}{1,295} = \$14.88$

Productivity seems to have increased, but in reality there is no change. The same menus are being used; the same items are being sold; the same number of guests are being served; the same working schedules are being used. The only change is that the guests are being charged more. If there were a standard for sales per man hour, it would obviously have to be increased so that management would have a valid frame of reference for comparison. There would, in fact, need to be a complete recalculation of all the department standards. If the sales increase came only in foods, with no change in alcoholic beverage prices, it becomes even more complicated. The figures just used increase total sales by 8 percent, but if only the dining-room food prices were raised, the increase in total sales would be less. The resultant change in sales per man hour would also be less. The same thinking would apply if only banquet food prices were increased or total banquet prices or alcoholic beverages or even wines alone.

Many operations will not merely just increase prices, however. They generally attempt to mask the increases with some changes in the operating system. At a minimum, they will make some menu changes. This could make the sales change difficult to interpret. It could also alter the workload, particularly in the kitchen. There would be different items being prepared, perhaps resulting in greater or lesser labor intensity in production. Consider the effects of a menu change that eliminated many high-labor-intensity products and replaced their sales with standing ribs. There certainly would not be as much work to do in the kitchen. The dining room would benefit as well. Orders could be filled much faster; guest turnover could increase, or larger stations could be assigned. The point here is that while determining standards for sales per

man hour is always difficult, it becomes even more so when changes are incorporated into the system.

Another problem here, which also must be reconciled with any of the analytical systems discussed, is what payroll hours to use. Management presents an obvious problem, as do other salaried personnel, for there may not be any payroll hours calculated for them. It is common practice to exclude such employees from the calculation. There are other types of employees who may be excluded as well, such as supervisors paid on an hourly basis or even such employees as cashiers who must be scheduled regardless of the expected level of business. The thinking here is that their productivity is solely a function of the sales level; including them only confuses the analysis. This is the basis for the analytical tool discussed under the heading "Variable Cost Employee Analysis," and it will be addressed in more detail in that section.

To summarize, sales per man hour cannot be recommended as the only analytic technique because of its tendency to increase whenever pricing adjustments are made and because of the difficulty in assessing the true impact of those changes. It can, however, be useful in the short run or as one of several statistics compiled on labor productivity.

Dollar Payroll Cost-Guest Analysis

This analysis uses a ratio obtained by dividing the dollar payroll cost by the number of guests.

1. Total weekly payroll cost = $4,750.00
2. Total guests = 1,675
3. Payroll cost per guest = $2.84

This eliminates the problem of menu price and check average variances, but it creates new problems. The most obvious is that wages increase over time, resulting in an increase in the wage cost per guest which then indicates an apparent decrease in productivity. As the discussion on sales per man hour showed, this is not necessarily the case. If the guest count were stable, the change in wage cost per guest indicates only that it is now more costly to operate; employee productivity has nothing to do with the change. As a matter of fact, it is entirely possible for actual productivity to increase and still have an upward trend in the wage cost per guest.

Assume the same guest count, and assume that management reduced the payroll hours somewhat but not enough to reduce the total wage cost (at the new rates). Under these conditions, there are fewer employees (or the same number of employees working fewer hours) servicing the same number of guests. This is truly an increase in labor productivity, but it does not show up in the wage cost per guest statistic.

Another factor to consider is the applicability of this analysis to all operating departments. It is a workable concept in the dining room, where guest counts are of primary importance. In the banquet department, though, the number of people served is not as important as the sales dollars because there can be such a wide variance in the types of groups served. You might handle a local service club on Tuesday (forty people at $6.50, tip and tax included) and have a wedding for two hundred on Saturday, generating $4,000.00 in food and beverage sales. Under these conditions check averages are meaningless, and guest counts are not much better.

Lounge and beverage operations are similar to banquets in that guest counts are not as important as sales dollars. In a bar, one patron may stay for three hours and spend $50.00 while another may have only one beer. There is such variance between individual spending patterns that the concepts of check averages and customer counts become blurred. In both the banquet and beverage departments, therefore, wage cost per guest is not a useful analytical tool.

Depending on whether or not there are banquet sales and, if so, their relationship to dining room sales, it may or may not be possible to use wage-cost-per-guest in the kitchen analysis. As with sales-per-man-hour analysis, management wages are generally excluded.

Variable Cost Employee Analysis

The unique aspect of this technique is that it not only excludes management from the analysis, but it also eliminates all personnel whose scheduling is not dependent on the guest counts or sales levels. These types of employees are called fixed. Examples of fixed employees are:

Management

Host or hostess

Cashier

Porter

Bartender

Some cooks

Bookkeeper

These people must be available in order to open the doors for business. Their schedules are generally fixed regardless of the level of business. A porter will vacuum the carpet once, whether 200 or 400 guests walked on it the previous night. When a bookkeeper makes out a daily report, the guest count and dollar sales volume have no effect on the time or effort required. With these fixed personnel, the level of sales activity has virtually no impact on the workload. The other fixed employees undoubtedly have to work harder when the operation is busier, but you usually cannot do anything about the scheduling. It may not be physically possible for additional bartenders to work behind the bar or more cashiers to staff the cash station.

Since management has little discretionary scheduling ability with these classes of employees, the theory is that they should not be included in the period-to-period labor productivity analysis. This approach calls for evaluation of all positions. The criterion for evaluation is that if sales increase or decrease significantly, will I need additional people, or can I get rid of some people? A true fixed employee cannot be removed from the payroll until the operation closes, but there are many others whose scheduling is somewhat dependent on the volume. It is with these types of employees that management can exercise control so the analysis concentrates on them. No classification of employees can be called totally variable—that is, scheduling being totally responsive to guest count—but the employees generally thought of as variable are:

Waiters and waitresses

Buspersons

Cocktail servers

Some cooks

Additional bartenders

Dish machine personnel

Banquet and catering employees (including bartenders)

Of these, the banquet and catering people come closest to a true variable classification as they are typically scheduled only for specific parties. This is another explanation of why banquets can be very profitable.

The analysis itself can be based on any of the techniques we have discussed, such as sales per man hour and/or wages per guest, even percentage analysis. The calculations are the same: the only change required is to exclude all nonvariable hours or wages from the computation. The result will be statistics that more realistically evaluate management's response to variable sales conditions.

Guest Count per Man-Hour Analysis

This approach compares guest count (or the covers served) with employee hours worked to come up with a ratio of guests to employees. Its value is that it is unaffected by both wage and selling price variances and, as such, is a fair and true indicator of changes in productivity over time. It recognizes that sales dollars result from guests and that the number of guests served is in

the long run the truest barometer of a foodservice operation's health. It also recognizes that wage dollars result from employees working a certain number of hours. The foodservice business is basically a people business although this fact is sometimes overlooked. This type of analysis puts the emphasis where it belongs—on people. The result is a ratio of people needed to serve other people eating and drinking. When there are more guests served with no increase in employee hours, there is a net increase in productivity. When the same number of guests can be served with fewer employee hours, there is also a net increase in employee productivity. When you require more employee hours to serve the same or smaller number of guests, there is a net decrease in employee productivity. All of the preceding statements are true, regardless of what the wage percentages are.

It is entirely possible for the payroll percentage to decrease if, for example, the menu prices are increased sufficiently to produce higher sales even if fewer guests are served. If the dollar payroll stayed the same, the cost percentage would decrease. Management would congratulate themselves on a fine job of labor control. A realistic appraisal of this situation, however, is that the same number of employees are now serving fewer guests. The only rational interpretation of that would be a poor job of management control. This is precisely the situation in which many foodservice operators find themselves during periods when menu price increases are constant and substantial, and guest counts are dropping. Since the sales dollars often increase in spite of the reduced guest counts, there is no perception of a sales problem. Since the payroll percentages are protected by the sales increases, there is no perception of reduced employee productivity. In recent years, incidentally, menu prices have risen dramatically, guest counts have slipped, and productivity has declined.

All of the foregoing point out the need for management to effectively analyze their labor forces so they can gain a more realistic appraisal of their actual situation. The guest-count-per-employee-hour approach can be very helpful in this regard. See the labor wage analysis case for an illustration of these concepts.

Wage Analysis Case

Exhibit A: Partial Operating Statements for October and November 1983

	October		November	
	$	*%*	*$*	*%*
Sales (all food)	65,000	100	69,000	100
Payroll				
Management	3,500	5.4	3,500	5.1
Direct wages	19,500	30.0	19,600	28.4
Total payroll	23,000	35.4	23,100	33.5

Exhibit B: Wage Analysis

	Hours		Wages	
Department	*Oct.*	*Nov.*	*Oct.*	*Nov.*
Kitchen	2,127	2,130	$11,700.00	$11,715.00
Dining room	2,400	2,426	7,800.00	7,885.00
Total	4,527	4,556	$19,500.00	$19,600.00
Management				
Manager	168	168	$ 2,000.00	$ 2,000.00
Assistant manager	168	168	1,500.00	1,500.00
Total	336	336	$ 3,500.00	$ 3,500.00
Total	4,863	4,892	$23,000.00	$23,100.00

Exhibit C: Sales Analysis

	Oct.	*Nov.*
Guest count	15,000	13,800
Check average	$ 4.33	$ 5.00
Sales	$65,000.00	$69,000.00

Case Analysis Examples

1. *Percentage analysis.* There are no problems here. The payroll (see Exhibit A) has gone down from 35.4 percent to 33.5 percent. Management is doing a fine job. Sales are up and payroll is down.

2. *Sales-per-man-hour analysis.* In October, the sales-per-man-hour figure was $13.37 ($65,000 ÷ 4,863), while in November it increased to $14.10 ($69,000 ÷ 4,892). Management is doing an excellent job, and labor productivity is increasing.

3. *Dollar payroll cost per guest.* October 1983 showed a dollar wage cost per guest of $1.53, and the November 1983 cost was $1.67. We begin to see a problem here. The main drawbacks of using this analysis system are increasing wage rates and the lack of valid guest count figures from catering and lounge sales. Neither of these problems occurs because this is a food-only operation, and the wage rates have not changed. We therefore get a clear indication of increased personnel costs regardless of what the operating statement shows.

4. *Variable cost employee analysis.* Here we will calculate both the *sales per man hour* and the *wage cost per guest* using only the variable wages—the *direct wages* from Exhibits A and B. It would be more useful if the wages were broken down by employee category as well as by department, but at least we can evaluate hourly employees exclusive of management, and we can evaluate the two main departments separately.

The sales per man-hour in October was $14.36 ($65,000 ÷ 4,527), and in November it was $15.14. The pattern is similar to the calculation that included management and is really not useful. The increase is due to a price increase; productivity cannot be measured. Looking at the kitchen and dining room individually, we find the kitchen went from $30.56 in October ($65,000 ÷ 2,127) to $32.39 in November ($69,000 ÷ 2,130). The comparable dining room statistics were: October = $27.08 ($65,000 ÷ 2,400) and November = $28.44 ($69,000 ÷ 2,426). The trend is the same in both cases and equally misleading, although it does indicate greater productivity in the kitchen. This is useful information.

The *wage-cost-per-guest* results are:

Entire operation

October—$1.30 ($19,500 ÷ 15,000)

November—$1.42 ($19,600 ÷ 13,800)

Kitchen

October—$ .78 ($11,700 ÷ 15,000)

November—$ .85 ($11,715 ÷ 13,800)

Dining Room

October—$ .52 ($7,800 ÷ 15,000)

November—$ .57 ($7,885 ÷ 13,800)

This information also shows, as did the previous wage-per-guest calculation, an increasing labor cost. But this is much more useful since it excludes management (fixed) costs and shows the controllable portion of the cost (direct labor or variable wage costs). There is other useful information here as well. The kitchen and dining-room labor costs are both increasing but at different rates. The kitchen cost per guest is up $.07 or 9 percent. The dining room shows a plus $.05, which is 9.5 percent. We evidently have a problem, and it appears to be slightly worse in the dining room. To put it another way, both the production and service functions are becoming more expensive to operate. Of the two, the service cost is increasing at a greater rate.

We can also calculate a percentage for both the kitchen and dining rooms by using the direct wages from each area.

Kitchen wage cost: October = $18% ($11,700/$65,000)
November = 17% ($11,715/$69,000)

Dining-room wage cost: October = 12% ($7,800/$65,000)
November = 11.2% ($7,885/$69,000)

We have a cost ratio between the two departments (18 percent to 12 percent) that

could be useful if there were a standard against which to measure it. Otherwise, these percentages are dangerously misleading. We are led to believe payroll cost is decreasing and that of the two departments, the dining room is decreasing faster (6.7 percent to 5.6 percent). As has been shown, the cost is probably increasing, and—of the two departments—the dining room is increasing faster.

5. *Guest-count-per-labor-hour analysis*: (Note: This analysis was done using the variable labor hours, not the total labor hours.)

October = 3.31 (15,000 ÷ 4,527)

November = 3.03 (13,600 ÷ 4,556)

Kitchen

October = 7.05 (15,000 ÷ 2,127)

November = 6.48 (13,800 ÷ 2,130)

Dining Room

October = 6.25 (15,000 ÷ 2,400)

November = 5.69 (13,800 ÷ 2,426)

Here we have a clear statement of decreasing worker productivity. The income statement is completely misleading. What has actually occurred in this operation is that it now requires more employee hours to serve fewer guests! The employee hours have increased only 0.6 percent, but the guest count has decreased by 8 percent. This is reduced productivity, and it doesn't matter what the labor costs are or what the percentages are. If this pattern were to continue, the unit would eventually be out of business. The only thing keeping it afloat is the increasing price structure. As a long-term strategy, there is not much to recommend in that.

In October, each hour that an employee worked, he or she handled 3.3 guests, while in November the rate dropped to 3.03. This is a decrease of 8.2 percent in personnel efficiency. Each of the departments should then be evaluated separately. The kitchen decreased by 8.1 percent, and the dining room by 9.0 percent. These results are consistent with the ones from the *wage-cost-per-guest* analysis: Both departments are in trouble, but the dining room is worse.

Analysis, as pointed out, is basically a comparison process. Here we compare figures from two consecutive months. We would also want to compare these figures to October and November of last year and perhaps even the year before that. We should compare them to the two to three months preceding October. We need as much information as we can get. We need to know whether this is a trend. If so, did it just begin in November, or has it been developing for some time? Another important comparison, perhaps the most important, is to compare these figures to a standard. In other words, what should have happened? In doing this with the guest-count-per-labor-hour figures, the follow-ing sequence occurs:

1. Since the guest count was down, they certainly did not require additional employee hours.

2. A major decrease in the guest count, which this was, should be accompanied by some attempt to reduce employee hours. Merely maintaining the same schedule would not be adequate.

3. Since it is reasonable to expect manage-ment to reschedule employees, attempting to cut hours where possible, it is logical to assume they would focus on the employees whose workload is most responsive to guest counts—the variable employees.

4. There are variable employees in both the kitchen and dining room, but by far the greatest number are in the dining room.

5. The reasonable expectation, therefore, is that management should have responded to the problem by rescheduling the employees, primarily the variable ones. The effectiveness of this attempt should be more apparent in the dining room than in the kitchen.

Case Summary

There is a problem here of reduced produc-tivity of the hourly employees. It is caused by declining guest counts and is made worse by management's failure to respond. The cost

percentages are temporarily protected by price increases, but it is unlikely that this will continue. The declining guest counts, in fact, could well be due to the rather substantial price increases. If so, the trend may continue. The result of the reduced productivity, shown by the lower guest-per-labor-hour ratios, is that the wage cost per guest has increased. The proper response for management would have been to reduce payroll hours, especially among variable employees and particularly those in the dining room. Not only was this not done, but the dining room—which offers the best hope of coping with this problem, at least in the short run—was actually mismanaged the most. It is the dining room that showed the greater increase in wage cost per guest and the greater decrease in guests per labor hour.

Importance of Proper Breakdown of Costs

The basic breakdown or division of costs is by departments, as shown. This often is inadequate, especially when there are cost problems. Management then requires more detailed information than a department analysis can provide. Basically, whenever there is variance, unpredictability occurs. Management cannot cope efficiently in an unpredictable environment and must obtain whatever information is needed to reduce the uncertainty. The use of depart-mental rather than total operational figures is an example of this concept. If one department is up and the other down, they could cancel each other out. The combined, overall results would seem okay. Only by evaluating each department separately would management become aware of the problem(s). There are other ways to do this, and we will look at three of them:

1. Meal periods
2. Days of week
3. Job classification

Meal Periods

Most operations have a luncheon and dinner meal period. Many serve breakfast, and a few may even have a fourth period, late evening or supper. From an analysis standpoint, this is important because in a sense there are two, three, or four foodservice units operating under one roof. The menus are different, production and service personnel are not the same, and the table setup changes with each meal period. Often the market varies as well; the types of customers who patronize the operation at lunch may be completely different from the dinner guests. When this is the case, it is senseless to try making decisions based on consolidated figures. Use of the guest-per-labor-hour analysis could reveal that the breakfast and luncheon figures are stable, but the dinner period shows a decline in the ratio. If management had only one statistic, averaging all three meals, they would draw incorrect conclusions. If the dinner guest count accounted for a large portion of the total, the overall guest-per-labor ratio might well decrease enough to cause concern. In this case, management would probably waste time looking into breakfast and lunch along with dinner. A more dangerous situation results if the dinner guest count, relative to breakfast and lunch, were small enough not to have much effect on the overall ratio. In this case, the problem would be overlooked; management would not even be aware it exists. In the first instance, management acts when there is no necessity to do so. In the second, they fail to act when it is called for. Both situations occurred due to lack of adequate information—information that, first, revealed the existence of a problem and, second, showed exactly where the problem was. The difficulty exists, as it usually does in foodservice operations, not in solving problems, but in identifying them.

There is a current trend, which seems to be picking up, for certain types of restaurants to serve the same menu throughout the day (breakfast is typically not offered). Under these conditions, there are no natural breaking points for analysis, but the productivity variances probably still exist. Management should determine what these variances are and whether they warrant separate analysis.

Days of the Week

The key here, as it was with the meal periods, is whether there are significant differences in patronage patterns over the week. In most commercial operations, there are. Many institutional foodservice units maintain very consistent guest counts, and this greatly simplifies the analysis. In essence, they have one meal period, and it is no different on Monday than on Thursday.

A typical pattern of luncheon activity for commercial operations shows a gradual build-up through the week, peaking on Friday. Saturday is generally well down. On Sunday, if open, the restaurant may serve brunch and then run the dinner menu for the rest of the day. Dinner would show a similar increase throughout the week, but Saturday is probably the best night, and Sunday could be either quite good or quite poor. An operation like this should look at the productivity indices on various days, not only to aid in efficient scheduling but also to evaluate basic operating policies, such as when the unit should be open and closed and what operating hours are best.

Job Classification

Management must also look at the different employee classifications. The productivity of dining-room service personnel should be analyzed separately from buspersons, bartenders separate from cocktail servers, cooks separate from dishwashers, and perhaps even dishwashers independent of pot washers. The necessity for this lies in the fact that just as there are variances between departments, meal periods, and days of the week, there are significant differences between labor categories. Standards must be established for each category. Analysis not only provides information for measurement against the standards, but it also aids in the development of standards.

Summary of Cost Breakdown

Just as management should use several procedures to analyze productivity in order to balance the strengths and weaknesses of each method, they should also decide where productivity variances are to be expected. This generally means that departments, employee categories, meal periods, and even days of the week will be evaluated separately to determine whether productivity is increasing or decreasing.

Analysis of Employee Schedules

Proper employee scheduling is critical to labor cost control. The question is, how can management determine whether the employees are scheduled efficiently or not? There must be some attempt to correlate the schedule with some criteria of activity. The two criteria that appear to have the most importance are guest counts and workloads. These two do not necessarily coincide over the day since obviously a lot of work has to be done before any customers arrive. Because of this, it is suggested that both methods be used, although the workload is most valid in production scheduling, and the guest count is best in service scheduling. Bar charts are very useful in these types of analysis. They are simple to prepare and present the information in a manner that, compared to statistics and computer printouts, can be understood and evaluated more easily. An example of a bar chart is given in Exhibit 9.2.

The left column consists of employees (individual or categories), and the hours of operation are listed across the top. The pay rate for each employee and number of hours scheduled is also given; this is optional and allows management to track total scheduled hours and dollar payroll. On this type of chart, each employee or position has a line drawn across the hours worked. This could be a schedule for specific employees (see Exhibit 9.3) or a master schedule by positions (see Exhibit 9.4). Exhibit 9.4 is really a *Staffing Chart*, showing how many people are required and when they are needed. This information can be even more useful and easier to interpret when, for example, the various job categories are color coded. If, in Exhibit 9.4, the dishwashers were in red, it would

be simple to see at a glance that there are a total of four scheduled and never more than two at any one time. Other types of coding can also be used. Exhibit 9.5 shows the various activities performed by the receiving and storage clerk. He might, for example, be expected to work from 7 a.m. to 11 a.m., receiving deliveries and putting them away; from 11 a.m. to 11:30 a.m. he has lunch; he works on the dish machine from 11:30 to 2; and the balance of the day, he is expected to be in the storeroom, preparing orders, taking inventories, issuing stock, and so on. A chart like this clearly shows management what work activities are to be performed and when. Dishwashers, by the use of different colors, could have their activities separated into dishwashing, meals, breaks, general kitchen cleaning, and trash removal—all at time periods management has determined are the optimal ones. With a little imagination, bar charts can be quite useful in both analysis and control.

These are all examples of straight schedule analysis, but they can provide analytical data when combined with the two criteria previously mentioned.

Guest Count Analysis

On this chart (see Exhibit 9.6), the number of guests served during each hour is depicted in a graph. The pattern is then compared with the employee schedule. The two can be put together if desired (Exhibit 9.7), or the hourly guest counts can be incorporated into the basic schedule as a constant reminder and guide (Exhibit 9.4).

Workload Analysis. In this chart (see Exhibit 9.8), instead of evaluating the number of persons served each hour, you attempt to determine how much of the total work is performed during each hour. This is particularly useful for analyzing production personnel schedules, for they do not correlate at all well with guest counts. One problem with this method is that it is not based on quantitative data, as the guest count chart is. Estimates must be made as to what percentage of the total work is performed during each hour (or period) of the day. The more accurate the estimates, the more useful this method will be. As Exhibit 9.8 shows, the chart looks similar to the guest count analysis, and the graph plots the activity peaks and valleys over the day. The idea is to match the labor hours as closely as possible to the graph. It can be superimposed over the schedule (Exhibit 9.9), or the workload percentages can be placed on the basic schedule for guidance (Exhibit 9.4), as was done with the guest counts.

Exhibit 9.2. Bar Chart

Operation _____   Date(s) _____

Position	Pay Rate	Hours	Total Pay	A.M. 12 1 2 3 4 5 6 7 8 9 10 11 12	P.M. 1 2 3 4 5 6 7 8 9 10 11 12

Exhibit 9.3. Employee Schedule

Operation ——————   Date(s) ——————

Position	Pay Rate	Hours	Total Pay	A.M. 12 1 2 3 4 5 6 7 8 9 10 11 12	P.M. 1 2 3 4 5 6 7 8 9 10 11 12
James					
Ron					
Celia					
Becky					
LARA					
Curt					
MR. DRAKE					

Exhibit 9.4. Staffing Chart

Operation _____   Date(s) _____

Position	Pay Rate	Hours	Total Pay	A.M. 12 1 2 3 4 5 6 7 8 9 10 11	P.M. 12 1 2 3 4 5 6 7 8 9 10 11 12
Dishwashers					
Pot washer					
Pantry					
Workload % or				0 0 0 0 0 0 2 4 4 4 7 9	9 4 4 4 4 7 9 9 9 3 1
Guest counts				0 0 0 0 0 0 0 0 0 22 70 53 16	0 0 0 11 41 46 51 34 11 0

Exhibit 9.5. Scheduling Specific Activities

Operation _____   Date(s) _____

Position	Pay Rate	Hours	Total Pay	A.M. 12 1 2 3 4 5 6 7 8 9 10 11 12	P.M. 1 2 3 4 5 6 7 8 9 10 11 12
Peter					

Exhibit 9.6. Guest Count per Hour

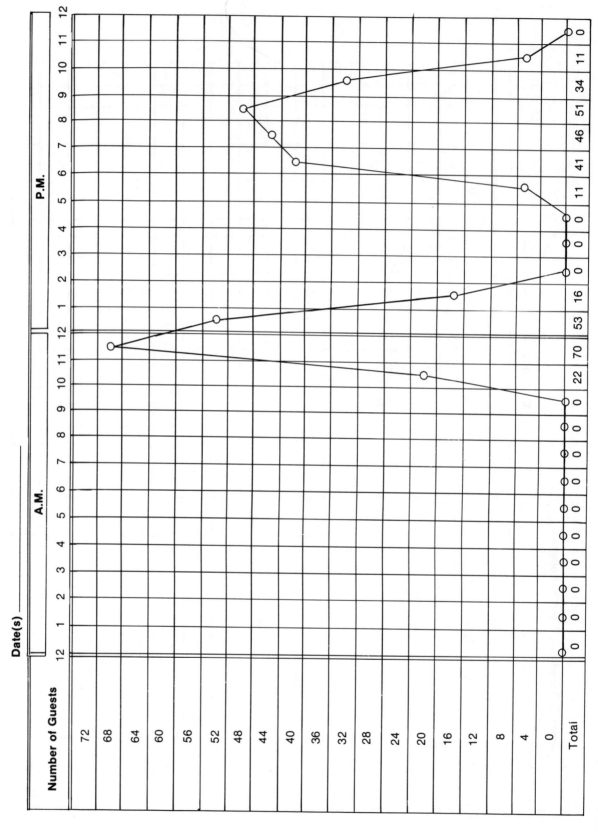

Exhibit 9.7. Employee Schedule Compared with Guest Count per Hour

Operation _____   Date(s) _____

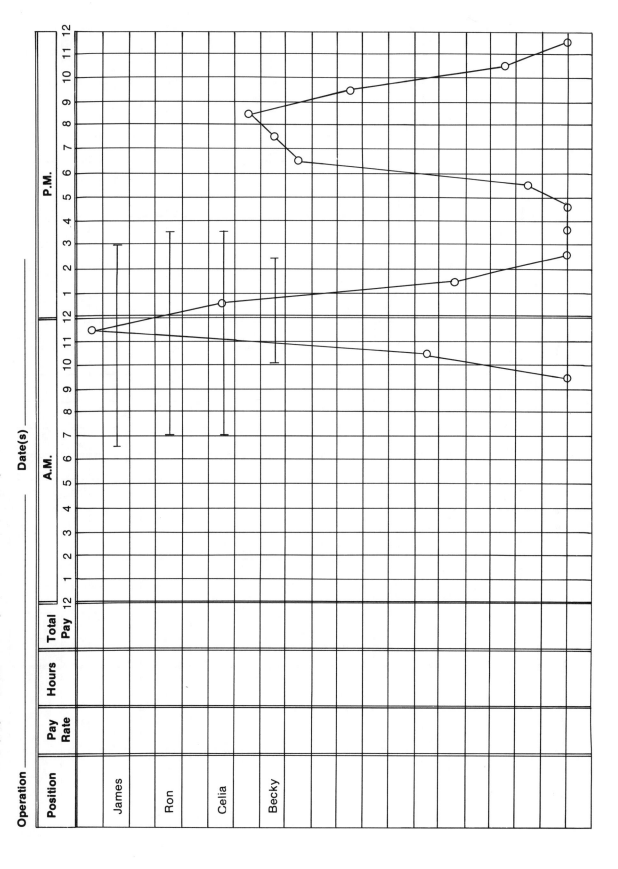

Exhibit 9.8. Workload per Hour (Kitchen)

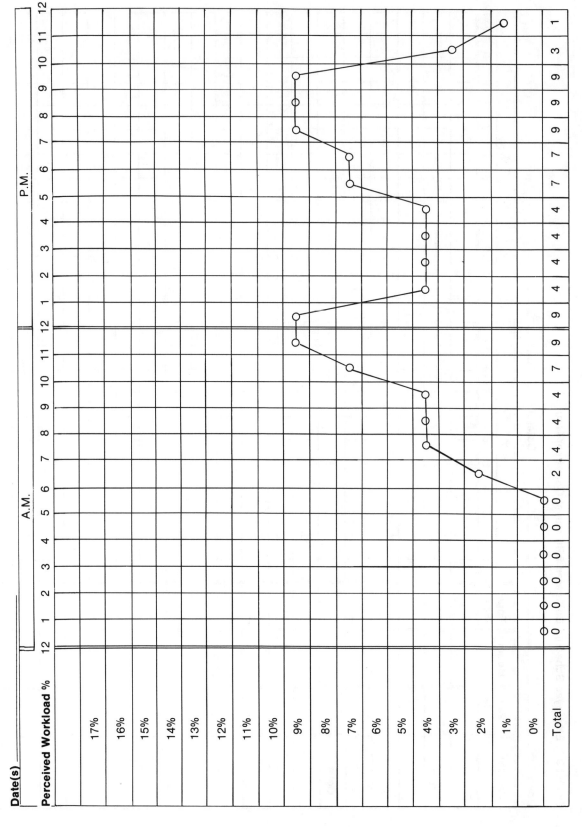

Exhibit 9.9. Employee Schedule Compared with Workload per Hour

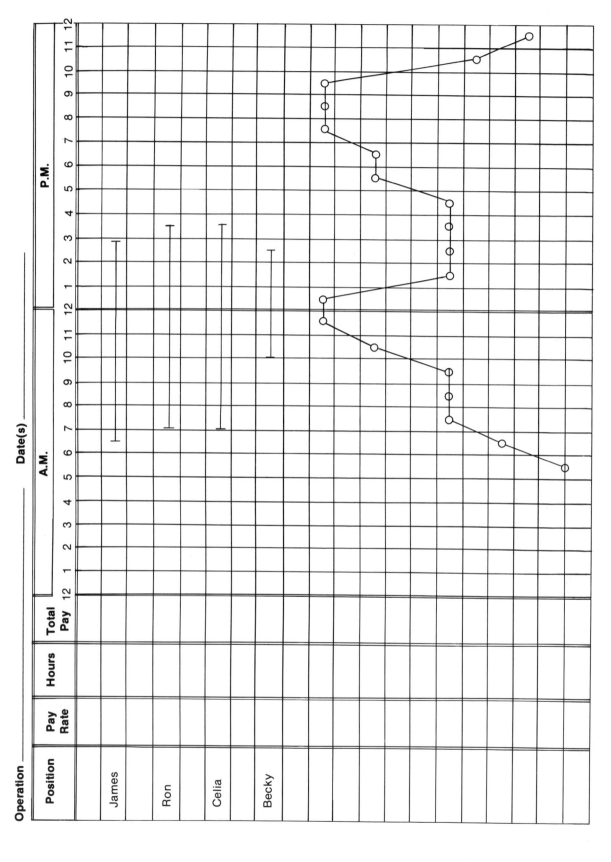

10 Control of Labor Costs

Fixed, Semivariable, and Variable Employees

The varieties in types of employees have been discussed from an analytical viewpoint, but employee variety is equally important in control. In analysis, the various types make it difficult to use percentages to compare payroll costs from one period to another. In control, it means management's ability to influence costs by effective scheduling is limited. Control must begin in the planning stages. All operations have a minimum staffing level below which they cannot go, except by closing. This is the paradox of labor cost. In periods of increasing sales, fixed labor can be the main generator of increased profits; while during periods of decreasing sales, it becomes a larger and larger proportion of sales. In such cases, the percentage goes up. If you recall the definitions of fixed and variable employees, you can readily understand why this occurs. A fixed employee is generally not responsive to changes in volume. Therefore, when guest counts increase, you do not require

additional help in the areas of fixed employees. This increases productivity and should generate higher profits. On the other hand, when guest counts are down, you cannot respond by reducing or eliminating fixed employees or perhaps even their hours. Thus productivity is reduced, as are profits.

A variable employee is, to some degree, responsive to the changes in guest demand. In periods of increasing sales, they are not so much a source of potentially increased profits as the fixed employees are because you must keep adding to the work force. The dollar cost increases, and changes in the percentage, if any, are generally minimal. The effect on profits of a sales decrease can be lessened by reducing the variable employees. They can, and should, be cut back by whatever degree possible.

It is apparent then that the volume level and ratio of fixed to variable employees are of critical importance to potential profitability. This is why planning is important. If the sales volume is incorrectly estimated, or if the wrong mixture of fixed and variable employees is put together, there may be little that operating management

277

can do later on to significantly alter the cost structure.

There is a third type of classification, that of semivariable employees. These are defined as employees who are responsive to changes in demand (removing them from the fixed classification), but who require major increases or decreases in volume levels before scheduling changes can be made. Some preparation personnel fit into this category as do some of the dishwashers and utility people.

From a control standpoint, management has the greatest influence on the scheduling of variable and, to some extent, semivariable employees. This, therefore, is where the control emphasis should go. Training is very important, and these employees should be trained as well as, if not better than, the fixed employees. This will increase management's flexibility in responding to volume variances. Poorly training variable employees—for example, dining-room service personnel—could result in their being handled like fixed employees. They are so inefficient that even with a drop in volume management cannot consider a manpower reduction. On the other hand, when sales increase, they are variable to an extreme in that even the slightest gain in guest count requires additional people.

Work Production Standards

Control consists of structuring and organizing the operation so that the organization's standards can be attained. Without standards, therefore, there is no control since no one can determine if the control was effective or not. Work production standards clearly outline the amount of work that is expected to be accomplished in each job classification. These standards are an important part of a labor control program.

Standards can be based upon many types of measurements. One of the most common is dollar sales. We discussed the drawbacks of this measure in the sales-per-labor-hour analysis method, but it can be very useful with dining room or lounge service personnel. Similar but a little different is a check-average standard; this would be legitimate for waiters or waitresses but not for cocktail servers. As pointed out, the dining room has more consistent and predictable check averages than does the lounge or bar. Patrons in the dining room are there to eat. In general, they all have some sort of a main course, supplemented by salads, desserts, alcoholic beverages, and so forth. There are certainly eating and spending variances between guests, but the overall average is fairly steady. The sales of most nonentree items are discretionary with the guests, as is the specific entree a guest chooses. Management should want to sell certain menu items in preference to others, presumably those that have higher than average prices (and profits). Management should also want to sell as many other items, both food and beverage, as possible. When these sales are quantified, a check average standard results. By doing this, management is stating that merely taking an order and serving it properly is not adequate performance. It would not be fair to impose this idea in the lounge in many cases, because drink selection decisions are not as open to suggestions as food selections are. Also there is no variety of side items available to build up the check average. The best way to build the check average in the lounge is to keep the guest drinking, and this is not always a desirable thing to do. Use of total dollar sales, however, is equally valid with food servers and beverage servers.

Another common base for work standards is units served. This, like the sales standard, is good with employees who serve foods and beverages. The third type of standard is units produced, which can be used to measure performance of kitchen personnel. Still another could be time. How long should it take to perform a particular task?

Diverse classifications of employees require different standards because their job assignments can be so dissimilar. Exhibit 10.1 is a listing of the types of standards that could be used with each variable type of job classification. It is difficult to put these types of standards on fixed employees.

Exhibit 10.1. Work Production Standards

Position	Performance or Production Standard

Waitress or Waiter
1. Total dollar sales
2. Check average
3. Time to approach table
4. Wine sales: bottles and/or dollars
5. Dessert sales: number and/or dollars
6. Appetizer sales: number and/or dollars
7. Cocktails: number and/or dollars
8. Sales of particular menu items, either daily specials or items management wishes to sell in preference to other menu items
9. Side work: number of napkins folded for next shift
10. Number of guests served

Busperson
1. Time needed to clear table
2. Time required to reset a table
3. How to stack a tray

Cocktail Server
1. Total dollar sales
2. Number of drinks sold

Cook (Service Line)
1. Number of orders (it would not be fair to *measure* performance by this criterion since the cook has no control over how many orders to prepare, but this is useful as a *staffing* standard)
2. Time to prepare each menu item
3. Plate and food appearances
4. Condition of equipment at end of shift
5. Number of returned (or otherwise lost) products
6. Number of portions from unportioned menu items, such as rib roasts (also applies to covers on buffets which are served)
7. Number of portions from prepared foods such as stews, soups, and so on
8. Number of portions from packaged foods such as frozen shrimp, french fries, vegetables, and so forth
9. Line set up by a specific time

Cook (Production)
1. Time needed to produce various soups, sauces, and menu items
2. Volume of food produced (also a staffing standard)
3. Number of portions from unportioned foods (such as when cutting steaks)

Dishwashers
1. Number of dishes washed
2. Time needed to wash (dishes from a meal period must be finished by a specific time)
3. Breakage
4. Number of items rejected and returned to dish machine for rewashing

Fixed Employee Standards (Although it may not be feasible to apply production standards for these people, time standards are appropriate)

Porter
1. Time required to vacuum dining room(s)
2. Time to clean and sanitize public restrooms
3. Time to perform other assigned tasks

Cashier
1. Time to check out and prepare reports

Storeroom Personnel
1. Time needed to take inventories
2. Time required to clean storage areas
3. Condition of storage areas

How Are Work Production Standards Determined?

If production standards are to be useful and fair, they should be unique to each operation. Industry standards are helpful as a frame of reference, but they should not be considered fully applicable because of the great diversity in foodservice operations. The type of industry standards that would be most helpful in developing unit standards are specific task standards, such as wrapping silver in napkins for a cafeteria, clearing a table of soiled tableware, or stacking a tray. Company and organizational standards generally come close to specific unit needs, but a national chain may have two or more different foodservice concepts, making generalizations difficult. It is also likely, even if all the units are basically the same (such as a hamburger chain or coffee shops), that there could be considerable variation in the type of location, the work force, and often the layout of equipment. It is thus the responsibility of each operating management to determine their own standards. If local standards are higher than those of the company, to use the overall company standards would deny potential profits. If they are lower and can be justified, to use the higher standards would be foolish, for by definition the work force would be unable to attain them.

It is obviously not possible to establish rational standards without a thorough and detailed knowledge of the tasks to be accomplished. Once determined, these standards are not immutable or engraved on stone tablets for posterity. A stable crew, one with little or no turnover, undergoing constant training should be expected to show improved performance over time. This ultimately means that performance standards should be evaluated on an ongoing basis and that even a unit's own specific standards are only a frame of reference as to what can reasonably be expected.

Once management has some idea of what should be expected (from their own knowledge of the operation and from industry and company standards), they can develop their own specific standards. These should be established using good employees as a basis. It would be senseless to set a standard based on poor performance; this negates the entire concept. It is also unwise to use superior or superstar employees' performance levels except as an eventual goal. The employee must be challenged but not discouraged by management's expectations. Time studies and job breakdown are proven techniques for determining standards.

How Are Work Production Standards Used?

Once the standards have been established, management can analyze each employee for a short period—perhaps a week—to see whether he or she meets the standard. It would be a mistake to assume that the sole objective is to find below-standard employees. Above-standard output is just as important and would indicate one of three things: (1) the standard may be too low; (2) the employee could be overworked; (3) the employee is a superior worker. It is important to establish which one of these applies. Superior workers must be recognized so they can be properly handled and rewarded. Conditions that create overworked employees must be corrected, not only to avoid losing the employee, but also to prevent a staff morale problem. When an employee consistently exceeds a reasonable standard, management should attempt to determine how or why this person is more efficient than the other employees. The individual may be doing the job differently, and better, than the way management set it up or instructed them. In this case, if possible, the job procedures should be altered, especially if that would enable the other employees to increase their output. If the standards are found to be too low, they will have to be increased. This could cause a difficult employee relations problem. The workers are given a standard of output that was developed by management in their supposed infinite wisdom, and when the employees begin exceeding it, the standard is raised. One does not have to be trained in the behavioral sciences to predict the attitude of the employees when that happens. Standards are important and necessary, but unless they are rationally developed, they could do more harm than good.

An employee performing below a reasonable

standard could indicate a problem either with that employee or with management. Personnel who are scheduled improperly may find it impossible to produce adequately. If, for example, the dining-room service staff were overscheduled, the guest count per employee would drop, as would the dollar sales average. Employees may fall below the standards, but is it their fault or management's? Say that a service crew is supposed to fold 200 napkins to leave for the next shift, but due to a fouled-up linen order there are no napkins to fold. Is it the employee's fault for not meeting the standard? If the portion standard for beef stew is 8 ounces, but management fails to supply the cooks with 8-ounce ladles, whose fault is it if the stew is not portioned properly? It is management's responsibility to analyze *all* the unit's needs and fill all the employees' working day. Management should also provide whatever support is necessary in the way of equipment, time, facilities, and other personnel to assure standard performance. Estimates as to what percentage of time foodservice personnel are actually working vary from as low as 40 percent to perhaps 60 percent. This means that these employees may not be working from 40 to 60 percent of the time they are paid to work. What are they doing the rest of their scheduled hours? They are smoking, talking, walking, trying to find something, and so on. This is due to poor management. If the storage areas are disorganized, people cannot find food and supplies very quickly, so they waste time. If food production is not well thought out, employees may not be kept busy, and they waste time. If the dish machine is not cleaned properly (or not at all) at night, the morning crew has to do it. Time is wasted. If cooks have to trim poorly specified or purchased steaks, roasts, chops, or seafood, they waste time (in addition to products). Much nonproductive activity is of course due to loafing; the employee simply does not want to do anything. But even in this case, inept management is at least partially the cause. Who, after all, hired these nonworkers? Who was responsible for the training they never received? Who provides inadequate supervision? Who is incapable of motivating the employees? Who cannot realistically evaluate

performance and determine whether or not it is sufficient? The use or lack of use of production standards will not solve any of these problems, but in a well-managed operation standards are a critical part of measuring and thus controlling employee activity.

Scheduling

The importance of scheduling has been well documented up to this point. What must be covered now is how management can most effectively schedule the various employees and their required tasks. The latter is often overlooked. Scheduling is frequently regarded as merely deciding when each employee works, but unless these decisions are based on the work to be performed, employee scheduling will seldom result in maximum production.

Effective scheduling begins with an accurate forecast of expected business. Once this is done, the actual scheduling of production and service employees is done much differently, as the decision on productivity analysis brought out. There are several methods to choose from in scheduling service employees. We will examine each for its advantages and drawbacks.

Scheduling Methods Based on a Forecast

1. Forecast dollar sales and multiply by a predetermined percentage. The result is the budgeted payroll, and management schedules within its parameters. The advantage is simplicity. Once a desired payroll percentage has been set, you merely calculate what the dollar payroll should be. It is then the task of management to prepare schedules that, when costed out, yield an acceptable dollar payroll. The drawbacks are many. The main one is that it is payroll management by percentage, and payrolls can no more be managed by percentage than they can be analyzed by percentage. Percentages are useful as guidelines, as warning signals that the relationship of payroll cost to sales is becoming unacceptable in regards to overall profitability. This is their primary function, and this is how they should be used.

The method described ignores the vital statistic of guest count and concerns itself only with sales dollars. Under such a system, if sales increase as a result of menu repricing, the payroll would automatically be increased. In such a case, any increase in labor hours would be totally unjustified and an unnecessary, incremental expense. The sales have increased solely due to repricing, and the employees have not contributed to the additional sales. If, however, the sales went up because the employees sold more drinks or higher priced menu items or more desserts, then they have certainly contributed to the added sales. Management may then decide that wage rate increases are justified. Even in this case, though, increases in hours would not be. If this first technique is used at all, it should be limited to establishing the *maximum allowable labor cost*. When a rationally arrived at schedule then yields an unacceptably high cost, management knows of the need for a reevaluation of the entire operation. The point has been made that these wages are necessary to support the anticipated volume according to the desired level of service. Reduction of the wages with no changes in the basic production or service systems generally results in reduced operational capability to satisfy the customers. Their perception of the operation's value will go down, and patronage will inevitably decline. The challenge is not how to prepare a schedule that meets the percentage requirements, but rather how to reconceptualize the operation so that the level of services does not decline and to figure out how to do this in a fiscally sound manner.

2. Forecast dollar sales and multiply by a percentage figure that excludes some or all fixed employees. This percentage is thus based upon variable employees, the one sector that is reasonably responsive to changes in demand. In this case, the use of a percentage can be legitimate. The usefulness of this system would vary considerably among units, but it should be considered. In general, the higher the sales volume, the smaller the ratio of fixed to variable wages. High volume restaurants may have many more cooks, waitresses, buspersons, and cocktail servers than lower volume operations, but they may not have any more managers, cashiers, bookkeepers, chefs, receiving clerks, porters, or

pot washers. This method would therefore probably be more effective in relatively high volume foodservice operations. In smaller units, with a higher ratio of fixed to variable wages, the payroll is less flexible and cannot respond quickly to volume changes; while the larger units, being more responsive, can use percentages more effectively.

3. Forecast dollar sales and have an expected dollar return for each hour of labor used. For example: If the standard were $10.00 sales for each labor hour, and forecasted sales were $1,150.00, the number of scheduled hours would be 115 ($1,150.00 ÷ 10). The disadvantage of this system is that it is sales based, and fluctuating sales are not necessarily indicative of equivalent workload changes, particularly when menu prices are going up. This system has the virtue of making management aware of the importance of each labor hour and the necessity of generating, in this case, at least $10.00 for every hour added to the schedule. When management thinks in these terms, scheduling is generally done more carefully.

4. Forecast guest count and base the schedule on the guests-per-labor-hour standard(s). This is similar to number 3 above but has certain advantages over it. If the check average were to increase due to higher prices, increased sales of side or auxiliary foods, changes in the sales mix, or more sales of alcoholic beverages, the schedule would not necessarily be altered, especially if there were no change in the guest count. Using this system insures that basic schedules would be revised only when there was a real change in the sales base.

5. Recommended scheduling method: The best and most effective scheduling would probably result from a combination of numbers 3 and 4. In this case, the recommended sequence of activities would be:

A. There should be standards for the various departments and shifts. These would be both for sales per labor hour and guests per labor hour.

B. Forecast on a weekly basis. The forecast should reflect total dollar sales, ratio of food to beverage sales, and guest count. It should also be broken down into department and shift.

C. Prepare the weekly schedules using the guest count and/or the dollar sales forecast with the standards.

D. Cost out the completed schedule, and calculate the cost percentage, hoping that the percentage meets the organizational goals. If it does not, attempt to reschedule without weakening the operation. It would not be unusual to have fairly significant sales shifts from week to week, so temporarily failing to stay within a desired percentage is not serious. These sales imbalances come about mainly due to the calendar. Mother's Day occurs only one Sunday in the year; school starts once a year; New Years Day the operation is closed; and so on. These are regular and predictable occurrences. Others are less so. You may expect a major snowstorm or a large convention in town or some such event. Temporary and explainable shifts in sales do not justify major schedule changes whereas permanent ones do. This is the point when management must seriously consider the current direction of the operation. When reasonably arrived at schedules cost too much and the situation is expected to persist, major changes in the operation are required.

E. Follow up on a *daily* basis to determine whether the schedule is being followed or not. The best way to do this is by comparing hours scheduled to hours worked by department and by shifts. Management should have some sort of a daily payroll-hours reporting system. Payroll hours have a habit of growing and expanding unless checked constantly and unless supervisors are held accountable for them. To wait until the end of the week, or perhaps even two weeks when that is the payroll cycle, to find out that the scheduled hours were exceeded is the same as having never attempted to control the scheduling at all. It must be done on a daily basis. If, for example, the scheduled hours in the dining room on Monday were ninety, and on Tuesday morning the daily payroll report showed ninety-one hours, the person responsible for the dining room must justify the overage. It may well be legitimate. Guest count could have been up, or there may have been a significantly higher than average count near closing time, necessitating holding two employees half an hour longer. It often is not legitimate, however: a busboy wanted an hour of overtime, so he stayed. These kinds of overages are readily identified as problems; others are not. What about a situation in which the night supervisor decided some extra work needed to be done and kept an employee over an hour? The schedule was based on management's best estimate of what was needed. If there was a need to deviate from it, the supervisor should have cleared it with management ahead of time. The purpose of scheduling is to control the wages and to insure that the work force is utilized as efficiently as possible. In this case, the supervisor was wrong. On the other hand, if the dining room had been exceptionally busy late in the evening and the scheduled side work not completed because the supervisor had not kept anyone to complete it, he or she would be just as wrong. Supervisors should be trained to think, make decisions, and accept responsibility. One way to do this is to require them to defend deviations from the schedule (or lack of deviations when they are obviously called for). When payroll hours are checked daily, when department heads, supervisors, and assistant managers are held accountable, there are no surprises at the end of the payroll period. It should be obvious, however, that this system depends first on accurate forecasting and then on management competent enough to develop realistic schedules.

F. A variation on this method would be for management to prepare the forecasts and then give department heads or assistants scheduling guidelines. They could be based upon payroll dollars or hours or both. The actual scheduling would then be done by the department heads. The advantages of doing this are many. It is effective delegation by management. They make the basic decision; the department heads merely implement it. It develops the administrative skills of the subordinates and gets them involved in the cost-control procedures. It is also easier to hold them accountable for the costs when they share the responsibility.

Back-of-House Scheduling

The basic scheduling principles as outlined in the previous section are valid, but there are enough differences to warrant a separate discussion. Front-of-house activities are closely tied to the guest count. Therefore, the total number of guests expected and the time they are expected will be the controlling factors for scheduling there. In the back of the house, the workload is only partially determined by the expected guest count. Daily production schedules limited to that particular day's expected sales will be inefficient. Production scheduling must be done by looking at the demand over time. If an operation has pea soup on the menu each day and sells one gallon daily (about twenty orders), it would not be a productive use of either the cook's time or the equipment to prepare one gallon every day. Depending on the availability of equipment and adequate storage facilities, the production could be done two times per week in larger batches and held refrigerated for three to four days, or it could be done weekly or monthly in even larger batches and frozen in 1-gallon containers. It is unlikely to take the cook any longer to prepare a 4-gallon batch than it would a single gallon, nor would it take the pot washer any longer to clean the pot. Very large batch production could require specialized equipment and could take longer, but when the production volume is considered, the labor cost per unit again decreases and often dramatically.

Production scheduling should therefore be based upon management's attempt to make the most efficient use of all the factors of production. These are personnel, products, equipment, time, and space.

With personnel, the objective is to keep them as busy as possible and to obtain the maximum output over time. To use the soup example again, if it required 1/2 hour to get the soup started, another 1/2 hour to prep another soup, and one hour to prepare a stew, the cook would have spent 2 hours on three products and then additional time checking them as they continue to cook. If these three products are served Monday thru Friday at lunch, a minimum of ten hours per week would be needed. By rescheduling the prep so that on Monday a week's supply of pea soup is made (perhaps one hour), on Tuesday a week's supply of the other soup (1 hour), and on Wednesday, a week's supply of the stew (two hours), a total of four hours would be required, and the same amount of food would have been produced. This is a rational approach unless the six hours saved cannot be made productive. If the cook has nothing else to do, there is no advantage. In fact, it could probably be disadvantageous in the long run. With only one cook working, it would be difficult to take this approach. In that case, the cook is a fixed employee, and there is no scheduling flexibility.

The greater the number of production personnel, the greater the possibility of actually reducing the scheduled hours and perhaps even the number of employees. Reducing the number of employees is much more important than cutting hours. Each employee has a built-in fixed cost that is fairly independent of the hours worked. Employees have to be hired, trained, supervised, clothed, and fed. Also an increasing number of records must be maintained on each employee. Reducing the number of employees, even though the total hours are not affected, would reduce operational costs in all the areas mentioned—hiring costs, training expenses, supervision, uniforms and linen, employee meals, and administrative costs. Creative production scheduling offers employee and labor-hour reduction potential. Management should evaluate the demand over time and schedule accordingly.

The typical production scheduling technique,

however, is to use the daily demand as the basis. Evaluation of the products to be prepared is thus of great importance. It would be a mistake to assume that only the daily menu items can be more efficiently scheduled. To refer to our previous production example, say that some of the six hours of labor saved were put to use in preparing hours d'oeuvres for freezing. It is then possible that when these items are needed, which is irregularly, extra help would not have to be scheduled to prepare them. In general, most foodservice operations have a basic production personnel schedule that is supplemented or added to when banquets and catering events occur. This is regarded as a good approach, but if some or part of this additional product demand could be met by the basic crew, there would be fewer extra employees required for the special or nonregular events. Management must therefore consider not only the regular menu items and the items for banquets already booked, but also those types of items that are likely to be needed. This approach demands a thorough knowledge of food. Some products lend themselves to this type of production scheduling, and others do not. Hollandaise sauce would not, whereas many soups and other sauces would. It would not make much sense to roast off all the standing ribs needed for the week on Monday, but the horseradish sauce served with the ribs could easily be prepared in weekly batches. The Stroganoff may be cooked to order, but the sauce could be prepared weekly, and the meat could be cut and portioned every two or three days. Production scheduling should also consider consolidation of certain recipe steps. If four different people in the kitchen preparing four different products are all required to peel, chop, dice, cut, mince, and so on various foods, the scheduling is inefficient. It would be far better to have one person at one station at one time do all these activities for all the products. This would be a more efficient use of personnel, products, equipment, time, and space.

Production scheduling, like service scheduling, is based on forecasted demand, but it requires more than knowledge of guest counts and sales levels. The back-of-the-house work force is more fixed and less responsive to sales changes than is the front of the house; therefore much attention must be paid to assuring that the work load, over time, is distributed as evenly as possible.

Types of Activities and When They Should Be Performed

There are two basic types of activities—those that directly benefit the guests and those that are of indirect benefit. Productivity can be affected by the time when these activities are performed. The terms used in the industry to describe this situation are *prime time* and *slack time*. Prime time is that period when the guests are there. In most operations, this does not account for a major portion of the total operating hours. In some operations, the prime time can be only a fraction of the total time. One objective of operations that use the same menu throughout the day is to increase the proportion of prime time. Some of the facilities (such as the kitchen) can be utilized during nonprime or slack time. The dining room generally cannot be. The result is that when there are no guests, a major portion of the foodservice operation is wasted. This explains the attempt to spread the business over a wider range of hours. Slack time is defined as the rest of the operating day—the time when there are no or few patrons.

During prime time, the only activities that should be performed are those of direct benefit to the guests. These would include:

1. Greeting and seating guests
2. Obtaining food and beverage orders
3. Preparing those orders
4. Serving foods and beverages
5. Table maintenance during a meal
6. Collection and cash handling
7. Table cleaning and resetting
8. Dining-room maintenance (keeping floor free from debris, side stands stocked, and so on)

It is during slack time that all the other necessary activities are done. The distinction between prime type and slack type activities is often blurred. Work scheduling should attempt to assure that nothing of a noncustomer nature, which can be done during slack time, should be performed during prime time. One of the reasons why productivity is low in the foodservice industry is that often much nonessential activity is being done during prime time with the consequent requirement of a large labor staff. When this happens, the operation is overstaffed during slack time. Management should be aware that the larger the work force scheduled during prime time, the greater the likelihood of low overall productivity. An obvious exception to this is part-time employees who can be brought in only for prime time. Part-time employees are desirable for this reason, but overreliance on them can cost more than is saved because, among other things, it increases the number of employees. As pointed out, the lower the number of average hours worked per employee, the higher the indirect payroll costs.

During prime time, all tasks performed should be of direct benefit to the guests. Some examples of activities often and improperly done during prime time are:

1. Receiving. Nothing should be received during meal periods. This is not only to assure better labor productivity but also for product control purposes as well.

2. Washing all the dishes required for a particular meal. (See the next section, "Equipment Productivity," for an explanation of this concept.)

3. Office work. The bookkeeper comes to mind first here, but many employees have some record-keeping responsibilities. One often finds them doing their "book-work" during meal periods. Even the bookkeeper could assist with seating or cashiering during the lunch peak.

4. Preparation work. Management must distinguish between food handling necessary to serve the guests and that which can be done ahead of time. When basic prep or preprep is being done during the meal, it reduces the efficiency of preparing the food for the customers. It could result in less food being served as well.

5. Pot washing. Pots and pans do not generally need to be washed during a meal. The materials to be washed are mainly generated by preparation prior to meals and by the meal service itself. In the first case, they should be pretty well caught up by the time service begins and in the second, the bulk of pans to be cleaned are not available until the meal is at least partially over. Thus, the pot washer could be used elsewhere during the serving peaks.

6. Kitchen cleaning.

7. Storeroom maintenance and/or inventory to prepare orders.

Engaging in duties like these during prime time reduces the number of people available to service the guests, which is the reason the operation is in existence. Taking care of guests is far and away the most important activity a foodservice unit can perform, and all of the unit's resources must be directed toward providing goods and services to the guests.

Uses of Slack Time

1. Washing dishes. This presupposes a large supply of china, glassware, and flatware, as well as a reduced crew who would work more steadily over a longer period of time. (See equipment productivity.)

2. Preparation of items normally purchased in convenience form. It is probable that decreasing foodservice worker productivity is partially due to poorly thought-out convenience food programs. If an operation requires six cooks and pantry employees to serve the customers, changing over to a lot of preprepared or convenience foods will not necessarily affect the labor needed to serve the food. A soup or stew or french fries take just as long to serve if purchased prepared as when made from scratch on the premises. If the service-labor demand is unaffected while the production labor demand is decreased, the result will be a crew with less to do during slack time. Productivity will decrease even if the guest count, sales, and payroll remain the same. It may thus be possible to increase output by using those full-time employees who are needed during meal periods for slack time preparation. The types of products that could be made, providing of course the right equipment is available, are breads and rolls, desserts, entrees, hors d'oeuvres,, and salad dressings. Some of these can be frozen and stored for later use.

3. General preprep. Breading chicken,

grinding bread crumbs, browning swiss steaks, peeling, dicing, and chopping vegetables for use in basic production and on the service line, blanching (precooking) vegetables and pastas for completion on the service line.

4. Bulk preparation. As described previously, some products can be prepared in large batches for future use. This can make dining-room production more efficient and could eliminate the need for extra people to handle banquet production. It is worthwhile to consider menu revisions to accommodate this type of production program.

5. Banquet setup. This type of work is usually done on demand. For example, when a group is to be served on Friday night, the room is prepared Friday afternoon. If, however, the room was empty Wednesday or Thursday and there was slack time available, it could be partially (or even completely) set up one or two days early, possibly saving extra setup labor on Friday. At the minimum, the tables and chairs (if available) could be placed in position. It is also possible to cover the tables with linen and set them with china, glassware, flatware, salts, peppers, sugar containers, candles, ash trays, and so on. These materials must also be available in sufficient quantities to spare. Often operators will not carry enough materials to do these types of things because of the extra capital expenditure and the increasing cost of money. These are important considerations, but expenses of this nature are basically one-time and written off over an extended period whereas labor costs occur day after day and cannot be amortized; they affect the current operating statement. Another factor to consider is that investments in tables, china, and glassware do not then require an additional investment in uniforms, training, supervision, meals, fringe benefits, and so on, as do labor investments.

6. Side work. This is a difficult area to judge. It is recognized that activities such as folding napkins, wrapping flatware, cleaning and polishing silver, refilling salt, pepper, and sugar containers, and so forth should be completed before or after the meal period. If the operation were unusually slow, however, it would be desirable to have these things done during prime

time. Management must evaluate each situation independently. Normally, however, this should seldom occur during meals; otherwise the forecasting and scheduling coordination has broken down. The most important job any service person has is to attend to the guests' needs. It would have to be quite slow indeed before the servers' and buspersons' time would be better spent in folding napkins than in being on the floor. An unfortunate paradox in this business is that when business is the slowest, the service is the worst. This is management's fault. They must not permit any other activities (or no activity at all) to take precedence over guest satisfaction. This problem is not confined to the dining room. Kitchen personnel also tend to become very unproductive when business is slow. In these cases, slack time has been created for at least some of the employees during what would normally be prime time. Management must anticipate this and train workers so that in this situation they automatically switch over to slack time tasks or at least check with supervisors as to what the priorities are. A cook may think that some chicken should be breaded, but management may want a specific piece of equipment cleaned or an inventory taken in the freezer or some vegetables cleaned and blanched for a party the next day. Buspersons in the dining room may begin folding napkins when, instead, the banquet room could be set up. As with regularly scheduled activities, management must control irregular, nonscheduled work as well. Abraham Lincoln once said that war was too important to be left to the generals. In foodservice operations, work is too important to be left to the employees to decide what to do, when to do it, and how to do it, at least without management guidelines.

7. Preportioning. This is a potentially valuable approach to food control and is a useful type of slack time activity. As pointed out in the chapter on food control, portioning should be done, whenever possible, prior to the service line. By definition, then, it becomes a slack time job.

8. Washing and folding linen. More and more foodservice operations are going back to doing their own linen. This type of activity pretty much

disappeared years ago due to the equipment, time, and personnel commitment required. With newer types of equipment (often available on a lease basis) as well as new, wrinkle-resistant fabrics, it has again become feasible to do linen in-house. Linen costs can be reduced, and slack time can be filled. Hiring employees specifically for this job would, of course, eliminate the labor advantage.

Equipment Productivity

Analyze the productivity of machines and equipment as well as personnel. Unproductive equipment generally goes hand in hand with unproductive employees. A classic example of this was a foodservice operation, located in a large, downtown office and trade building. It consisted of a 200-seat dining room, a 450-seat coffee shop, and a 75-seat lounge. The hours of operation were basically consistent with the working hours of the building's nearly 20,000 employees: 8 A.M. to 6 P.M., Monday through Friday, closed evenings and most weekends. This restaurant had a high volume, most of it coming in a limited time. In fact, nearly 75 percent of the sales occurred between 10 A.M. and 2 P.M. The dish room was organized similarly to most foodservice operations; that is, the dishes used for the first luncheon guests had to be washed immediately or else the guests in the mid luncheon period would have no clean plates. Because the volume during that period was so massive, the dish room operation was scaled massively as well. There were ten employees with an assistant manager as supervisor. This assignment was nearly a full-time job for the assistant manager. Since the materials coming into the dish room all had to be recycled quickly, the pace was furious. The turnover in the crew was very high, and employee morale was quite low. Breakage was at an awesome level. Within an hour after the luncheon period ended, the dishes were finished, and management was faced with trying to control ten basically transient, unskilled, untrained employees who would either loaf, wander about the operation, or attempt to steal everything not nailed down.

There was not sufficient slack time activity to keep them busy. The problems arising from this department were many:

1. High labor cost
2. High employee meal cost
3. High uniform cost
4. High hiring and training cost
5. High supervision cost
6. High breakage cost
7. Excessive department turnover
8. High fringe-benefits cost
9. Difficulty in controlling crew during slack time

A new general manager assigned to this operation came up with a revolutionary idea. He wanted to make a major investment in china, glassware, and flatware, cut the dish crew, and spread the dishwashing over a longer period of time. As with most ideas that go against the conventional wisdom, this one was not well received; but the manager persevered and was allowed to go ahead. The results were dramatic:

1. Number of dishwashers eventually cut in half, to five
2. Labor cost dropped
3. Employee meal cost decreased
4. Uniform cost decreased
5. The work was distributed over most of the eight-hour shift. The requirement was now not to maintain pace with the dining room but merely to have all materials cleaned by the end of the shift.
6. The working environment was more attractive, leading to improvement in employee morale. People, as a rule, do not enjoy working in a chaotic environment. The former situation, where the workload during prime time was excessive and during slack time dropped to virtually nothing, was chaotic.
7. The crew turnover dropped significantly, which meant that over time the remaining employees became much more proficient.
8. The hiring and training cost and effort was reduced.
9. The cost of supervision was reduced. A

more skillful crew requires less super-vision, and a crew that is constantly busy also requires less supervision.

10. Breakage was reduced
11. The payroll fringe-benefits cost dropped

These are all positive results, but there was obviously a substantial investment in china, glassware, and flatware. As brought out earlier, this is a capital expenditure and can be amortized over a long period. The impact on each month's operating statement was minimal. The impact of the lower labor cost, however, was sizable, and it did show up favorably each month. The other major potential drawback is operational. There may not be adequate room for dirty dish unloading and storage. If this is the case, it would not be practical to consider this type of program. In this operation though, there was no problem as the space available was more than sufficient. A third drawback, a minor one as it turned out, was that the dish machine had excess washing capacity most of the time. This was solved shortly as it was an old machine in poor condition due to its intensive use over the years. It was replaced by a smaller piece of equipment. Not only had the employees not been fully productive prior to the change, but the dishwashing equipment had not been either. It was used intensively for only a portion of the day, and much of the remainder of the time it was used little or not at all. It was expected that the capacity of the replacement would be determined by the total daily demand divided by the number of washing hours. The operation would have a smaller, less expensive piece of equipment that would be working more productively.

The basic lesson is that when a major portion of the total work has to be completed in a small portion of the time, the operation has to concentrate both personnel and equipment. This is expensive since neither will be productive the rest of the time. All such situations should be carefully evaluated to determine whether the workload can be spread out over a longer period using fewer people and smaller equipment. Another example of improved operation commonly practiced today is the use of individual

coffee pots instead of large urns. The primary impetus for the change was to increase coffee quality (fresher coffee) and reduce costs (less waste from having large batches leftover). Overlooked by many operators was the fact that previously they had a large, expensive, fairly complex piece of equipment that was used infrequently to make large batches of coffee. Often specialized personnel made the coffee and took care of the equipment. The smaller, less expensive equipment that has since been installed was used continuously throughout the day, producing small, quickly consumed batches. Making coffee was no longer a specialized job. It became one of the side duties of the service and bus crew, as was the cleaning of the equipment. The result was not only potentially increased quality and reduced product cost, but also reduced labor cost and increased equipment productivity.

The equipment productivity referred to here is not calculated the same way as labor productivity is. In the two examples, the same amount of dishes are being washed as before and the same number of cups of coffee are being served. In both cases, though, the output is now being accomplished with less expensive machinery. The result is increased productivity. This is not a viable concept with all equipment. If you have a 400-seat banquet room and put broiled steaks on the menu, you will need to have sufficient broiler capacity to prepare 400 steaks more or less at one time. This would require several broilers, a large investment, and considerable kitchen space. It also would mean the broilers would sit idle much of the time. The equipment is nonproductive, but because of the menu policies, this is unavoidable. Were, however, the policies altered, even this situation would be improved. The steaks could be seared to simulate grill marks and placed on elevated racks and on sheet pans during preprep. When service time came, they could be cooked in a very hot forced-air convection oven. The final product, when properly done, is quite acceptable. Evaluation of the net results would show reduced space requirements in the kitchen, and space today is expensive and valuable. There would also be no investment in broilers, another significant saving. It is likely that personnel cost would be reduced because there would be no need for several highly skilled, highly paid broiler cooks during service.

To repeat, when you concentrate equipment and personnel to maximize output at one time, you not only have an increased investment in equipment and personnel at that time, but the equipment is wasted the rest of the time and the personnel may be as well.

Labor productivity is closely tied to that of the equipment, and management should pay particular attention to situations such as those described in which there appears to be a concentration of both. The best time to make changes, of course, is during the planning stages. If the dish machine had not needed replacing, the first restaurant would not have realized the full potential benefits of their operating modifications. If the coffee urns were installed and operating, it would require additional investment to bring in the pot brewers. If the former restaurant were designed and built with several broilers to handle the banquet steaks, changing the production system would insure their nonproductivity all the time rather than part of the time and totally waste expensive equipment.

Up to this point, we have been discussing the advisability of spreading the use of certain types of equipment. Other kinds of equipment call for the opposite strategy, however, that of concentrating activity that was formerly spread out. For example, when grinding meat, do you grind a few pounds three or four times daily or do you grind many pounds two or three times per week? If you cut meats in the operation, do you do it for an hour every day of three hours twice a week? These examples are similar in concept to the bulk production scheduling discussed earlier. Among other things, it is more efficient due to setup, breakdown, cleanup, and time. A meat grinder takes the same time to clean regardless of whether 1 pound or 30 pounds was ground. The same principle applies to the meat block, the stock pot, the braising kettle, and most other pieces of equipment. It takes a certain amount of time to set up equipment or a station for a particular job, but that time is not particularly

dependent upon the volume of products used. If the pantry cook sets up a slicer to slice sandwich meats, why not slice all the cheeses, tomatoes, and other foods as well? While they are at it, they could do the onions, garnishes, lemons, and other sliced products required by the production and line cooks. This is a more efficient use of the slicer and the total production labor hours. We say *total* because it obviously will be more work for the pantry person, but if 15 or 20 minutes extra are used it may well save several hours of labor elsewhere.

Ingredient Room and Stored Labor

Some of these efficiency concepts are similar to two ideas known as the *ingredient room* and *stored labor*. The consolidation of preprep activities is the basic idea behind the ingredient room. To implement it requires a separate area and separate personnel who fabricate, measure, and package all the recipe ingredients. The cooks' jobs are thus made easier; the equipment is more productive; and, of great importance, food quality and cost control are significantly increased. The concept of stored labor is that when products are prepared for later use, the operation is holding labor as well as products. A tray of portioned steaks in the walk-in represents not only food products that are readily available when needed, but also possibly $10.00 to $20.00 in labor as well. This is labor that is generated during slack time but will be used during prime time. It indicates an efficient use of labor hours. The concept is not limited to food; wrapped flatware, folded napkins, preset banquet rooms, and glassware prepared for banquets are also examples of labor purchased during slack time and used during prime time.

Overtime Control

Overtime is expensive and responsible for a large portion of payroll cost overages. Any rational payroll control program must pay a great deal of attention to overtime, its causes, and how to control it. In addition to the extra hours, the overtime rate of pay is usually higher than regular wages. When this happens, the payroll increases even if the total hours of work do not. Overtime is caused by a variety of reasons, some of which are unavoidable and legitimate. When employees cannot work for whatever reason, they should be replaced if possible. Some managers and supervisors will consciously avoid replacement in the mistaken belief that this helps the operation. Employees are either required or they are not. If they are scheduled, it is assumed they are needed, and, therefore, should be replaced. If the operation can get along without them, they should not be scheduled in the first place. Working "short" when people fail to report is a foolish way to reduce the payroll, even though the replacement labor is often paid time and a half. This then is one reasonable explanation for overtime. Supervisors should be trained to make decisions in the best interests of the entire operation. The most important thing is to fill the job slot with a qualified person. They should attempt to replace the straight-time labor with straight-time substitutes. If that can be done, there is no overtime problem. Building a steady, reliable crew that experiences little turnover is the best insurance against the operation being faced with these situations.

Another cause of justifiable overtime is when the unexpected occurs. The hotel front desk informs the dining room manager that it looks as though the occupancy will be close to 100 percent for the next day or two rather than the usual 70 percent, or a tour company informs the restaurant that they are going to bring a bus load of people for lunch tomorrow. When this happens, the most rational thing is to add whatever hours are necessary to handle the increase. To not do so is again a foolish way to cut payroll. If possible, the staff should be augmented with straight-time labor, but the first priority is to assure that an adequate work force is on hand when needed.

One type of overtime often considered reasonable, but which may not be, occurs when a supervisor or department head decides additional help is needed for some special task(s). The evening dining-room supervisor may keep a busperson to clean tables, or the assistant manager may feel the dish machine should be delimed. The decision that this work ought to be done may not be incorrect, but the timing of the decision certainly is. Needs like these do not suddenly spring up, rather they build over time, and it is the supervisor's responsibility to be aware of them and to schedule the work during slack time, using regularly scheduled employees. If this cannot be done, a standard procedure should be established so that overtime can be requested and approved or disapproved as management desires. The policy should be that the schedule will be followed except when the prime time work load increases—in other words, when additional guests are expected or show up unexpectedly. Deviation from the schedule should not be permitted for any sort of slack time activity.

The type of overtime that is totally unacceptable is when employees themselves decide to work extra hours. They may do so because they were not able to get their job done. Perhaps all the dishes were not cleaned by the end of the shift, and they simply stay. It is commendable of them to not want to leave the job unfinished, but management or the supervisor must make that decision. The decision may well be to keep the dishwasher(s) until the work is all caught up, and that is fine if that is consistent with operational policy and if the supervisor makes the decision. Another example is an employee who may simply loaf during the shift, hoping to be kept overtime to finish something that has to be completed such as the dishes. Here is another justification for performance standards. If they were in effect, and if they were reasonable and enforced, the employee(s) could not get away with this type of action.

Employees may simply want to pad their paychecks, and so they stay on the clock past the end of their shift. Even worse are the situations in which employees are not even working. They punch out long after they have stopped working, or a friend punches them out an hour after leaving, or worst of all they are carried on the clock for an entire shift and aren't even there! Coworkers punch in the absentees' time card along with their own, no doubt in return for the same favor at a later date. The best control against these activities is the daily labor hour report. If the supervisors or department heads check the time cards and prepare a daily report, and if management makes them explain and justify any deviations, these actions will not take place. Or if they do, it will happen only once. It is also a good policy to require the shift supervisor to initial the time cards daily at the end of the shift. When overtime is not discovered until the end of the pay period, the likelihood of anyone remembering the circumstances is remote. Even if they did remember, hundreds of dollars would have already been lost.

The overall policy guidelines concerning overtime should focus on two areas. One is to anticipate the need and submit requests for schedule deviations. Management can then decide whether or not to approve them. The other is to require an overtime report after the fact. This should state the employee(s) involved, the time worked, and the reason. If the overtime had been previously approved, this would be noted on the overtime report, but all the other information should still be required. These are both formal reports and should be filed and kept. A supplementary benefit is that they can be useful in evaluating the performance of supervisors, department heads, and assistants.

Absenteeism

Absenteeism has been noted as one of the factors contributing to labor cost problems. It is, for example, directly responsible for some of the overtime expenses just discussed. As with overtime, if management ignores absenteeism, it becomes implicitly permitted, and the problem worsens. There are many reasons why employees do not go to work. Some of these management can directly control, and others they have some, but only limited, influence on. The causes may be work related: the job conditions are poor, the supervision inept, the pay rate low (in comparison to comparable establishments), the other employees are difficult to work with, the performance demands are excessive, the operation is dirty or without

any standards at all, the meal and break policies are not reasonable, none of the equipment works properly, the department is poorly equipped with essential tools. There could probably be an endless list developed as to why employees do not enjoy their work and voluntarily stay away. These types of motivations for absenteeism are entirely under the control of management because they originate in the work place. It would not be reasonable to expect management to provide perfect working conditions so that no employee would ever have any complaints, but is is reasonable to expect that these work-related causes of absenteeism should not have the impact they typically do.

The other causes could be termed environmental and personal. The foodservice operator has little if any control over environmental factors. If the employee depends on public transportation, a strike could make it nearly impossible to get to work. If an employee's car was stolen, or her apartment burglarized, she may be unable to work. These types of incidents do occur, and they are uncontrollable by management as well as beyond the control of the employees. The location of the foodservice operation has a great deal to do with these situations, and these factors should be considered in a feasibility study.

The remaining cause—personal reasons—is one over which management can exercise some degree of control, but it is probably limited. People can and do have many personal problems. To name just a few: alcoholism, drug addiction, personal illness, family illness, injury (nonwork related), financial problems. Again the list could probably be endless. The most effective control for these problems is to avoid them by hiring carefully. If you hire an alcoholic, you are going to have absenteeism problems. Other than avoiding potentially troublesome employees, management can be supportive when personal problems do occur. Like the external or environmental causes, they may be beyond the control of the persons themselves, and assistance or support from an employer could help them cope. If a person cannot cope, one thing is certain; his or her value as an employee may be nil.

Staffing

Staffing is not the same as scheduling, though the two are sometimes confused. Staffing is a planning function, that of making the basic manpower decisions. Scheduling is an operating function, that of deciding who works where and when, and what specific tasks they do. Staffing decisions, when made properly, do provide operating management with guidelines that aid in control.

Manning tables or *Standard staffing guides* should be prepared. They will provide the specific number of authorized personnel in the various positions. One of the causes of profit erosion is the growth factor in foodservice operations. This refers to the tendency of inventories and the numbers of employees to grow over time, seemingly by themselves. If management does not make a conscious effort to control this growth, it will occur. It happens in the absence of staffing guidelines. A supervisor or kitchen manager may feel another dishwasher is needed to get the job done, and so one is promptly hired. A cook who is brought in a couple of times to assist with banquet preparation impresses the chef and suddenly is on the payroll full time. Production schedules are then altered to accommodate the additional person. If the dish room staffing table authorized only five dishwashers, and if this were enforced, it would not be possible to hire a sixth dishwasher. If the supervisor was correct in observing that the five were not getting the job done, the problem is not an insufficient number of personnel, but inadequate personnel—a critical difference. This implies either that the wrong persons were hired, or that they were trained inadequately, or that they are incompetently supervised, or all three.

Manning tables or staffing guides are based on production standards and forecasted levels of business. They are complex and difficult to prepare. They presuppose detailed knowledge of all the activities in a foodservice operation as well as the ability to correctly forecast the future. This latter is so difficult to do that it is best to prepare guidelines for varying levels of sales. Thus, the dish room staffing table may well

authorize a sixth person but only under specific sales conditions.

Job numbering is a similar concept. The authorized positions within a department are numbered. Then the only time someone may be hired is when a numbered position is vacant. There should be more numbers available than are initially authorized so that when sales conditions change, additional positions can be added without altering the numbering sequence. See Exhibit 10.2. As this table shows, numbers 1 through 20 are reserved for dining-room servers. At the present time only eleven positions are active. The bus crew has numbers 21 to 30, while positions 21 to 24 are those currently active. A server or busperson could not be hired unless there were an open position number. This is an excellent way to control the hiring of personnel.

Exhibit 10.2. Job Numbers

Position	Job Number	Active	Inactive
Waitress or	1	x	
Waiter	2	x	
	3	x	
	4	x	
	5	x	
	6	x	
	7	x	
	8	x	
	9	x	
	10	x	
	11	x	
	12		x
	13		x
	14		x
	15		x
	16		x
	17		x
	18		x
	19		x
	20		x
Busperson	21	x	
	22	x	
	23	x	
	24	x	
	25		x
	26		x
	27		x
	28		x
	29		x
	30		x

Summary: Labor Management

The issue of labor management is of vital importance for two reasons. One is due to the cost of labor, which is the largest single cost in most foodservice operations. The other is due to the importance of the labor force. They are, without exaggeration, the second most important asset any foodservice operation has. The most important, of course, is the customers. If an operation is to be successful, the employees will ultimately make it so. When an operation fails, the employees usually did not perform adequately. We say *usually* because there are situations where failure has little to do with the operational efficiency. If management insists on locating a Mexican restaurant in an Italian neighborhood, it may fail regardless of how well it is run.

Assuming that the location and concept design are suitable, however, the success rests upon how well the operation can satisfy its guests. This, in turn, depends on the skill, enthusiasm, and dedication of the employees. It is often said that the hospitality industry is a people business. What that means is simply that it is a business based upon people attempting to satisfy other people. While our customers may be our most important asset, they come and go and often change frequently. Our employees do too, of course, but this need not happen. If our ultimate goal is to achieve profitability through satisfying our guests and if most of what goes into customer satisfaction—the products and service—is the responsibility of our employees, it makes sense to attempt assembling the most competent staff possible and keep them together and happy. This business is not easy, but it certainly is not as complicated as some would maintain.

Labor management, then, has dual goals. The foodservice operation must be managed profitably. This means that the cost of labor must be controlled, and discussing this has been the primary purpose of this section. The foodservice operation also must satisfy its employees; and while this aspect is beyond the scope of this text, it must be recognized as equally important to the eventual success of the enterprise.

Section V

Operating Management— Other Areas

11 Management and Control of Other Operating Expenses

Fixed Versus Variable Expenses

We have discussed the major expenses to be found in foodservice operations. These consist of product cost (food and beverage) and labor cost. The total of these expenses is often referred to as the "prime cost." In a typical foodservice establishment, prime cost would range from a a low of about 63 percent to 72 percent or higher. In hotel foodservice operations, the prime cost ranges from about 65 percent to over 80 percent.

The other expenses are characterized in the *Uniform System of Accounts for Restaurants* (*The Uniform System of Accounts for Restaurants* was published by the National Restaurant Association in Chicago, Illinois, 1968.) as "controllable" or fixed. The controllable expenses are variable in that the dollar cost will vary according to the volume. As we pointed out in the discussion on forecasting, some of these expenses are much more controllable than others. The fixed expenses are exactly that; they do not vary regardless of how high or low the volume may be. Since operating management has no control over this cost, we will only identify the kinds of expenses that constitute fixed costs. With the others, the costs that are, to a greater or lesser degree, controllable by operating management, we will identify the specific costs in each category and also discuss control methods and procedures.

Fixed Expenses

In the *Uniform System of Accounts*, this is termed "rent or occupation cost." The categories are as follows:

Rent—minimum or fixed amount

Additional percentage rental

Ground rent

Real estate taxes

Personal property taxes

Other municipal taxes

Franchise tax

Capital stock tax

Sewer tax

Partnership or corporation license fees

Insurance on building and contents

Interest paid

The industry range for these types of expenses is from a little under 5 percent to over 8 percent, the average being about 6 percent. These types of statistics, incidentally, are developed by the National Restaurant Association in conjunction with the accounting firm of Laventhal and Horwath and are published in their annual *Restaurant Industry Operations Report*. The figures they cite are not for individual restaurants but for categories of restaurants, such as less or more than five years in business, or for type of restaurant (full-menu table service, limited-menu table service, all others), or for region (northeast, southeast, north central, south central, west). Statistics from individual restaurants would show much more variance than the figures shown here.

As mentioned, rent or occupation expenses are beyond the control of management on a day-to-day basis. They are, however, controllable by management in the planning stage. In fact, they are quite controllable in that management can choose to decline to build and operate the establishment if they consider these costs excessive relative to the volume expected. Volume is the key, and as pointed out in forecasting, volume is often overestimated. When this happens, fixed expenses that look very acceptable on paper can in fact become oppressive. We recall an organization that signed a lease under the expectation that the rent would be about 7 percent of sales. This was right in line with most of their other restaurants. The actual volume fell so far below their projections that the rent became 17 to 18 percent of sales. Since the average operating profit for the chain was less than 5 percent, you can guess what the effect on the operating statement was of an increase in the rent from 7 to 17 percent. This operation suffered massive losses for the corporation until it could get out of the lease. The situation was not really the managers' fault. As you can imagine, they had a lot of managers, but changing the managers in this case was not the answer, and it did no good at all.

Variable Expenses

On the *Uniform System of Accounts*, these expenses are identified as "controllable expenses." The largest one is payroll (including employee benefits); the others are the ones we will discuss in this section.

Direct Operating Expenses

The following list comes from *The Uniform System of Accounts*.

The Uniform System of Accounts

Uniforms

Laundry

Linen rental

Linens

China and glassware

Silverware

Kitchen utensils

Kitchen fuel

Cleaning supplies

Paper supplies

Guest supplies

Bar supplies

Menus and drink lists

Dry cleaning

Contract cleaning

Flowers and decorations

Auto or truck expense

Employee transportation

Freight, express, and cartage

Parking

Licenses

Administrative and general

Repairs and maintenance

Banquet expense

Typical Industry Costs. The average expense for direct operating is over 5 percent, though the range is from a little under 5 to as high as almost 7 percent. With the volumes most chain foodservice operations are running today, we are talking about a lot of money being spent for these kinds of things: over $50,000.00 for each $1 million in sales. In other words, expenditures of $100,000.00 or over are not uncommon. Hotels do not structure their operating statement the same way, but if all these kinds of operating expenses are totaled, they come to over 6 percent.

Control Procedures. We will examine each line item separately, first identifying what types of expenses are charged to the category, and then discussing what management can do, if anything, to control these expenses.

Uniforms. This category includes: aprons, blouses, caps, coats, collars, dresses, smocks, suits, gloves, ties, trousers, shirts, costumes, badges, and so forth. It covers the purchase costs, the cleaning costs, and the repairing costs of such items.

To control this expense, management must first have policies, then the proper equipment. Finally they must be willing to follow up. There should be policies covering who is authorized specific uniforms, how many they are authorized, and what the employees' responsibilities are regarding cleaning and maintenance. There should be inspection at the employee exit. This is important for other reasons, but it serves a useful purpose here as well. Employees should not be permitted, if possible, to wear uniforms out of the building. If this is not feasible, management should have some method of ascertaining that company uniforms are not being used for personal use. In most cases, this would not be a problem, but with a waiter's tuxedo, for example, it could be.

If the restaurant is responsible for cleaning, there should be a one-for-one exchange. There should never be any uniforms issued without accepting a dirty one in exchange. If the size of the operation permits, a linen room would be helpful, as would assigning the control responsibility to a specific person.

Use of canvas hampers for soiled uniforms is recommended. Uniforms should be kept separate from other soiled linen in this case. Pass-through control lockers can be used for control. These are sometimes provided by commercial linen companies and are used by employees for dirty-clean uniform exchange. The companies can do this because of the savings to them in loss of linen and uniforms.

In general, control is made possible by management knowing what should be on hand and following up to assure that it is being used properly. There should be a uniform inventory, and management should know not only what they have but also where they are. Employees should be required to sign for uniforms. There probably should be a financial penalty for loss or destruction of uniforms. We refer to loss or destruction of uniforms through real employee carelessness, not if they should happen to have a fire at home or if their auto should be stolen, for example.

Laundry. Laundry expenses include laundering table linens, napkins, towels, and aprons. Management should have cost and usage guidelines here. Employees should not be permitted to work in dirty aprons, nor should they be encouraged to refrain from changing table linen when they are obviously soiled. Such occurrences are far too common due to the mistaken belief that an expense is being reduced. The expense itself may be reduced, but when management lets kitchen employees work in filthy uniforms and aprons (perhaps rationalizing that the customers cannot see them), the employees will have a hard time believing that the establishment really has any standards of quality. This uncaring attitude will inevitably extend to the foods being prepared.

The same thing will be true of dining-room employee attitudes when soiled linens are left on the tables. They will not take seriously any statements by management that the guests are important or that quality standards are important. The effect upon the guests' perception of the establishment are bound to be negative as well. If the guest count should drop as a result, where are the savings? Management must establish reasonable usage standards for these types of articles so that they can project realistic expenses. It is foolish to cut corners here, but it is obviously just as foolish to waste money through carelessness. If one employee seems to use twice as many aprons as anyone else, he or she should be provided with a clean one, but management should have a discussion with the individual to find out why the aprons get dirty so fast. Messy or sloppy employees seldom do quality work. Employees who cannot keep themselves clean will probably not keep their work areas or their equipment clean either.

Linen Rental. If the linen is not owned by the restaurant, the rental service cost is charged to this account although it is sometimes included in the laundry cost, especially when linen and laundry services are provided by the same company. The usual arrangement for restaurants has been to rent their linen, but some foodservice operations are now investigating the possibility of purchasing linen and cleaning it themselves. The combination of the availability of no-iron fabrics plus new efficient washing equipment (available either by lease or purchase) has made it possible for restaurateurs to consider owning and cleaning their own linen. The control procedures are the same as were described for laundry.

Linens. This is a line-item expense only when the operation owns its tablecloths, side towels, napkins, and so forth. The control procedures for these types of items have been described.

China, Glassware, and Silver. Although these are two different line items in the *Uniform System of Accounts* (china and glassware, and silverware), we will discuss them together since they are closely related. Hotel people include linen with these three expenses and refer to them as the "big four."

The replacement of these items was for many years regarded as part of the maintenance expense, but they are now considered to be direct-service costs and assigned to the direct operating expense group. One problem that arises with accounting for these items is that the purchases are often made infrequently and in large quantities, which tends to distort the operating statement for the period when they are purchased.

The recommended method is to spread the annual cost, and this is the usual accounting procedure in larger establishments and chain restaurants. If, for example, the expectation was that the total expense for the year would be $1,200.00, the expense would be charged to the income statement at $100.00 per month. Since monthly inventories are not usually taken with this type of equipment, expenses would be based on the actual purchases unless some sort of reserve account were established to spread the expense. With the example just given, if $100.00 were charged on the income statement each month and the actual cost at the end of the year were more or less than $1,200.00, the difference would be charged or credited to the last statement. The alternatives to this are either to charge these large expenses infrequently to the operating statements, or to take an inventory each month of china, glassware, and silverware to obtain the actual cost. Such an inventory would have to include materials in service as well as storage to provide totally accurate cost information. While this is not recommended as an ongoing procedure, it should be done from time to time for three reasons.

1. To provide usage guidelines so that standards can be established.
2. To check the actual usage against the standard.
3. To record actual usage when you suspect a cost problem.

The first of these, to provide guidelines, is necessary because standards are necessary. The operation should begin with realistic standards based on industry and/or company experience but should also develop its own actual usage figures. Taking inventories for the first few months will provide management with exact usage figures. Incidentally, *usage* with these products refers to breakage and pilferage. China, glassware, and silver are not consumed in the same manner that foods and beverages are. They are, however, broken and stolen and must be replaced continuously.

Pilferage is caused both by employees and guests. We once asked a manager how he calculated the amounts of silverware necessary to open a restaurant. His reply was to take the number of seats and multiply each piece (forks, knives, teaspoons, and so forth) by a predetermined percentage of the seat total. The reasoning was that he needed fewer iced teaspoons, for example, than forks. The fork multiplier might be 2 and the iced teaspoons only .5. The interesting thing was the remainder of his equation. To whatever number he came up with, he added a complete set of flatware for each employee. In other words, if there were expected to be fifty employees, he added fifty sets of flatware to the initial order! Once management has determined what their specific usage is, they can adjust the standards if necessary. When they have realistic standards, they can plan their replacement purchases more rationally.

The second reason, to check actual usage against the standard, refers to the necessity for follow-up to assure that the operation is running as expected. Without taking a physical inventory, management cannot know their actual usage and cost. We could compare this with yield testing. It was recommended that several yield tests be done in the beginning to determine what the average yields would be. It was also recommended, however, that management have a continuing yield-testing program so as to assure that the yields were being met over time. The principle here is the same. Management wants assurance, from time to time, that the usage has not deviated from the standards.

Finally, management needs the data from a physical inventory whenever they suspect that there is something wrong. If it is their impression that breakage and/or pilferage is increasing, they must know the exact magnitude

of the problem before they can take effective corrective action.

Except for these reasons, it should not be necessary to take monthly inventories of these categories. Purchasing needs would be based on the standard usage factors, which means that you replace the materials as needed. There are two ways in which china, glassware, and silver purchases can be planned. One method is to order infrequently from a purveyor specializing in these product lines. It would not be economical to place weekly or even monthly orders from such a supplier mainly because delivery costs will require high minimum orders. To prepare an order, management will project their needs for long periods, perhaps even six months, and order two or three times per year. The purchase cost, which will be substantial, will be written off in equal amounts over the order period as described. The other method is to purchase from a full-service distributor, one who carries these types of materials in addition to foods. There are many suppliers to choose from today since this is becoming common. In this case, large minimum orders are not necessary since each delivery will consist of foods, supplies, chemicals, kitchen utensils, china, glassware, and so forth. The foodservice operation (even small ones) will have no trouble meeting minimum order requirements. Purchases of china, glassware, and silver can be made weekly if the operator so desires. In this case, the purchase cost will probably be charged to expense as it is incurred. Both methods are effective purchasing techniques; the specific needs of the operation, and their suppliers' capabilities will determine which is the best.

Silver consists not only of table flatware, both stainless and silver, but it also includes hollowware, ladles, serving dishes, candelabra and decorative pieces, ice cream dishes, bowls, platters, and trays. The flatware is handled the same as china.

With these types of materials (those other than flatware), management should be sure to maintain inventories since they can disappear quickly, and some of them can be very expensive.

If management has accurate inventories, checks the count against the inventory frequently, and secures the more valuable pieces, serious problems should not arise. Silver has become prohibitively expensive, but some older establishments may already have substantial numbers of silver pieces in addition to silver flatware. In these cases, they must take extreme care to secure the pieces and maintain a perpetual inventory. In fact, when these pieces are used for banquets and catering, they should be accounted for each time they are used. When they are in general dining room use, they should be counted constantly.

China and glassware costs can best be controlled by using the proper equipment and maintaining effective employee training. Breakage of glassware can be reduced by using correct glass racks. Many restaurateurs attempt to save money on such items, but when glassware is run through dish machines in nonstandard racks, breakage tends to be high. Efficient dishroom design is important as well. When there is inadequate dirty and clean dish-landing space, excessive breakage will result. Just as proper washing racks are important, so are clean dish-and-glass holding equipment. Clean dishes are best stored on carts, while cups and glasses can best be stored in the same racks they were washed in. In addition to being ideal for storage, racks also reduce the handling of the glasses and cups, which in itself should reduce breakage.

Durability should be a purchase consideration. Excessive breakage is often the result of management attempting to save money when buying china and glassware. When you have a high incidence of breakage and chipping, not only will the replacement costs be high, but there will also be operating problems due to material shortages.

The largest single cause of breakage, however, is people, and as a result the importance of employee training cannot be overemphasized. Of particular concern are buspersons and dish-machine operators. Soiled dishes and glasses can be brought to the dish room in bus tubs, on trays, or on carts; if done properly, any of these will be effective. Bus tubs are probably the least desirable since employees can more easily mishandle the materials, but they can be satisfactory if used properly. In Chapter 4, we discussed the proper method of stacking trays. One of the rationales for standard tray organization was to reduce breakage. The most important personnel are the dish-machine operators. This position is typically regarded by employers and employees alike as a very low one, perhaps the lowest in the entire foodservice operation. Consequently, it attracts and is staffed with the least acceptable and most marginal employees in the operation. The pay scale is typically low also. The results are predictable: poor-quality employees who are then poorly trained, high personnel turnover, and excessive breakage.

To reverse this, start at the beginning. Hire quality personnel, train them properly and extensively, pay them adequately, and so keep them on the job. Turnover results in replacement of employees, which costs money and takes time. Breakage obviously costs money and, as pointed out, can disrupt the operation. Management can probably justify somewhat higher wages if they can reduce these costs. More important than the wages is the attitude of management. When they show, through interest and training, that the job (and thus the person holding the job) is important, they should be able to attract and keep better personnel.

Utensils. This category includes all the equipment routinely used in kitchens and food preparation. Examples would be knives, cleavers, pots, pans, kettles, stock pots, mixing bowls, whips, skewers, mixing spoons, measuring equipment, and so on. The total initial cost of such items can be considerable and so can the replacement cost if management does not pay attention to them. In general, such equipment is reasonably durable and, under normal use, will not become broken or damaged to the point where they cannot be used. This is in marked contrast to china and glassware for example. With the larger items, such as stock pots, pilferage is not much of a problem either.

Replacement costs generally are concentrated

in the smaller utensils that can be easily stolen and/or damaged. Knives are a particular problem in this regard. A good chef's knife can easily cost $25.00 (often more), and a careless cook can ruin the blade in a few minutes. Knives can also be easily hidden and carried out of the establishment. Measuring spoons and cups, spatulas, and other small equipment are constantly being misplaced and eventually lost. The best control is to have an inventory count of what is in service and to secure the back-up supply. When someone seeks replacement, find out what happened to the original equipment. Was it broken, damaged, or lost? Make the kitchen personnel responsible for taking care of such equipment.

It is also recommended to have specific storage locations in the production areas. In other words, there should be specific places to store measuring equipment, kitchen spoons, scoops, knives, and so forth. If this were done, and if there were standard numbers of each in use, it would be easy at the end of each shift for the cooks to check to see whether everything was accounted for. This should be part of the routine closing procedure.

Just as important as the replacement cost is the disruption of production that occurs when the proper tools are not available. Anyone who has ever cooked will attest to the frustration of trying to do a job properly without the right knife, or with a damaged knife, or without measuring spoons, ladles, scoops, sauté pans, and other small but essential equipment.

Kitchen Fuel. In the *Uniform System of Accounts*, this includes gas, coal, charcoal briquets, sterno, steam, electricity, hickory chips, and similar fuels. Ranges and ovens should be metered separately from fuels used for light and power. Where the use of electricity for cooking is minor, however, it is not practical to do this. The reason for separating the cooking expense from that of heating and lighting the establishment is that kitchens can consume huge amounts of energy, and management should be able to determine what the costs are in each area. A great deal of energy in the kitchen is used to produce heat. Much of this heat is wasted, not used by the foods being heated. The wasted energy then heats the kitchen, and more money must be spent to remove the excess heat.

Control procedures include not turning equipment on until needed. It is common for cooks to begin a shift at six or seven in the morning by turning on all the ovens, ranges, and fryers. In many cases, it could be hours before some of them are actually used. Steam tables are filled and heated at seven, although often nothing will be placed in them until 10:30 A.M. Aside from the energy wasted in heating and holding for all this time, the steam table releases a lot of moisture, which then must be removed. Chafers for buffets are often filled with water and heated with sterno long before the function begins instead of being filled with hot water at the last minute and then lighting the sterno. Management can do several things to assure that kitchen fuel is being used efficiently. The main one, however, is to keep the heat off until the equipment is needed.

Cleaning Supplies. According to the *Uniform System of Accounts*, the following types of materials will be charged to this expense: cleaning fluids, cleaning compounds, polish, BB shot (for silver burnishing machines), deodorants, brooms and sweepers, mops, mop pails, cleaning cloths, dust cloths, rags, steel wool, and similar items.

Control is achieved by training employees in the proper use of these materials. If they do not know how to use them, these materials will be wasted, and that is the primary cause of excessive costs. These are not attractive items for pilferage, so management is mostly concerned with getting maximum usage from them. Dish-machine compounds are generally metered, but waste will still occur if the equipment is not used properly. A lot of waste takes place because employees are trying to do a good job. Their reasoning is that if one cup will clean the floor, then two or three cups will really do a good job. We have seen employees do this for years. No one ever explained to them exactly how the compounds work and why it was unnecessary as well as wasteful to use more than the recommended amounts. This is another area where management should monitor the usage and compare it to standards. The chemical company that is providing your dish-machine compounds can tell you how much you should be using based on how many customers you serve and how many pieces will be washed.

Another source of waste in dishwashing is to run less than full loads through the machine. It takes the same amount of soap to clean a rack that is half loaded as it does a full one. Employees think they are doing the right thing by staying ahead, but they are merely wasting soap and hot water; the energy required to heat the water is another substantial source of waste. When management has usage standards to compare with actual consumption and when they provide proper training, costs are likely to be in line.

Supplies: Paper, Guest, and Bar. The *Uniform System of Accounts* gives these examples of paper supplies and other disposables: chop frills, cups (hot and cold), doilies, liners, napkins, plates, wrapping paper, boxes, plastic film, aluminum foil, soufflé cups, ramekins, holders, pastry bags, filter paper (including coffee filters), wax paper, and twine.

Examples of guest supplies are: matches, favors and small gifts, newspapers, souvenirs, toothpicks, and postcards.

Bar supplies include: corkscrews, mixers, bottle openers, shakers, bar spoons, fruit squeezers, fancy-drink decorations, favors and small gifts, souvenirs, measuring devices, knives, cutting boards, strainers, bottle stoppers, swizzle sticks, toothpicks, bar picks, bottle pourers, condiment or garnish holders, and other such items.

Some of these items would be attractive candidates for pilferage, and management must therefore not only control the usage but also maintain adequate security. Controlling the usage refers to avoiding waste; the situation here is similar to that just described with cleaning supplies. Management should have known consumption standards and should compare the

actual monthly usage to the standard. This is very important with disposable products.

Management should also assure that the employees know how to use the various supplies properly. Aluminum foil is wasted by not knowing how to wrap foods properly for the refrigerator and freezer. The same is true for freezer paper. Aluminum foil, freezer paper, and plastic bags can often be reused if care is taken in the wrapping and unwrapping. All such materials, especially the nondisposables, should be securely locked up, and inventory counts should be maintained on them. Any usage in excess of the standard should be investigated, and any missing items should be investigated quickly.

The expense for supplies is generally determined by the purchases. Monthly inventories are not taken for the purpose of calculating the exact cost as that would not be an efficient use of time. These types of supplies are being purchased on a continuous basis, more or less as they are being used, and the purchases generally are an accurate indication of the cost. The usual purpose of inventory counts when they are taken is to provide information for control purposes, not to prepare operating statements.

Menus and Drink Lists. These items, if the cost is small, are often combined with printing and stationary under the general heading of "administrative and general" expenses. These expenses could be out of line in several ways. One is that management has to pay too much money for the menus themselves. As with any purchase, an effort should be made to assure that the purchasing objectives are being met. As you recall, these were: to obtain the right quality, at the right time, in the right quantity, at the right price, and from the right supplier. The first decision management has to make is what is the right quality? There are many different types of menus and menu materials to choose from. The menu is so critical in creating a positive attitude on the part of the guest that great care should be taken to assure that the menu is consistent with the image of the establishment.

Once these decisions have been made, management should determine how many viable suppliers there are. There will probably be more than one who have the capability of meeting your needs. The task of management at that point is to determine which can do a good job at the lowest overall cost. As with most other products, the lowest selling price is not necessarily the lowest operating cost. A supplier who quotes prices 10 percent less than anyone else but who requires a six-months' supply as a minimum order could end up costing you money because of the cash you would tie up. There would also be the problem of menu revision inflexibility.

Another cause of excessive expense in this area would be guest pilferage. Many foodservice operators do not mind giving a menu to a customer; it can be an effective advertising tool. But when menus are costly, and many are, the establishment cannot afford this practice. The more expensive and unique the menu is, the greater will be the inclination of some guests to take it with them, with or without permission. Thus, management has to take steps to control guest pilferage of menus. This is done by training servers to pick menus up as soon as the order is placed. If the guest requests that he or she be allowed to look at the menu a while longer, the server will have to remember to retrieve it later.

Menus do not have an infinite life; they will eventually wear out, become dog-eared, soiled, and so on. Management can delay this process or accelerate it, and, again, training is critical. A well-trained crew will take care of everything they work with, including the menus. They will not leave them in the kitchen where food can soil them more easily. They will handle them carefully, not throwing them about or over-crowding them in a storage rack, and so forth.

A management program to control menu costs will concentrate on getting the most menus for the least price, preventing unwanted guest pilferage, and training employees to treat menus, drink lists, and wine lists with appropriate care.

Dry Cleaning. The *Uniform System of Accounts* recognizes dry cleaning expenses as the following: cost of dry cleaning curtains, draperies, wall hangings, the cost of washing or cleaning awnings, carpets, rugs, window shades, and chair coverings. Effective control begins with keeping them as clean as possible to start with. They are, of course, going to eventually become soiled, but an effort can be made on a day-to-day basis to maintain them and delay major cleaning expenses. One restaurateur, when asked whether he objected to the expense of cleaning the dining room carpet replied, "Oh no! I love to have to shampoo the carpet. The only people who get it dirty are my customers, and the more times I have to shampoo it, the more money I make." He made sure, however, that *only* his customers soiled the carpet, and, even then, not unnecessarily. In rainy and snowy weather, he had throw rugs available at the entrance for his guests to clean their shoes off when they entered. He also made sure that the kitchen floor was kept clean, in particular that there was not an accumulation of greasy dirt which could be tracked into the dining room. He had the kitchen mopped often, and the dining room was brushed frequently between vacuumings. When he finally did have to shampoo the rug, he did not mind because he knew it was only a reflection of the customer volume and not carelessness in his operation.

The other way to control this expense area is to select your suppliers carefully. When dealing with suppliers of services, you have to assure that there is mutual understanding as to what the work will consist of, when it will be done, and what the standards of inspection will be. If there is some sort of written agreement on these things, management has recourse if they are not satisfied with the work; they can withhold payment until it is done to their satisfaction. In the absence of any sort of clear agreement, the supplier can claim he or she did the work as promised and demand payment. In the case of no written standards, who is to say whether the service did or did not do a satisfactory or complete job? With a job such as carpet cleaning, one must be specific about whether or not the tables and chairs are to be moved, how they are to be moved, whether they are to be replaced when the job is finished, and so forth; are draperies to be removed and rehung by the cleaners or by the establishment? These details of service rendered will also affect the price quotations, and they must be clearly understood for that reason as well.

Contract Cleaning. The *Uniform System of Accounts* considers contract cleaning as all expenses incurred for service contracts for night cleaning, window washing, extermination, and disinfecting. Many restaurants show some of these expenses separately on their income statements. The control suggestions are the same as those discussed under dry cleaning.

Flowers and Decorations. These expenses include fresh flowers, artificial flowers, ribbons, flags, decorative pieces prepared for tables or display, cost of florist and decorator services, and ice carvings. Expenses for these or similar items are often incurred in banquet and catering functions, but they are not charged to this account.

There are two ways to handle banquet expenses. In many cases, the expense is passed along directly to the guest. For example, the restaurant may order floral centerpieces for a wedding. The bill prepared for the guest would itemize this cost separately from the foods and beverages. In this case, the income would show up as "other income," and the expense would be charged to that account also. When banquet expenses are actual operating expenses, they will be charged to a separate banquet-expense account. That account will be discussed shortly. Management does not have a lot of control options with this cost category. The primary interest of management will probably be to assure that they are getting quality products for their money. When services are being purchased, the guidelines discussed earlier should be followed.

Auto and Truck Expense and Employee Transportation. When it is necessary to provide transportation for employees located away from public transit lines or distant from the place of work, the expense is charged to employee transportation. When a company auto or truck is used for these purposes, the expense will be charged to the auto and truck account. A more obvious auto or truck expense is when a company maintains their own vehicle for the transportation of foods, beverages, and supplies, or for delivery purposes, in the case of outside catering. That account (auto and truck) should be charged with all vehicle operating expenses, as should car rentals or delivery-service contract costs.

Employee transportation costs are difficult to control; they are often a function of the location and should be considered when evaluating potential sites. We recall one manager who had to spend about $500.00 per month just to get employees to and from work. His restaurant was located in a wealthy suburb and was beyond the public transportation lines. He found it nearly impossible to recruit his work force from the local community; most of the employees came from the city. Unless they had their own automobiles, they could not get to work. Since limiting potential employees to those having cars was not practical, he accepted the financial responsibility of assuring that they could get to work. He paid taxi fares, paid other employees to make runs into the city to pick up people, bought gas for employees who had cars, and so forth. This expense of $500.00 per month, month after month, or $6,000.00 per year was caused solely by the location, and there was nothing he or anyone else could do about it once the location was fixed.

When an operation maintains its own vehicle, management will have to develop usage policies covering who can use it, under what circumstances, and how the operating expenses are to be paid. In the absence of clearly defined policies, the vehicle will probably be misused, and the operator will find herself paying employees for gas that has been used in their own automobiles.

Parking. Parking of guests' automobiles has become a major consideration for many foodservice operators, and any such expenses should be charged to this account. This would include parking-lot rental, garage costs, and so forth. Restaurants will sometimes make arrangements with a commercial parking facility to obtain a specific rate for restaurant patrons who will then turn their ticket in for reimbursement when paying their restaurant bill. These expenses would be charged to the parking account as well. Management will have to control this since there is an opportunity for fraud. The parking lot attendant, working in collusion with the restaurant cashier, could provide unused tickets to the cashier, and they would split the money that had supposedly been paid back to guests. Management can control this by having a standard as to how many guests are normally expected to use the parking facility and monitoring the usage and paid-outs. They could also require the guest to sign or initial the tickets or require the cashier to attach the ticket to the specific guest checks. None of these would make it impossible for fraud to take place, but such practices would probably make any fraud attempts more trouble than they were worth.

Banquet Expense. The *Uniform System of Accounts* includes those expenses incurred in connection with banquet and catering services that cannot properly be included with other expense groups. An example would be chair, table, or equipment rental. Operations will sometimes have to rent equipment of this type to accommodate large groups. The reasoning is that such functions occur infrequently enough that they would not be justified in purchasing and maintaining large numbers of chairs. Another example would be expensive audio-visual equipment. Unlike banquet expenses discussed earlier, these expenses are not normally charged back to the guests.

Music and Entertainment. On the average, this is not a high expense category for food and beverage establishments. Industry statistics show that restaurants range from about .5 percent up to 1.5 percent, and that the average is under 1 percent. In the *Uniform System of Accounts*, this expense is listed as a controllable expense. It is not controllable in the sense that food, beverage, or supplies are controllable, but it is controllable in that management signs

contracts with individuals or groups, and so they have complete control over how much they will or will not pay. If, for example, the budget limit for entertainment is $500.00 per week, then management will not sign a contract for $750.00 per week. They thus do have control over how much is spent. Once the contract is signed, however, they do not have any control. Food costs can be reduced on a continuing basis, so can beverage costs, and so can payroll costs; even energy expenditures can be controlled on a day-to-day basis. Music and entertainment expenses cannot. They are controllable from a planning standpoint but not from an operating one.

The types of expenses that will be included in this category are orchestras, musicians, professional entertainers, mechanical music, piped-in music, piano rental and tuning, films, records, sheet music, royalties to ASCAP and BMI, booking agents' fees, and meals served to musicians and entertainers.

Advertising and Sales Promotion. Sales promotion covers a lot of items. Included would be table tents, special menus, signs, brochures, matches, cocktail napkins, stationery, postcards, coupons, foods and beverages given away for promotional purposes, sugar packets, ashtrays, and any other items imprinted with the company logo.

On the average, restaurants spend a fair amount of money for advertising and sales promotion; and the successful ones probably spend quite a bit. The industry average is nearly 3 percent, but the reported range goes from less than 2 percent to nearly 5 percent.

One problem with attempting to control promotion and advertising items is that there are many sources of supply, and this complicates procurement. It also means that each expense tends to be regarded individually as minor and unimportant. Distribution is also a major problem. These items are small and numerous, and you can easily lose track of them. The fact that they are often stored loose and are available to many employees does not make control any easier.

Items with an organizational logo can pose a particular problem, for guests will take them as souvenirs. This can often be the intention of management, but it surely is not their intention to have each guest take three or four of an item.

Menus can be lost in this way as well, increasing an already significant expense. One effective technique used to protect menus is to print disposable menus for distribution to patrons. These are generally done in a miniaturized format, and the guests are encouraged to take them. This is very definitely a promotional type of expense; even when the regular menus are not charged to this account, these types of menus should be. Some operations print up such menus without any prices on them. This gives them a lot of flexibility in menu revision for management can change prices without having the menus reprinted, which is important because the menu pricing structure will change more frequently than the overall menu format.

Many people in the business feel that much of these types of promotional expenditures are wasted: one survey showed that up to 70 percent was wasted. The key to promotion is that such expense must be carefully budgeted, and there should be specific goals and objectives as to what is to be accomplished. This point was clearly brought out in the discussion on expense forecasting (Chapter 1). This is not often done, however, and these expenses are mostly incurred without any regard for what they are supposed to accomplish and how the effect is supposed to be measured. The important aspect of having objectives is that they be measurable. If they are not, the operator cannot determine whether the promotion worked or not.

Consider a manager who decided to spend $500.00 on a Mother's Day promotion. Without any measurable objectives, a sales increase of $200.00, $400.00, or $800.00 could not be evaluated. It would be meaningless unless there were some figure to compare it to. If the objective had been to spend $500.00 to increase the sales at least $500.00 over the previous year and to bring one hundred new customers into the establishment, management could easily determine whether the promotion had worked or not. Promotional spending would certainly be

done more carefully if such a procedure were followed.

Promotional items must be carefully distributed if there is to be any control over them. It is recommended to have a distribution center and to identify the individuals responsible for distribution. Establish a policy on how these types of materials are to be handled. Most important of all, assure that the customers who are getting them are those for whom they were intended. Promotions are, or should be, directed to specific markets, and they are wasted when the wrong individuals get them. If you had developed a quiche Lorraine luncheon plate, you would not be advised to put the table tents in your banquet room when you are serving the road crew from Massey-Ferguson! Few operators would miss their market to this extent, but they do frequently dilute a promotional effort by not assuring that it is entirely directed to the right market.

Utilities. The types of expenses charged to this account are electricity, electric bulbs, fuel, water, ice and refrigeration supplies, waste removal, and engineering supplies. On the average, the industry spends nearly 3 percent of its sales dollar on such expenses.

We have already discussed some ways to reduce energy consumption in the kitchens, and there are several other things to watch for as well. Leaking water faucets and toilets can waste huge amounts of water in addition to causing expensive damage to the plumbing. Many communities have very hard water, and cleaning with hard water increases the use of water and chemicals. Hard water can cause other problems too. The dish machine will have to be delimed much more frequently; water pipes can become clogged resulting in costly plumbing bills; and any steam-operated equipment can develop serious problems in a very short time. In these situations, a water-softening system can pay for itself quickly.

Insulation can dramatically reduce heat loss. Steam and hot water pipes should be insulated as should as much of the other equipment as possible. Pots should be kept closed since much less energy is required to heat covered pots, *bain maries*, kettles, and so forth than if they were uncovered. As pointed out, this provides a secondary bonus in the kitchen: less energy is required to remove the added heat and moisture. Automatic timers and thermostats can also reduce energy expenditures for heating and lighting as well as for kitchen operation.

Administrative and General. The *Uniform System of Accounts* lists these types of costs under "administrative and general":

Office stationery, printing, and supplies

Postage

Telephone and telegraph

Management fees

Executive office expenses

Data processing costs

Directors' or trustees' fees

Dues and subscriptions

Traveling expenses

Insurance—general

Fees to credit organizations

Collection fees

Provision for doubtful accounts

Cash shortages

Claims and damages paid

Professional fees

Protective services

Bank deposit pickup services

Royalties

Franchise fees

Sales taxes

Personnel expenses, help-wanted ads, and so forth

The average expense here is about 6 percent, with a range of from 4.5 to about 8 percent. Many of these are not very controllable by operating management, though inept or poor management can result in excessive expenses as far as these categories are concerned. In that case,

however, there would be much more serious waste in the areas of food, beverage, and labor utilization. These items would account for only a fraction of the total cost overruns.

When we say they are not very controllable, we mean that there is not much money for management to save here. It would not be a productive use of management time to spend too much of it in trying to control such expenses. There are some categories that will respond to a good control program, and we will look at those.

The first three items listed are definitely in the controllable category. Management should pay close attention to office stationery and supplies, postage, and telephone expenses. Telephone expenses in particular can really mount up without close attention. The biggest problem with all of these is that of personal use by employees.

There should be a telephone log, especially for long-distance calls, so management can see who is calling whom, and for what reason. Telephone locks can be a deterrent to unauthorized use, particularly in the evening after office hours. The kitchen and dining-room phones should be specified as incoming only. In other words, these phones will accept calls, but no one can make a call out on them. Some operations will install pay phones for the employees, which keeps the company lines free for business and even provides a little income for the establishment. Employees should be discouraged from accepting or making routine personal calls. We are not, of course, referring to emergency calls. These, by definition, occur infrequently and should not cause any problems.

Control of stationery and postage can generally be done by management knowing exactly what the usage and expenses are. When they seem to be getting out of line, management should find out why. As we pointed out, there is no sense in management spending a lot of time on this or in assembling reams of statistics, but they should pay attention to it nonetheless and know what "normal" costs should be.

Cash shortages is another account that should be given attention. It is not only an expense but could also be an indication of a much more serious problem, that of fraudulent cash handling. Cash overages, while less common than shortages, do sometimes occur and could be credited to this account or listed on the income statement as "other income."

Other than these, the administrative and general expenses are mostly a function of the type of operation and the company operating policies. Management should monitor them and be aware of how much they are spending, but the returns for investment of management time here are slim.

Repairs and Maintenance. These expenses are highly controllable by management. They include the following:

Painting and decorating

Repairs to:

    dishwashing and sanitation equipment

    kitchen equipment

    office equipment

    refrigeration

    air conditioning

    plumbing and heating

    dining room furniture

    electrical equipment and appliances

    elevators and lifts including dumbwaiters

    floors and floor coverings

    buildings

    gardening and grounds

    parking lots

Building alterations not in the nature of an improvement

Plastering

Upholstering

Mending curtains, draperies, hangings

Maintenance contracts

Industry statistics show an average expenditure of around 2 percent, with most segments reporting either slightly above or slightly below that figure. There appears to be a narrower range here than with the other expense categories.

People have a tendency to neglect things that are not their own; they will also misuse them, even abuse them. As an example of this, we will use microwave-oven door standards. The usage standards on noncommercial (home) models is based on X number of openings and closings by a user who is also an owner. The commercial standards are based on usage by a nonowner and they are different. Manufacturers consider the distinction between owner-users and nonowner-users to be an important one, and the projected durability of their equipment is based on it.

Repairs often receive inadequate attention; corrections are done quickly and often prove to be temporary. We recall the maintenance man of a small restaurant chain who had the reputation among the managers of being able to fix anything, absolutely anything—for about a week! What a great example of planned obsolescence! This individual guaranteed himself a job forever. Expert repairs and quality work will actually lower overall costs.

Control comes from information that allows management to anticipate problems, plan for their correction, and, finally, follow through and do it. A strong employee-training program is also essential for control. When the machines and equipment are being abused, you are always playing "catch up." You are the reactive manager we referred to in the first chapter, a firefighter, a crisis manager.

Keep an inventory of all equipment and maintain inspection records. These should describe weaknesses and the corrections that will have to be made. A maintenance requisition system should be used that provides for management review and approval of all repairs and maintenance. These expenses can, and must, be planned, scheduled, and controlled, just as the other expenses have to be.

12 Cash Control and Security

Protection of the cash generated by a foodservice operation is an important part of the total control system. As in the case of food and beverage control, information is essential. Knowledge of how much cash should have been accumulated, when, where, and by whom is basic to an effective cash control system. When such information is available, management can fix responsibility and establish accountability. Employees who are truly accountable and upon whom responsibility can be fixed are not high-risk employees.

When knowledge of how much cash *should* have been taken in is not known, it is likely that cash will be missing. When cash losses, even if recognized, cannot be placed as to time and/or location, it is likely that cash will be missing. When cash losses cannot be traced to specific individuals, it is likely that cash will be missing.

Security is concerned with protecting all the assets of an establishment. Cash would be one of these, along with the food and (especially) beverage inventories, supply and other inventories, property, and equipment. Security is partially controlled by having the type of information just discussed available, but it goes well beyond that. Control of access is probably the most important aspect of security management. We will discuss specific cash control techniques first and then discuss the policies and procedures to be followed in establishing security.

Sales and Cash Control

Bunching Checks

Cashiers often like to accumulate and/or bunch several checks together and ring the transaction all at once. This makes it difficult to audit the tapes at a later time and increases the possiblity of an error. It also enables a cashier, particularly in the bar, to slip other checks onto a guest's bill; checks that may already have been paid or checks for drinks that may have been "given away." The recommended procedure is to ring all checks separately.

Use Consecutively Numbered Checks

Any guest checks—whether used in the bar or in any of the dining rooms, coffee shops, for room service, and so forth—must be consecutively numbered. There is one exception to this rule: some computerized point-of-sale registers have the capability of performing check-numbering operations. In these cases, management can save money on guest-check purchases and still have guest-check control. The purpose of numbered checks is to fix responsibility upon specific individuals for product disbursement and cash collection. In the absence of numbered checks, it is quite easy for employees to sell food and beverages, collect the money, and destroy the check. Control of guest checks was covered in detail in the food control section.

Audit Guest Checks Regularly

Someone should examine the checks on a regular basis. Correct prices are an obvious thing to look for, as are tax rates, tips, and whether register ringing policies are being followed or not. As with any control, follow-up is the key. When errors are discovered, the individual(s) must be held accountable. This is done by discussing the error, attempting to determine how it happened, and establishing procedures to assure it will not occur again. The two most important things such a process does is to make the employees aware (1) that management knows what is going on and (2) that the organization's policies and procedures are important and must be followed. Lack of control is often a result of employees not taking the organizational directives seriously.

Place Cash Registers in a Highly Visible Location

This would seem to be self-evident, but if observations of many diverse foodservice operations are taken into account, it must not be. Cash registers are sometimes very poorly located. The location should not only be visible, but it should also be well lighted.

Separate Cash Drawers

When two or more persons are working out of one cash drawer, it becomes nearly impossible to fix cash responsibility. Assigning separate register keys to each person will not be effective if they both have the same drawer. Some registers have multiple drawers. This is more effective, but it is still possible for one person to use more than one drawer. In that case, a shortage would appear to be the responsibility of one particular individual, but there would be an element of reasonable doubt. Use of separate registers is recommended, but this is not always possible. This is more of a problem in the lounge (several bartenders) than in the dining room, where there is generally only one cashier.

Spot Cash Checks

Do this randomly by preparing a cash drawer with a starting "bank." This is taken to the cash station and exchanged with the drawer being used. A register "reading" is taken at this time. This reading shows the cash that should have been collected and it is compared to the cash actually in the drawer (after deducting the starting bank). Overages are what management is really interested in, not shortages. An accumulation of cash significantly in excess of what should have been collected is fairly conclusive evidence that the establishment and/or the customers have been cheated. Cash shortages could indicate sloppy cash handling or that excess cash *had* been accumulated, but too much had been removed. Probably the least likely expectation would be that the cash would be exactly what it should to the penny. This is generally an indication that the cash has been tampered with, for most people can be expected to make some errors. This later statement would be especially true in a bar, cafeteria, or high-turnover foodservice operation. In a high-check-average, slow-turnover restaurant, however, the cash may reasonably be expected to balance most of the time.

Drop Cash Regularly

This is a basic procedure that is not followed surprisingly often. The recommended procedure is as follows: establish a deposit amount—say $200.00. When the cashier accumulates $200.00 above the starting bank, she or he would count out the money (using the largest bills in the drawer), place it in an envelope, and make an entry in a cashier's book. This would be to record the number of the deposit envelope and the amount. A manager or supervisor would be called to verify the deposit, seal the envelope, and place it in an inaccessible safe or drop box. The cashier's book would be initialed by both the cashier and the manager or supervisor. The purpose of these procedures is to maintain only those cash amounts necessary for business. This provides a deterrent against cashiers accumulating cash in excess of the checks paid, for much of it would end up being deposited. It also offers protection in the event of a robbery. The thief could obtain only the amount currently in the cash drawer, probably only a small fraction of the total cash receipts.

It is important to place the drop envelopes in a safe or box not accessible by unit personnel, including management. This protects not only the cash, but the establishment personnel, none of whom can be placed in the position of being forced to open the safe. The most common way this is done is to contract a cash pickup service. These companies will place a safe in your operation that requires two keys for opening. One key will be given to management, while the other will be carried by the collection personnel. These people will typically arrive in an armored vehicle and will be armed. They will not count the money; they merely sign for a certain number of envelopes, said to contain X number of dollars. The money will be counted when received by the collection service, Brinks, for example. Any discrepancies will be reported to the operation. Such variances are uncommon since two people have counted the envelopes in the unit.

An actual example will illustrate the necessity for such procedures. A consultant, in evaluating a client's restaurant, found that they made no drops at all. They did not even change drawers when changing cashier shifts. On a typical Friday and Saturday, when the unit closed at about midnight, there would usually be over $2,000.00 on hand at the cashier station. At that time, the restaurant would be staffed by three or four high-school-age employees under the direction of an

assistant manager. It would, in other words, be an attractive candidate for a robbery. It might also be mentioned that the unit was located in a city where armed robberies were hardly an unusual occurrence. The owner's attitude was that it was a waste of money to have such a service. He saw nothing wrong with leaving all the day's receipts at the cash station, holding it in a safe overnight that was accessible by the store management, and then hand carrying the deposit to the bank the next day (or, as frequently happened, every two or three days).

Use of Cash Banks

Start each shift with a fresh bank. The purpose of this is to make each cash-handling individual accountable for his or her own cash. Each cashier should count the bank and sign for it when beginning a shift. When the deposit is made, the bank will be returned, verified by management, and the employee will sign it back in. Sometimes cash handlers are required to provide their own banks. Although this reduces the cash needs, it is generally not recommended. One problem is that employees would be expected to come and go with fairly large amounts of cash. This would naturally make a lot of managers nervous. Another problem is that management has no control over the bank amount or the paper and silver money denominations. The purpose of a bank is to assure that all normal transactions can be handled, right from opening. The best way to do this is for management to determine how much money is needed and what denominations are required, and then to issue it.

Review Overages and Shortages

Management should make it a point to discuss all significant overages and shortages with individual cashiers each time they occur. We cannot define the value of *significant* here; it would vary according to the circumstances, but each operator must establish reasonable expectations of accuracy for the cashiers. It is likely that there would be different accuracy standards for various cash stations. For example, a dinner cashier would probably be expected to be more accurate than would a luncheon cashier who may handle more checks for smaller amounts and in a much shorter period of time. Aside from one-on-one meetings, this is a legitimate subject for cashiers' meetings and training sessions.

Register Tapes

Make sure registers have sufficient tape on hand at the beginning of each shift. If a register were to run out of tape, some or nearly all of the individual transactions would be lost. The totals would not be; they could be recovered when making a final reading (assuming a new tape had been provided), but losing the separate transactions could be a serious problem. At the very least, it would make it easier for unscrupulous employees to defraud the establishment.

Change Handling

When needed, change should be brought to the cashier, not the reverse. Aside from the potential operating and control problems arising from leaving the cash station unattended, it is a bad policy to allow cash-handling personnel access to the safe or other change supply.

Do Not Make Assumptions as to Honesty

More specifically, don't make assumptions about the legitimacy of cash transactions. The point here is not to assume anything is either wrong or right but rather to check all cash transactions completely—constantly. Many managers waste a lot of their own time and do their employees a disservice by trying to figure out who is likely to cheat them or who is cheating them. A good control system will not make theft impossible, but it will quickly reveal that it has occurred and probably who was involved as well.

Audit Register Tapes

This should be a regular procedure, just as you would have someone check all food and beverage invoices for price errors and extension mistakes. Some of the things to look for are:

Continuity of Transaction Numbers. Each time the register is used to record a sale, collection, or even just to open the drawer to make change, it will be recorded on the tape. This will take the form of a transaction number, and each time the register is used, the number will advance. This can be used to show whether the machine had been cleared prior to closing. When the operation actually closed, the register would be cleared again, and any income after that period could be kept by the cashier. If this were to happen, however, the transaction number sequence would show a gap. The starting number for day two would not correspond with the ending number from day one. If your register has this capability, be sure to train your office personnel to check for continuity *daily*.

Overages and Shortages. Whenever significant overages and shortages occur, review the tapes for any transactions that appear out of the ordinary. Included would be prices, foods, drinks, ringing patterns, time of sales, and so forth.

Blank Spots on Tape. This indicates some sort of nontypical activity and should be questioned. If the register is operating properly and is used correctly, such blanks will not occur.

Number of No-Sale Transactions. Cash personnel have to open the register for no-sale reasons from time to time, but management should have an idea as to how many times per shift is reasonable. *Any* time the standard is exceeded, the personnel involved should be questioned and asked to justify the variance. We are not suggesting that they should be accused of doing anything wrong, but management has the right, the *duty* in fact, to look into variances, especially when they occur in cash-handling situations.

Post Prices

Posting prices, especially when they can be seen by the customers, can be a deterrent to overcharging. When the guests are totally unaware of what they should be paying, it is relatively easy for cashiers and service personnel to cheat them. This is more likely to happen in the bar than in the dining room where it is standard practice to use a menu. Even in the dining room, however, many establishments will have their service personnel recite a list of "specials" that do not appear on the menu. Prices are often not quoted, or, if they are, the guest typically finds it impossible to remember them. Under these circumstances, the servers could charge (within reason) nearly anything they wanted. If they collected more than what was expected, they could keep the difference.

Use ID Marks on Guest Checks

Randomly place an identification mark on the checks. This is a bar control gimmick and is combined with a promotion. The promotion is that any guest getting a check with one of the special marks on it (a star or some such symbol) gets a free drink or a discount. The control is that the guests will begin to pay a lot more attention to their checks than they formerly had. Some unethical bartender or waitress activities obviously would not stand up under such scrutiny.

Use Machines for Check Calculations

Nonregister additions must be performed on a machine with a tape. It is preferred that personnel not make any calculations, but unless the right type of point-of-service equipment (POS) is available, they will have to make some. In such cases, the operation should provide a good calculator with a tape and require that a tape be attached to all such checks.

Close Cash Drawers

The cash drawer must be closed between all transactions. The reason for this has been discussed in detail in the section on bar personnel frauds.

Missing Check Policy

Personnel must be held accountable for missing checks. As explained previously, it is not recommended to hold employees fiscally responsible, that is, to charge for missing checks. They must nonetheless be responsible for all checks issued to them and be held *accountable* for any missing ones. This means they would have to participate in an investigation as to what occurred and who was at fault. It also means that repeated mistakes will result in dismissal.

Recording Wrong Selling Prices

If a cash-handling person can ring amounts lower than those actually collected, the difference is theirs. Checks should be examined to assure that proper prices are being charged. This is easier to do in the dining room than in the bar for two reasons. One is that there are probably many more transactions in the bar. The other is that food orders are generally written on the checks while bar orders often are not.

Reading Registers

Do not allow cashiers to read registers. A register should be "read" only by management or a member of the office or accounting staff. One of the purposes of reading a register is to determine how much cash *should* have been collected. This figure is then compared to the deposit. It is an obvious violation of control to allow cashiers to have this information. For the same reason, it is recommended not to reset registers to zero at the end of each day. When this is done, it is easier to calculate how much cash should be deposited. Even then, however, the cashier would have to be able to take a reading. In the one instance, we refer to the necessity for denying cashiers the reading information. In the other, we refer to the fact that were this information available, it would be more meaningful if the day had opened with the register at zero. The recommended closing procedures are as follows: cash personnel should remove sufficient cash and in the proper denominations to make up their bank at the end of each shift. They then should prepare all additional monies for deposit. If the $200.00 drop system described earlier is used, there would not be much cash accumulated, and this final deposit would be simple and should proceed quickly with minimum error. The final deposit would be handled just as earlier ones were. The money would be placed in envelopes, recorded in a cashier's deposit book, initialed by the cashier, coinitialed by the manager or supervisor, and dropped in a suitable safe.

Customer Frauds

Beware of customer frauds with cash collection. The most common source of fraud would be the employees, but the guests can and will cheat the establishment. The severity of the problem seems to depend upon the location, and some places can be expected to have more problems than others. It can also be a more general problem during recessionary periods. Here are some things to look for.

Guest Walks Out Without Paying. Unfortunately, when this happens, some service person or the cashier is suspected of dishonest activity. This is a greater problem with the more expensive operations. Inexpensive restaurants often collect before the guest eats (fast food establishments and some cafeterias), or they put the guest into a closed dining environment, the only exit from which is the cashier station (cafeterias, coffee shops). Another advantage inexpensive restaurants have is that they are inexpensive! Expensive, elegant restaurants are more attractive targets, and it is easier to just get up and walk out. If the customer were to be stopped or challenged, there are any number of explanations that could be used. The best control is probably a well-trained and vigilant service staff, but proper design of the facilities can also be helpful.

Guest Consumes Food or Beverage and Then Claims Something Was Wrong. The foodservice operator would probably like to respond "it took the *entire* steak to determine that it was no good?" This may not be the recommended procedure, however. Like a walkout, this is often an easy thing to pull off, since most foodservice operators are eager to satisfy their guests and will go to great lengths to assure that satisfaction. This is difficult, if not impossible, to control against, *the first time.* It is not difficult to control when someone continually asks for a credit due to poor quality.

Guest Says Something Was in the Food or Beverage and Refuses to Pay. There are certain stories that make the rounds among foodservice people. One is about the lady who kept a supply of deceased insects in her purse. Following her meal, she would produce one or more of them and artfully arrange it (them) on her plate. When management was confronted with such graphic evidence of poor—perhaps even criminal—housekeeping, they could be expected to cave in completely. Like all stories, it probably has some element of truth in it. Certainly it is possible. The restaurateur is very vulnerable to such tactics, and, as yet, we have developed no foolproof methods of identifying "previously used" flies!

Deposit All Receipts Intact

Depositing all cash receipts intact on a daily basis is or should be standard accounting procedure. Whenever an operation allows cash receipts to be taken from the drawer and used for a variety of purposes, there is real potential for misuse. The most common violation of this principle is in the use of daily cash receipts for petty cash purposes.

Another, often unavoidable, cash demand occurs when all deliveries are on a COD basis. This is usually a result of a poor credit rating; the suppliers feel that the only way they can be assured of payment is to collect on delivery. This puts large and inconsistent cash demands on the operation and makes cash control extremely difficult. For one thing, large sums of cash must be held in the operation at all times. Sometimes these sums will exceed the average daily cash receipts, especially when there are appreciable amounts of charge sales. This means that the unit will have to hold receipts from two or more days. It would obviously make it impossible to use the drop system described earlier, and the problem of cash security could become a serious one. The best and safest thing to do with your cash is to drop it in an inaccessible safe and deposit it, intact, the next day with an armored pickup service.

Petty Cash Policies

Make paid-outs from a petty cash fund. All cash needs should be handled out of a petty cash fund. This permanently removes cash from the system, much as cashiers' banks do but, as pointed out above, is the lesser of two evils. For this reason, the petty cash fund should not be any larger than necessary. All disbursements from the petty cash fund should be approved by management personally and in advance. When someone requires foods or supplies, she should submit a cash request to the management. This request should be on a standard form, which should have the date, estimated amount needed, and reason for the request. The request should be signed by a supervisor. Foods and supplies are the most common materials needed on an emergency basis. Alcoholic beverages could also be needed, but it is usually illegal for a bar or restaurant to purchase them from nonapproved sources. All disbursements must be replaced by a receipt or legal proof of payment. At all times, the total of the cash on hand and the receipts should equal the original petty cash fund. When the fund needs replenishing, a check should be drawn against the organization's bank account for the amount needed. As with any other payments, there should be something tangible to support the expense. In the case of normal food, beverage, and supplies payments, there are invoices. In the case of petty cash reimbursement requests, they must be supported by the cash receipts. As with other payments, they must be charged to the appropriate income statement account.

Make All Other Payments by Check

Except for petty cash, all expenses should be paid for by check, and checks should be written only after the payment is authorized by management. Petty cash payments should be kept to a minimum. Often when there are large petty cash demands, there is no cash control. Payment by check also assures better expense records.

Compare Cash Receipts with Bank Deposits

Management should continuously monitor the cash deposits to assure that they equal the amounts supposedly taken in by the operation. This is one reason why it is recommended to deposit cash receipts intact. When the cash drawers are used to support daily cash needs, it becomes quite difficult to compare receipts with deposits.

Voids, Bad Debts, and Sales Allowances

Bad debts, sales allowances, voids, and so forth must be personally approved by management. *All* instances that result in cash not being collected from a register transaction *must* be personally approved by management. These should be accompanied by a form that shows the date, time, department, amount, and reason for noncollection. It should be signed by an authorized person.

Bond Cash-Handling Employees

This is an additional operating expense, but to avoid it on the grounds that it is too expensive is foolish. There is one circumstance in which the expense would become prohibitive; that is when there is such a high turnover in cash-handling employees that you are continually bonding new people. The high bonding expense would be only one of several problems arising from such a circumstance, however, and it is best to avoid such a situation entirely.

Mail Handling

Have mail opened by someone other than a cashier or bookkeeper. This is to protect checks and/or cash sent through the mail. It is simply another application of the separation-of-functions concept. Whoever opens the mail should have a method of recording all payments received prior to turning the materials over to the bookkeeper or accounting office.

Separate the Cashiers and Bookkeepers

Again, this is an example of separation of functions. Any person who handles both these functions could easily skim considerable sums of cash with minimum risk of exposure.

Pay All Employees by Bank Check

Making cash payments to employees for wages is a poor practice, from both a cash control as well as an accounting standpoint. It would require considerable sums of cash to be accumulated, and the payroll records would probably be unsatisfactory as well. It is also recommended that you distribute the paychecks yourself, at least periodically. You may find that checks are being made out to nonexistent persons. Another possibility is that they are excessive, and some sort of kickback arrangement has been made. It is possible for supervisors or management to hire persons on the condition that any wage overpayment will be returned to that supervisor. This individual will then authorize a higher-than-normal wage scale or overtime that was never actually worked.

Change Safe Combinations

Do this periodically. It is not an inexpensive thing to do but is necessary for cash protection. It must, of course, be done whenever someone with the combination leaves the organization. This refers to management as well as office employees. It should not generally be necessary when management is reassigned within the corporation, but some companies may want to do it then as well.

Security

The recommended procedures and policies for establishing and maintaining the security of an operation's assets are described in detail below.

Only One Exit

There should be one authorized entry and exit point for all employees. This may be the same as the guests use, but it should *never* be a door at a receiving area. If employees are allowed to come and go via the back door in the kitchen, it will be impossible to keep it locked and secured. Ordinarily, the only time this door should be opened is when deliveries are being made or when trash is being removed from the operation. A variety of problems could arise from not having such a policy; one is security. Employees could find it much easier to remove food, beverages, and supplies from the establishment if they could go out the back door. When they are required to enter and exit via the guest entrance, it is more difficult to remove materials. There is also a potential sanitation problem in allowing the back door to be unlocked and probably open much of the time. Flies, rodents, and other undesirable creatures—including two-legged ones—will have ready access to your operation. Some managers do not want their employees coming or leaving through the front of the house. One was quoted as saying, "I cannot afford to let my customers see my employees. They will not eat here any more!" If this excuse is a valid one for an operation, and it may well be, then that operation has more serious problems than a violation of security procedures!

Package Policy

There should be a policy whereby management has the right to inspect any packages brought in or removed from the restaurant. As with any policy that has an irritant potential, this one should be made very clear during the hiring and orientation periods. In other words, if an employee's package were ever inspected, it should not be a surprise. Employees would be fully aware that this is normal operating procedure. When this policy is enforced, it must be done fairly. It would be a serious mistake to examine the packages of only certain employees because it would tend to be discriminatory, showing those employees that they are not trusted. This practice also puts management in the position of making a judgment as to each employee's honesty. As pointed out, the best attitude for management to take regarding honesty is to neither trust nor distrust employees. It is management's responsibility to establish and maintain an adequate control system so that such judgments are not necessary.

Another recommended procedure is to have a

package storage area. Any packages that are brought to work must be stored in some place management has designated. This could be the cashier stand, the office, or behind the front desk in a smaller hotel. When either of these policies is instituted, it *must* be enforced. There is no sense in having a package inspection policy if no one ever checks the packages. There is no point in a package storage policy if employees are allowed to bring in packages and take them to their lockers or work stations. In fact, in both cases, nonenforcement of the policy will cause more harm than if there were no policy at all because employees would tend to disregard all policies.

Employee Parking Policies

Specify employee parking areas as a matter of policy. Deciding where employees ought to park is always a difficult problem. There are two areas where they should *not* park. One is near the rear entrance. Regardless of whether they are allowed to come and go through the kitchen door, security problems arise in allowing employees to park their cars by the back door. It is simply too easy to store illegally removed materials. The other area they should not use is the prime parking area in the front of the establishment. These should be reserved for the guests. Management often makes a mistake here by parking themselves right in front but forbidding the employees to do so. If management really wants the employees to believe that the customers are important, they should not take up these valuable spaces themselves. The best parking places for the employees are those that are neither by the kitchen door nor by the front entrance. The fact that they have to walk a few extra steps should not cause significant problems.

One real problem that may arise, however, is when employees, especially female employees, have to walk a considerable distance in a dark and potentially dangerous area to get to their cars at night due to parking policy. Management will have to deal with this, for they may have a legal responsibility to insure the safety of their employees. In the absence of legal responsibility, they certainly have a moral commitment to protect their employees.

Discarding Materials for Later Retrieval

Employees can throw articles out of windows (onto a roof, for example) and get them after leaving work. This would be especially easy for employees leaving after dark. Management should patrol and inspect the premises, particularly after dark. Wherever the physical design of the facilities permits this to happen, managers should be especially vigilant.

Hiding Items in Garbage for Later Pickup

This is an old trick but still a useful way to get stolen articles out of the operation. For sanitary reasons, nonfoods lend themselves best to this practice, but the procedure is not limited to them. Control is obtained by spot checking the garbage area and by assuring that garbage removal occurs at specified times, is done by particular employees, and is *supervised*.

Locker Room Security

Here management is as interested—perhaps more so—in protecting the employees' property as in securing their own. A work crew that is constantly having personal articles stolen, with management seemingly helpless or unwilling to do anything about it, will not be a happy crew, and an unhappy group of employees will seldom be very productive. Here are some things that can be done to make the locker room more secure.

Bright Lighting. The better the lighting is, the less inclined dishonest employees will be to steal.

Discourage Keeping Valuables in Personal Lockers. There would ordinarily be no reason for employees to have to store valuable items in their lockers, but when these occasions do arise, management should let it be known that they would rather the items be stored in the office safe during the shift.

Have Random Locker Checks. When the employees are hired, they should be made aware of a locker inspection policy. This policy should provide for unannounced, randomly scheduled, inspections of all employee lockers. The most efficient way to do this is for management to provide the locks. This way they have keys to all lockers. The employees should not be allowed to have their own locks on their lockers. The often high turnover in our industry can cause security problems with this policy, however: An employee could conceivably be assigned to a locker that had belonged to four different employees during the previous five months. To avoid this problem, management should have a greater supply of locks than lockers and should periodically change locks, especially when an employee leaves. It should not be necessary to throw away the locks; merely put them on "leave" for a time.

Key Control

This topic was covered in both the food and beverage control sections, and we will only reiterate here the necessity to assure *maximum* control over all keys at all times. Keys in restaurants appear to have amazing reproductive abilities, rivaling even rabbits and minks.

Bar Liquor

Many operations do not take sufficient measures when they lock the bar because the stock is left open. When there are night cleaning personnel or a cleaning service is hired, liquor left on open shelves is a clearly worded invitation to disaster. Even in the absence of evening workers, all the liquor should be secured when the operation closes, if for no other reason than that there will be other employees on the job the next day and probably long before either management or the bar personnel arrive for work.

Burglar Alarm

There are many types of burglar alarms available. Some are sensitive enough to react to the mere movement of people prowling around after closing hours. Other alarm systems can be attached to all entry areas, including windows. Some systems can secure the perimeter of the establishment. Most security experts strongly urge restaurateurs, particularly those in urban areas, to invest in some sort of alarm system. This is unfortunate, but it appears to be wise advice.

Closed Circuit Television

The use of a VTR (videotape recorder) as a beverage control device was discussed in the bar control section, and it has other uses as well. Other cash-handling stations would be good areas to monitor, as would the back door and, perhaps, the locker rooms. It is likely that such surveillance systems will increase in popularity during the 1980s.

Use of a "Shopping" or "Spotter" Service

These are services offered by specialized consultants. They will visit your establishment as guests, unknown to your employees, and will order a variety of foods and beverages, offer opportunities for employees to cheat them or the house, and give management a written report. This report can be expected to cover cash-handling procedures, quality of products, guest impression of cleanliness and housekeeping, employees' attitudes, quality of service, and so forth. In a way, it should be a management dream come true: a complete report of what the guest's experience is, bad and good, and for their eyes only. If it is bad news, the work is not spread about like a brushfire.

Proper Closing Procedures

Assure the unit is properly closed. A closing checklist is useful, helpful, and highly recommended. An example is shown in Exhibit 12.1. Probably the most important things to assure when closing are that no one is left in the operation, that all exits are secured, and that all storage areas and offices are locked.

Check Windows and Doors

Periodically check all windows and doors to assure that they are in good working order.

Employees may tamper with them in order to ease after-hours entry.

Patrol the Operation

The entire operation, both inside and outside, must be checked on a regular basis. A good manager will take walks around the unit from time to time, at least once daily, to look at where the employees' cars are parked, examine the garbage area, and look for items or articles that may have been thrown out of the unit for later pickup. The manager will test the windows and exits to assure that they are secure and in good working order and check the exterior lighting system. In other words, there is no use securing the interior of an establishment without securing the exterior.

Exhibit 12.1. Closing Checklist

Kitchen
_____ 1. Is the garbage removed from the kitchen?
_____ 2. Is the garbage area outside clean and sanitary?
_____ 3. Have the following areas been secured?
    _____ Meat walk-in
    _____ Vegetable walk-in
    _____ Dairy walk-in
    _____ Walk-in freezer
    _____ Reach-in refrigerators
    _____ Reach-in freezers
    _____ Dry storeroom
    _____ Beverage storeroom
    _____ Soap and chemicals storage
    _____ Supply storage
_____ 4. Kitchen floor swept and mopped?
_____ 5. Employee restrooms clean?
_____ 6. All dishes washed?
_____ 7. Dish machine cleaned?
_____ 8. All foods properly stored, covered, and wrapped in all storage areas?
_____ 9. Kitchen equipment cleaned?
    _____ Slicer
    _____ Range tops
    _____ Steam kettles
    _____ Steam table
    _____ Work tables
    _____ Mixers
    _____ Food choppers or processors
    _____ Carts
    _____ Mobile ovens
    _____ Mobile hot-cold carts
    _____ Grills
_____ 10. Frying fat filtered?
_____ 11. Pots and pans all cleaned, area clean?
_____ 12. Back door locked?
_____ 13. All walls wiped clean?
_____ 14. All reach-in-walk-in exterior surfaces wiped clean?
_____ 15. Walk-in interiors clean?
_____ 16. Reach-in interiors clean?
_____ 17. All temperature gauges checked?

Dining Room

_____ 1. Public restrooms clean?
_____ 2. Side stands restocked with flatware, glassware, china, linen?
_____ 3. All soiled dishes removed?
_____ 4. Tables reset for next meal?

Bar

_____ 1. Glassware all washed?
_____ 2. Trash removed?
_____ 3. Alcoholic beverages all properly secured?
_____ 4. Empty bottles placed on bar for replacing next day?
_____ 5. Daily requisition prepared for next day?
_____ 6. Cash register empty, left open?
_____ 7. Equipment cleaned?
　　　_____ Sinks
　　　_____ Mixers and blenders
　　　_____ Glasswashers
　　　_____ Bar top
　　　_____ Back bar
　　　_____ All work surfaces
　　　_____ Jiggers, spoons, knives, cutting boards, and so on
_____ 8. Refrigerator temperatures okay?
_____ 9. Beer cooler stocked?

Office

_____ 1. Cash deposit(s) made?
_____ 2. Cashier and bartender banks secured?
_____ 3. Safe secured?
_____ 4. All keys secured?
_____ 5. All report materials assembled?
　　　_____ Register tapes (bar and dining room)
　　　_____ Guest checks (bar and dining room)
　　　_____ Register readings (bar and dining room)
　　　_____ Sales counts
　　　_____ Voids record (bar and dining room)

General

_____ 1. All windows and doors secured?
_____ 2. Alarm system activated?
_____ 3. Exterior inspection made?
_____ 4. Interior premises checked to assure that no one remains in the operation?

13 Management Information Systems

We have referred to the use of computers constantly throughout this text, and by now it should be obvious that they can be a very valuable management tool when used properly. The computer revolution everyone has been predicting for some years is in fact upon us. Two factors are of great importance to foodservice operators considering computers. One is the downward spiral of computer prices. They are becoming more and more affordable, and it is now possible to purchase powerful computers for less than $2,000.00. Information processing capability and memory capacity are both increasing at the same time as the prices are dropping. The other factor is the increasing availability of software, which are the programs themselves. A computer without a program is like a cassette deck without any cassette tapes; it does not do anything.

If you attend any of the hotel or foodservice trade shows, you will see an expanding number of companies selling specialized food service control programs: inventory programs, menu planning programs, menu analysis programs, recipe programs, food cost programs, and so

forth. What this all means is that even the smallest foodservice and bar operators can now afford to computerize at least a portion of their information gathering needs, while many units can install complete management systems.

The purpose of this chapter is to familiarize readers with the types of programs generally available today. We will do this by evaluating the applications as they affect the operating functions in a foodservice establishment, such as forecasting, purchasing, receiving, and so forth. We will also describe a system developed by a full-service food distributor. Finally, we will discuss how a foodservice operator should go about evaluating a potential system.

There are two basic types of systems that the restaurateur will be looking at. One we will call the POS system (point of sale), and the other the operating system. The POS systems, at their most basic level, consist of food and/or beverage terminals only. These are used by the service personnel to record items sold. Employees do not ring up prices on checks; instead they punch buttons representing specific menu items. The registers will print the checks with the standard name (or abbreviation) and selling price. Employees do not decide how to identify an item or how much to charge for it. If the production system is set up so that this type of preregistered check is the only authorization for either foods or beverages being produced and released to the servers, a great deal of control has been established. We have discussed the necessity for standard abbreviations to reduce production mistakes and increase production speed, and we discussed the need for standardized pricing. We also said it is necessary for every sale to be recorded prior to production. This equipment performs all these functions. It will also maintain a running record of what is being sold. Management can then obtain accurate sales records, something else that was described as necessary. Although this type of system is quite basic, it is a powerful management tool. It provides both control and information, which is itself necessary for control.

An upgrading of such a system provides for linking the terminals together. When this is done, the information from all the terminals becomes available at one time on one report. Further upgrading provides for remote printers. When the server enters the order, regardless of whether he or she receives a check, the check is printed in the kitchen or the bar. Thus the server does not have to physically deliver the order and has to go to the production area only to pick up a completed order. In the case of a kitchen using the expeditor-runner system, servers would not even have to pick up the order; it would be delivered to them. There are other refinements, but this is the general idea. This type of equipment is generally available from companies that have traditionally offered cash registers and checking machines. Names like NCR, Sweda, and Data Terminal Systems, to name a few, are familiar to foodservice operators.

The other type of management we will consider is the complete operating system. There are three ways to go here. A computer manufacturer will offer a complete package, which is their computer together with the software they have developed. The second is for an independent software company to sell programs modified to run on different computer systems. The third way is for a software manufacturer to write programs designed to run on specific computers, and these are sold with those computers. An example is the HAL system (Hotel and Leisure) sold by Qantel, a well-known computer manufacturer. The entrance of IBM into the personal computer field has opened up the second area. Computer programmers in all fields are writing programs for the IBM PC (personal computer) as fast as they can. It is reasonable to expect that an increasing number of hospitality programs will become available.

What Can Computers Do?

Before we get into how a foodservice operator can evaluate his or her computer needs, we should describe the capabilities of the various systems and programs that are available today. To do this, we will look at each of the operating functions.

Menu Planning

These functions are more useful for institutional operations than for commercial foodservice units. With some institutions, nutrition is of great concern, and there are programs that aid in developing menus which provide the required balance of nutrients. The computer is given the nutritional needs—how much protein, fats, vitamins, minerals, calories, and so forth—and it will develop satisfactory menus. It can be programmed to meet cost constraints as well. There is nothing mysterious about how the computer does this. It has the current costs of all foods used, the nutritional parameters desired, possible menu items, recipes for all those items, and the nutritive values of all ingredients. The menus could be developed just as well without a computer if one had all this information, but it would take much, much longer, with a higher risk of error. This is an important point about computers; they generally do not do anything that management cannot do or provide information that cannot be obtained manually. The problem is that without a computer it is so time consuming that management will not do it.

Forecasting

We will discuss two types of forecasting here. One is the type described in Chapter 1, short-term budgeting. The other is production forecasting. With short-term budgeting, it is necessary to know as much as possible about the sales patterns in each operating department, on the various days of the week, and throughout the four seasons of the year. It is necessary to know this in terms of both dollars and guest counts. The computer makes it feasible to extract this information. Very detailed sales records can be obtained with minimal expenditure of management time.

Production forecasting depends on sales mix information, and even the most basic system will provide this. If you want to know how much stew to prepare for lunch tomorrow, you need to know how much you sold the same day the last three or four weeks and perhaps the same day last year. When sales mix information is available by pushing a button, it will probably be obtained. Otherwise, it has been our experience that it generally is not. Some programs will make the production forecast for you. All that is necessary is to give the day and menu (or menu items), and the computer will prepare the forecast. This would be quite feasible in an operation with standardized menus and consistent demand. It would be less feasible where menus change constantly and guest counts fluctuate widely.

Purchasing

Effective purchasing is achieved by satisfying the five purchasing objectives: to buy the right product at the right time in the right quantities at the right price from the right supplier. Once the right item is determined, the computer can be programmed so that other products cannot be purchased. In other words, the computer can have all the operation's specifications stored in its memory. Quantities can easily be handled by

computers. The operator can use the minimum-maximum concept whereby whenever the inventory falls below a predetermined level, an alert is given (or an order can automatically be prepared). The order volume will depend on the upper stock limit, that is, the maximum amount you wish to carry. Or the concept of par stocks can be used. Here there is no minimum, but when the order is prepared, the current stock level is compared to the par.

With many products, a par stock will not be useful. This is true with products that have a high value and varying sales. Portioned steaks, lobster tails, crab legs, and similar items would be examples. With these types of products, the buyer needs to know how many will be consumed during the period between orders, be it a day or week, and how many are currently in stock. Thus the computer can increase the production forecasting accuracy, and it can provide current inventory levels without physically counting the stock. Even with items where the order tends to be different each time, the computer provides the information required to make the "how much" determination easy and accurate.

What is the right price? An operator would probably want to have a record of what prices have been charged over time by various purveyors as well as a listing of what current price quotations are. We are assuming here that the operation has adequate specifications. Without them, as was made clear in the purchasing section, price quotations mean little. A computer program designed to analyze supplier prices would be worthless without specifications.

Purchase orders can be prepared by computers. Many operations do not use a formal purchase-order system. By this we mean that they do not send their suppliers purchase orders as the legal authorization for an order and delivery. Even in such cases, there should be some sort of purchase notification prepared for the receiving clerk so the delivery can be checked properly. Purchase orders printed by the computer would be perfect for this. They could also be used on an informal basis in communicating with salespeople. It would save a lot of time in dealing with sales representatives if purchase orders were available.

Receiving

The objectives of receiving are to assure that all incoming goods meet the organization's standards, that the proper quantities are delivered, that the prices charged are the same as the ones quoted, and to assure that the foods, beverages, or whatever are adequately stored. Management should want a permanent record of all these procedures, and the computer is fully capable of providing it. When the delivery invoices are entered into the computer, it can automatically compare the amounts and prices to see whether any variances occurred. An ideal system would require only one entry of this sort. From this information, ingredient prices could be updated, which means in turn that all recipes and menus would reflect the current costs. The inventory levels would be adjusted to reflect the just-delivered goods, and this could be done for as many storage areas as management desires.

Many operations will issue some goods when they are received instead of sending them to one of the storage locations. In these cases, management would want to charge the goods directly to production so the costs will be reflected on the current day. The computer can make the necessary allocations.

Inventory

The computer can make the use of a perpetual inventory feasible in most food systems. The reason a perpetual inventory is not recommended for many foodservice operations is that they cannot assure that all issues are recorded. With a computerized system, the sales forecast can result in an issues requisition being prepared. This is a listing of all ingredients needed to prepare the menu items expected to be sold. If these items are deducted from the inventory, we have a perpetual inventory: a list of what is currently available. Of course, this is what is *supposed* to be available, and its accuracy depends upon the kitchen actually using what the recipe calls for. If such a system were used,

and if any variances were promptly discussed with the production personnel, it is likely that they would soon begin using exactly what the recipes called for.

Taking physical inventories can also be made easier with computers. There are programs that will print an inventory form, complete with all current prices, with blank spaces for the current count. If the operation has organized storage areas, the inventory forms will follow the order in which the materials are shelved. All that is necessary after the count is taken is to enter it into the computer. The result will be a print-out with all the price extensions. The inventory value could be used in turn for preparing an operating statement if the computer has such a program. Food and beverage transfers, employee meals, and promotional food would not cause any problems since they could be programmed as part of the cost calculation equation. At least one company offers a hand-held computer that resembles a calculator; the physical inventory is recorded directly into it, and it is later electronically transferred to the main computer system. The advantage of this is that there is no writing to do, and the stock does not have to be in any particular order. One just goes from shelf to shelf, recording whatever happens to be there. The computer will organize it all later. Each entry has to be coded, however, and in the absence of stock numbers written on all the products or on the shelves, looking up the numbers could be tiresome and time consuming.

Most systems can handle multiple inventory locations easily, enabling each location to be treated as a distinct cost center. These locations could be separate storage areas, or they could be different foods stored in the same areas. It would thus be possible to track meats separately from dairy products, for example, or to keep portion-cut steaks separate from roasts.

The transfers we mentioned can also be accommodated. When food is sent to the bar; when wines, spirits, and beers are used in the kitchen; or when food is moved from one kitchen storage area to another, as in a large hotel, each product category or location is updated.

Processing foods can cause difficulties in costing and inventory maintenance. This occurs when one inventory item is transformed to another—for example, when a boneless strip loin is cut into strip steaks. The inventory records show the presence of a loin but no steaks; yet now there is no loin and we have steak. Some programs can track even these changes. You simply schedule strip steaks for production and issue strip loins to the kitchen. The computer takes care of the necessary calculations.

Some operations, especially fast-food units, will use the sales totals to update the inventory. If a hamburger consists of one 4-ounce patty, one bun, one pickle chip, 1 ounce of "special sauce," one tomato slice, and one paper wrapping, each time the cash register records a hamburger sale, the inventory of all the items mentioned is automatically reduced by one. This function is also useful in alcoholic beverage operations.

Many things can happen during food handling that result in product loss. Waste, spoilage, and poor yield are causes of this, as are theft and pilferage. Most systems allow management to make the necessary adjustments for these as needed to keep the inventory totals correct.

Production

The most obvious need here is to forecast the production requirements. In other words, what should be made and in what quantities? We have already discussed how a computer can furnish this information. It can provide management the information as well as print out production schedules for the kitchen. Computers can also print the recipes needed and in the desired amounts. They can provide the actual requisitions needed to remove materials from storage. Even if a formal requisition system is not used, the print-out will tell the production personnel what they need for that day or shift. In many operations, a lot of time is wasted in traveling back and forth to the storage areas to collect foods and supplies. When the total needs are known prior to beginning production, the employees can organize their activities much

better, getting all the ingredients in one or two trips.

Recipe costing is made difficult by the fact that many different units of the same foods are used. Tomato puree may be measured in one recipe by teaspoons, in another by tablespoons, in another by cups, and in still another by number 10 cans. A cook could be instructed to use one bunch of parsley in one instance and 1/4 cup in another. These types of measurement variances are quite common. As pointed out in the recipe costing section of Chapter 4, these variations make accurate costing nearly impossible in some cases.

One solution, forced on operators who wish to computerize their production costing, is to convert all recipe ingredients into standard units. If the units are to appear on the recipes, they have to be in weights or volume measurements, but if they will be only used for costing purposes, they can be in abstract numbers. For example, a case of tomato puree could be divided into 1,000 units. If the case was priced at $24.00, each unit would have a value of $.024. A recipe using 15 units would have $.36 charged to it. The information would have to be given to the cook in a more useful form, but at least the ingredient could be costed with accuracy. With these systems, goods received do not have to be converted to standard units manually. They are entered as the unit received, and the computer does the conversion. With the tomato puree example, the receiving entry would be for one case costing $24.00. The computer knows that there are six number 10 cans in each case, and that there are 1,000 recipe units in each case. Each time the case price changes, all recipes using tomato puree are automatically updated. This makes costing many different recipes using tomato puree very easy and accurate as well.

Does your chef have "secret" recipes? One company has come to your rescue. Access to computer programs is usually done with a password; without the password, one cannot get the computer to do anything at all. This particular recipe program requires a second password. Thus access to the recipes does not have to be shared with everyone in the operation and can be restricted to a few persons. This may not be a bad idea. If you allow a cost accountant to see the recipes, he or she will probably start substituting all sorts of less expensive ingredients.

Yield testing is another production function that could be made easier by a computer. If you recall the discussion on yield testing, it would be necessary only to input the starting weight and cost per pound as well as the by-products removed during the breakdown. The calculations would then be made by the computer. This could be tied in to the recipe costing procedures as well. The computer would keep track of the yield tests and use the average yield over time to determine the ingredient costs. It would not be necessary, or even advisable, to do this with a major portion of the ingredients, but if you are cutting your own meats, it certainly would be a worthwhile thing to do.

Service

The basic control requirements described as necessary in the service section of Chapter 4 were:

Assuring that a record is made of all orders prior to their preparation

Documentation of all finished goods that leave the kitchen

Guest check control

When we described the POS systems earlier in this chapter, we were describing how the first two of the above may be attained. When the waitress prechecks the order, there is a record of the order. There is also a record of what left the kitchen, who took it, and—if the computer has a time clock—a record of when as well. Some systems have the capability of bypassing the item price when preparing the check. This is useful when employee meals, for example, are entered into the register. In this case, management does not want sales dollars recorded that will later have to be removed.

The important thing is that all foods leaving the kitchen be properly accounted for. One word of warning, however: if it is possible for employees to register foods without prices, they may be tempted to do this with a regular guest check. In this case, they would write in the prices, collect, and keep the money. The guest would probably not notice anything wrong since most guest checks are handwritten.

We previously described how a guest check control system can be set up and implemented. It is time consuming and requires a lot of record keeping. With some computer systems, however, it is not necessary. They automatically assign a guest check number whenever a new check is started. This number is assigned to a specific employee and must be used each time the check is reused, as when dessert is ordered or when drinks are reordered. If a waitress did not use the number when adding items to an active check, the computer would assign it a new number. As far as the computer is concerned, there would be two separate checks. If the waitress attempted to collect the full check and turn in only the money resulting from the additions, the first number would show up as a missing check, and questions would be asked. This strikes us as an efficient and easy way to obtain guest check control. An added benefit is that numbered guest checks are not required. Most operations could save money by purchasing unnumbered guest checks. The major benefit, however, is the time and effort saved.

When a computer does have a time clock, the chef and management can track item preparation times and preparation patterns over the meal period. Complaints about service delays can be evaluated more effectively if the time an order was submitted is posted. Since the computer would not time the check when the preparation is completed, the expeditor or waitresses would have to do it. This information is so useful that it is worthwhile to train the employees to do it. When the check is paid, the time will be recorded as well, and management should regularly review the guest checks to determine whether any service employees appear to have a problem with slower-than-normal turnover times.

Accounting and Other Uses

One of the advantages of having a computer in the operation is that you have a computer! Computers have many uses beyond the ones we have discussed. Computers can prepare operating statements. Programs are available for accounts receivable and accounts payable. There are also many things that can be done with payroll. One is that the computer can become the time clock: employees punch in and out on the POS terminal, and the hours worked as well as total pay for each employee can be obtained at any time. It is quite easy to prepare the payroll summaries for an outside payroll service. With the proper program, it is even possible to do the payroll in-house. Word processing can be added to most systems, as can filing and mailing programs.

Many companies include gross margin reports in their program packages, and some are quite complete. There is even a menu engineering program in use that not only gives the total CM of every menu item but also classifies each item as a plow horse, star, dog, or puzzle. The type of profitability analysis we discussed really becomes easy when tools like these are available.

In the area of labor control, the computer could be an invaluable tool. The types of bar charts we described in scheduling analysis can be prepared by the computer. If the computer is used as a time clock, management has a variety of labor and wage statistics available to them. Guests per labor hour can be determined for the different departments. Wage cost percentages are easily determined, and on an hourly basis if you want. Productivity analysis is made easier by the computer, which can also be used in scheduling employees.

This is not meant to be a complete listing of computer capabilities. We merely wanted to show how computers can be used in those areas we specifically discussed in the previous chapters. Considering present and projected costs and what a computer can do for an operator, we feel that the attitude should not be: should I get a computer system? but rather, what kind of system is best suited for my operation?

A System Description of a Food Distributor's Approach

An interesting example of how the computer can be used in purchasing is illustrated by a system recently developed by Gordon Food Service, a full-line distributor located in Grand Rapids, Michigan. Their approach was to commission the preparation of several proprietary software programs and provide them, along with the necessary hardware, to whichever of their customers wished to purchase the system. An interesting sidelight is the fact that GFS also became a distributor for the computers themselves, thereby enabling them to sell the entire system, software and hardware, at a very reasonable price. The foodservice operators not only obtained several customized purchasing and food control programs but also ownership of the computers. This obviously opened the way for many more operating uses, such as word processing, office management, accounting, and so forth.

What Can the Customer Do with the System?

Foods Listing. All food items stocked can be listed along with a notation of whether or not each is a key item. A key item would be defined as one that the operation cannot or should not be without. With such items, there would have to be suitable substitutions agreed on to assure a constant supply. With non-key ingredients, a temporary shortage would be acceptable.

Other ingredient information would be: the purchase unit for each item (case, box, pound, bottle), the purchase price per unit, the unit net weight, and the cost per pound. Each inventory food item is broken down into recipe units, such as: cup, 2 cups, 5 ounces, tablespoon, teaspoon, pound, 10 pounds, and so forth. The recipe quantities are then given according to these units.

Recipes. Each recipe used in the operation can be listed, giving such information as the number of servings, portion sizes, selling price, contribution margin (CM, or gross profit), and food cost (dollars and percentage). A recipe report prints whichever recipes are needed for the day's production. Added flexibility is obtained by allowing the recipe to be altered for an increased or decreased yield. When this is done, the batch cost of producing that product is automatically adjusted. This is possible due to one of the unique features of the system: the computer is tied into the distributor's inventory system. Whenever GFS changes their prices, they are automatically available to each participating customer.

Menus. The computer will provide a print-out of each menu used in the operation, and it lists all recipes used to present that particular menu. Included in the listing is the selling price, portion cost, and total CM of each menu item. The portion cost reflects the actual current cost of producing each item since, as pointed out, the operator's computer has access to the distributor's current prices.

Precosting and Postcosting. This program enables the operator to insert the sales forecast into any of the meal periods. The resulting precost sales report gives, for each menu item, the total sales, total cost, and total CM. It provides a summary of the overall menu totals as well. From the sales forecast counts entered into the computer, it will then print a production sheet, showing the amount to be produced for each menu item as well as the preparation area to be used. Another feature is an ingredient usage report, showing the ingredients and quantities (in inventory units) that will be required to prepare the forecasted menu.

The postcost reports are the same as the precost except they would be adjusted for the actual sales. Interfacing with appropriate point-of-sale equipment would automatically provide the computer with the necessary sales information; otherwise it would have to be entered manually. The ingredient usage report would then show the food quantities that *should* have been used

Inventory. When a physical inventory is scheduled, the computer will produce an inventory work sheet. This is a listing of all inventory items in the order in which they appear in the various storage areas. The par stock for each is given as is the inventory unit. The form also has a blank line labeled stock-on-hand. When the inventory is taken, the actual count is entered into this space. This would have the effect of greatly improving the typical inventory-taking procedure in most foodservice operations. Ingredients can be moved, added, or eliminated with ease, enabling the operator to always have an up-to-date inventory work sheet.

Once the physical count is entered into the computer, the inventory valuation report can be run. This reproduces the entire inventory, the current cost per unit, the current quantity on hand, and the extended value of each stock item. The total inventory dollar value is also given. It is quite easy to break the inventory into as many subunits as desired. The operator could, for example, divide it into storage areas or into meats, seafood, poultry, dairy, and so forth.

A product usage report is also extremely useful to management. There are two parts. One is the report itself, which calculates the actual usage of each inventory item. It starts with the beginning inventory, adds all purchases, and deducts the ending inventory. This is done both for units and dollars. Management, therefore, has the usage in units as well as the cost for each item in stock. The second part is the usage variance report, which compares the actual usage to what the usage *should* have been according to the actual sales recorded. This provides the variance for each inventory item (if any) in units and in percentages. It also gives, for each item in variance, the amount of the total variance each item accounts for. This is given as a percentage and enables management to focus their attention on the important variances. For example, if two items account for 60 percent of the total variance, and no other single product is responsible for more than 2 percent, it is obvious where management's attention should be directed. On the other hand, a substantial variance that is spread evenly over hundreds of items may indicate a more difficult problem to control: general overall sloppiness in food operations. In either case, management has an accurate indication of what the problem is.

Purchase Orders. Two types of purchase orders can be generated. One is for GFS orders, and the other is for non-GFS orders. It is hoped, of course, that the majority of the orders would be placed with GFS, but no distributor can handle *all* its clients' needs. For example, few if any would carry many dairy products. Alcoholic beverages would be another obvious product line that would not be available through the food distributor. The food-service operation can thus prepare purchase orders for whatever products are required. The purchase order (PO) form itself is quite simple. It gives all products needed, along with the stock number, quantity desired, purchase unit, cost per unit, and the extended order cost. The unit costs for all the GFS items are automatically provided, while other unit costs would have to be manually entered and updated. Many foodservice operations do not use a formal PO system, but it is difficult to conceive of an operation that could not utilize these PO's. We have pointed out how they provide the information for proper receiving: the receiving clerk needs to know what is expected, how much of it, and what the price should be.

The PO is generated from the sales forecast. Once management gives the computer the information about what is expected to be sold, the computer—drawing information from a variety of files (inventory, recipes, unit costs)— can prepare the list of what is needed for production during the order period.

Menu Engineering. The capabilities of this system obviously go well beyond purchasing requirements; they address, in fact, many of the control necessities described in the food control and analysis chapters (as well as beverage control and analysis; the major difference there being that current product costs are not automatically provided).

In addition to the capabilities described, it also provides a menu engineering program. The operator has to provide the current menu sales counts, and the computer, using the information it contains, will run a menu engineering analysis.

This would provide all the information previously discussed: standard percentage cost for each menu item, percentage MM share for each menu item; MM ranking, CM, and CM ranking for each menu item; and classification of each item as to dogs, puzzles, stars, and plow horses. By simply changing the actual sales counts to proposed or hypothetical ones, the operator can play the "what if" game: What if I sold 200 lobster tails instead of 100, and what if these 100 additional sales came at the expense of liver? The operator, in a minute or two, would know the effect upon total profitability. This is a valuable adjunct to the system; one which in the long run could have a more positive effect on profits than any of the primary programs.

How to Evaluate a Computer Purchase Decision

As we stated earlier in this chapter, any decision should not center on whether to computerize but what kind of system you should purchase. When an operator begins to make the selection, she or he will find that there are many systems now available and many more about to come on the market. This can make evaluation difficult and confusing. The purpose of this section is not to recommend any particular brands or manufacturers but to develop some selection criteria that the operator can use in making a rational choice.

The best overall guideline is the same one we used in determining what the best quality is in food purchasing. The best food quality depends on the use and cost, and the best product is that which fulfills a specific use at the lowest cost. It is the same with computer systems. The operator must first decide what the computer will be used for. Then a specification can be developed. Once this is done, the best purchase is a system that meets the specifications at the lowest cost. We would suggest the following sequence of activities.

Evaluate Present Operation

What information are you presently gathering from your operation? Some of what you are now obtaining may well be suited to manual retrieval, for the computer is not always the best method from a cost-value standpoint. Much of what is now being gathered, however, can probably be acquired more economically and faster by a computer.

What information would you like to have that is not available to you now? Throughout the book we have discussed information that management must have to make rational and timely decisions. Much of it, for a variety of reasons, is probably not being gathered at the present time. Make a list of information you would like to have. Think of this as developing a specification because that is what you are actually doing. Do you want to use the computer as a time clock? Do you want an inventory management system? Do you want to put your recipes on the computer? Do you want a food cost control system? Do you want a word processing system for your office? Figure out what you need and put it down. It is the same process you go through when buying any other product, be it dish-machine soap, portion-cut steaks, frilly tooth-picks, or a tilting braising kettle.

While you are doing this, look ahead and define your future needs and goals. There should be organizational objectives, and the computer program should be planned into them. Determine how computerization can aid in achieving those goals.

One thing that must be mentioned is the importance of management commitment to the concept. Without that, it will simply not work. Installation involves redesigning many of the operating systems. A simple example would be the implementation of a computerized pre-checking terminal system in an operation where the waitresses were handwriting all checks. The way they will write the checks will be different, and the way they handle the check totaling and billing will be different. Personnel will have to learn to use a much different register. We have seen several examples where excellent equipment proved a disaster due to inadequate attention to such details as employee requirements. Personnel will have to be retrained, layouts will often need altering, job descriptions

will have to be rewritten, and so forth. It is a lot of work and is potentially disruptive to the operation. As in all aspects of the operation, management must set the example and provide leadership. When management has really thought the process through (involving the employees in the decision), and when they are enthusiastic and let the employees know what is going on, including exactly what is going to happen, there will seldom be any problems. When the computerization process is poorly thought out and forced on the employees, it will seldom be successful. In fact sabotage is not out of the question, and an employee attempting to cause computer problems can result in a real nightmare.

Software Selection

Once the needs have been determined and you know exactly what you want the system to do, the next step is to evaluate the available software. Software is programs or instructions that tell the computer how to accept data, process it, and what to do with it after processing. Most experienced computer users strongly recommend selecting the software prior to the hardware (the computer itself). We can use the tape analogy referred to earlier to illustrate this. When you decide to listen to music, you select a particular piece to listen to. It may be a jazz recording, an opera, or country western, but it will be a unique work, different from your other tapes. Once you have the tape, you can play it on any tape recorder. It is much the same with computers. The program is the important thing. If you want to process payroll, you purchase payroll software; or to forecast costs, you get software designed to cost recipes; or to do inventories, buy software that maintains inventories. Then you run them all on the same computer.

Basically, what you are trying to do is to match your requirements to the software available. At this point you may well eliminate some things from your list. You might drop, for instance, an expensive program that meets a need you do not consider critical or really necessary. You are modifying your specification, something you do all the time in purchasing foods, beverages, and supplies.

Software evaluation can be complex, frustrating, and time consuming, but information can be obtained from other foodservice and lodging operators. Trade shows and conventions are particularly valuable sources of information. As mentioned earlier, software is getting increasing attention at these shows.

As you begin to narrow your choices, begin testing them. This is very important. Some systems are a lot easier to use than others. A term one often encounters with computers is *user friendly*, which refers to the ease with which noncomputer-trained people can use the systems. Our experience is that some software is not friendly at all; in fact it could be described as overtly hostile. Testing can be done at a supplier's booth at a convention, in the supplier's office, in your own operation (if possible), or in an establishment already using it. Along with actually using the equipment and programs, or even before, read the directions. These (the users' manuals) are called the program documentation and provide real insight into how easy the system is to use. Some have been written by computer programmers. While this may seem to be reasonable, they assume a lot of computer knowledge that most users, especially foodservice users, do not have. If you do not understand the manual, you will not be able to use the system effectively, if at all.

Think of your employees at this point. The acronym KISS is quite appropriate for foodservice operations. It means, keep it simple, stupid. We are not suggesting that foodservice employees are stupid; far from it, but simple, clear, and easily understood systems work best. Computer systems are no different in this regard. To make this changeover, you are going to have to retrain your present employees and train all future ones, so easy-to-use software is essential.

You will probably be using several software modules. These are sets of software programs designed to perform specific functions. For example, you may have a food-costing module. When you enter your receivables, they are posted

to the inventory. If any prices have changed, the inventory cost is automatically updated. Price changes alter recipe costs, which will be taken care of automatically also. When you make your production forecast, the computer will tell you what the food cost should be, based on the actual current product costs. Modules are then combined to form a software system. This is complicated stuff, and you will want to prove to yourself that it works.

Flexibility is another area you will want to explore. It is unlikely you will want to become a computer programmer, but if the system allows modification of reports, financial statements, and so forth, it may be more suited to your specific needs in the long run. Some systems provide something called a *report generator*. These allow the user to create report formats without hiring a programmer. Say, for example, you decide someday that you want a report comparing the sales per man hour for the dining room, kitchen, lounge, and catering department. As long as all the necessary statistics are somewhere in the computer, you can pull them together and create a new report. This is what a report generator is, and its usefulness is obvious.

Hardware Selection

Once your software selection has been made, the hardware decision is relatively easy. The best computer is the one that is most compatible with the software you have selected. Specific software systems will not run on all computers, nor will they run equally well even on those computers that do accept them. The most important aspect of your hardware specification, therefore, is compatibility with your software. Other elements of the specification are:

How may terminals do you need?

How much memory will you require?

What volume of reports will you be printing?

Reliability of the equipment is another critical decision factor. As pointed out in the discussion of computerized beverage systems, a breakdown could put you temporarily out of business. Try to select equipment that is proven in the field. When you talk to others who are using it, discuss this point in particular. Along with reliability, you want to know about the service and support network. One reason for the rapid acceptance of the IBM personal computer is undoubtedly their long-standing reputation for service and support.

In summary, this is a complex and time-consuming decision to make, but successful food and beverage operation today requires that management receive certain types of information and get it as quickly as possible. Reasonable speed is essential if managers are to make rational and effective responses to a quickly changing environment. Manual retrieval systems are no longer capable of providing adequate information, and what they do provide is often available too late to be useful. Computer systems are no longer a luxury; today they are a necessity.

Glossary

Advertising: Attracting public attention to a product or service with *paid* announcements, using the media, direct mailing, printed giveaways, and so forth (*see also* Publicity).

AP (As purchased): Food items as they are received from the purveyor; before they are treated by the foodservice operation.

Average check (AC): Money value of sales divided by total number of customers. For example, if receipts = $868.00 and customers served = 47, then AC = 868/47 = $18.47.

Blind receiving: A receiving system in which the receiver must record the delivery on a blank invoice from the supplier.

Bonding: A form of insurance that reimburses the enterprise for cash stolen by a particular employee.

Brand: The name by which an individual product is known. For example, Kelloggs Cornflakes, Heinz Catsup, Chivas Regal Scotch.

    - Call brands: Drinks that customers often call for (order) by the brand name; for example, Chivas and water, Jack Daniels on the rocks.

    - Well brands (also house brands): The stocks of liquor regularly used when the customer does not specify a particular brand; for example, gin and tonic, bourbon and water.

Breakdown: Analysis of situations and operations by dividing them into smaller components to which a cost can be attached; for example, the breakdown of July's sales shows that the prime rib was the most profitable menu item.

Break even: When the sales revenues equals the total cost of operations, so there is no profit and no loss.

Contribution margin (CM or gross profit): The amount remaining when the product cost of a menu item (both food and beverage) is subtracted from its selling price. The CM can also be calculated for the entire menu:

$$\text{Average CM} = \frac{\text{Total CM of menu}}{\text{Number of menu items}}$$

Costing: The process of determining the exact food or beverage cost of a ready-to-consume item by calculating the cost of each ingredient in the recipe.

Costs (or expenses): All the payments the enterprise must make to provide products and services for the customers. These costs are identified in different ways:

- **Controllable:** Costs that can be increased or decreased by management action.
- **Fixed (or uncontrollable):** Costs that the management can do little to change; for example, rent, interest payments, property taxes, and so forth.
- **Food cost:** The money spent to purchase the food that, after processing, is served to the guests (and also to the employees). The food cost is often expressed as a percentage of total sales.
- **Beverage cost:** The money spent to purchase the beverages (and foods) that will be sold as alcoholic beverages.
- **Labor cost:** The total money spent to reward the workers (including management) in the operation. This includes direct wages, fringe benefits, meals, uniforms, and so forth.
- **Overhead:** A grouping of all costs except product costs (food and beverage costs) and labor costs.
- **Percentage cost:** Expresses the cost as a percentage of sales.

$$\text{percentage cost} = \frac{\text{cost}}{\text{sales}} \times 100$$

- **Prime cost:** Product cost (food and beverage cost) plus labor cost.
- **Standard Cost:** The cost, under ideal conditions, of preparing each item on the menu (foods and beverages).
- **Unit cost:** Usually the cost of each portion (see Yield testing).
- **Variable costs:** Costs that change with the quantity produced and which are more or less proportional to the sales volume.

Direct wages: The hourly wages, salaries, and overtime paid to employees. The gross wages, before deductions, that appear on an employee's paycheck.

EP (Edible portion): Food items ready to serve, after preparation is complete.

FIFO (*See* Inventory rotation).

Forecast: A prediction, estimate, projection, or expectation. An expression of the expected future situation in a measurable form. The two types of forecasts discussed most frequently in the text are the operating forecast, which is a formal projection of sales and expenses for a period of (generally) a year, and the production forecast, a listing of the sales expected for each menu item.

Fringe benefits: Rewards received by the employees other than direct wages; for example, paid holidays, meals, uniforms, and so forth.

Gross profit (*see* contribution margin).

Inventory: The stocks of goods that are maintained in the foodservice operation. They include food and beverage stocks, supplies, china, glassware, flatware, and so forth.

- **Perpetual inventory:** Stocks calculated according to the following formula: original inventory plus goods received minus goods issued. It provides current stock levels without having to take an actual count.
- **Physical inventory:** The actual counting and recording of these stocks (usually monthly). This gives the closing inventory for one period and the opening inventory for the next.
- **Valuation:** Putting a money value on the physical inventory. Since purchase prices change frequently for many items, management must decide whch price, original or current, to use for inventory valuation.
- **Rotation:** Making sure that older items in the storeroom are used before newer items. A term commonly used to describe the recommended technique is FIFO (first in, first out).
- **In-process inventory:** Items held in the kitchen (or bar) for current use. This also includes foods partially or completely

prepared.

- *See also* Turnover

Issue: The release of items from storage. This is normally done only when authorized by a signed requisition. Issues records are used to keep the perpetual inventory up to date. They can also be extended to determine the daily/weekly cost of goods.

Job analysis: Lists all the work to be done and decides who is responsible for each task.

Job description: Lists the tasks to be performed by the employee given the job.

Job specification: Lists the qualifications necessary to hold the job such as age, education, experience, and so forth.

Low-balling: When a supplier quotes an attractive price to obtain business and then raises the price. The key here is whether the supplier intends to increase it when quoting.

Menu engineering: The gross profit approach to menu analysis. It compares the popularity and profitability of menu items (indicating which items need changing in some way), of old and new menus and of similar menus in different establishments (such as with chain operations).

Merchandising: Whatever management does in the operation to promote sales.

Menu mix or **Sales mix:** The total of the individual sales patterns of each of the menu items.

Monitor: To check and to indicate any variances from standards.

Par stock: The quantity of each item in inventory that will be maintained. It must be sufficient to supply the normal expected sales plus a reasonable safety margin.

Personal selling: One of the most effective ways with which to control the sales mix and, hence, the gross profit is to train the dining-room service staff to sell as opposed to simply taking orders.

POS (Point of Sale): Associated with an electronic register into which all food and beverage items are preregistered prior to being ordered.

Pricing: The process of establishing the prices to be charged to the customers. It is a complex process and depends on such factors as food cost, labor cost, overhead costs, desired profits, expected sales volumes, and so forth.

Prime time: Those periods of the day when there is heavy customer traffic. In many foodservice establishments, this only comprises a small portion of the total operating hours.

Productivity: A term used to indicate the output of employees. Increased productivity is taken to mean better or increased performance.

Profit factor (PF): For each item on the food and/or beverage menu, the PF is calculated as a ratio:

$$\frac{\text{Total CM for one menu item}}{\text{Average CM for entire menu}} = PF$$

A result of 1 (one) indicates that the item is providing exactly its mathematical share of the total profit. A figure of less than 1 means that the menu item is not producing average profits; the lower the PF, the lower the profitability of that item. It is an indicator of the relative profitability of all menu items.

Promotion: Any form of communication with the objective of selling a product or service. It includes advertising, personal selling, publicity, and merchandising.

Publicity: Public awareness created by unpaid mention in the media, or oral recommendation (*see* Advertising).

Purchase order (PO): A document specifying the items being purchased, the prices, the quantities, and the purveyor. With organizations that have a formal PO system, the PO becomes the only legal authorization for a supplier to ship goods.

Purveyor: An organization or individual that provides or sells goods to the foodservice operation. Also called supplier.

Receiving: Covers the reception of goods from the purveyor, checking quantities and specifications against the original order, noting any variation(s), accepting or refusing the delivery, and transferring it to suitable storage. It requires a very competent, responsible, highly trained, and honest employee.

Requisition: A signed form authorizing the issue (or release) of specific goods from storage.

Schedule: A detailed list of requirements usually specifying time, place, and quantity. A production schedule lists food items, recipes, quantities, and so forth. A work schedule specifies what each worker has to do, where, and when.

Scheduling: The process of production and/or labor planning.

Shrinkage: Loss of weight or volume during cooking, especially for meat.

Slack time: Those periods in the day when there are few or no customers (*see* Prime time)

Specifications (Specs): Detailed descriptions of all items being purchased, especially important with foods, but also used for beverages and supplies. They are used to assure attainment of standards.

Supplier (*see* Purveyor).

Staffing: Determining the optimum amount of labor needed to service the expected demand.

Standards: Established levels of quality and performance that provide a basis for comparison. They provide a frame of reference for evaluating an operation's performance.

Stock rotation: (*see* Inventory rotation).

Trade-up: To substitute a more expensive (and/or profitable) menu item for a less expensive or profitable one. Usually used in reference to customers' decisions.

Transfer: Movements of items from one department to another (but not from the storeroom). Food transfers are foods sent to the beverage department and charged to the beverage cost. Beverage transfers refer to alcoholic beverages sent to the kitchen for cooking purposes and charged to the food cost.

Turnover (T/O): A measure of activity used in several ways. Examples are:

- **Guest turnover:** Average number of customers per seat per day (or per meal period). A restaurant with 150 seats and 450 customers per day would have a guest turnover of 3.0.

- **Inventory turnover:** A figure indicating the number of times the inventory was sold or used during a period, generally one month. It is calculated as follows:

$$\frac{\text{cost of goods}}{\text{average value of inventory}} = \text{T/O}$$

- **Labor turnover:** A figure that indicates the stability or lack of stability of the work force. It is calculated by dividing the total number of employees on the payroll during a period by the number of employees normally scheduled. For example, if an operation normally employs sixty persons, but the payroll records show that ninety-six were employed during the year, the labor turnover would be 160 percent.

Variances: Differences between what actually occurred and the established standard. The purpose of analysis is to determine where and why the variances occurred, and the purpose of control is to reduce or eliminate variances.

Yield: The usable physical quantity remaining after processing the AP item. Yield is of extreme importance in a food system since few food products will be served in their AP (as purchased) form. The yield is the EP (edible portion).

Yield testing: The process of establishing the yield and calculating the unit cost.

Bibliography

Dittmer, P., and Griffin, G. *Principles of Food, Beverage, and Labor Cost Controls for Hotels and Restaurants.* Boston: Cahners Books, 1976.

Kasavana, M., and Smith, D. *Menu Engineering: A Practical Guide to Restaurant Pricing.* Lansing, Mich.: Hospitality Publications, 1982, (1801 N. Fairview Ave., Lansing, MI 48912).

Katsigris, C., and Porter, M. *The Bar and Beverage Book: Basics of Profitable Management.* New York: John Wiley & Sons, 1983.

Keiser, J., and Kallio, E. *Controlling and Analyzing Costs in Food Service Operations.* New York: John Wiley & Sons, 1974.

Kelly, H. *Food Service Purchasing: Principles and Practices.* New York: Chain Store Publishing, 1976.

Keister, D. *Food and Beverage Control.* Englewood Cliffs, N.J.: Prentice-Hall, 1977.

Keister, D. *How to Use the Uniform System of Accounts for Hotels and Restaurants.* Chicago: National Restaurant Association, 1977.

Kotschevar, L. *Quantity Food Purchasing.* 2d ed. New York: John Wiley & Sons, 1975.

Levinson, C. *Food and Beverage Operation: Cost Control and Systems Management.* Englewood Cliffs, N.J.: Prentice-Hall, 1976.

Miller, J. *Menu Pricing and Strategy.* Boston: CBI Publishing Co., 1980.

Ninemeier, J. *Planning and Control for Food and Beverage Operations.* East Lansing, Mich.: The Educational Institute of the American Hotel and Motel Association, 1982.

Pedderson, R. *Specs: The Comprehensive Foodservice Purchasing and Specification Manual.* Boston: CBI Publishing Co., 1977.

Stefanelli, J. *Purchasing: Selection and Procurement for the Hospitality Industry.* New York: John Wiley & Sons, 1981.

Uniform System of Accounts for Restaurants. Chicago: National Restaurant Association, 1968.

Warfel, M., and Waskey, F. *The Professional Food Buyer.* Berkeley, Calif.: McCutchan Publishing Corp., 1979.

Index